My love STORY!!

Story **KAZUNE KAWAHARA**

Art **ARUKO**

2

MY love STORY!!

STORY Thus Far...

Takeo Goda, a first-year high school student, is a hot-blooded guy who is 6'6" tall and weighs 265 pounds. Boys look up to him, but the girls he falls in love with all end up liking his handsome best friend, Sunakawa!

One morning on the train to school, Takeo saves a girl named Yamato from a molester. When she visits Takeo to thank him for his help, he immediately falls in love with her. He suspects she's after Sunakawa, so he does what he can to get the two of them together. But it turns out that Yamato is actually in love with Takeo!

Takeo gets his first girlfriend ever and tries his best to look after his pure-hearted Yamato, but Yamato seems depressed for some reason... She eventually reveals that she actually wants to hold hands and touch Takeo. After Takeo hears that, he forces an unwilling Sunakawa to practice kissing with him through plastic wrap!

CONTENTS

2

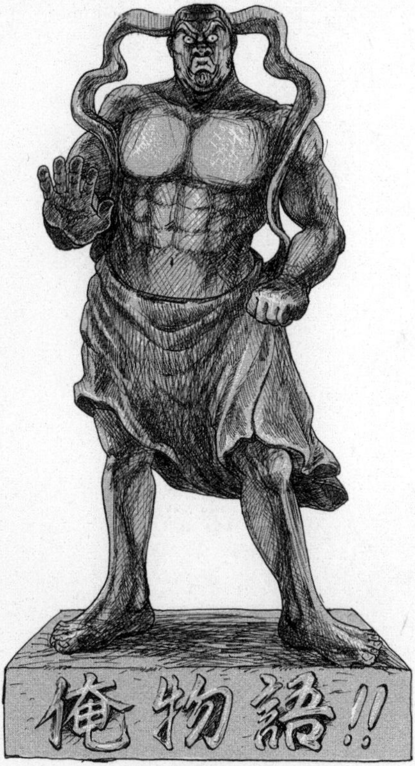
俺物語!!

*MY LOVE STORY!!

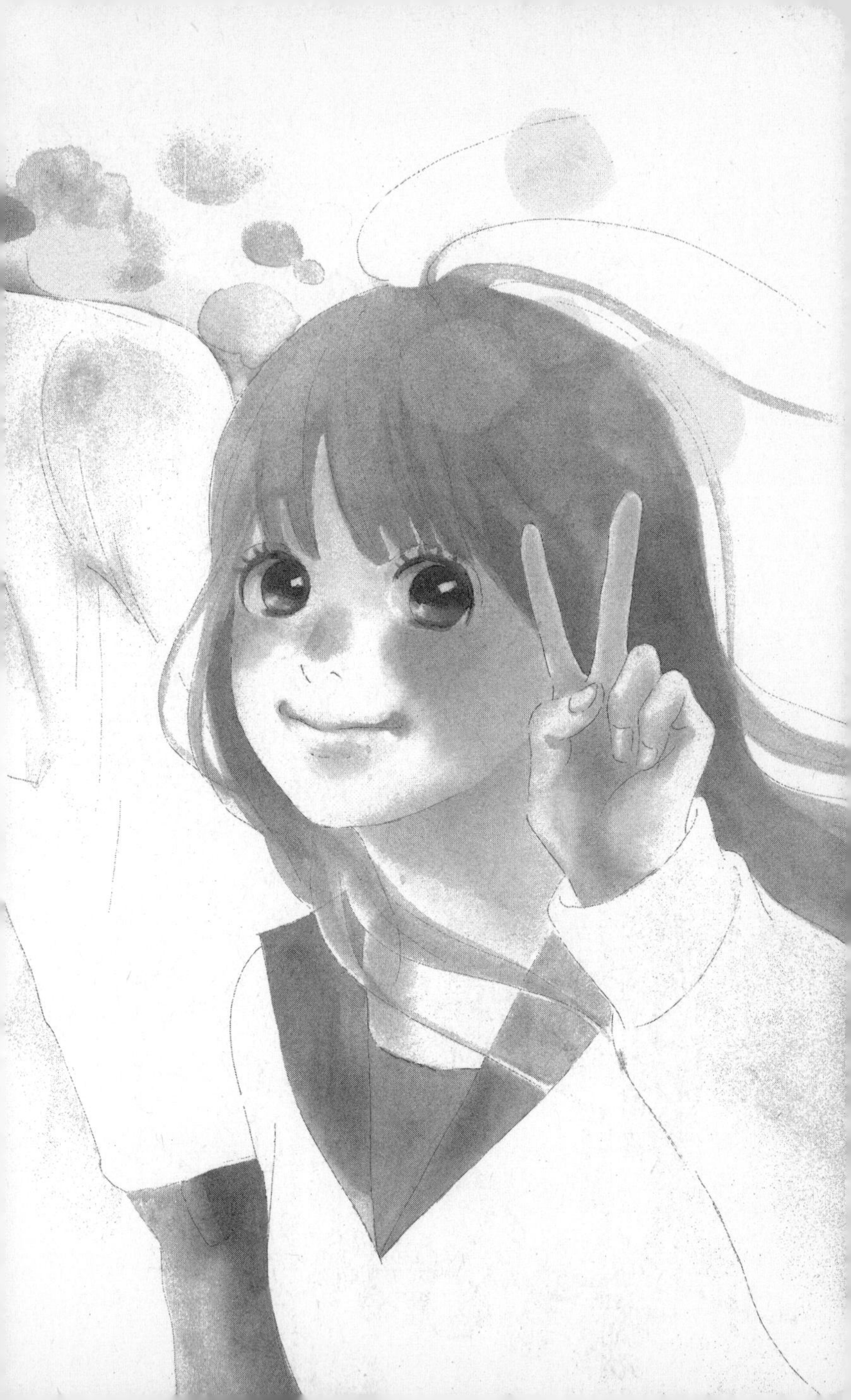

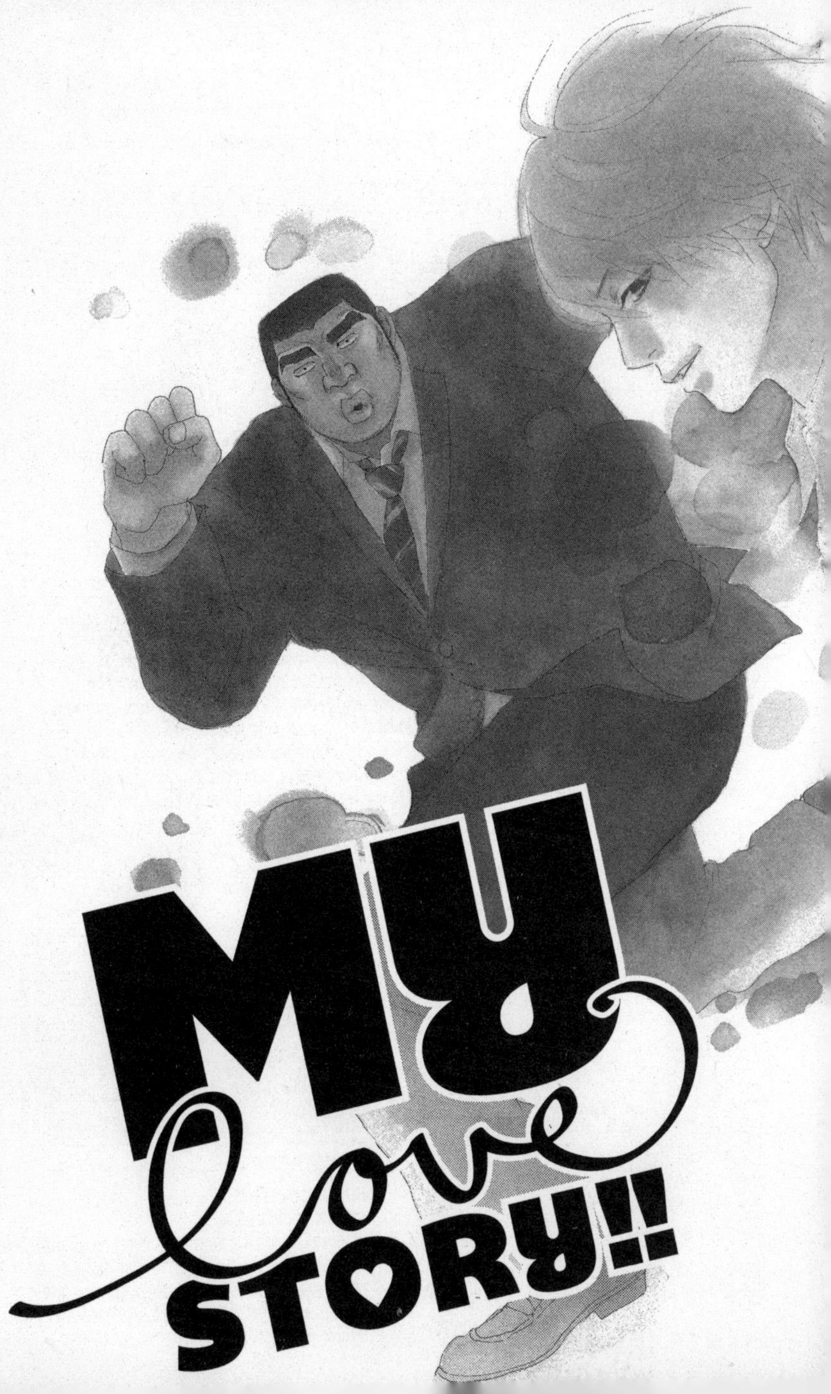
MY love STORY!!

My Love Story!!

SWEETS of LOVE RECIPE COLLECTION 1

Presenting the recipes for some of Yamato's delicious baking! ♥ Recipe Creation and Preparation: Nana Hoshitani Photography: Akiko Honda

Sweet No.1 SACHERTORTE of HAPPINESS

Requires a 6-inch or 7-inch cake pan with removable base

Chocolate Cake Ingredients:

- 70g [2.5 oz] chocolate, grated
- 70g [4 2/3 tbsp] unsalted butter
- 3 eggs
- 40g [2 2/3 tbsp] cake flour
- 1 caramelized chestnut
- 70g [4 2/3 tbsp] sugar

Decorations:

- 50g [3 1/3 tbsp] apricot jam
- 50ml [3 1/3 tbsp] fresh cream
- 100g [3.5 oz] chocolate

Preparation:

- ♥ **Line the cake pan with parchment paper.**
- ♥ **Grate the chocolate finely.**
- ♥ **Separate the egg whites from the yolks and chill the whites in the fridge.**
- ♥ **Preheat the oven to 170° C [338° F].**

From *My Love Story!!* vol. 1

INSTRUCTIONS

1 Place the butter and chocolate in a small bowl; heat over a pot of hot water. (Or use a double boiler.) Gently mix until melted.

2 Place the mixture from step 1 into a larger bowl and add half of the sugar, the egg yolks, and the cake flour. Mix well with a spatula.

3 Beat the egg whites in a different bowl. Once they start to foam, gradually add the remaining sugar one third at a time, and beat until you get fluffy peaks.

4 Add the mixture from step 2 to the mixture in step 3 one third at a time, and fold them together with a spatula.

5 Pour the mixture into the cake pan and place a dry chestnut on top. Bake for 40 minutes at 170°C [338° F]. Poke it with a skewer. If the skewer comes out clean, remove the pan from the oven and let it cool.

6 Pour the apricot jam in a heat-resistant container, and place it in the microwave for 30 seconds. Flip the cake over and remove the parchment paper. Spread the jam on the surface while the cake is still hot.

7 Pour the fresh cream into a small pot and bring it to a boil. Turn off the heat and add the chocolate. Slowly mix it in until melted. Pour it over the cake, and spread it evenly with a palette knife or a spatula.

FLUFFY VEGETABLE SAVORY CAKES Sweet No.2

From *My Love Story!!* vol. 1

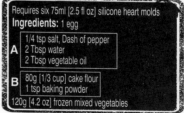

Requires six 75ml [2.5 fl oz] silicone heart molds

Ingredients: 1 egg

A
- 1/4 tsp salt, Dash of pepper
- 2 Tbsp water
- 2 Tbsp vegetable oil

B
- 80g [1/3 cup] cake flour
- 1 tsp baking powder

120g [4.2 oz] frozen mixed vegetables

INSTRUCTIONS

1 Place the egg in a bowl and beat it. Add the "A" ingredients and mix well.

2 Combine the "B" ingredients and sift into the mixture. Add the frozen mixed vegetables. (It's fine if they're still frozen.) Fold them in with a spatula.

3 Pour the mixture into the molds and bake for 25 minutes in an oven preheated to 190° C [374° F]. Poke them with a skewer. If the skewer comes out clean, you can remove them from the molds and let them cool.

◀◀◀◀◀◀◀ More recipes on page 94!

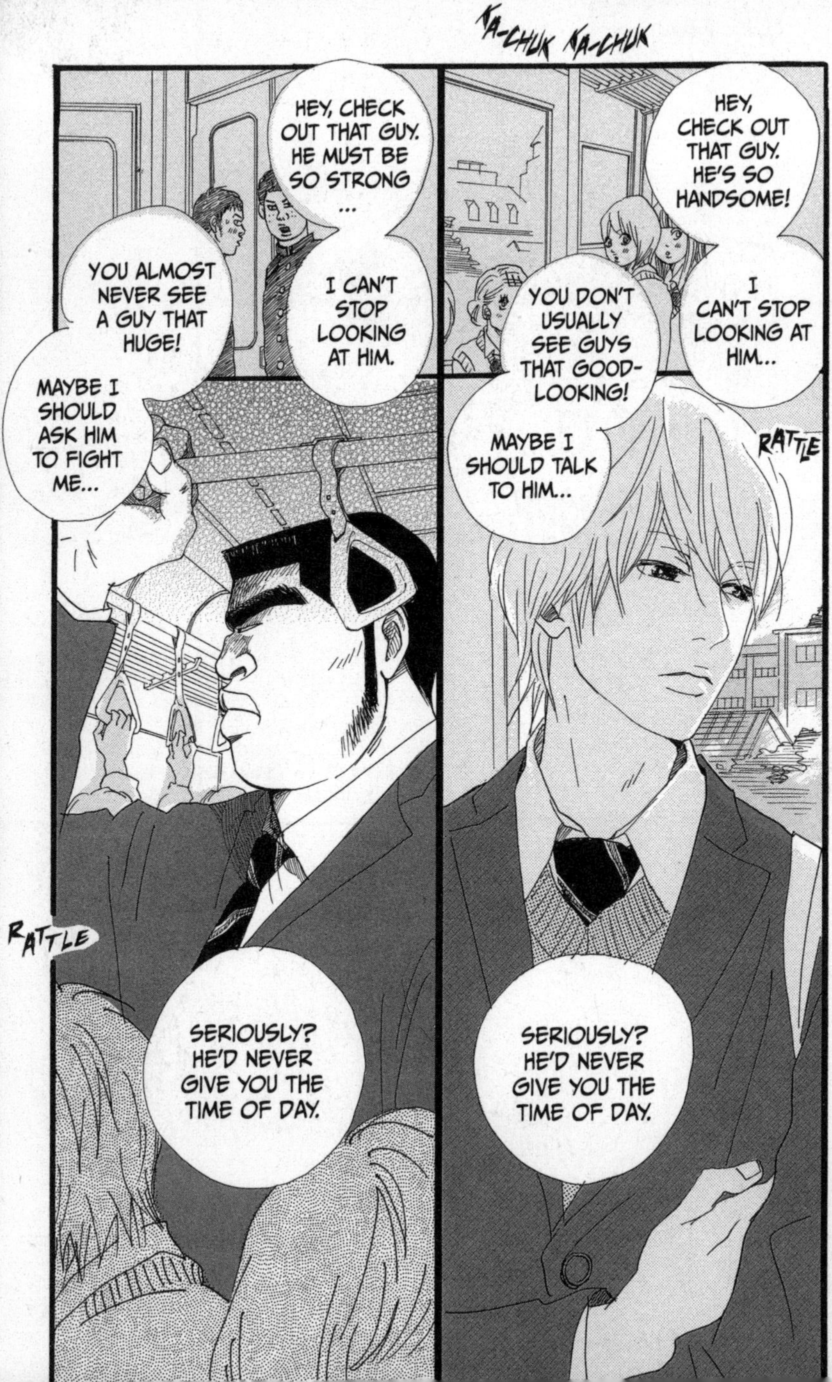
KA-CHUK KA-CHUK
HEY, CHECK OUT THAT GUY. HE'S SO HANDSOME!
I CAN'T STOP LOOKING AT HIM...
YOU DON'T USUALLY SEE GUYS THAT GOOD-LOOKING!
MAYBE I SHOULD TALK TO HIM...
HEY, CHECK OUT THAT GUY. HE MUST BE SO STRONG...
I CAN'T STOP LOOKING AT HIM.
YOU ALMOST NEVER SEE A GUY THAT HUGE!
MAYBE I SHOULD ASK HIM TO FIGHT ME...
RATTLE
SERIOUSLY? HE'D NEVER GIVE YOU THE TIME OF DAY.
RATTLE
SERIOUSLY? HE'D NEVER GIVE YOU THE TIME OF DAY.

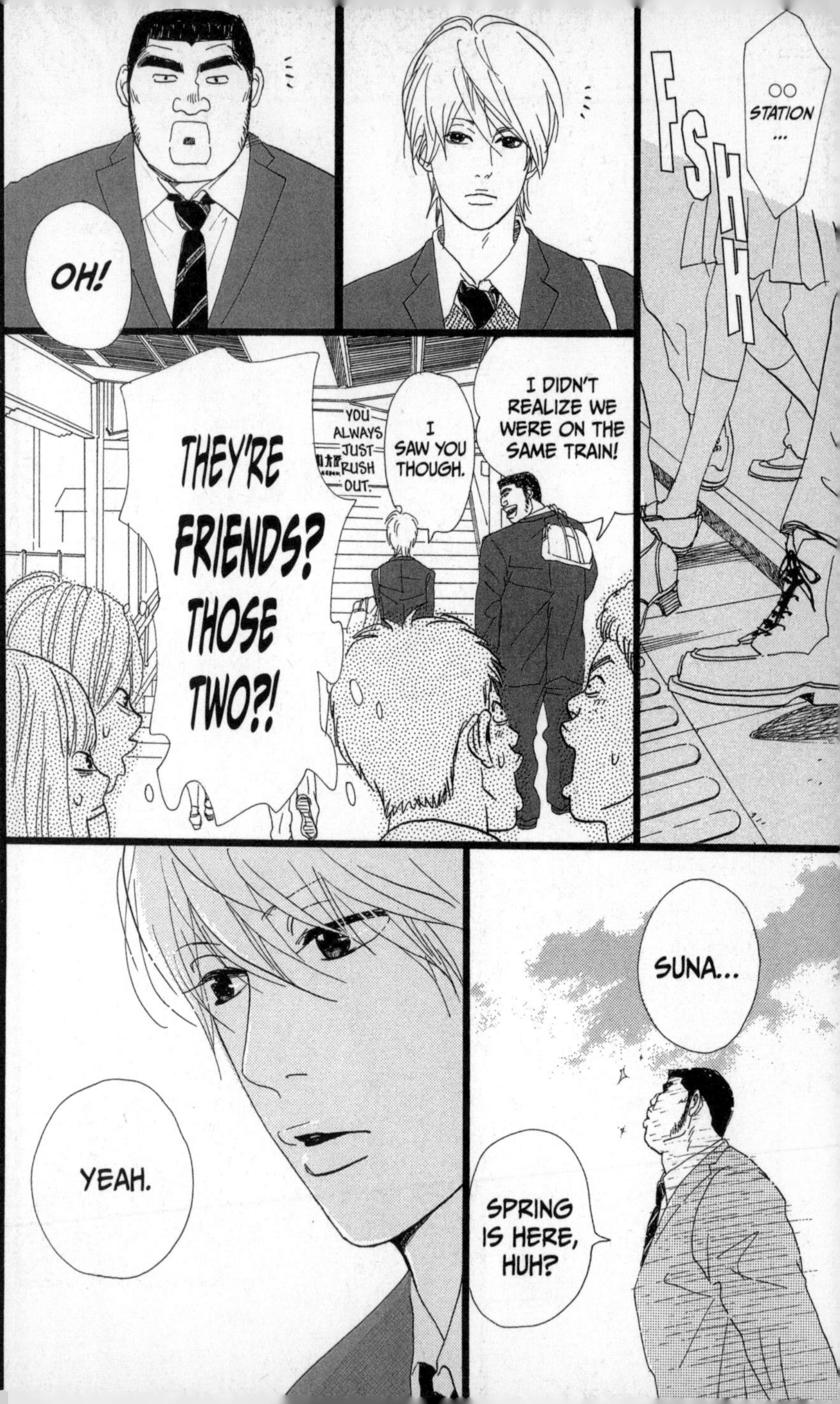
○○ STATION ...
FSHHH
OH!
I DIDN'T REALIZE WE WERE ON THE SAME TRAIN!
I SAW YOU THOUGH.
YOU ALWAYS JUST RUSH OUT.
THEY'RE FRIENDS? THOSE TWO?!
SUNA...
SPRING IS HERE, HUH?
YEAH.

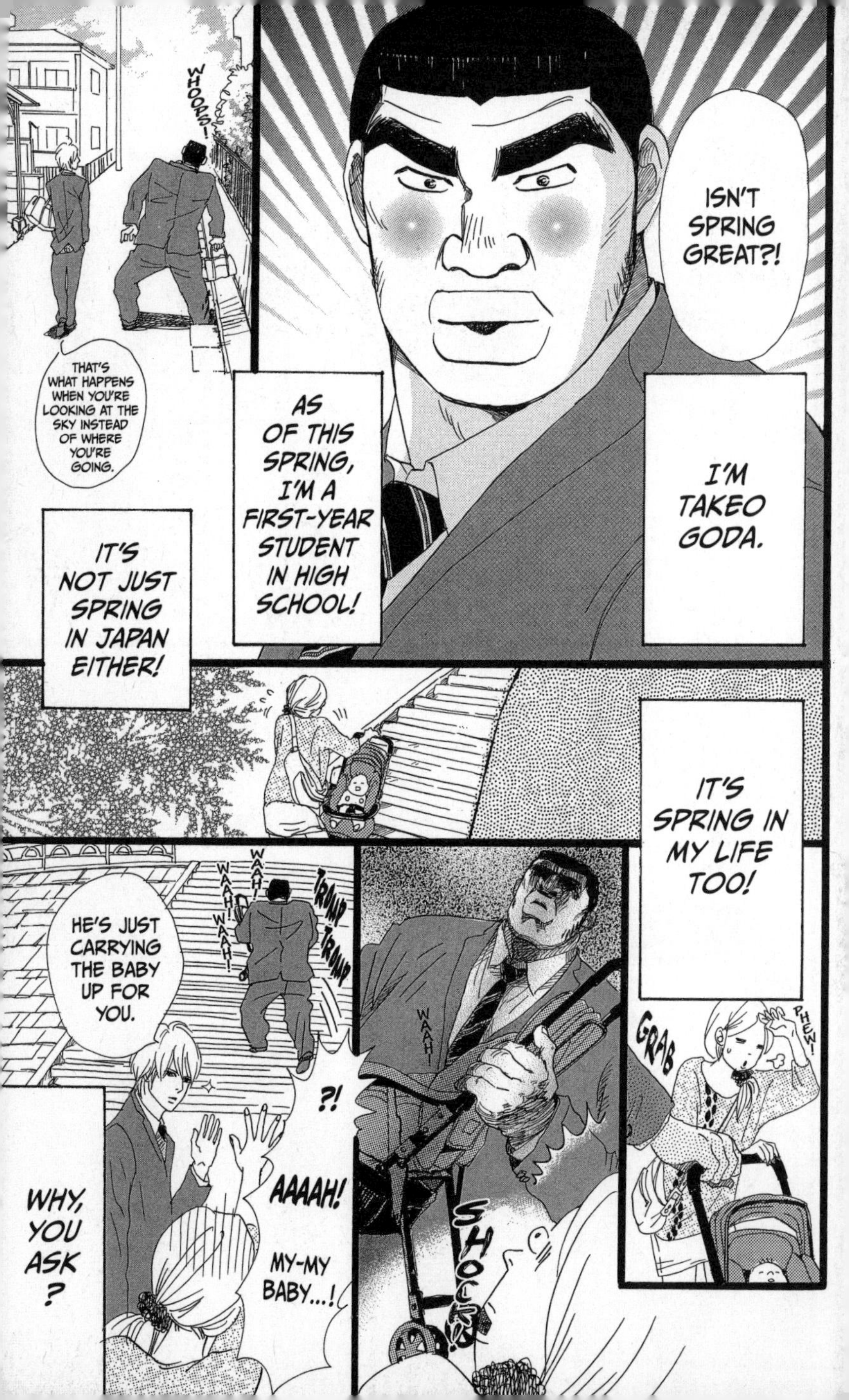
ISN'T SPRING GREAT?!
I'M TAKEO GODA.
AS OF THIS SPRING, I'M A FIRST-YEAR STUDENT IN HIGH SCHOOL!
WHOOPS!
THAT'S WHAT HAPPENS WHEN YOU'RE LOOKING AT THE SKY INSTEAD OF WHERE YOU'RE GOING.
IT'S NOT JUST SPRING IN JAPAN EITHER!
IT'S SPRING IN MY LIFE TOO!
GRAB
PHEW!
WAAH!
SHOCK!
TROMP TROMP
WAAH! WAAH! WAAH!
?!
AAAAH!
MY-MY BABY...!
HE'S JUST CARRYING THE BABY UP FOR YOU.
WHY, YOU ASK?

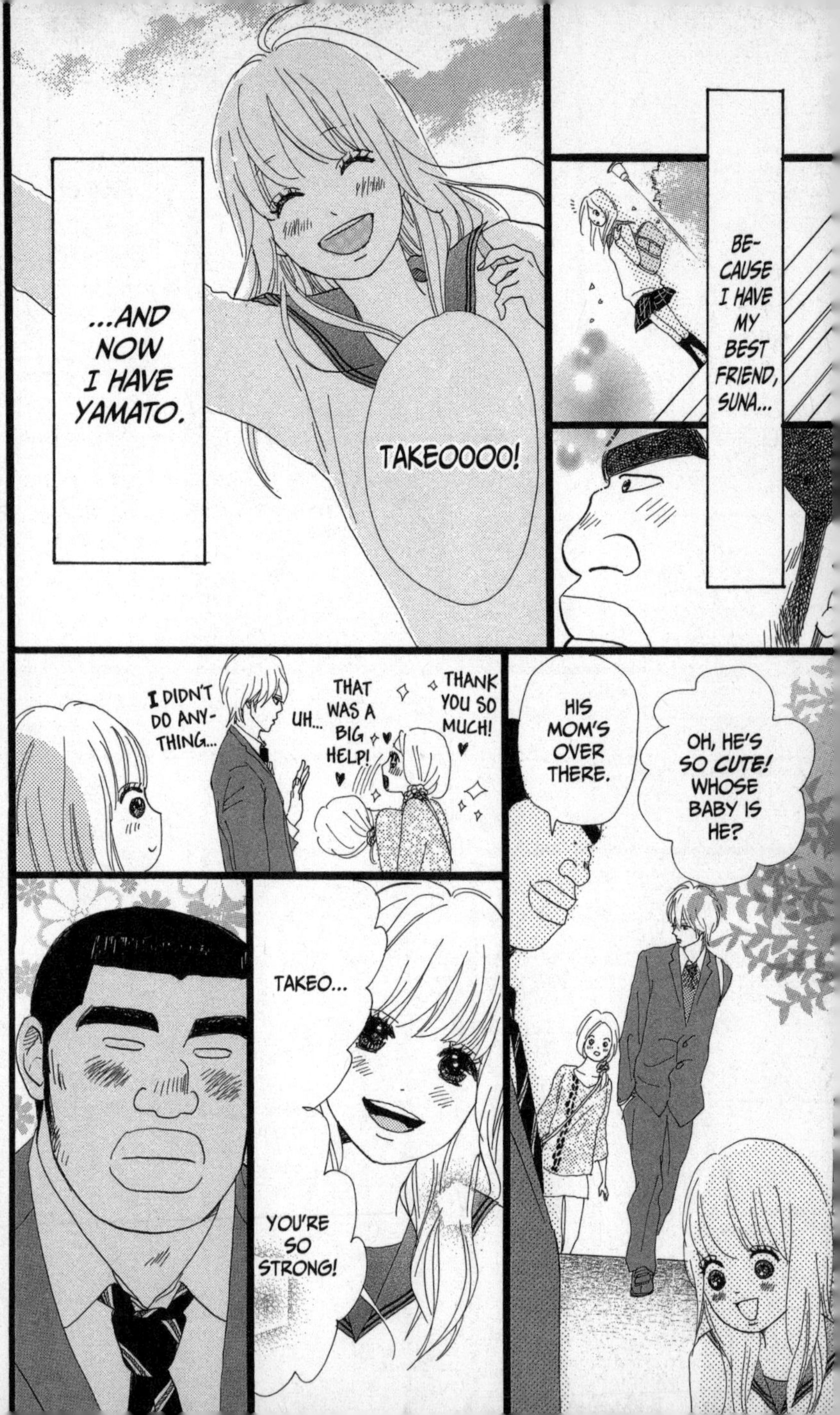
BE-CAUSE I HAVE MY BEST FRIEND, SUNA...
...AND NOW I HAVE YAMATO.
TAKEOOOO!
OH, HE'S SO CUTE! WHOSE BABY IS HE?
HIS MOM'S OVER THERE.
THANK YOU SO MUCH!
THAT WAS A BIG HELP!
UH...
I DIDN'T DO ANY-THING...
TAKEO...
YOU'RE SO STRONG!

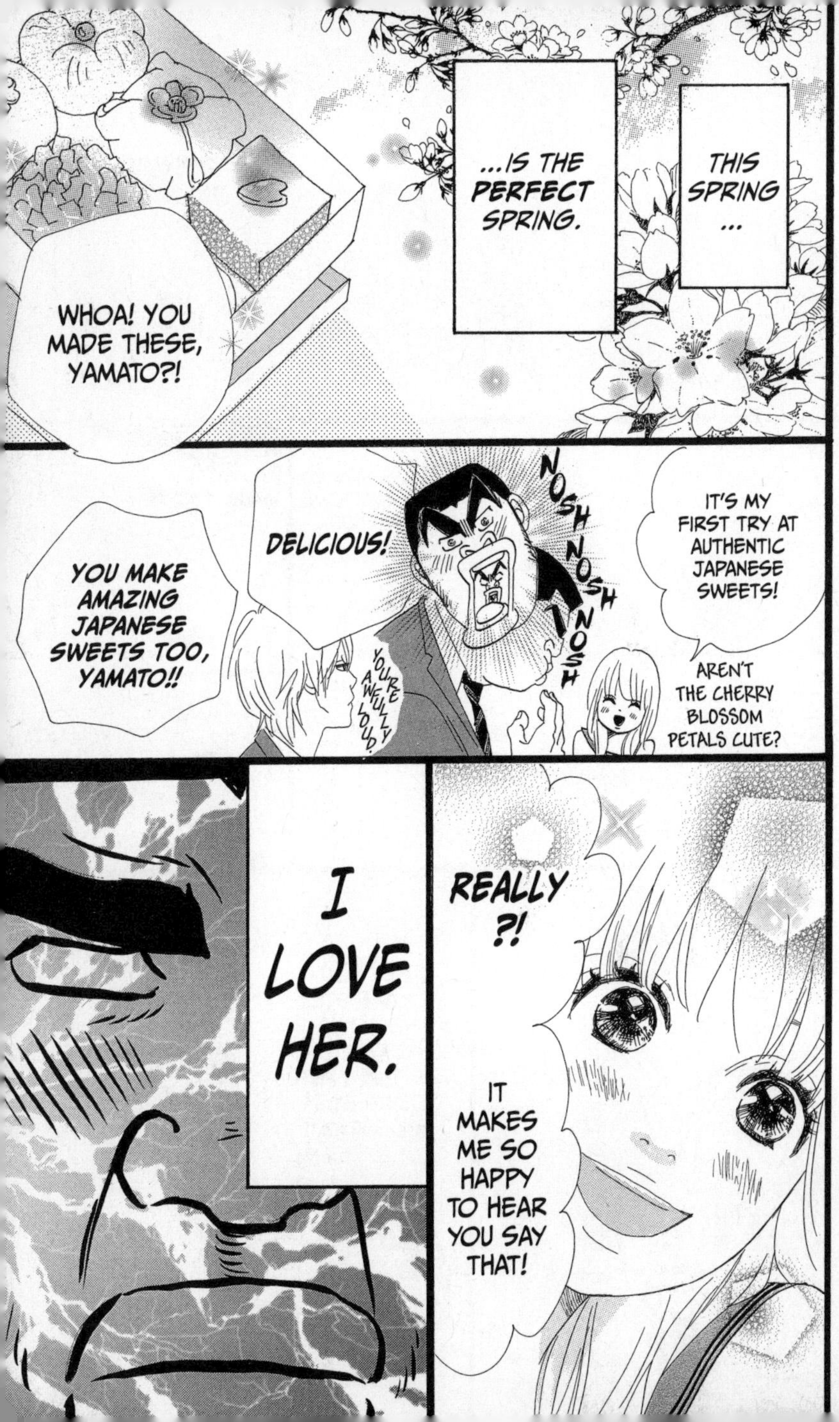
THIS SPRING ...
...IS THE PERFECT SPRING.
WHOA! YOU MADE THESE, YAMATO?!
IT'S MY FIRST TRY AT AUTHENTIC JAPANESE SWEETS!
AREN'T THE CHERRY BLOSSOM PETALS CUTE?
NOSH NOSH NOSH
DELICIOUS!
YOU'RE AWFULLY LOUD.
YOU MAKE AMAZING JAPANESE SWEETS TOO, YAMATO!!
REALLY ?!
IT MAKES ME SO HAPPY TO HEAR YOU SAY THAT!
I LOVE HER.

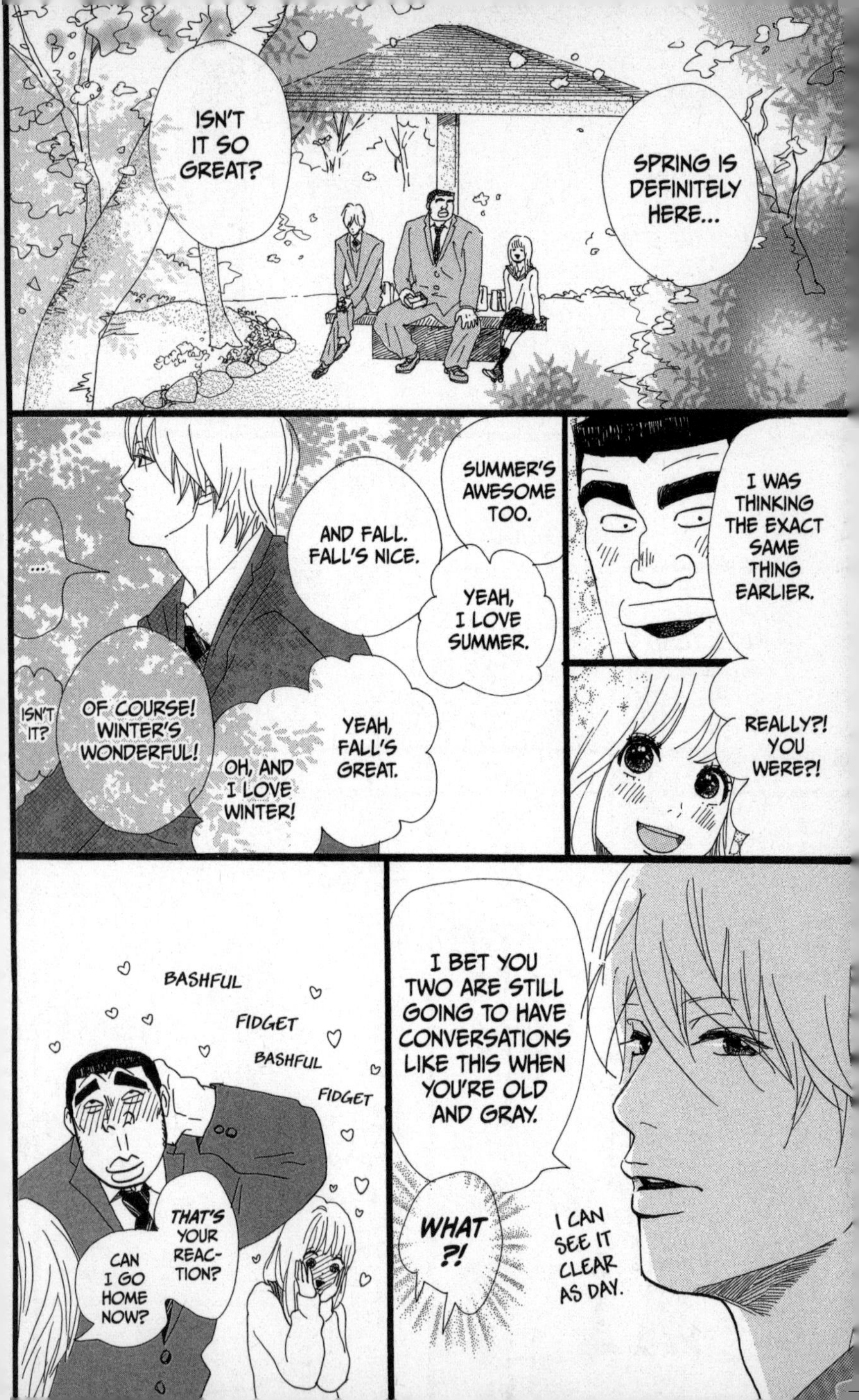
SPRING IS DEFINITELY HERE...
ISN'T IT SO GREAT?
I WAS THINKING THE EXACT SAME THING EARLIER.
REALLY?! YOU WERE?!
SUMMER'S AWESOME TOO.
YEAH, I LOVE SUMMER.
AND FALL. FALL'S NICE.
YEAH, FALL'S GREAT.
OH, AND I LOVE WINTER!
OF COURSE! WINTER'S WONDERFUL!
ISN'T IT?
...
I BET YOU TWO ARE STILL GOING TO HAVE CONVERSATIONS LIKE THIS WHEN YOU'RE OLD AND GRAY.
I CAN SEE IT CLEAR AS DAY.
WHAT?!
BASHFUL
FIDGET
BASHFUL
FIDGET
THAT'S YOUR REAC-TION?
CAN I GO HOME NOW?

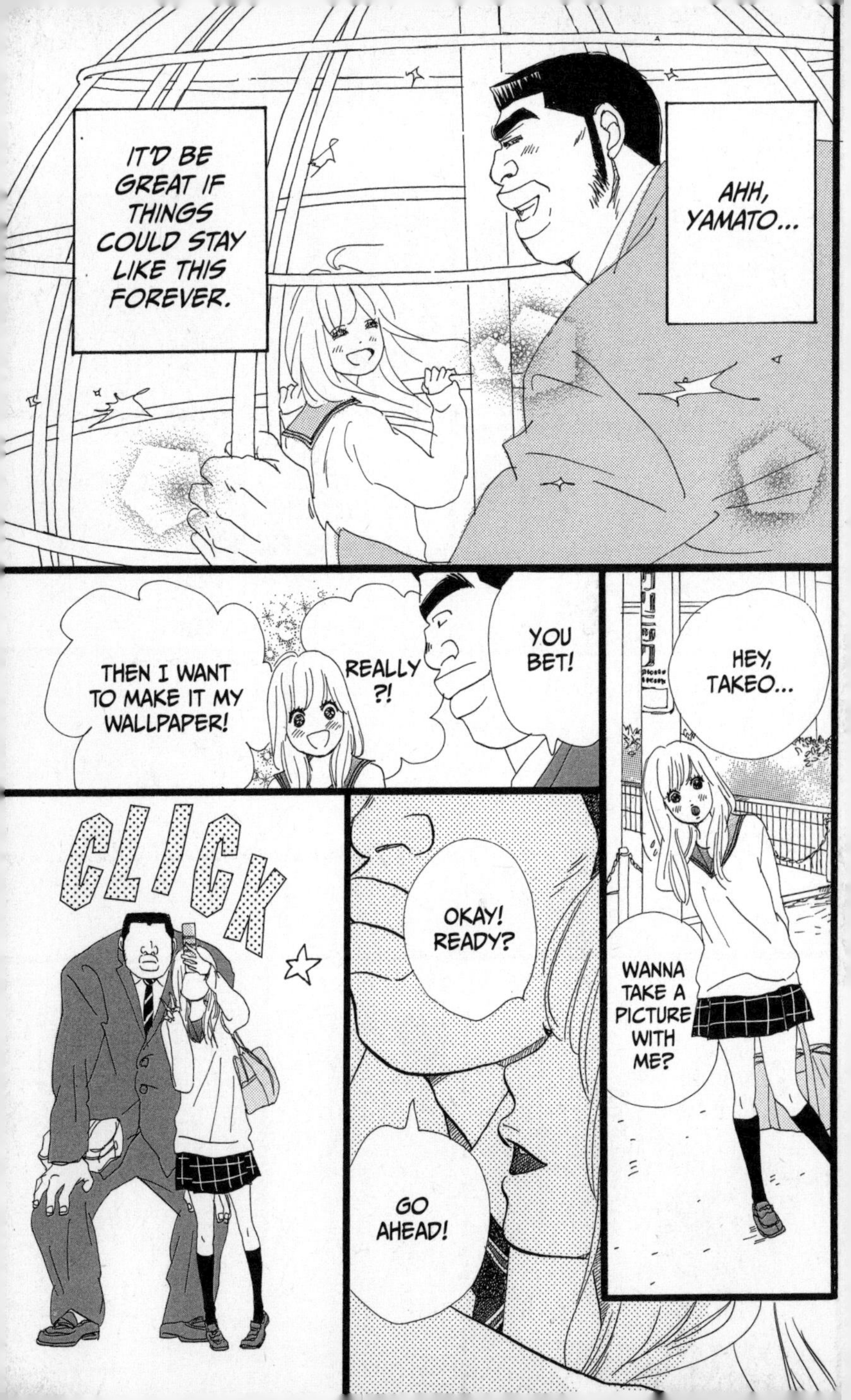
AHH, YAMATO...
IT'D BE GREAT IF THINGS COULD STAY LIKE THIS FOREVER.
HEY, TAKEO...
WANNA TAKE A PICTURE WITH ME?
YOU BET!
REALLY?!
THEN I WANT TO MAKE IT MY WALLPAPER!
OKAY! READY?
GO AHEAD!
CLICK

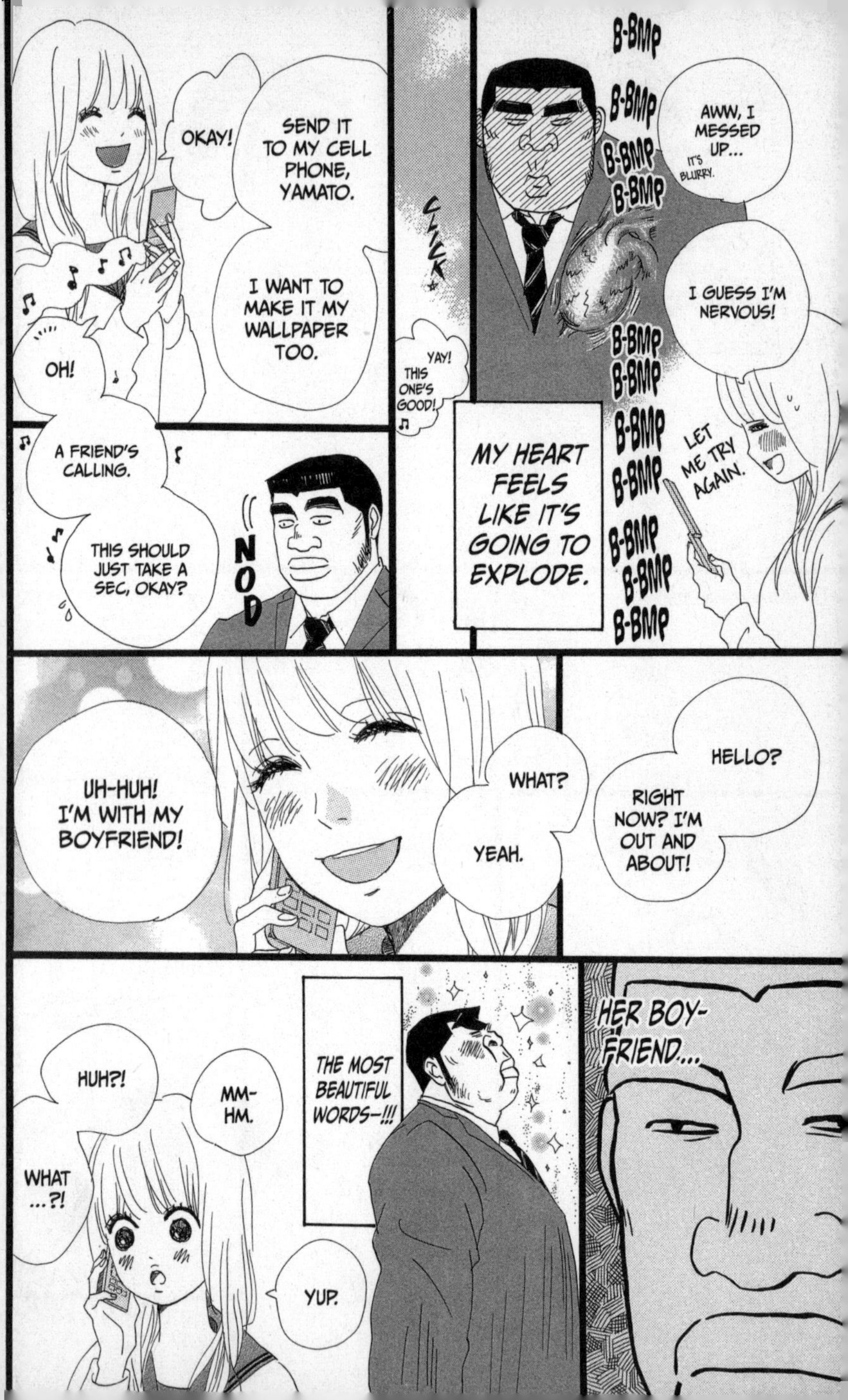
B-BMP B-BMP B-BMP B-BMP
AWW, I MESSED UP...
IT'S BLURRY.
I GUESS I'M NERVOUS!
B-BMP B-BMP B-BMP B-BMP B-BMP B-BMP B-BMP
LET ME TRY AGAIN.
MY HEART FEELS LIKE IT'S GOING TO EXPLODE.
CLICK
YAY! THIS ONE'S GOOD!
SEND IT TO MY CELL PHONE, YAMATO.
OKAY!
I WANT TO MAKE IT MY WALLPAPER TOO.
OH!
A FRIEND'S CALLING.
THIS SHOULD JUST TAKE A SEC, OKAY?
NOD
HELLO?
RIGHT NOW? I'M OUT AND ABOUT!
WHAT?
YEAH.
UH-HUH! I'M WITH MY BOYFRIEND!
HER BOY-FRIEND...
THE MOST BEAUTIFUL WORDS—!!!
MM-HM.
HUH?!
WHAT ...?!
YUP.

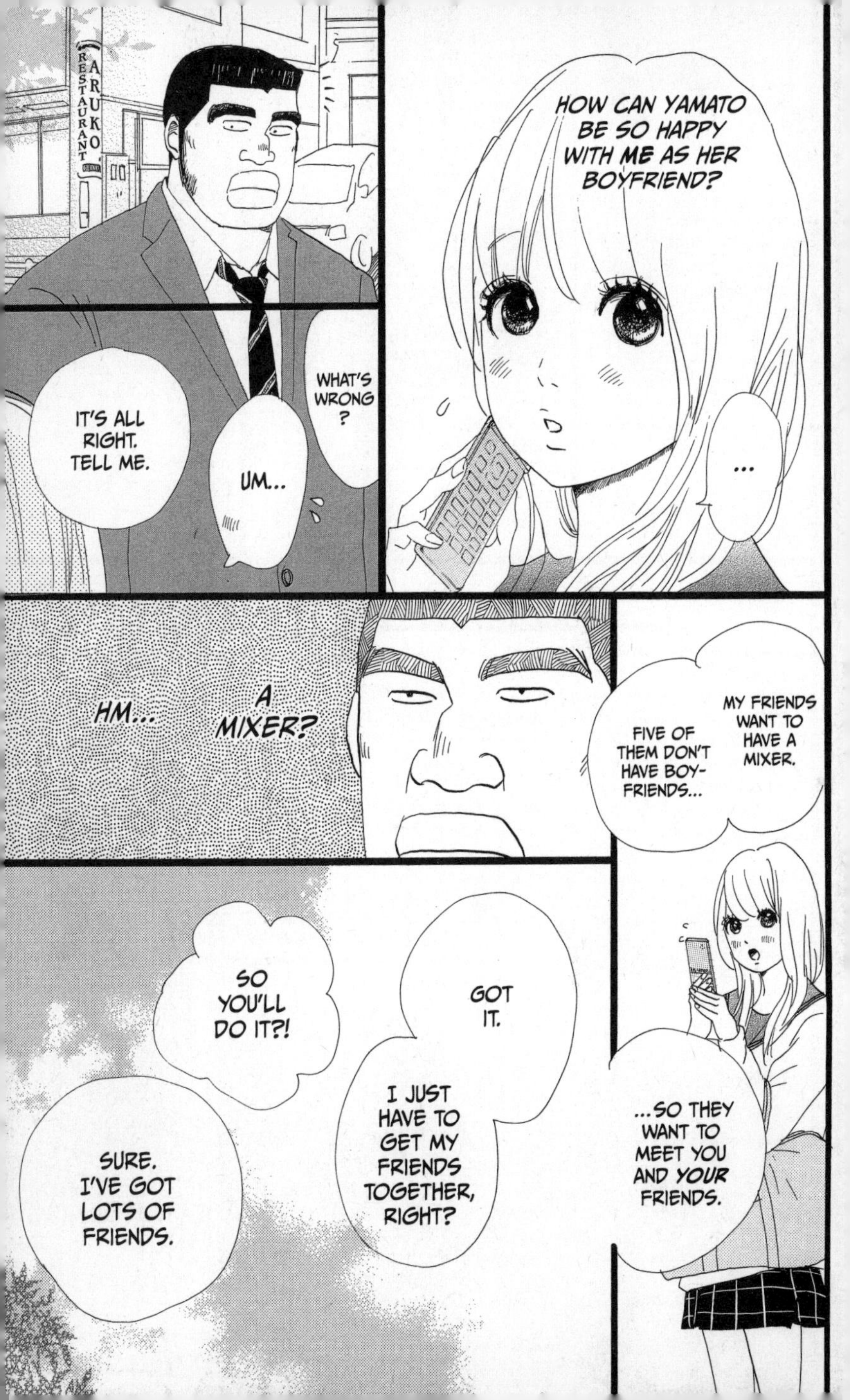
HOW CAN YAMATO BE SO HAPPY WITH *ME* AS HER BOYFRIEND?
...
RESTAURANT
ARUKO
WHAT'S WRONG?
UM...
IT'S ALL RIGHT. TELL ME.
MY FRIENDS WANT TO HAVE A MIXER.
FIVE OF THEM DON'T HAVE BOY-FRIENDS...
...SO THEY WANT TO MEET YOU AND *YOUR* FRIENDS.
A MIXER?
HM...
GOT IT.
I JUST HAVE TO GET MY FRIENDS TOGETHER, RIGHT?
SO YOU'LL DO IT?!
SURE. I'VE GOT LOTS OF FRIENDS.

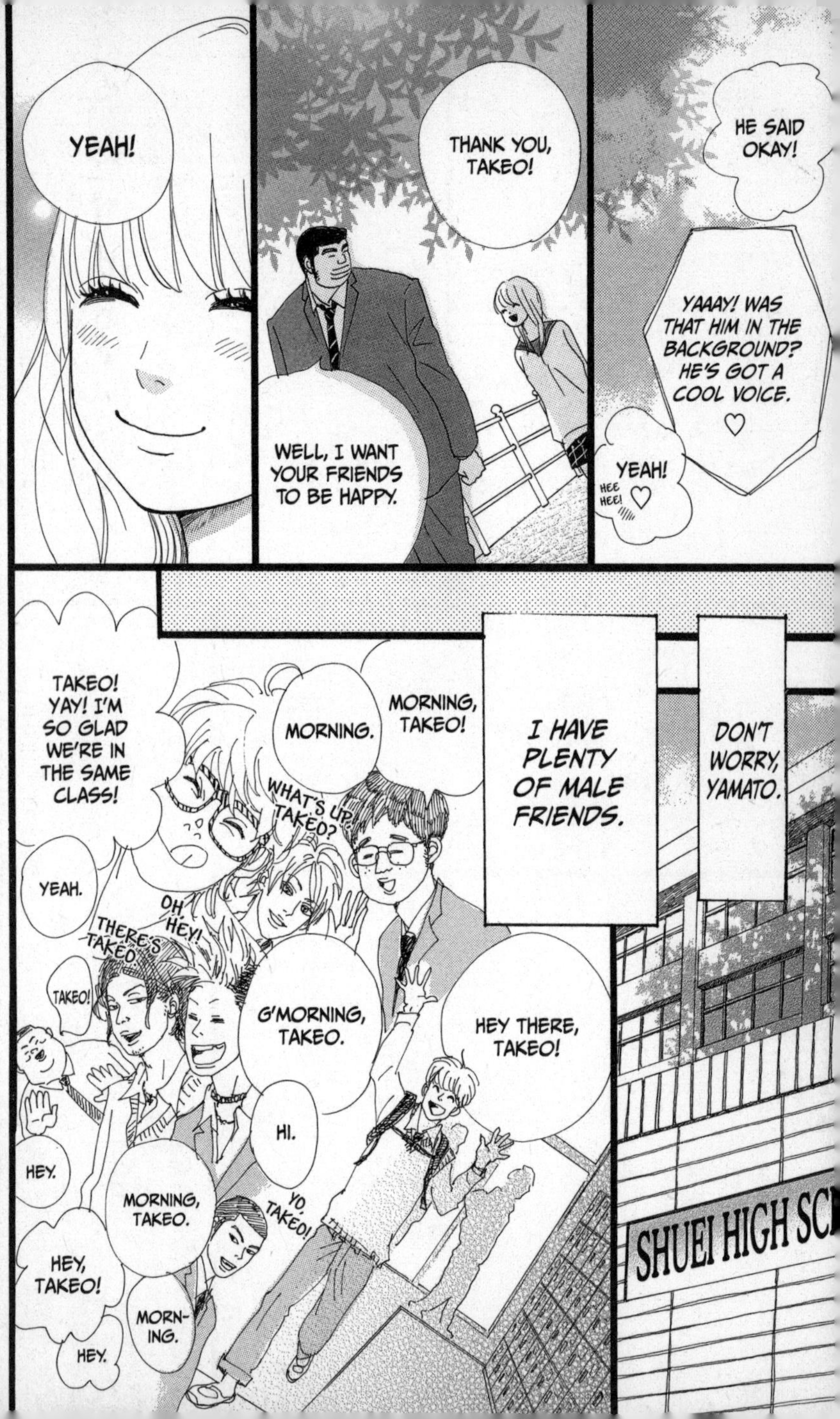
HE SAID OKAY!
YAAAY! WAS THAT HIM IN THE BACKGROUND? HE'S GOT A COOL VOICE. ♡
YEAH!
HEE HEE! ♡
THANK YOU, TAKEO!
WELL, I WANT YOUR FRIENDS TO BE HAPPY.
YEAH!
DON'T WORRY, YAMATO.
SHUEI HIGH SC
I HAVE PLENTY OF MALE FRIENDS.
MORNING, TAKEO!
MORNING.
TAKEO! YAY! I'M SO GLAD WE'RE IN THE SAME CLASS!
WHAT'S UP, TAKEO?
HEY THERE, TAKEO!
G'MORNING, TAKEO.
OH, HEY!
YEAH.
THERE'S TAKEO.
TAKEO!
HI.
YO, TAKEO!
MORNING, TAKEO.
HEY.
HEY, TAKEO!
MORN-ING.
HEY.

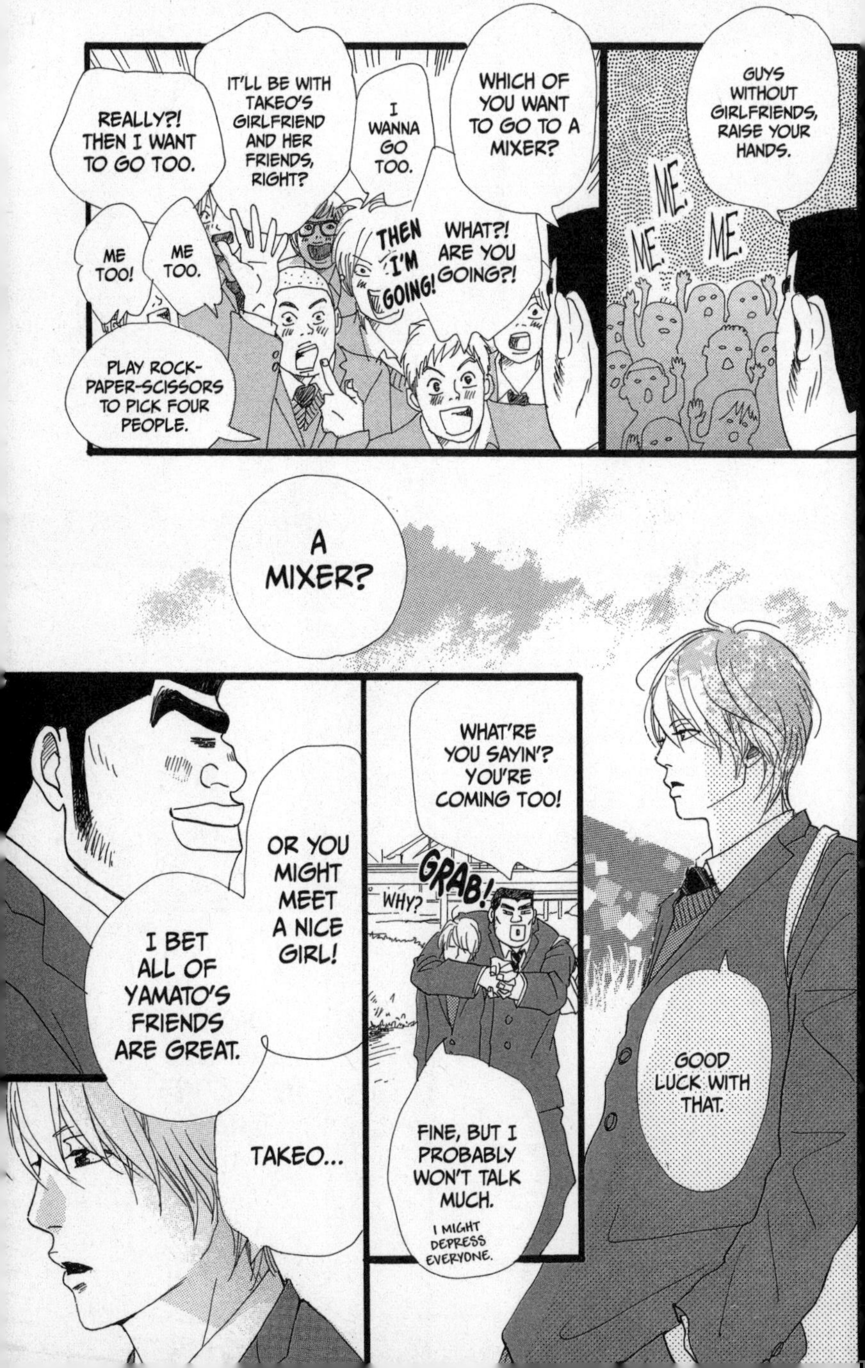
GUYS WITHOUT GIRLFRIENDS, RAISE YOUR HANDS.
ME.
ME.
ME.
WHICH OF YOU WANT TO GO TO A MIXER?
I WANNA GO TOO.
IT'LL BE WITH TAKEO'S GIRLFRIEND AND HER FRIENDS, RIGHT?
REALLY?! THEN I WANT TO GO TOO.
WHAT?! ARE YOU GOING?!
THEN I'M GOING!
ME TOO.
ME TOO!
PLAY ROCK-PAPER-SCISSORS TO PICK FOUR PEOPLE.
A MIXER?
GOOD LUCK WITH THAT.
WHAT'RE YOU SAYIN'? YOU'RE COMING TOO!
GRAB!
WHY?
FINE, BUT I PROBABLY WON'T TALK MUCH.
I MIGHT DEPRESS EVERYONE.
OR YOU MIGHT MEET A NICE GIRL!
I BET ALL OF YAMATO'S FRIENDS ARE GREAT.
TAKEO...

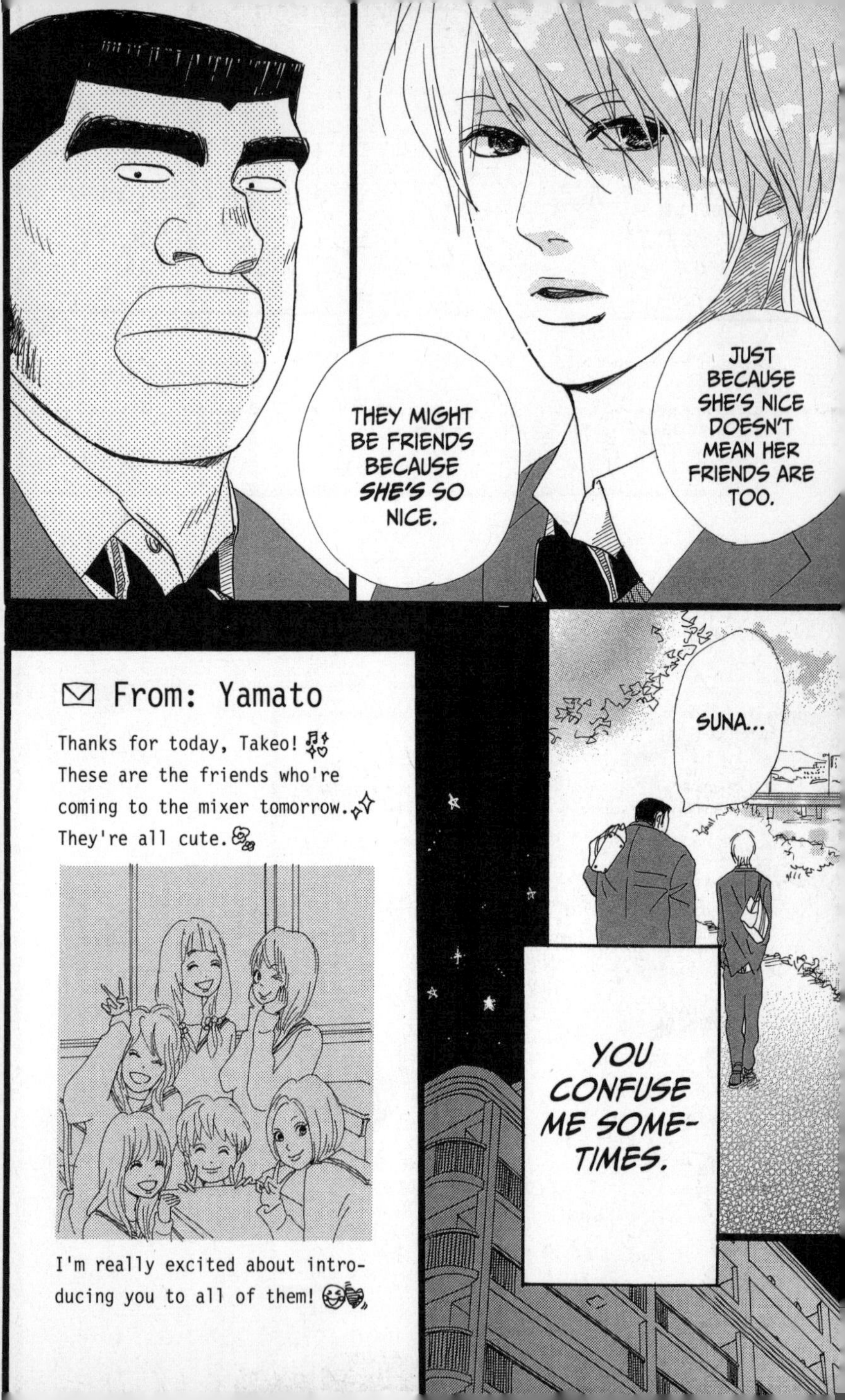
JUST BECAUSE SHE'S NICE DOESN'T MEAN HER FRIENDS ARE TOO.
THEY MIGHT BE FRIENDS BECAUSE SHE'S SO NICE.
SUNA...
YOU CONFUSE ME SOME-TIMES.
From: Yamato
Thanks for today, Takeo!
These are the friends who're coming to the mixer tomorrow.
They're all cute.
I'm really excited about intro-ducing you to all of them!

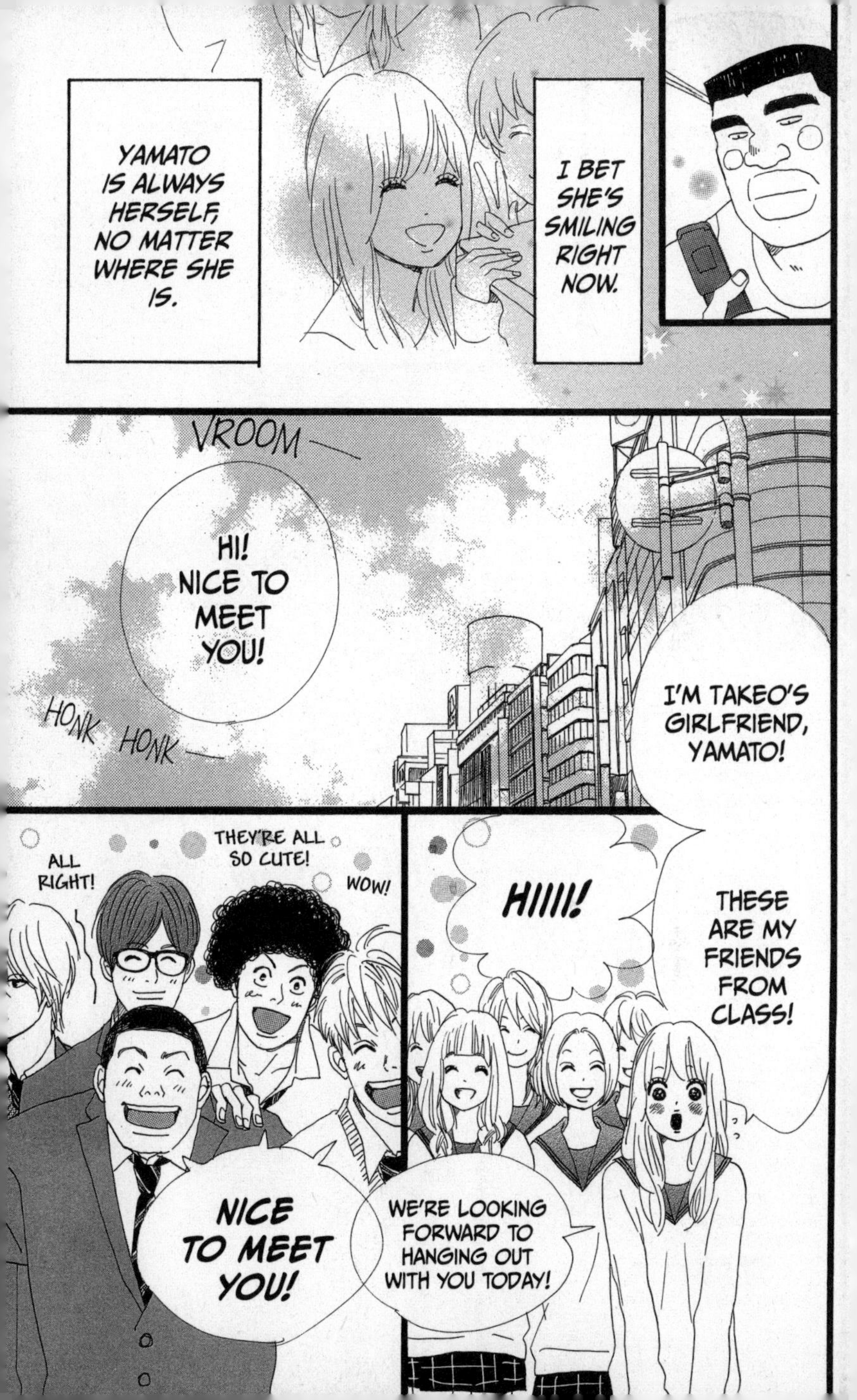
I BET SHE'S SMILING RIGHT NOW.
YAMATO IS ALWAYS HERSELF, NO MATTER WHERE SHE IS.
VROOM
HI! NICE TO MEET YOU!
I'M TAKEO'S GIRLFRIEND, YAMATO!
HONK HONK
THESE ARE MY FRIENDS FROM CLASS!
HIIII!
WE'RE LOOKING FORWARD TO HANGING OUT WITH YOU TODAY!
WOW!
THEY'RE ALL SO CUTE!
ALL RIGHT!
NICE TO MEET YOU!

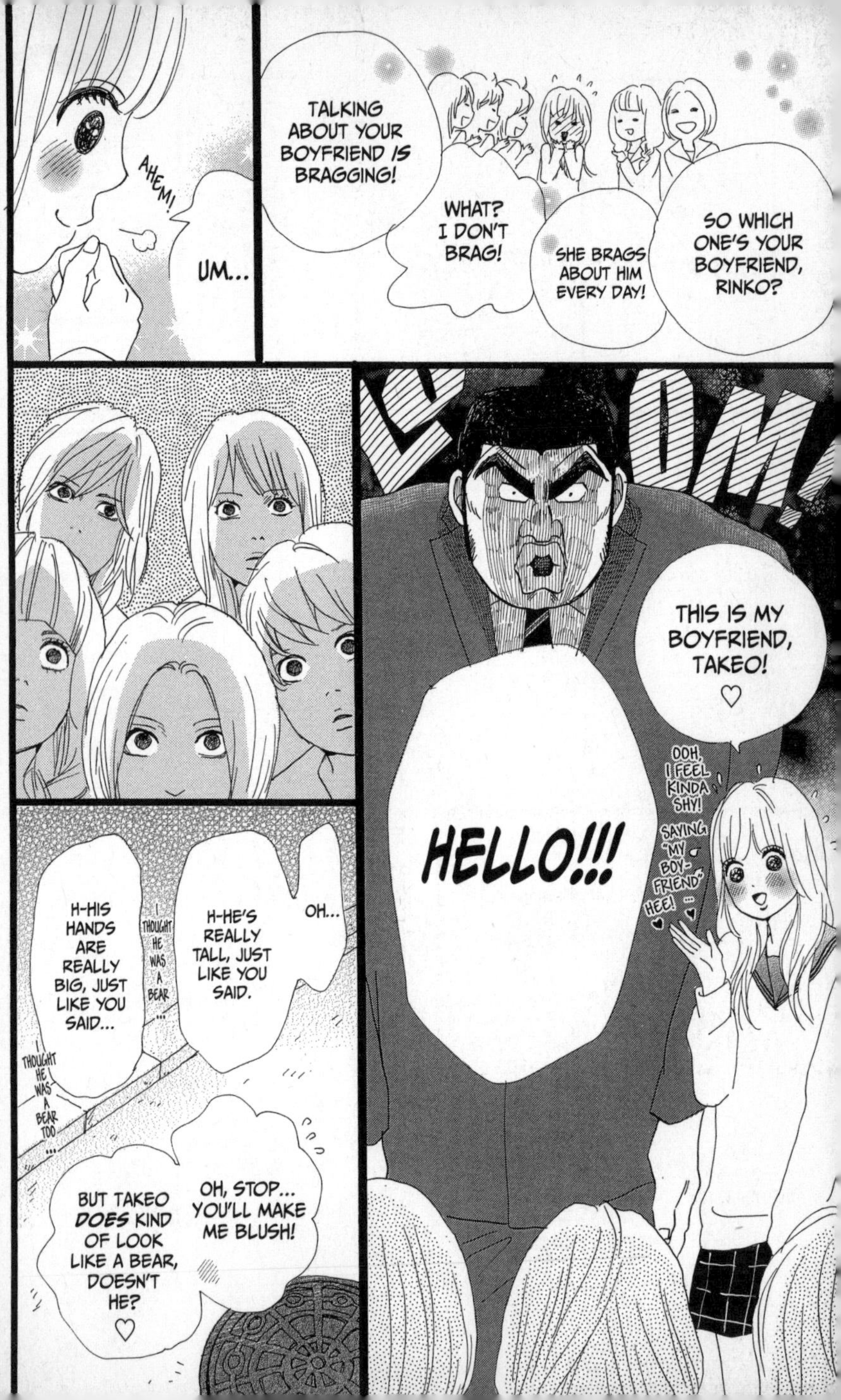
SO WHICH ONE'S YOUR BOYFRIEND, RINKO?
SHE BRAGS ABOUT HIM EVERY DAY!
WHAT? I DON'T BRAG!
TALKING ABOUT YOUR BOYFRIEND *IS* BRAGGING!
AHEM!
UM...
THIS IS MY BOYFRIEND, TAKEO! ♡
OOH, I FEEL KINDA SHY!
SAYING "MY BOY-FRIEND" HEE! ...
HELLO!!!
OH...
H-HE'S REALLY TALL, JUST LIKE YOU SAID.
I THOUGHT HE WAS A BEAR...
H-HIS HANDS ARE REALLY BIG, JUST LIKE YOU SAID...
I THOUGHT HE WAS A BEAR TOO...
OH, STOP... YOU'LL MAKE ME BLUSH!
BUT TAKEO *DOES* KIND OF LOOK LIKE A BEAR, DOESN'T HE? ♡

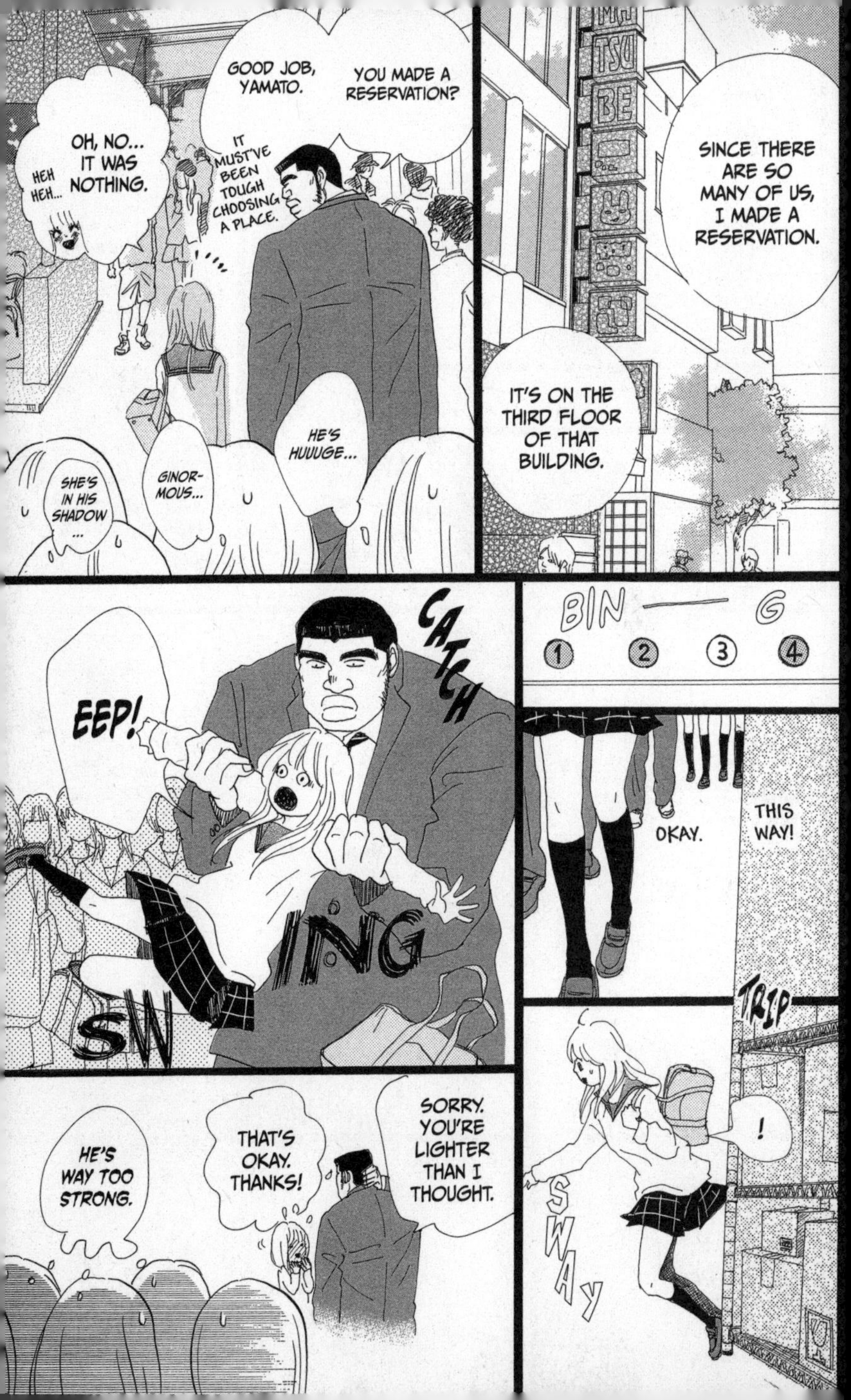
SINCE THERE ARE SO MANY OF US, I MADE A RESERVATION.
IT'S ON THE THIRD FLOOR OF THAT BUILDING.
YOU MADE A RESERVATION?
GOOD JOB, YAMATO.
IT MUST'VE BEEN TOUGH CHOOSING A PLACE.
OH, NO... IT WAS NOTHING.
HEH HEH...
HE'S HUUUGE...
GINOR-MOUS...
SHE'S IN HIS SHADOW...
BIN—— G
1 2 3 4
THIS WAY!
OKAY.
TRIP
!
SWAY
CATCH
EEP!
SW ING
SORRY. YOU'RE LIGHTER THAN I THOUGHT.
THAT'S OKAY. THANKS!
HE'S WAY TOO STRONG.

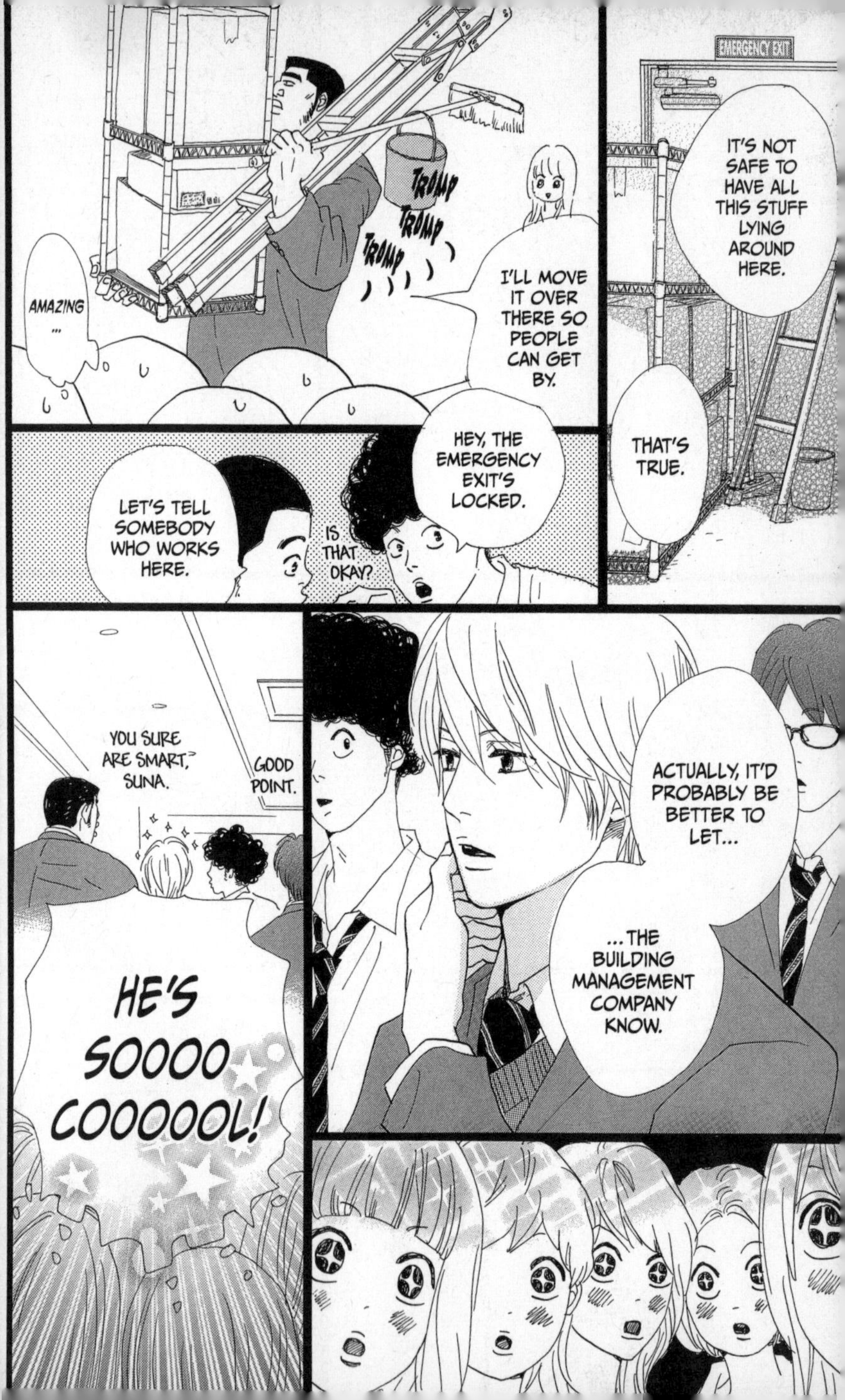
EMERGENCY EXIT
IT'S NOT SAFE TO HAVE ALL THIS STUFF LYING AROUND HERE.
THAT'S TRUE.
I'LL MOVE IT OVER THERE SO PEOPLE CAN GET BY.
TROMP
TROMP
TROMP
AMAZING ...
HEY, THE EMERGENCY EXIT'S LOCKED.
IS THAT OKAY?
LET'S TELL SOMEBODY WHO WORKS HERE.
ACTUALLY, IT'D PROBABLY BE BETTER TO LET...
...THE BUILDING MANAGEMENT COMPANY KNOW.
GOOD POINT.
YOU SURE ARE SMART, SUNA.
HE'S SOOOO COOOOOL!

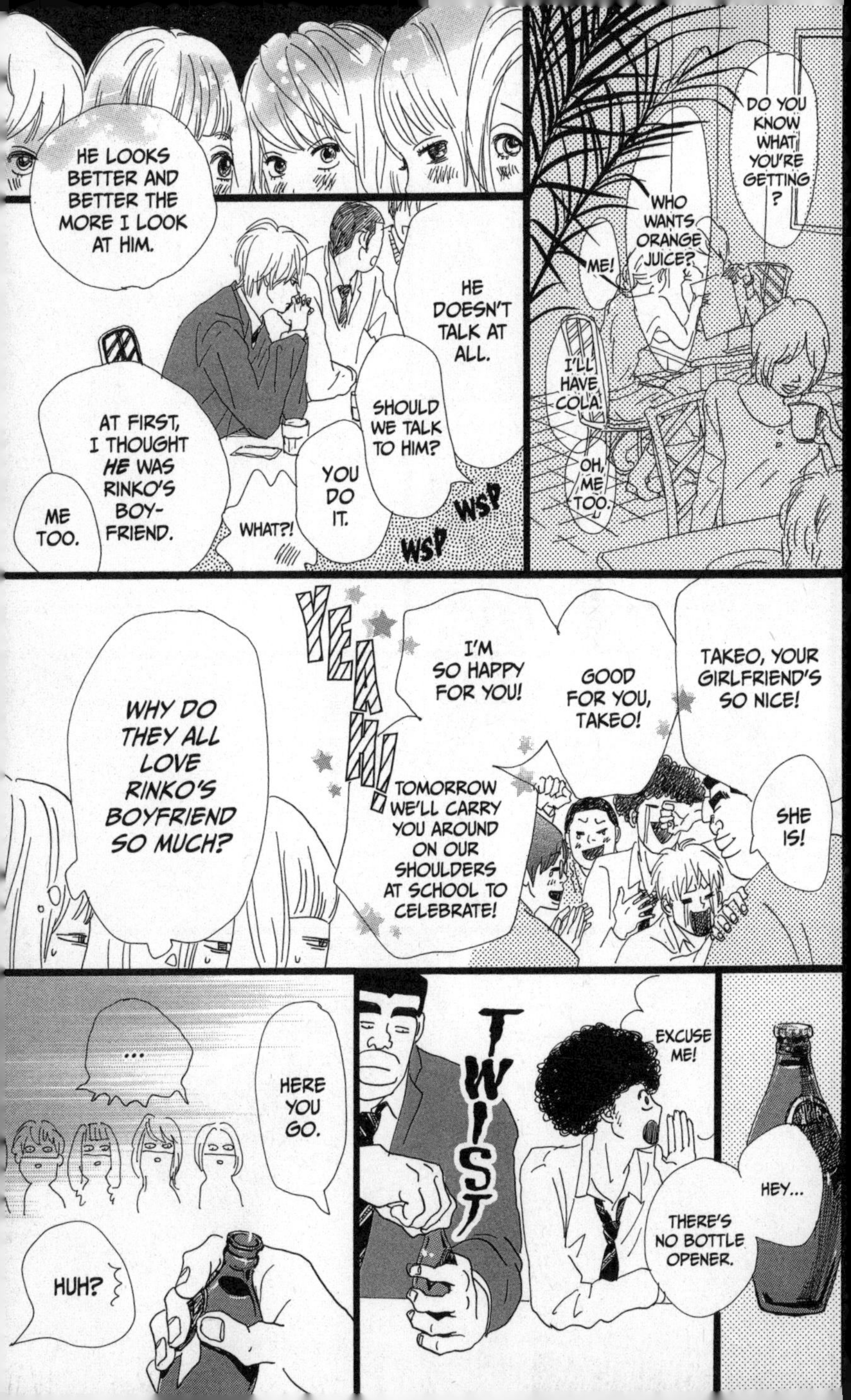
DO YOU KNOW WHAT YOU'RE GETTING?
WHO WANTS ORANGE JUICE?
ME!
I'LL HAVE COLA!
OH, ME TOO.
HE LOOKS BETTER AND BETTER THE MORE I LOOK AT HIM.
HE DOESN'T TALK AT ALL.
SHOULD WE TALK TO HIM?
YOU DO IT.
WSP
WSP
WHAT?!
AT FIRST, I THOUGHT *HE* WAS RINKO'S BOYFRIEND.
ME TOO.
TAKEO, YOUR GIRLFRIEND'S SO NICE!
SHE IS!
GOOD FOR YOU, TAKEO!
I'M SO HAPPY FOR YOU!
TOMORROW WE'LL CARRY YOU AROUND ON OUR SHOULDERS AT SCHOOL TO CELEBRATE!
YEAH!
WHY DO THEY ALL LOVE RINKO'S BOYFRIEND SO MUCH?
HEY...
THERE'S NO BOTTLE OPENER.
EXCUSE ME!
TWIST
...
HERE YOU GO.
HUH?

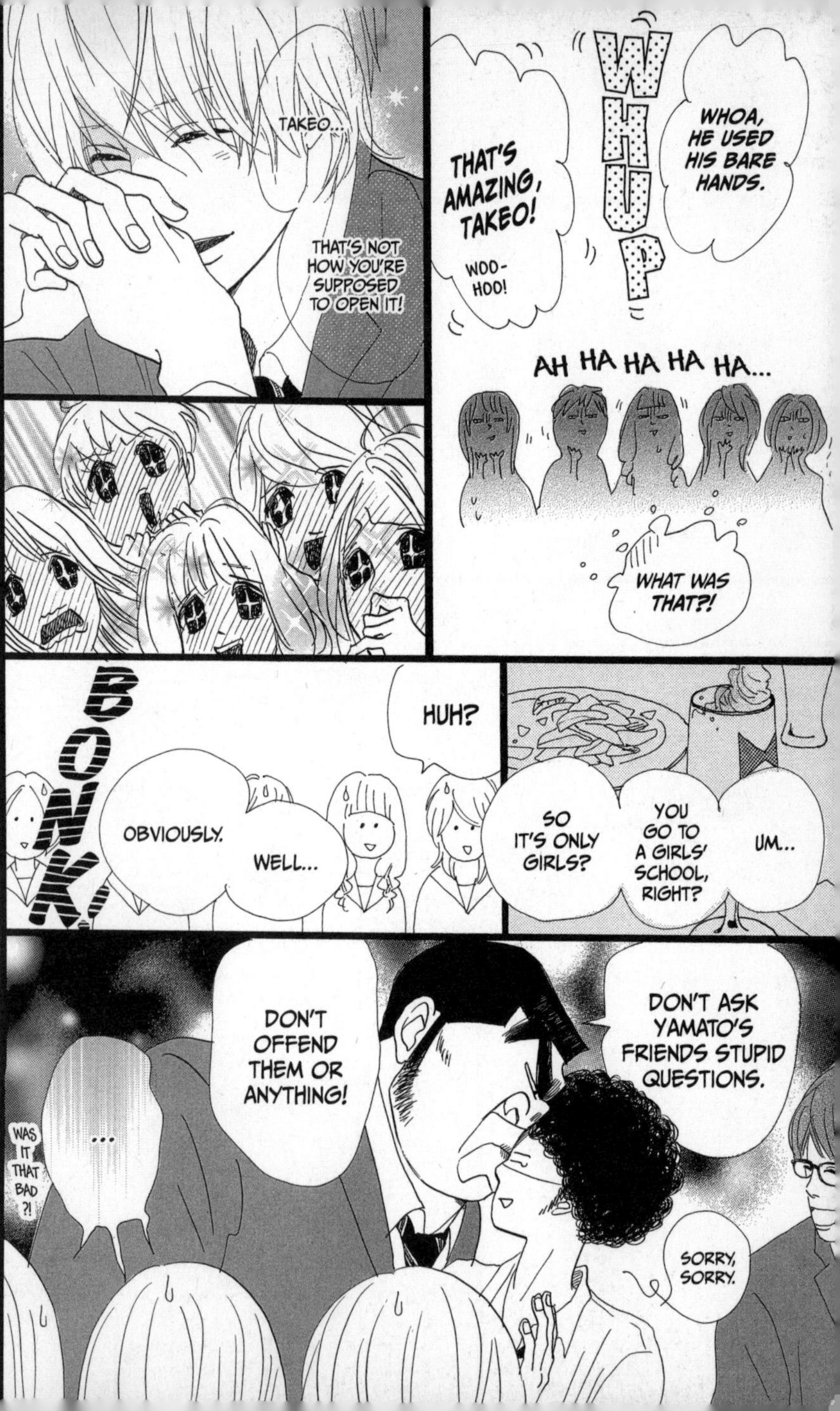
WHUP
WHOA, HE USED HIS BARE HANDS.
THAT'S AMAZING, TAKEO!
WOO-HOO!
AH HA HA HA HA...
WHAT WAS THAT?!
TAKEO...
THAT'S NOT HOW YOU'RE SUPPOSED TO OPEN IT!
UM...
YOU GO TO A GIRLS' SCHOOL, RIGHT?
SO IT'S ONLY GIRLS?
HUH?
WELL...
OBVIOUSLY.
BONK!
DON'T ASK YAMATO'S FRIENDS STUPID QUESTIONS.
DON'T OFFEND THEM OR ANYTHING!
SORRY, SORRY.
...
WAS IT THAT BAD?!

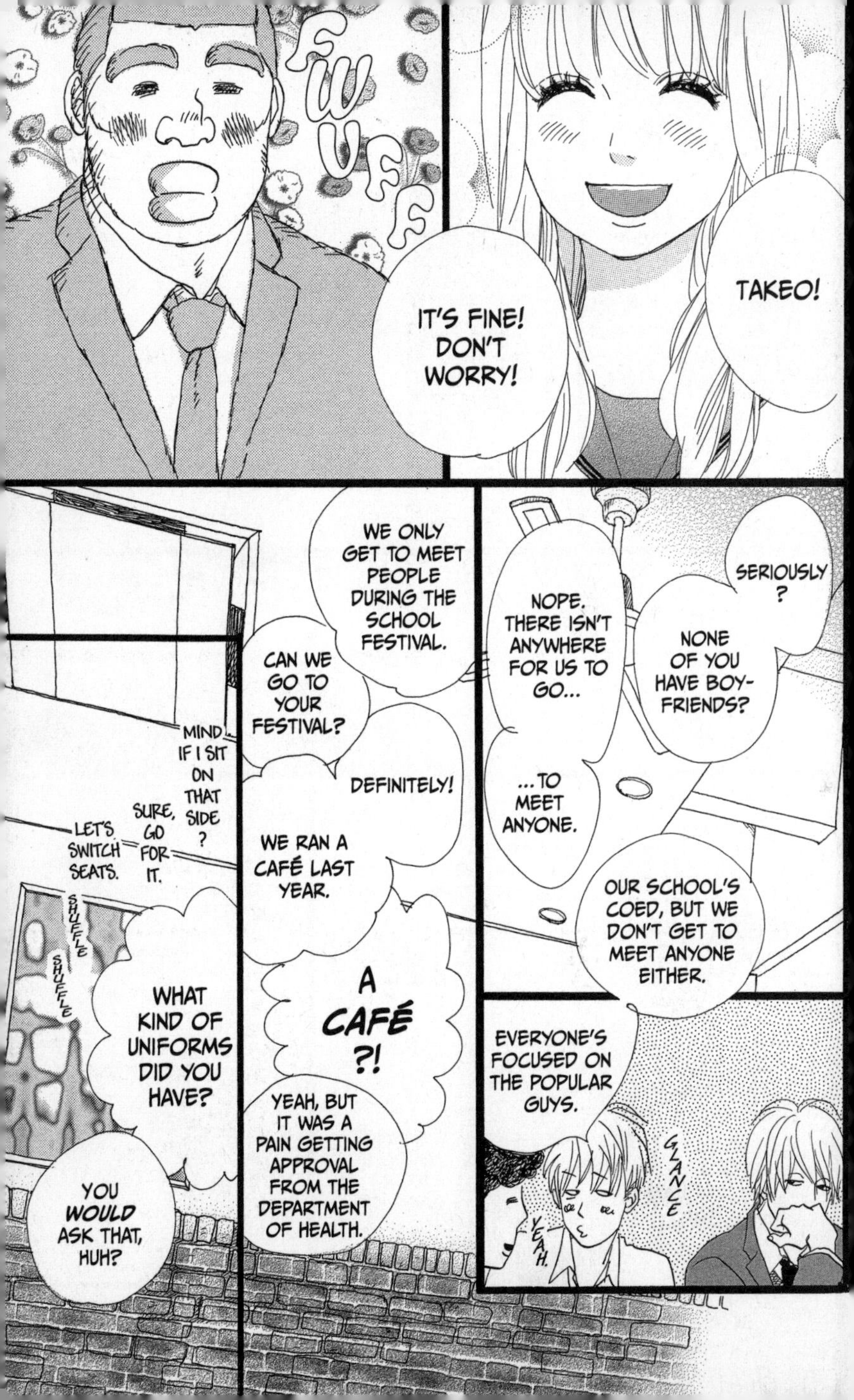
TAKEO!
IT'S FINE! DON'T WORRY!
FWUFF
SERIOUSLY?
NONE OF YOU HAVE BOY-FRIENDS?
NOPE. THERE ISN'T ANYWHERE FOR US TO GO...
...TO MEET ANYONE.
OUR SCHOOL'S COED, BUT WE DON'T GET TO MEET ANYONE EITHER.
EVERYONE'S FOCUSED ON THE POPULAR GUYS.
GLANCE
YEAH.
WE ONLY GET TO MEET PEOPLE DURING THE SCHOOL FESTIVAL.
CAN WE GO TO YOUR FESTIVAL?
DEFINITELY!
WE RAN A CAFÉ LAST YEAR.
A *CAFÉ*?!
YEAH, BUT IT WAS A PAIN GETTING APPROVAL FROM THE DEPARTMENT OF HEALTH.
MIND IF I SIT ON THAT SIDE?
SURE, GO FOR IT.
LET'S SWITCH SEATS.
SHUFFLE
SHUFFLE
WHAT KIND OF UNIFORMS DID YOU HAVE?
YOU *WOULD* ASK THAT, HUH?

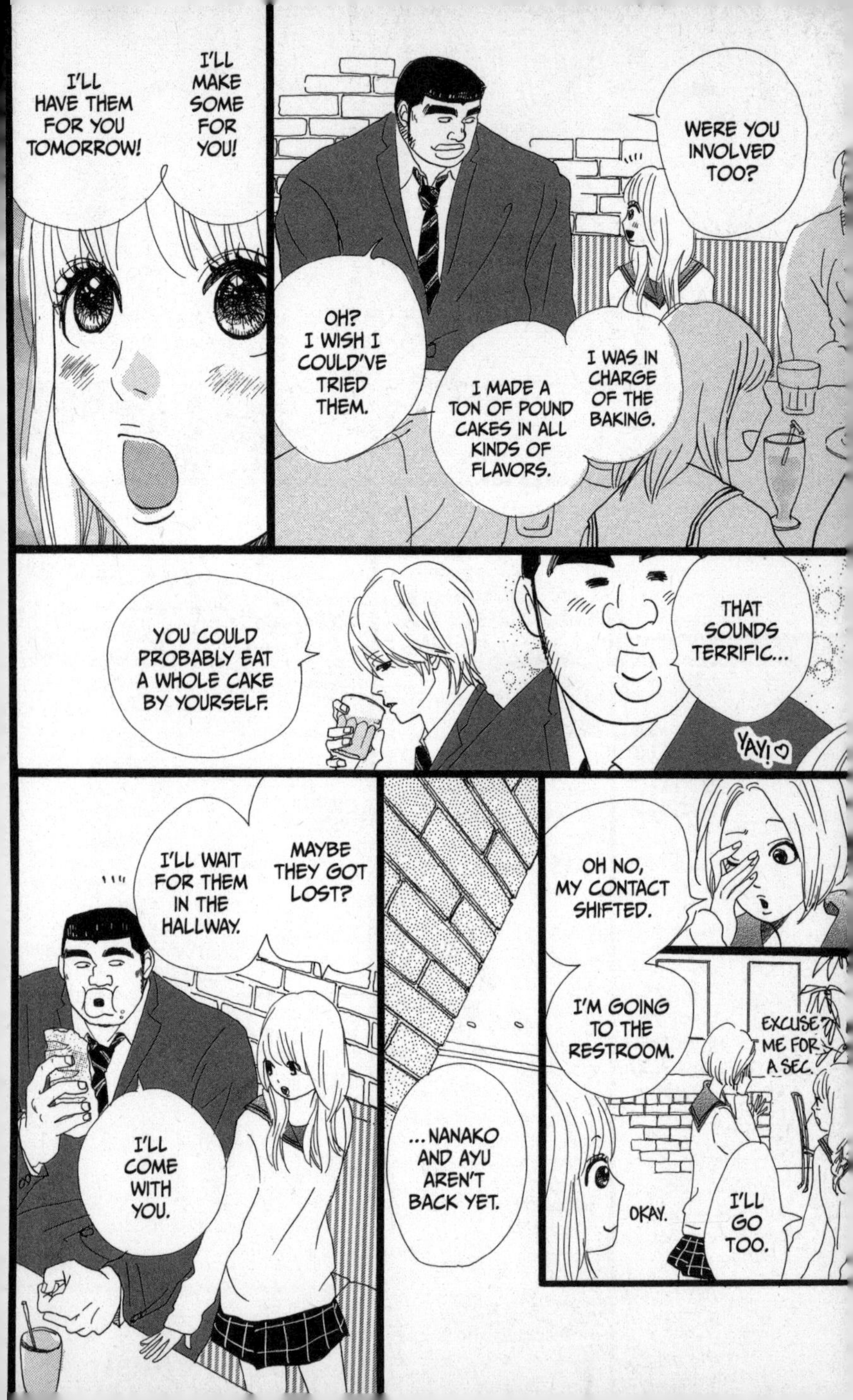
WERE YOU INVOLVED TOO?
I WAS IN CHARGE OF THE BAKING.
I MADE A TON OF POUND CAKES IN ALL KINDS OF FLAVORS.
OH? I WISH I COULD'VE TRIED THEM.
I'LL MAKE SOME FOR YOU!
I'LL HAVE THEM FOR YOU TOMORROW!
THAT SOUNDS TERRIFIC...
YAY! ♡
YOU COULD PROBABLY EAT A WHOLE CAKE BY YOURSELF.
OH NO, MY CONTACT SHIFTED.
EXCUSE ME FOR A SEC.
I'M GOING TO THE RESTROOM.
I'LL GO TOO.
OKAY.
...NANAKO AND AYU AREN'T BACK YET.
MAYBE THEY GOT LOST?
I'LL WAIT FOR THEM IN THE HALLWAY.
I'LL COME WITH YOU.

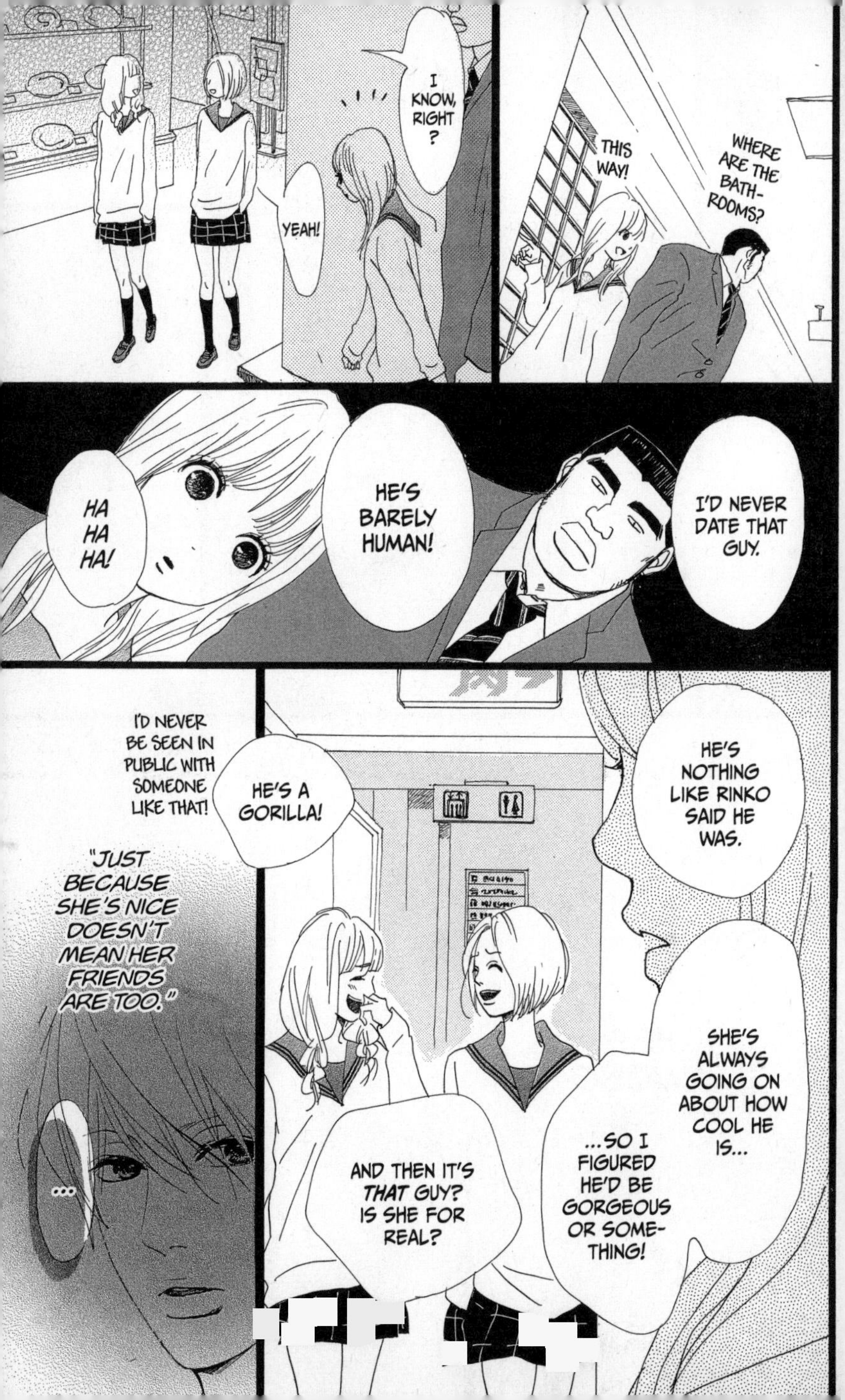
WHERE ARE THE BATH-ROOMS?
THIS WAY!
I KNOW, RIGHT?
YEAH!
I'D NEVER DATE THAT GUY.
HE'S BARELY HUMAN!
HA HA HA!
HE'S NOTHING LIKE RINKO SAID HE WAS.
SHE'S ALWAYS GOING ON ABOUT HOW COOL HE IS...
...SO I FIGURED HE'D BE GORGEOUS OR SOME-THING!
AND THEN IT'S *THAT* GUY? IS SHE FOR REAL?
HE'S A GORILLA!
I'D NEVER BE SEEN IN PUBLIC WITH SOMEONE LIKE THAT!
"JUST BECAUSE SHE'S NICE DOESN'T MEAN HER FRIENDS ARE TOO."
...

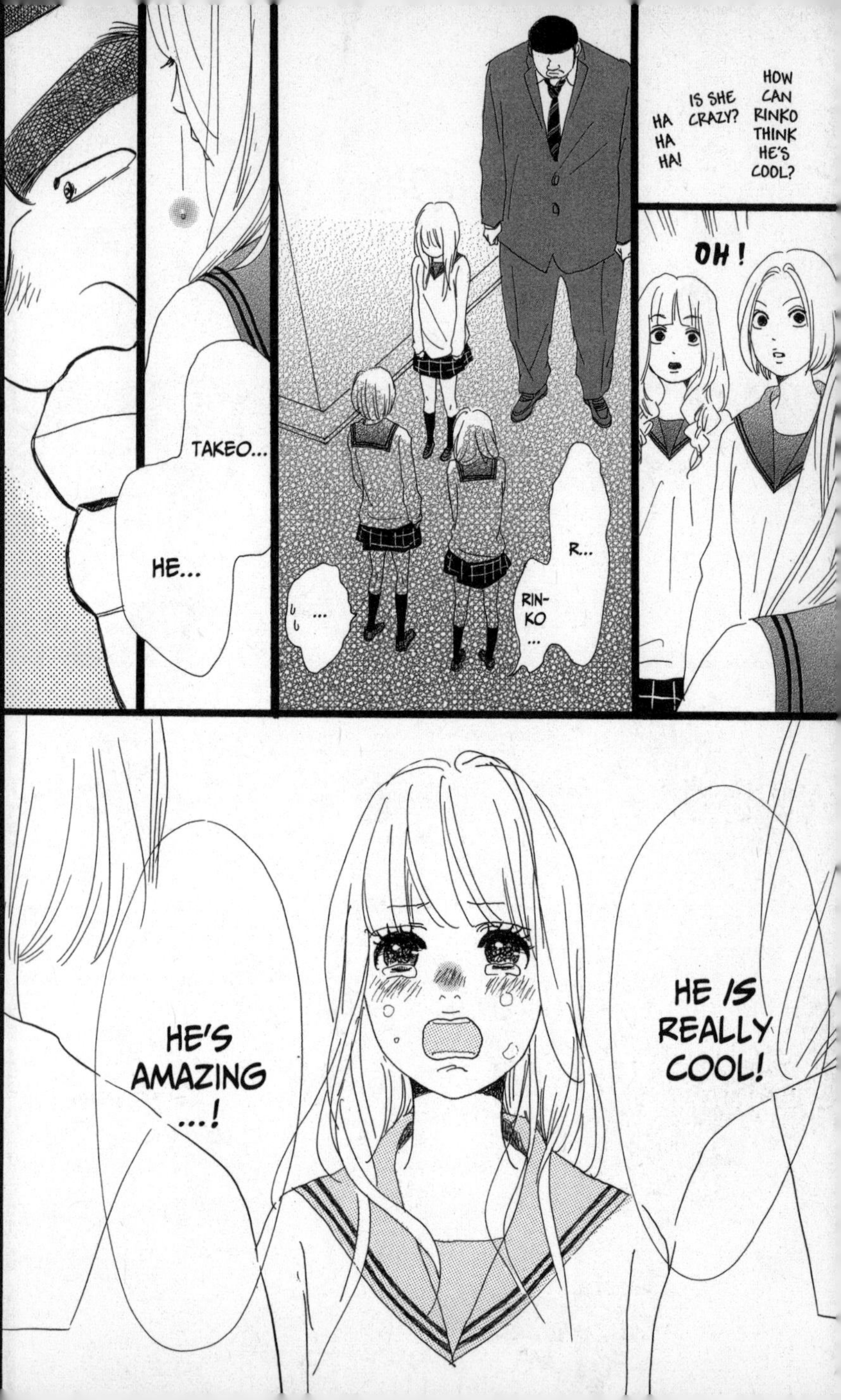
HOW CAN RINKO THINK HE'S COOL?
IS SHE CRAZY?
HA HA HA!
OH!
R... RIN-KO...
...
TAKEO...
HE...
HE IS REALLY COOL!
HE'S AMAZING...!

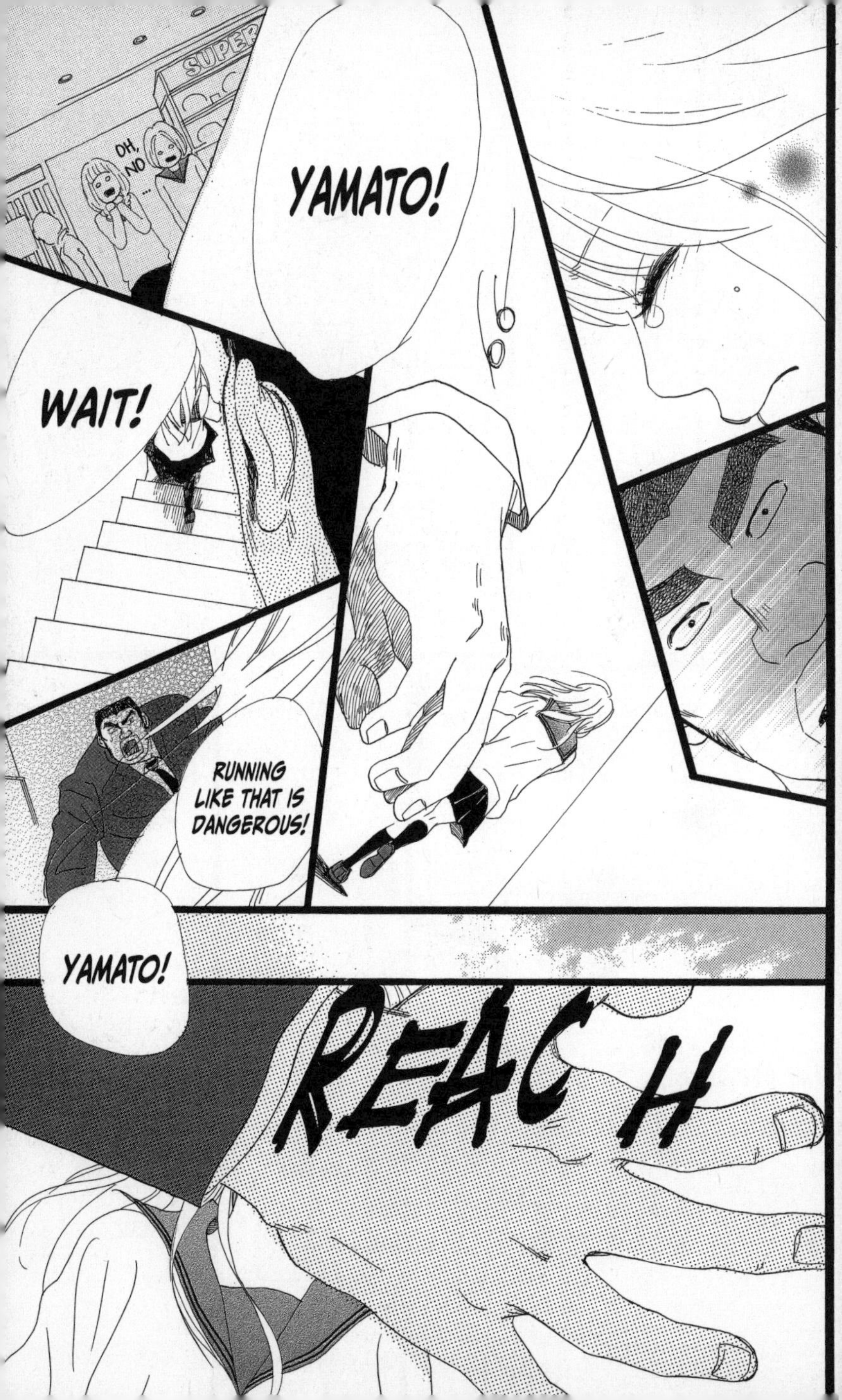
YAMATO!
OH, NO ...
WAIT!
RUNNING LIKE THAT IS DANGEROUS!
YAMATO!
REACH

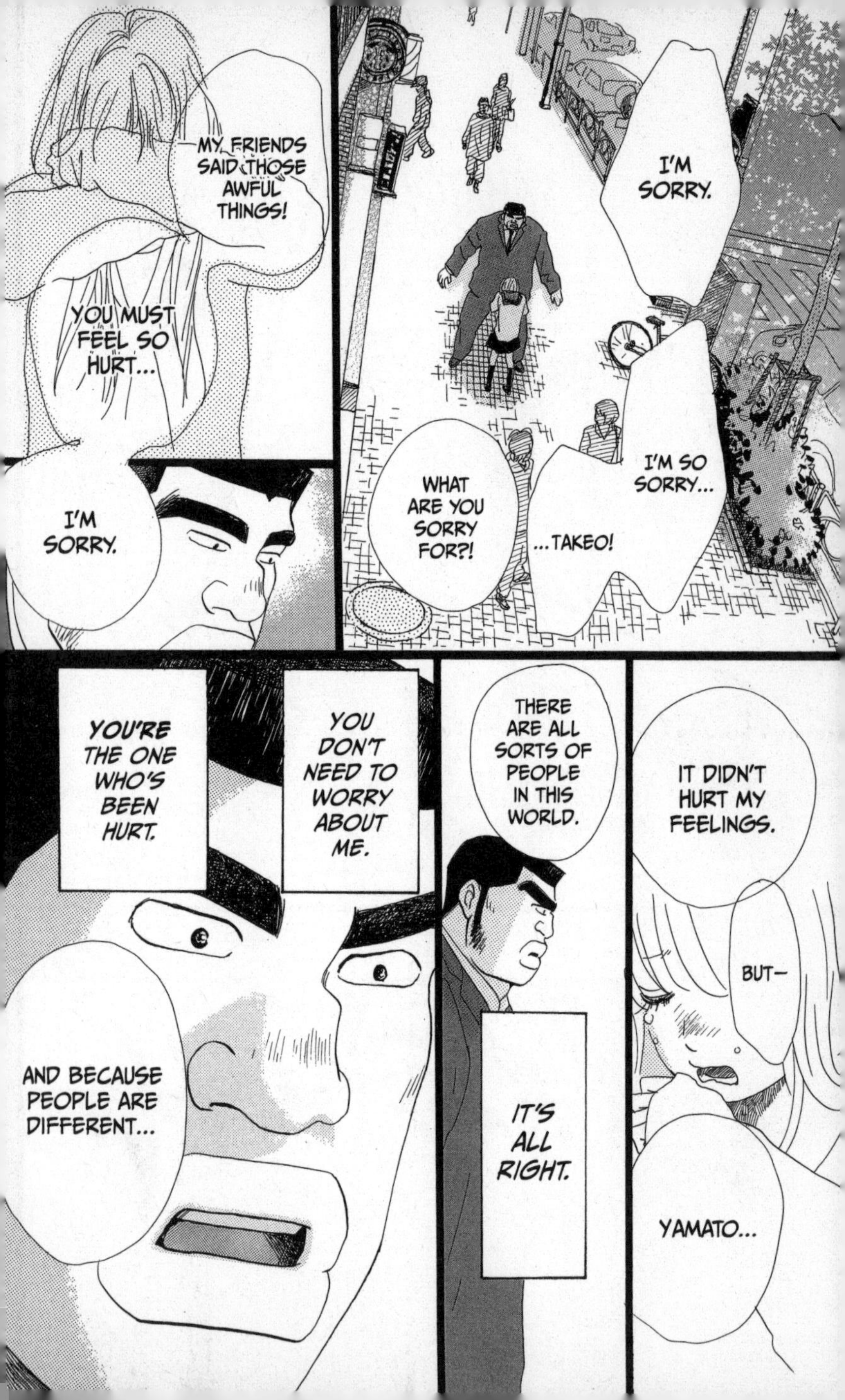
I'M SORRY.
I'M SO SORRY...
...TAKEO!
WHAT ARE YOU SORRY FOR?!
MY FRIENDS SAID THOSE AWFUL THINGS!
YOU MUST FEEL SO HURT...
I'M SORRY.
IT DIDN'T HURT MY FEELINGS.
BUT—
YAMATO...
THERE ARE ALL SORTS OF PEOPLE IN THIS WORLD.
IT'S ALL RIGHT.
YOU DON'T NEED TO WORRY ABOUT ME.
YOU'RE THE ONE WHO'S BEEN HURT.
AND BECAUSE PEOPLE ARE DIFFERENT...

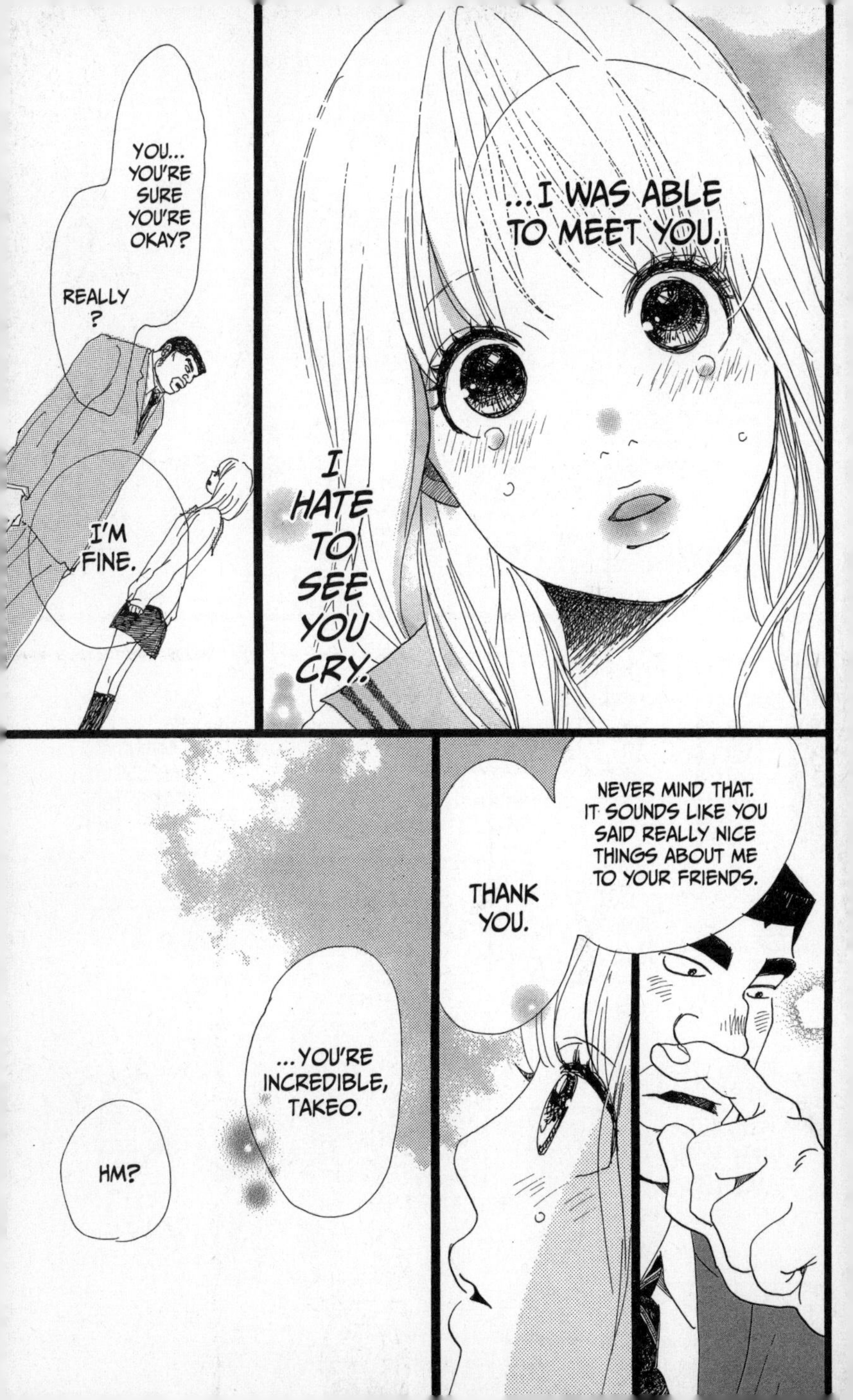
...I WAS ABLE TO MEET YOU.
I HATE TO SEE YOU CRY.
YOU... YOU'RE SURE YOU'RE OKAY?
REALLY ?
I'M FINE.
NEVER MIND THAT. IT SOUNDS LIKE YOU SAID REALLY NICE THINGS ABOUT ME TO YOUR FRIENDS.
THANK YOU.
...YOU'RE INCREDIBLE, TAKEO.
HM?

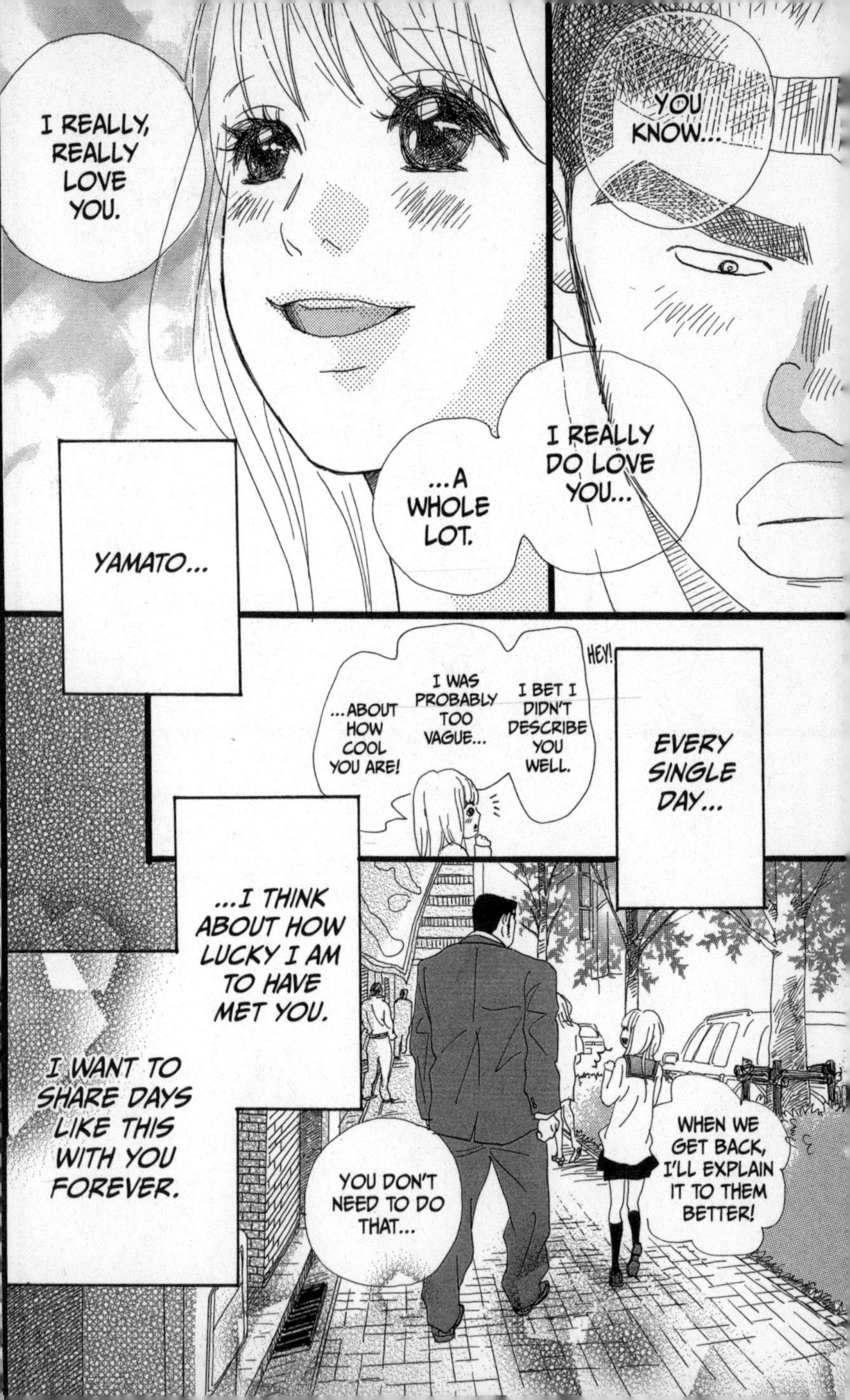
YOU KNOW...
I REALLY DO LOVE YOU...
...A WHOLE LOT.
I REALLY, REALLY LOVE YOU.
YAMATO...
EVERY SINGLE DAY...
HEY!
I BET I DIDN'T DESCRIBE YOU WELL.
I WAS PROBABLY TOO VAGUE...
...ABOUT HOW COOL YOU ARE!
...I THINK ABOUT HOW LUCKY I AM TO HAVE MET YOU.
WHEN WE GET BACK, I'LL EXPLAIN IT TO THEM BETTER!
YOU DON'T NEED TO DO THAT...
I WANT TO SHARE DAYS LIKE THIS WITH YOU FOREVER.

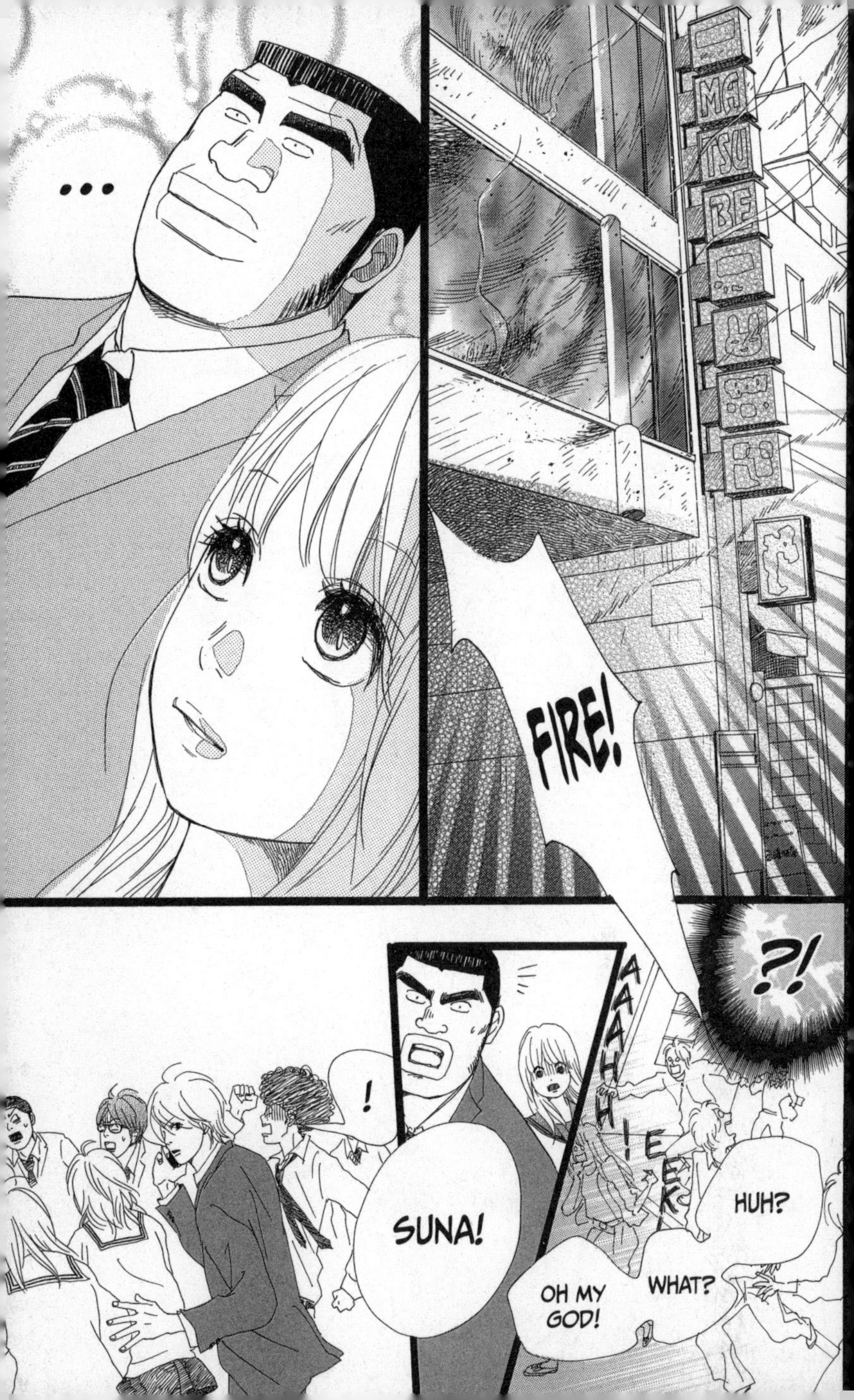
MA
TSU
BE
FIRE!
...
?!
AAAAHH!
EEEK
HUH?
WHAT?
OH MY GOD!
SUNA!
!

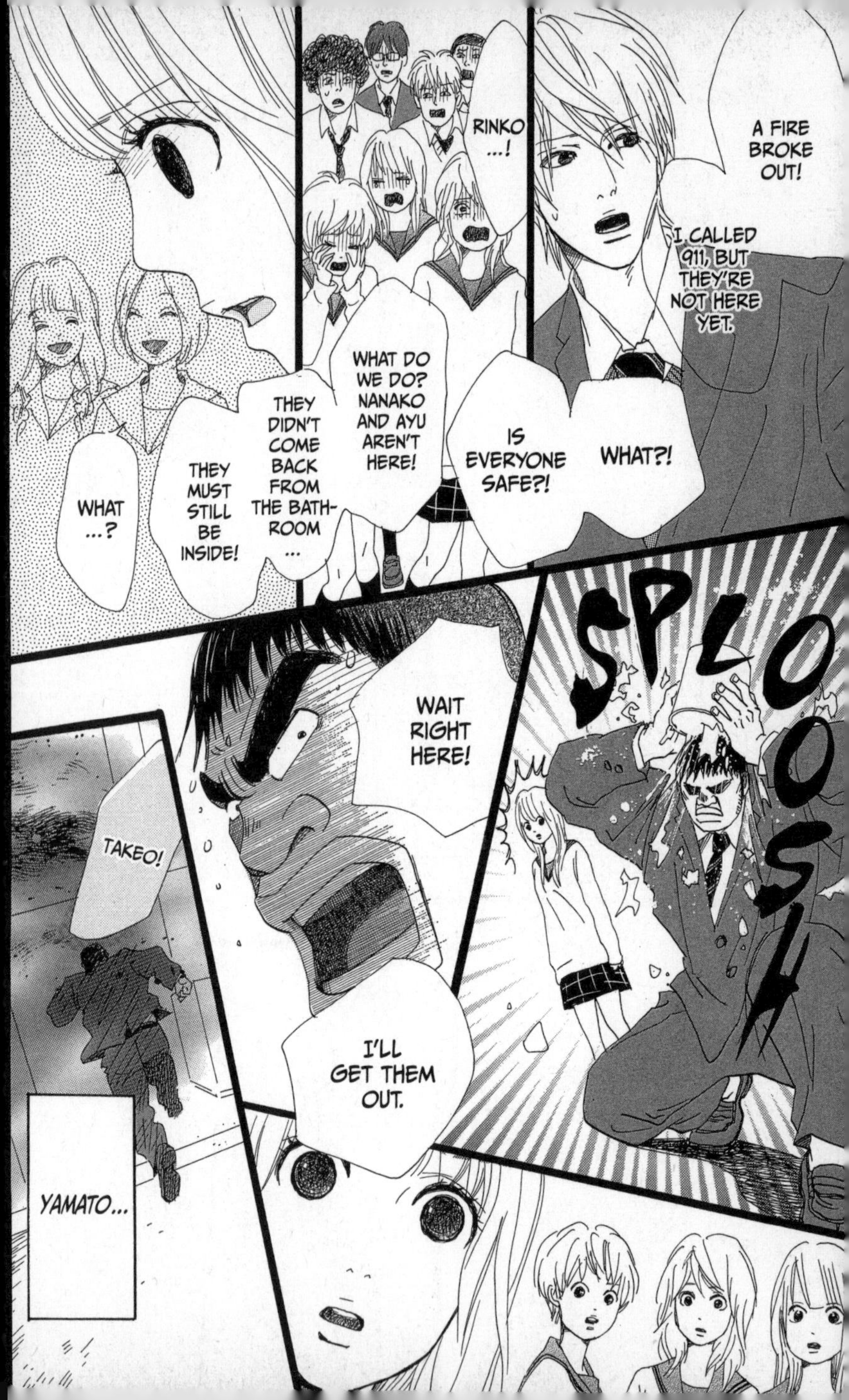
A FIRE BROKE OUT!
I CALLED 911, BUT THEY'RE NOT HERE YET.
WHAT?!
IS EVERYONE SAFE?!
RINKO ...!
WHAT DO WE DO? NANAKO AND AYU AREN'T HERE!
THEY DIDN'T COME BACK FROM THE BATH-ROOM ...
THEY MUST STILL BE INSIDE!
WHAT ...?
SPLOOSH
WAIT RIGHT HERE!
I'LL GET THEM OUT.
TAKEO!
YAMATO...

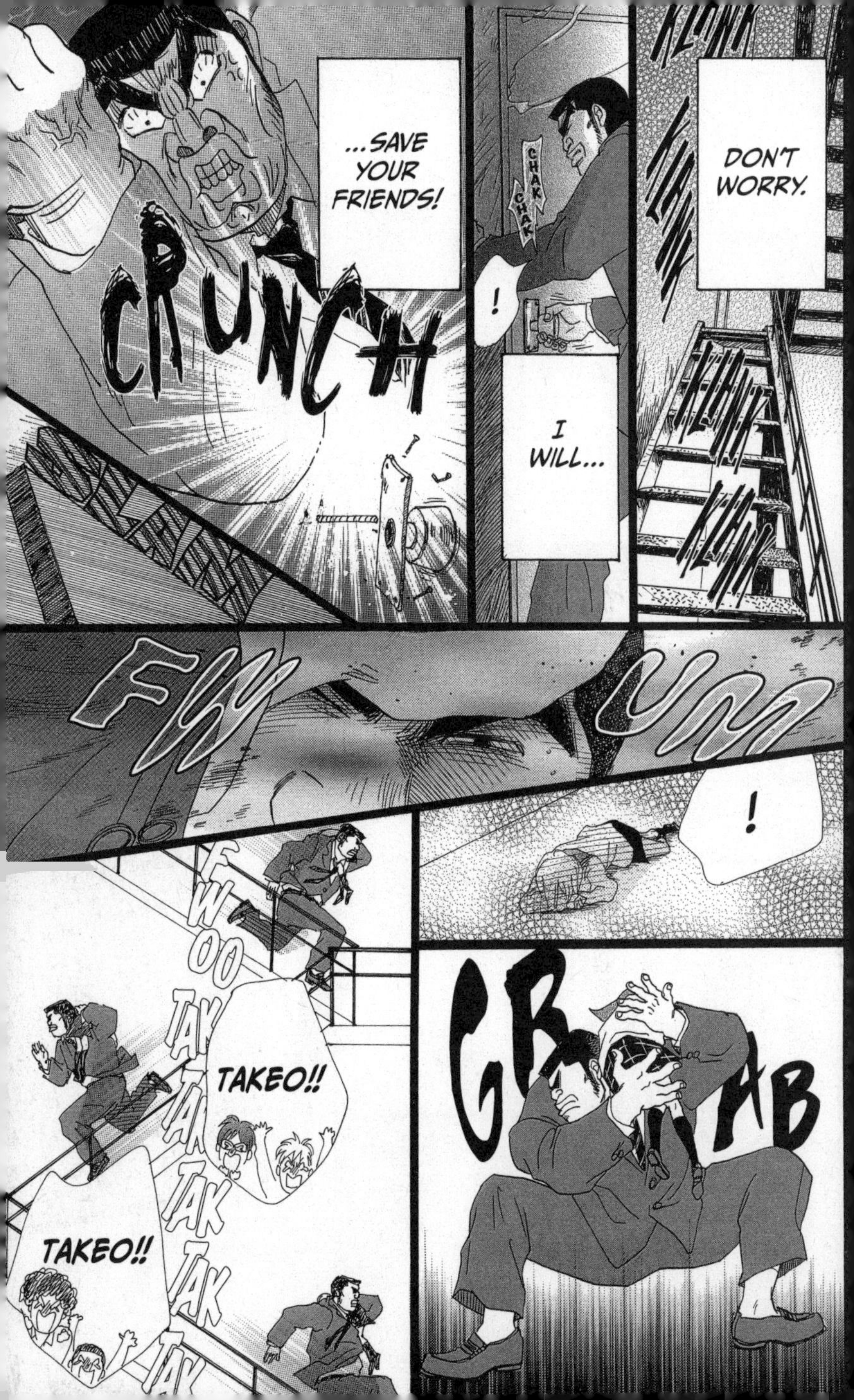
KLONK
KLANK
DON'T WORRY.
I WILL...
CHAK CHAK
!
...SAVE YOUR FRIENDS!
CRUNCH
FWUM
!
GRAB
FWOO
TAK TAK TAK TAK TAK
TAKEO!!
TAKEO!!

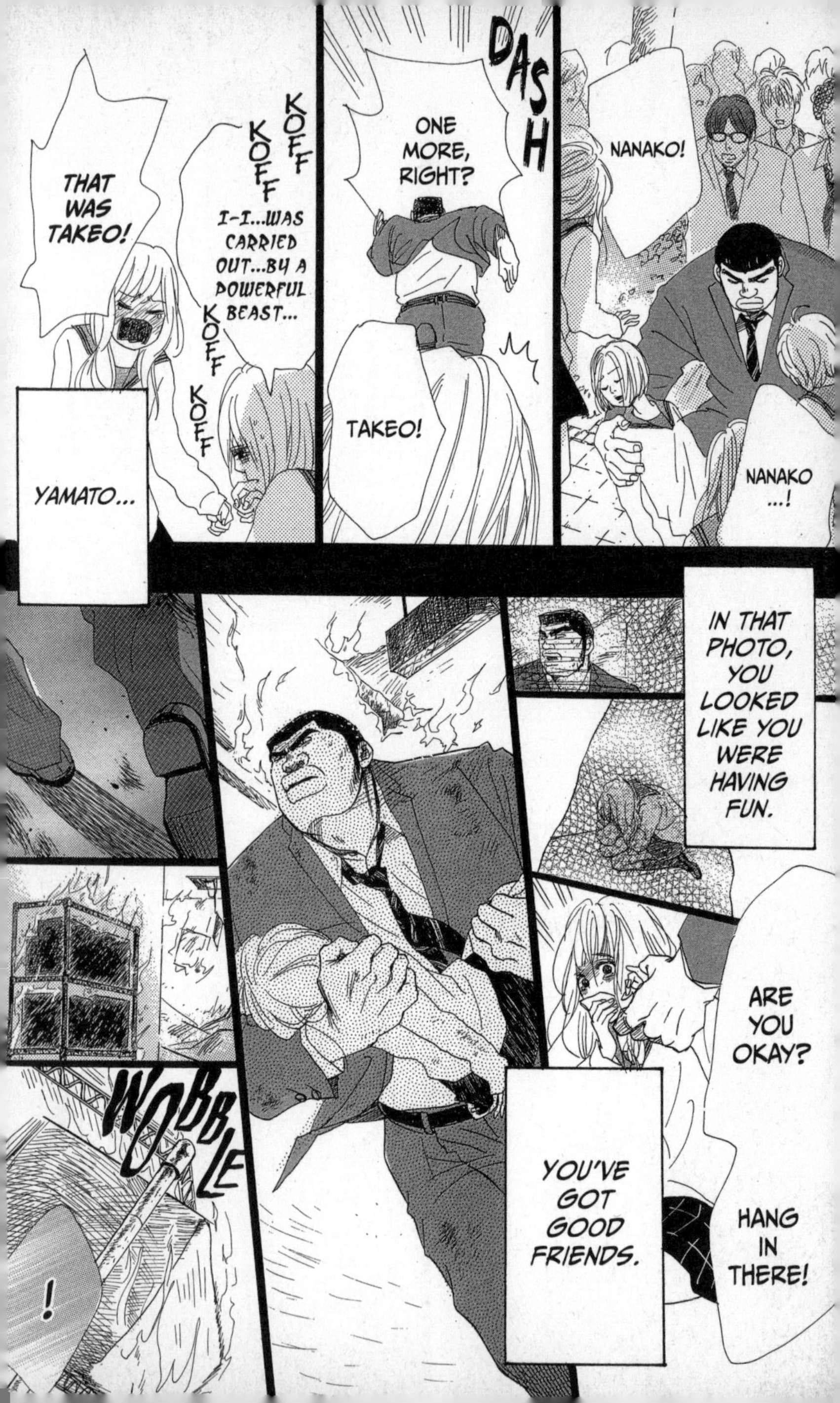
NANAKO!
NANAKO ...!
DASH
ONE MORE, RIGHT?
TAKEO!
KOFF KOFF
I-I...WAS CARRIED OUT...BY A POWERFUL BEAST...
KOFF KOFF
THAT WAS TAKEO!
YAMATO...
IN THAT PHOTO, YOU LOOKED LIKE YOU WERE HAVING FUN.
ARE YOU OKAY?
HANG IN THERE!
YOU'VE GOT GOOD FRIENDS.
WOBBLE
!

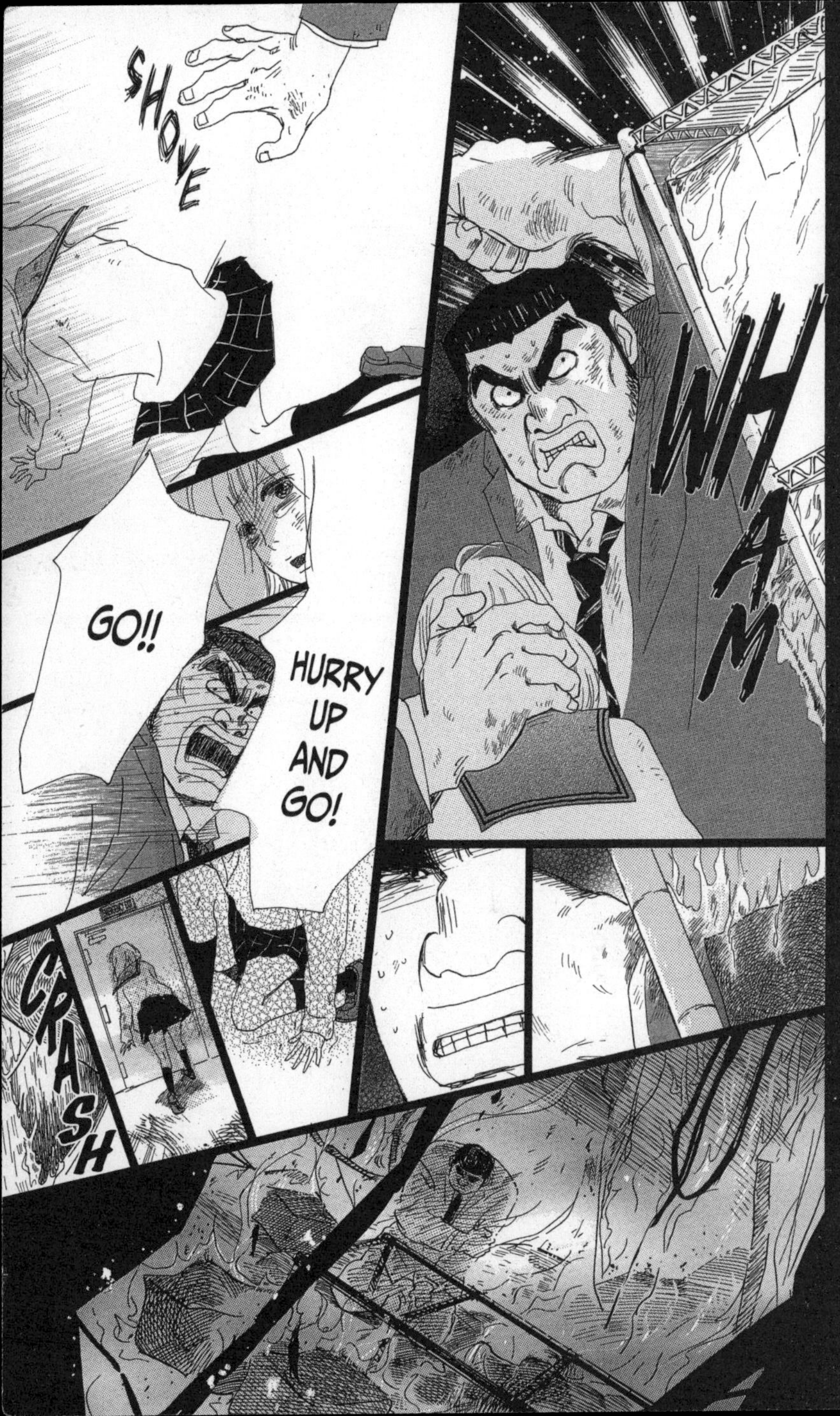
WHAM
SHOVE
GO!!
HURRY UP AND GO!
CRASH

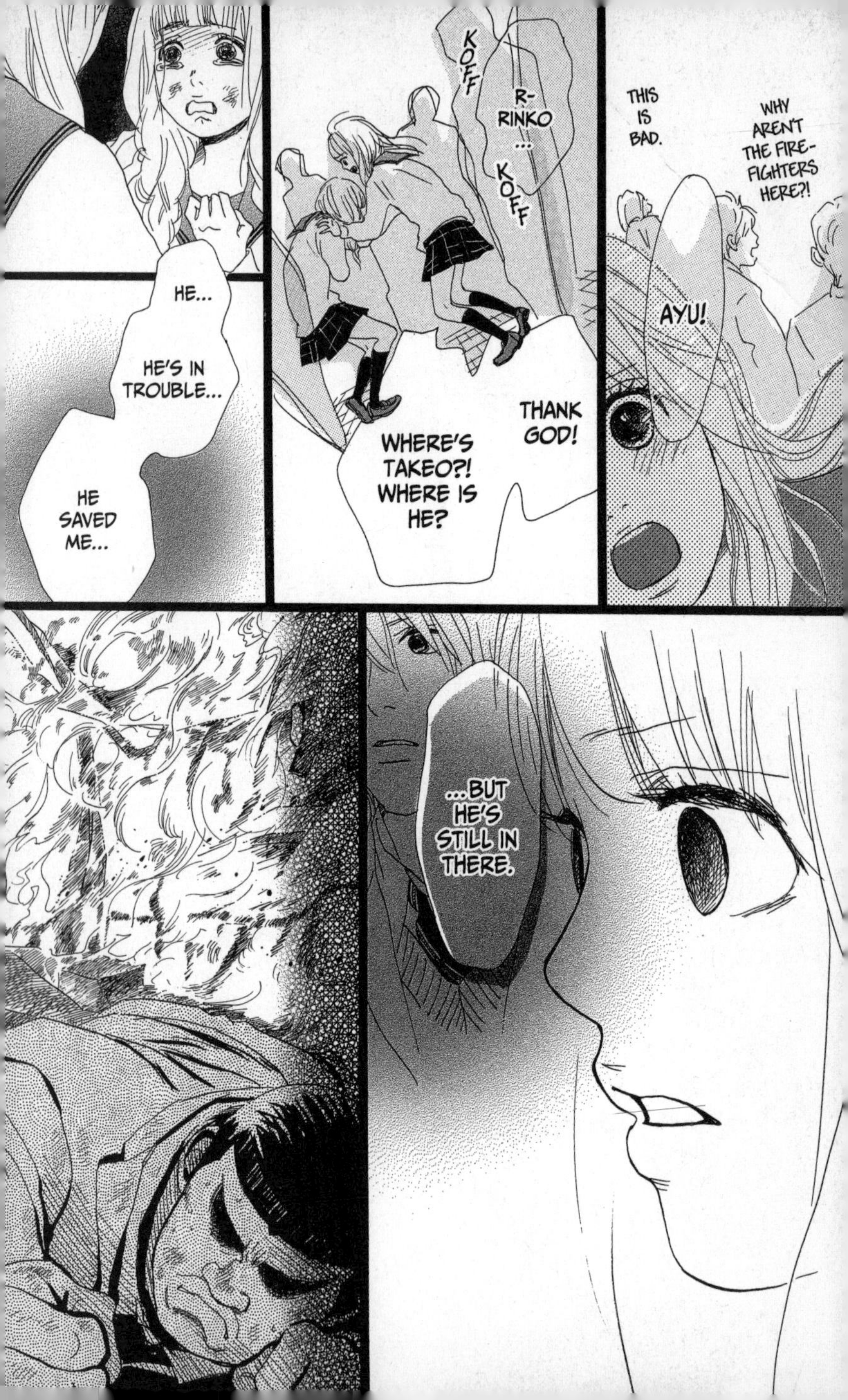
WHY AREN'T THE FIRE-FIGHTERS HERE?!
THIS IS BAD.
AYU!
R-RINKO... KOFF
KOFF
THANK GOD!
WHERE'S TAKEO?! WHERE IS HE?
HE...
HE'S IN TROUBLE...
HE SAVED ME...
...BUT HE'S STILL IN THERE.

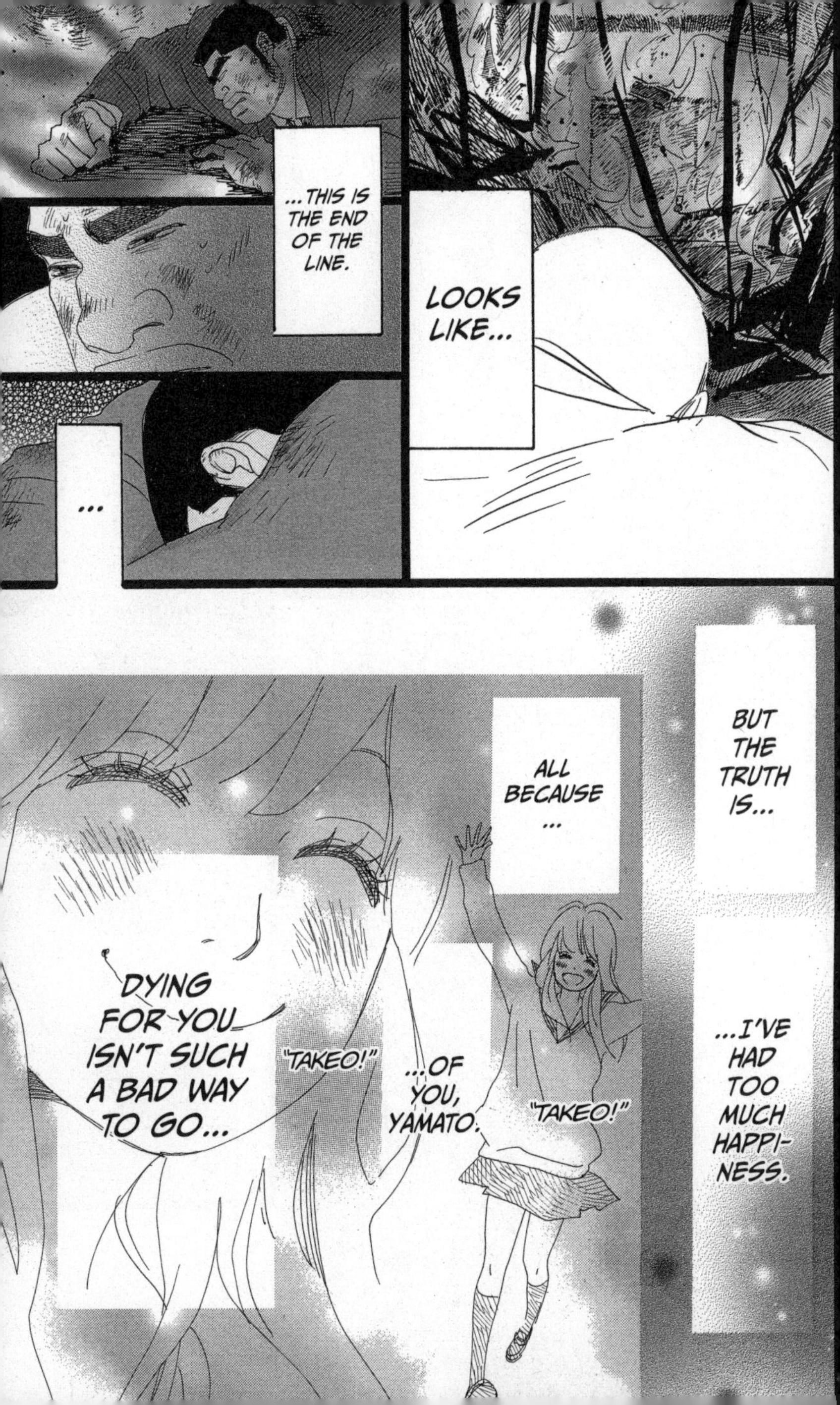
LOOKS LIKE...
...THIS IS THE END OF THE LINE.
...
BUT THE TRUTH IS...
...I'VE HAD TOO MUCH HAPPINESS.
ALL BECAUSE ...
"TAKEO!"
...OF YOU, YAMATO.
"TAKEO!"
DYING FOR YOU ISN'T SUCH A BAD WAY TO GO...

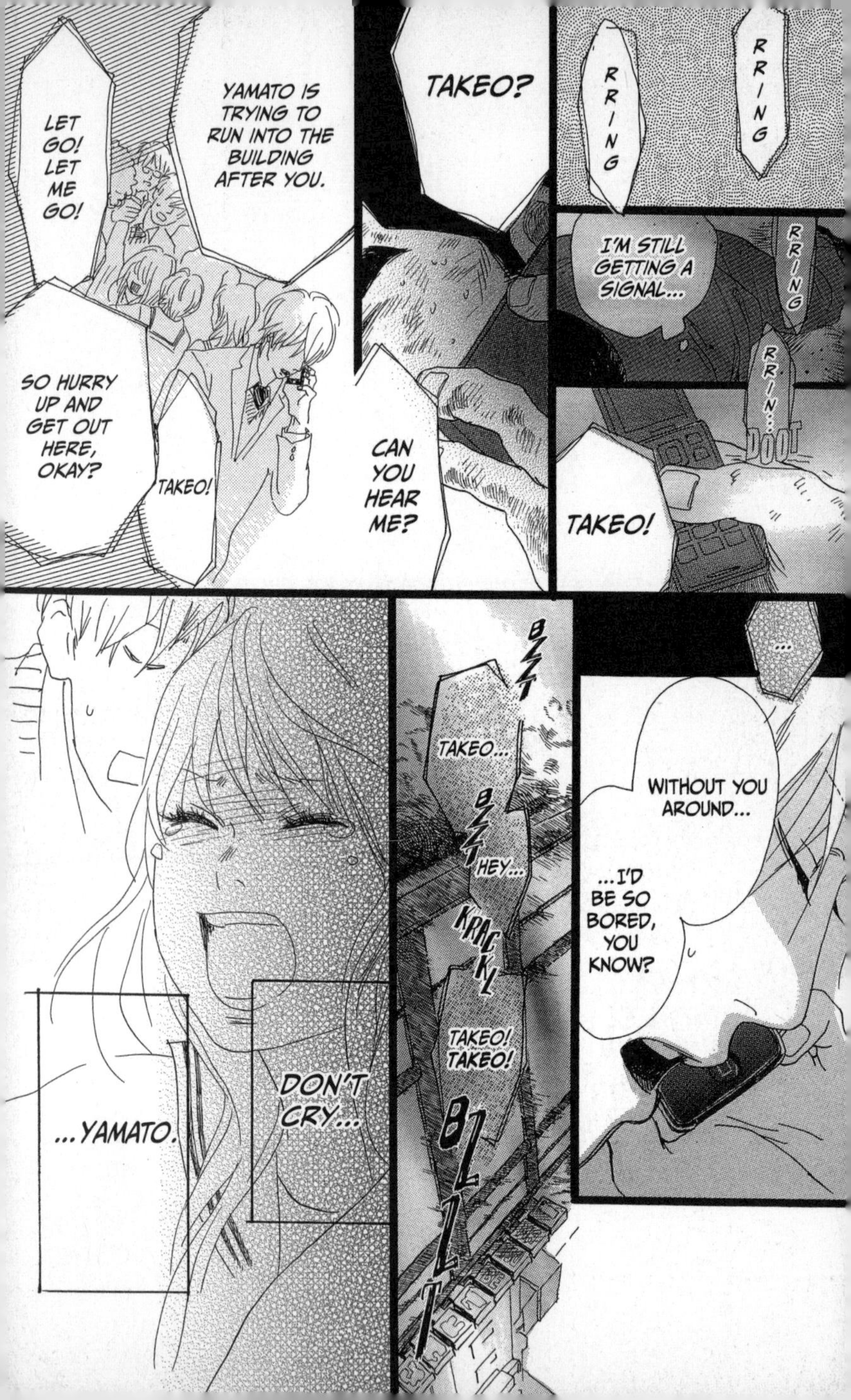
RRING
RRING
I'M STILL GETTING A SIGNAL...
RRING
RRIN...
DOOT
TAKEO!
TAKEO?
CAN YOU HEAR ME?
YAMATO IS TRYING TO RUN INTO THE BUILDING AFTER YOU.
LET GO! LET ME GO!
SO HURRY UP AND GET OUT HERE, OKAY?
TAKEO!
...
WITHOUT YOU AROUND...
...I'D BE SO BORED, YOU KNOW?
BZZT
TAKEO...
BZZT
HEY...
KRACKL
TAKEO! TAKEO!
BZZT
DON'T CRY...
...YAMATO.

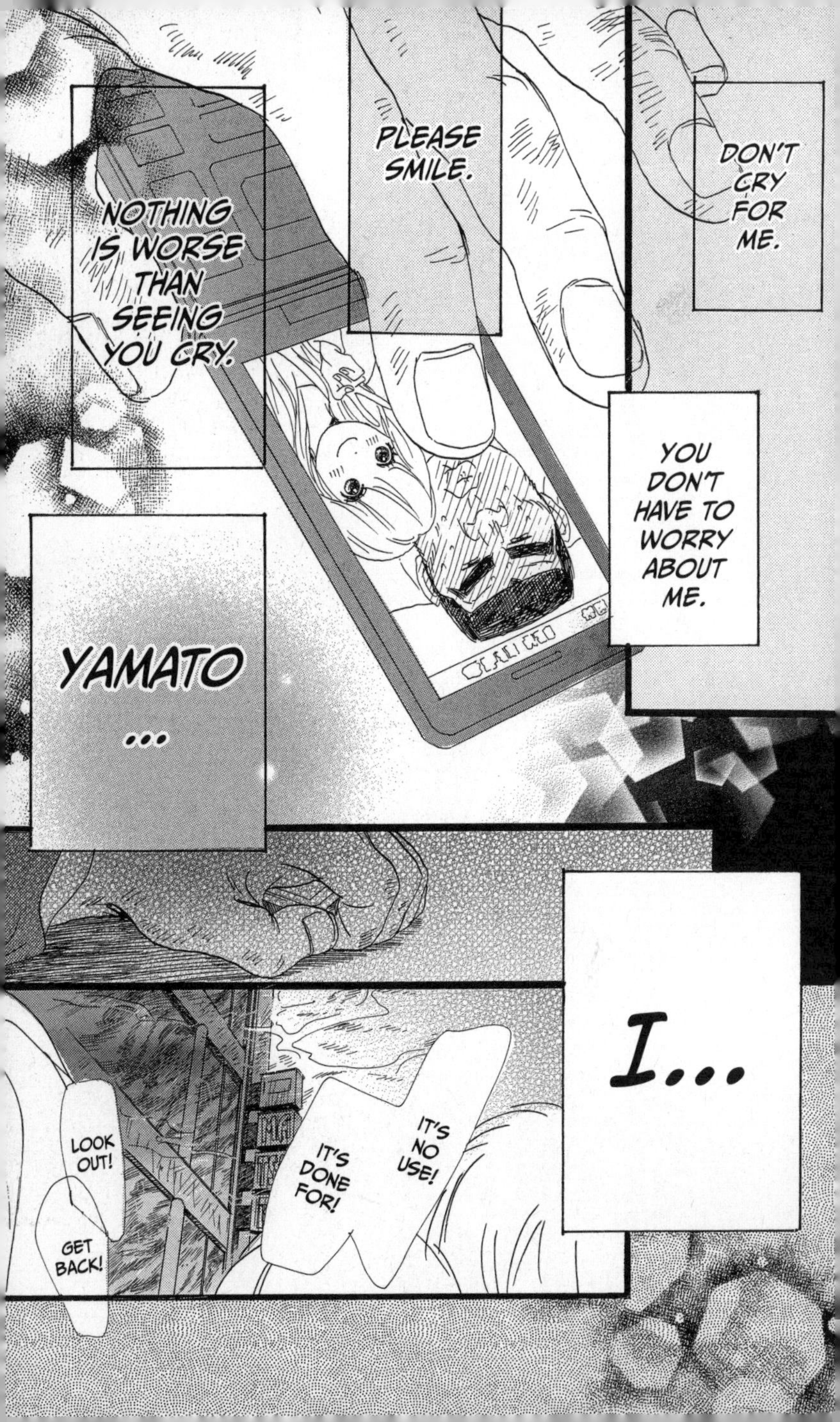
DON'T CRY FOR ME.
YOU DON'T HAVE TO WORRY ABOUT ME.
PLEASE SMILE.
NOTHING IS WORSE THAN SEEING YOU CRY.
YAMATO ...
I...
IT'S NO USE!
IT'S DONE FOR!
LOOK OUT!
GET BACK!

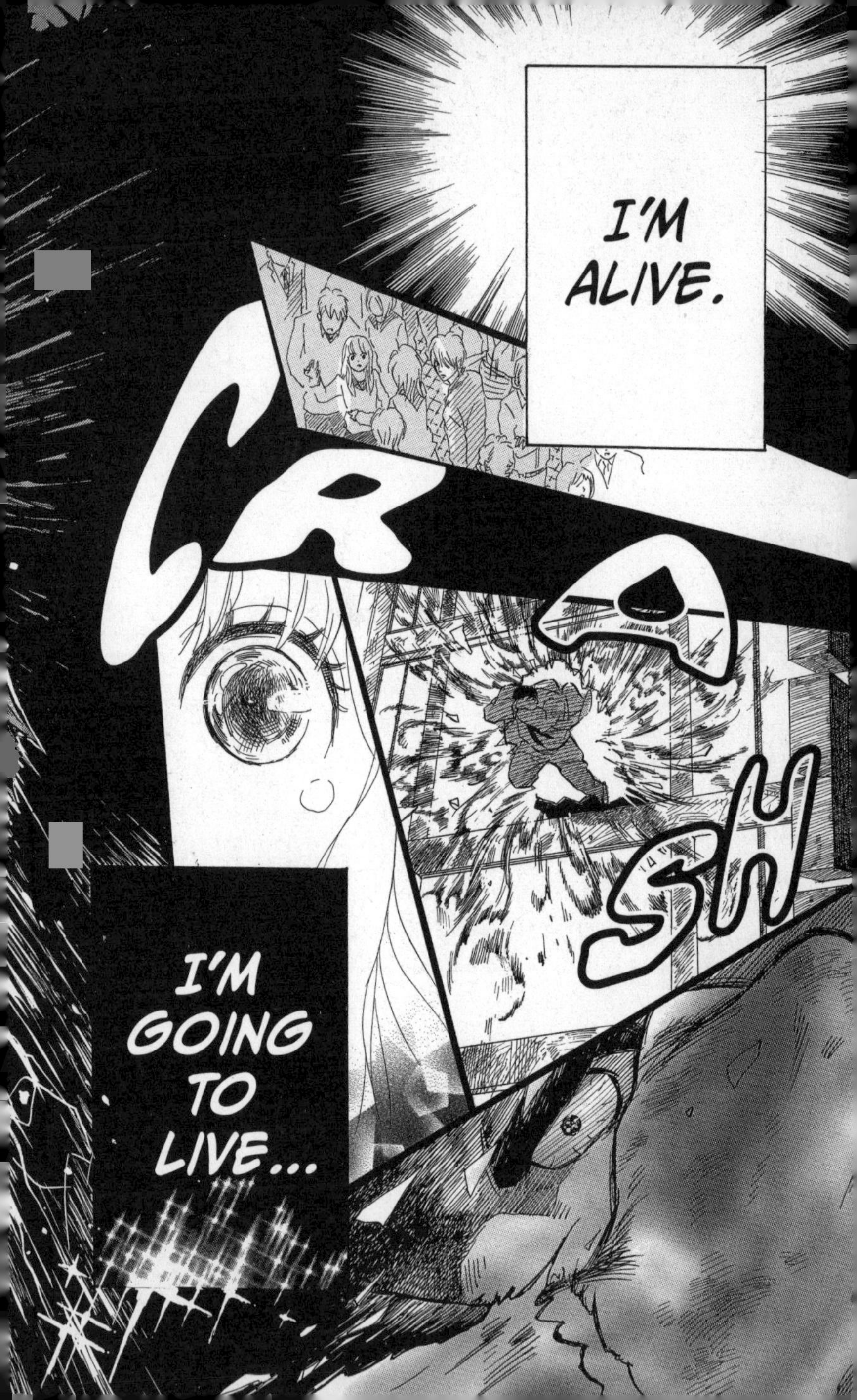
I'M ALIVE.
CRASH
I'M GOING TO LIVE...

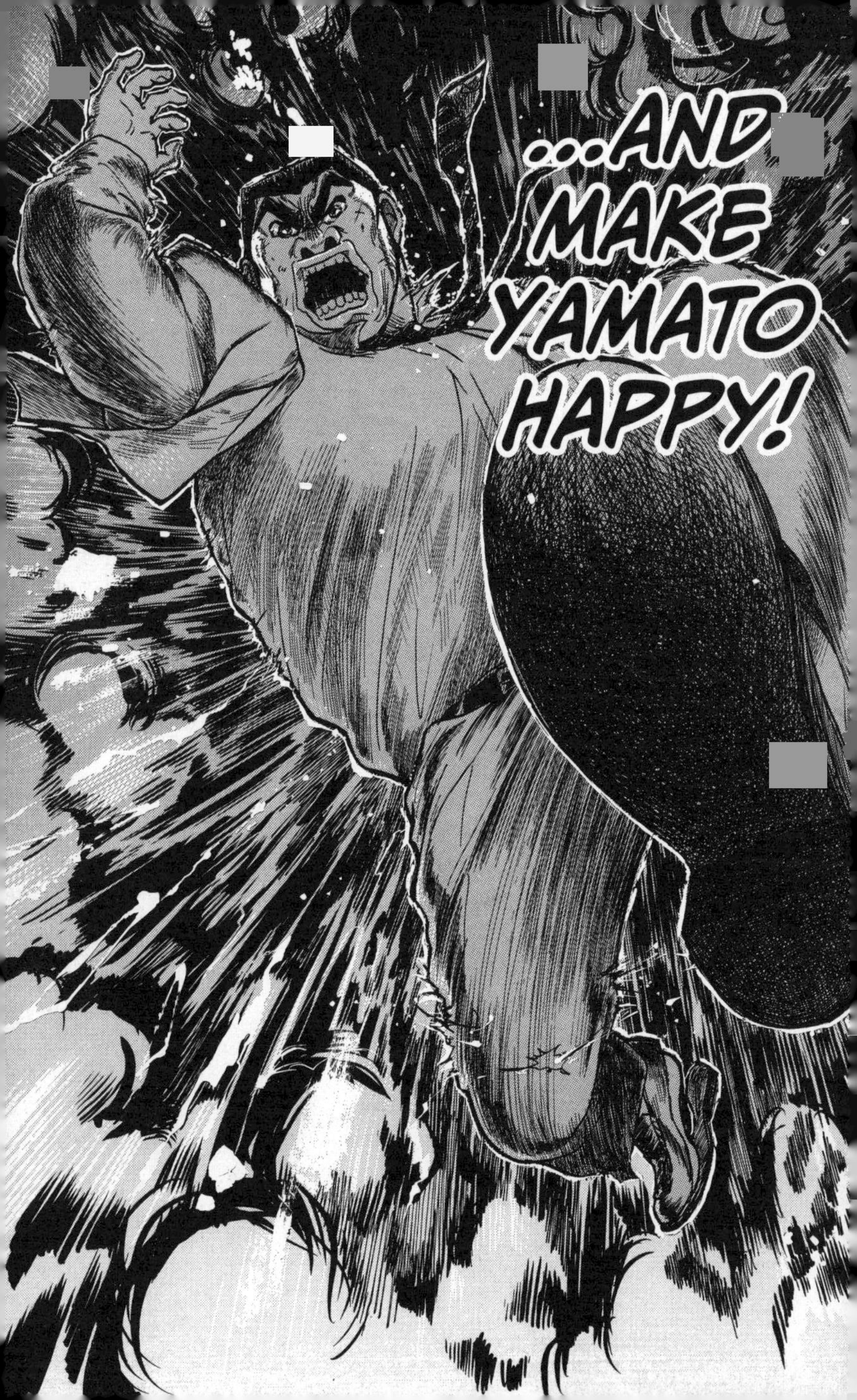
...AND MAKE YAMATO HAPPY!

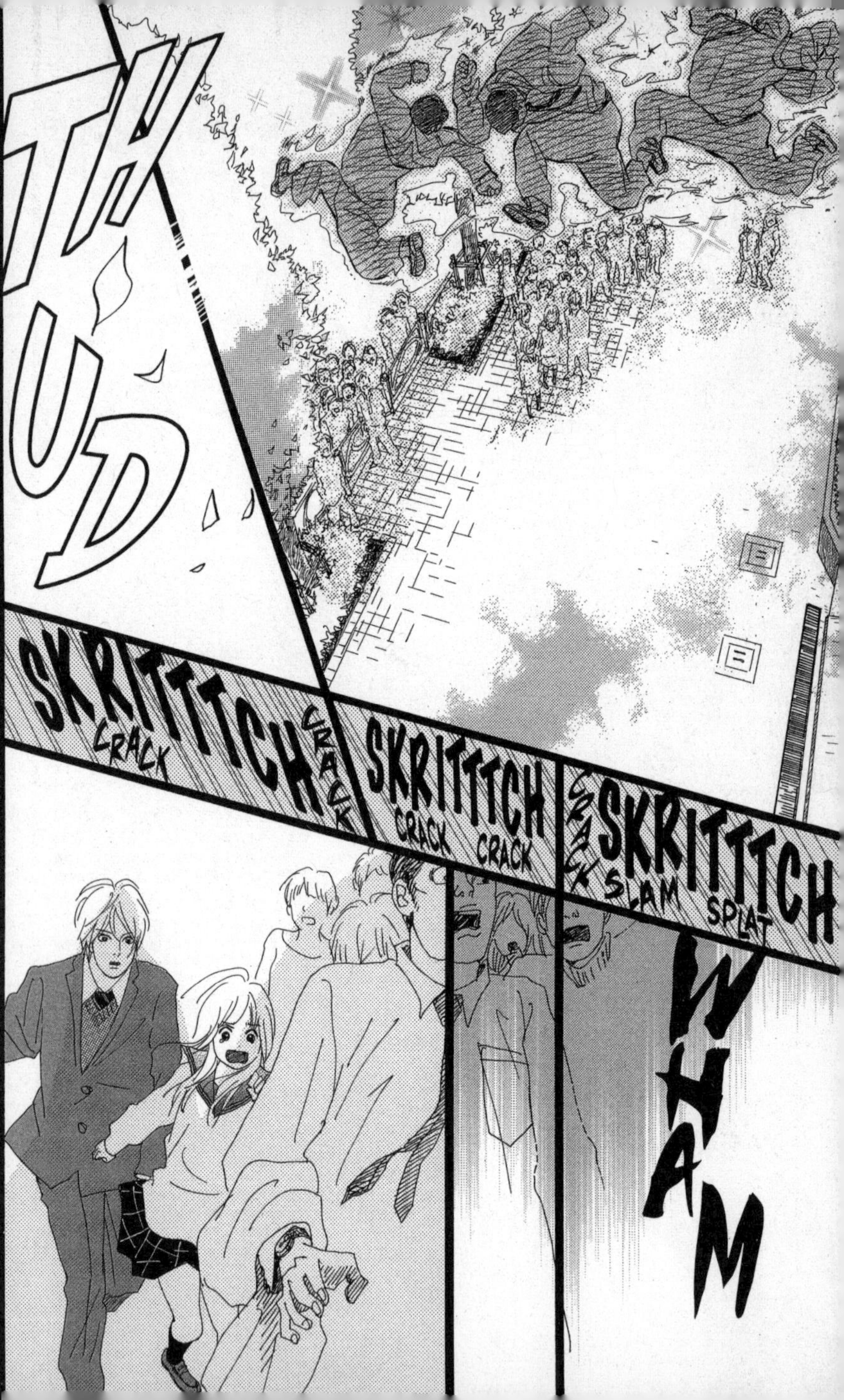
THUD
CRACK
SKRITTTCH
SLAM
SPLAT
SKRITTTCH
CRACK CRACK
SKRITTTCH
CRACK
CRACK
WHAM

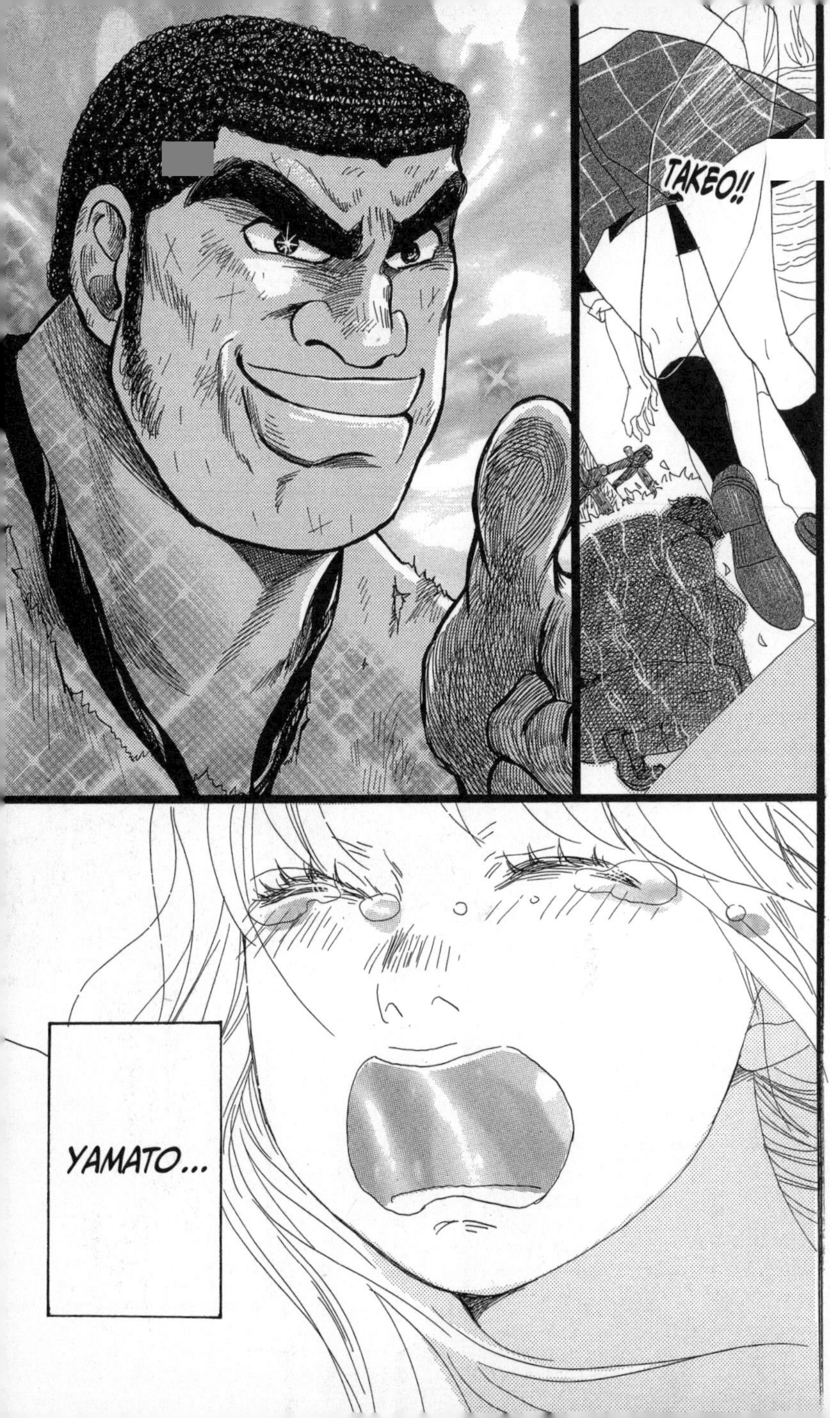
TAKEO!!
YAMATO...

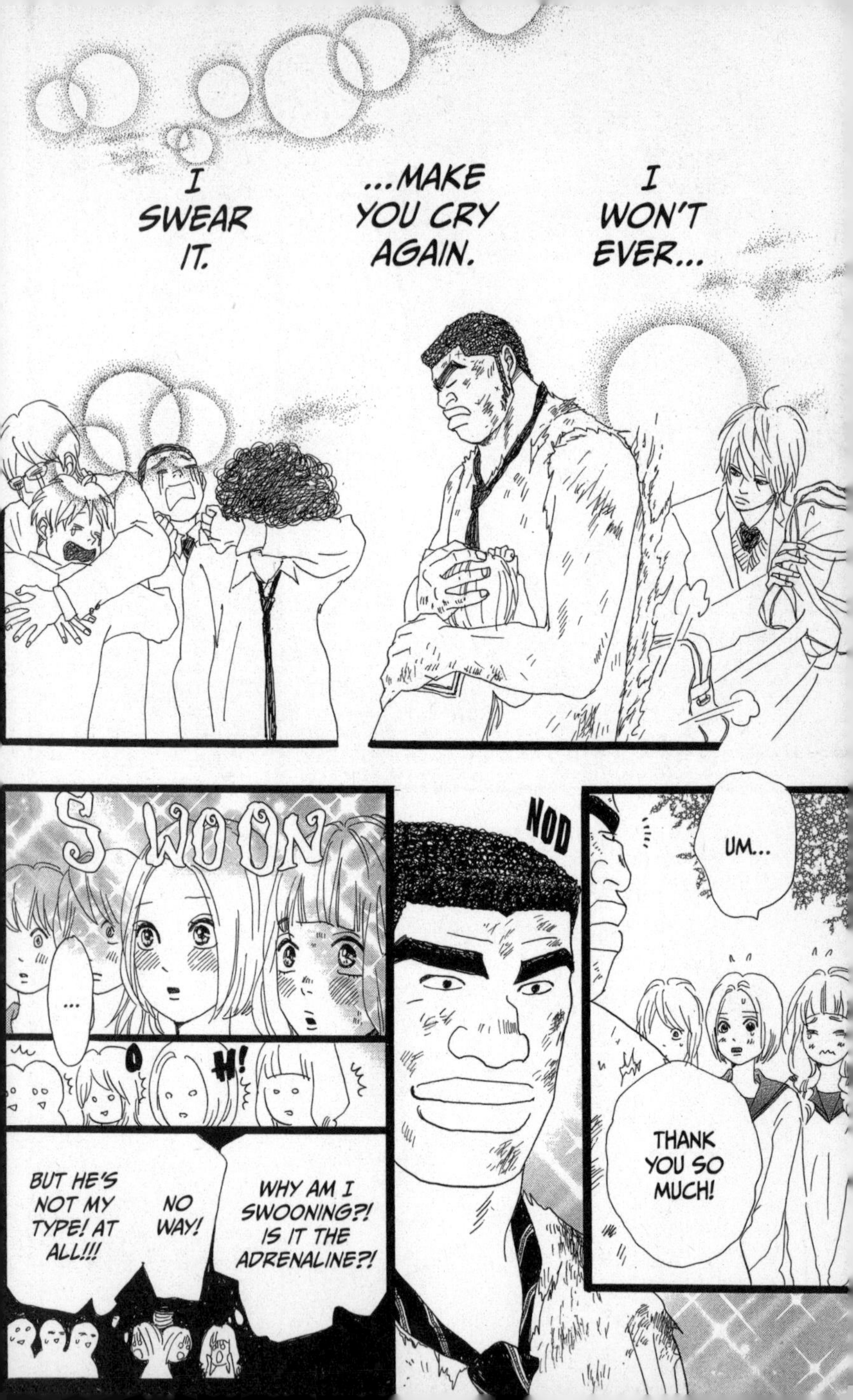
I WON'T EVER...
...MAKE YOU CRY AGAIN.
I SWEAR IT.
UM...
THANK YOU SO MUCH!
NOD
SWOON
...
OH!
WHY AM I SWOONING?! IS IT THE ADRENALINE?!
NO WAY!
BUT HE'S NOT MY TYPE! AT ALL!!!

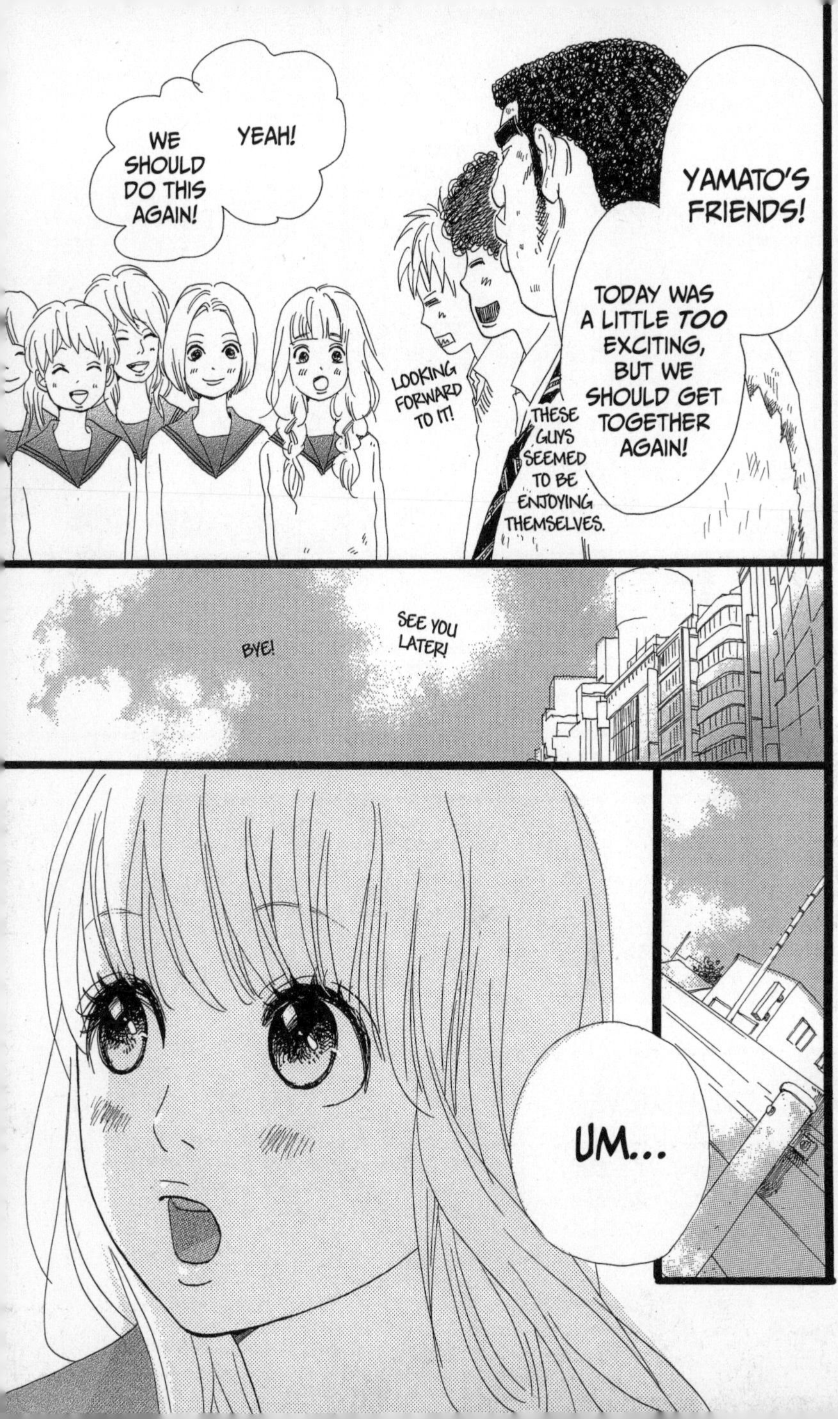
YAMATO'S FRIENDS!
TODAY WAS A LITTLE TOO EXCITING, BUT WE SHOULD GET TOGETHER AGAIN!
THESE GUYS SEEMED TO BE ENJOYING THEMSELVES.
LOOKING FORWARD TO IT!
YEAH!
WE SHOULD DO THIS AGAIN!
SEE YOU LATER!
BYE!
UM...

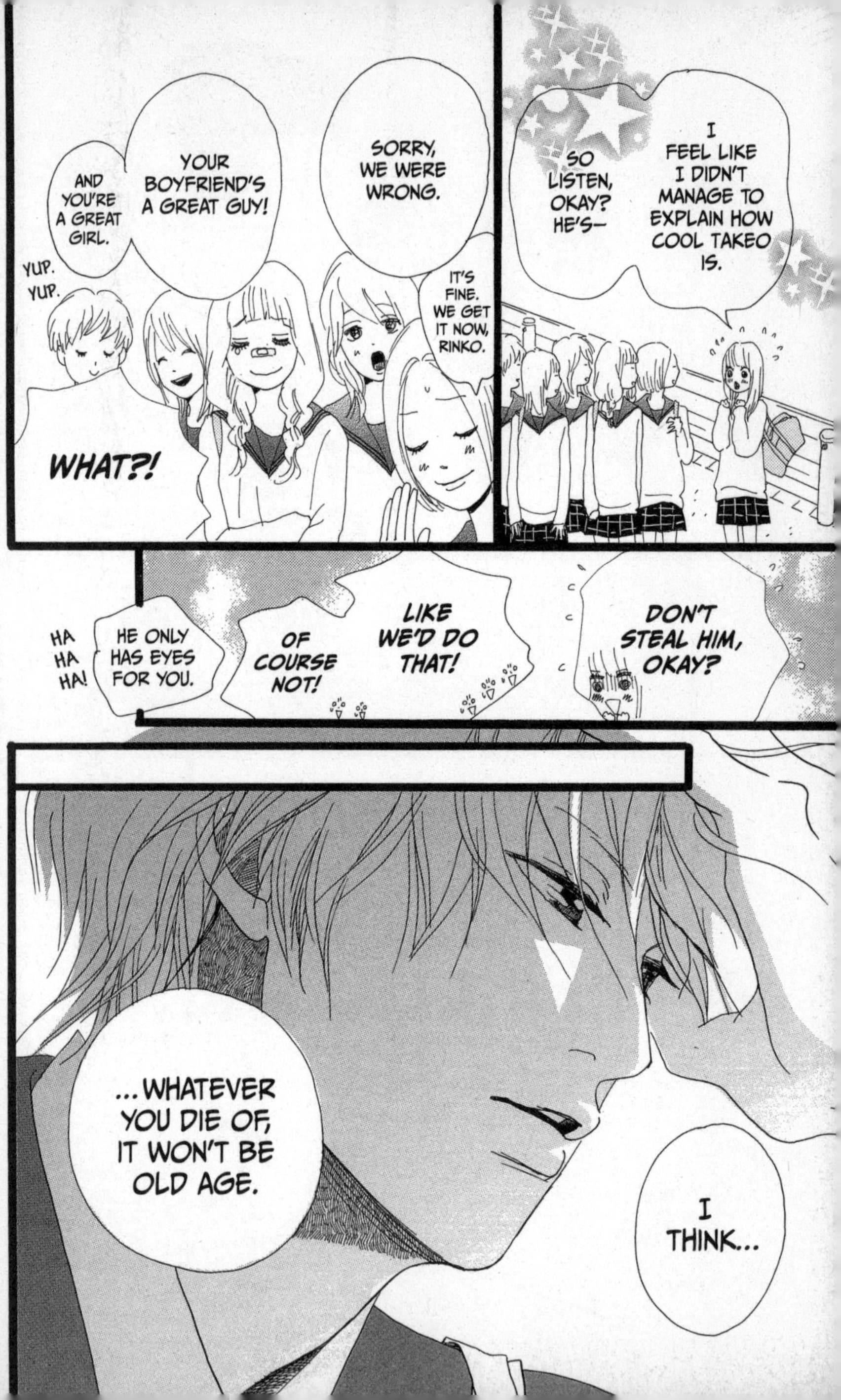
I FEEL LIKE I DIDN'T MANAGE TO EXPLAIN HOW COOL TAKEO IS.
SO LISTEN, OKAY? HE'S—
SORRY, WE WERE WRONG.
IT'S FINE. WE GET IT NOW, RINKO.
YOUR BOYFRIEND'S A GREAT GUY!
AND YOU'RE A GREAT GIRL.
YUP. YUP.
WHAT?!
DON'T STEAL HIM, OKAY?
LIKE WE'D DO THAT!
OF COURSE NOT!
HE ONLY HAS EYES FOR YOU.
HA HA HA!
I THINK...
...WHATEVER YOU DIE OF, IT WON'T BE OLD AGE.

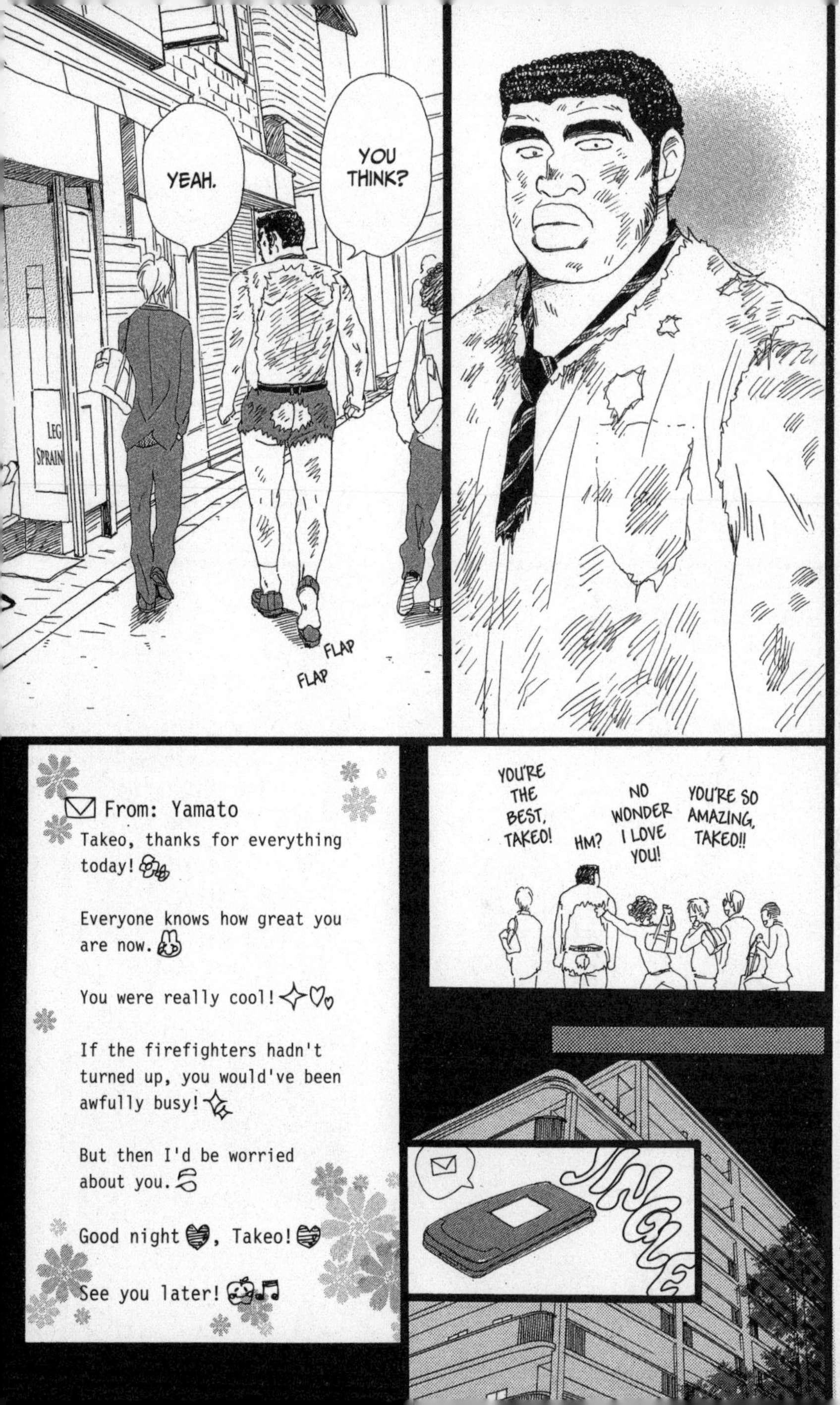
YOU THINK?
YEAH.
FLAP
FLAP
LEG
SPRAIN
YOU'RE SO AMAZING, TAKEO!!
NO WONDER I LOVE YOU!
HM?
YOU'RE THE BEST, TAKEO!
JINGLE
From: Yamato
Takeo, thanks for everything today!
Everyone knows how great you are now.
You were really cool!
If the firefighters hadn't turned up, you would've been awfully busy!
But then I'd be worried about you.
Good night, Takeo!
See you later!

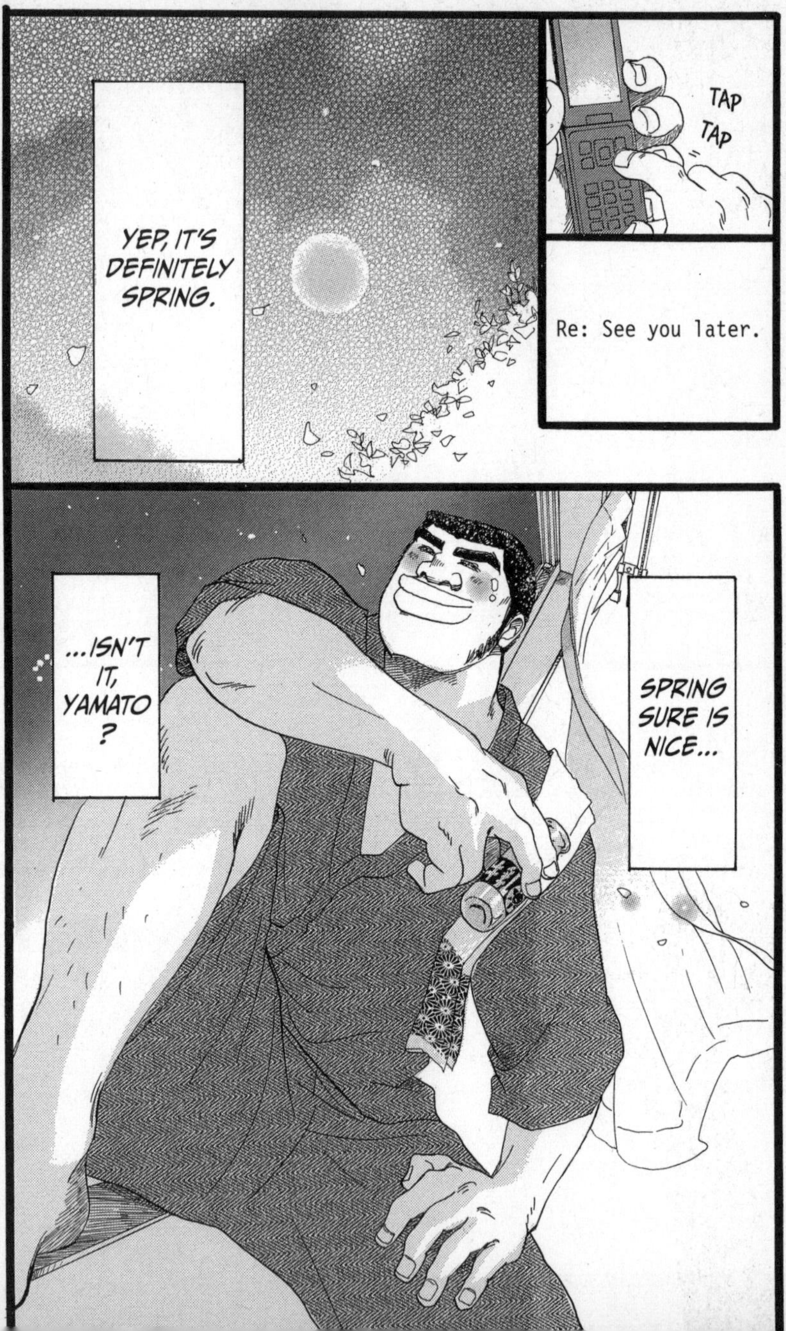
TAP
TAP
Re: See you later.
YEP, IT'S DEFINITELY SPRING.
SPRING SURE IS NICE...
...ISN'T IT, YAMATO?

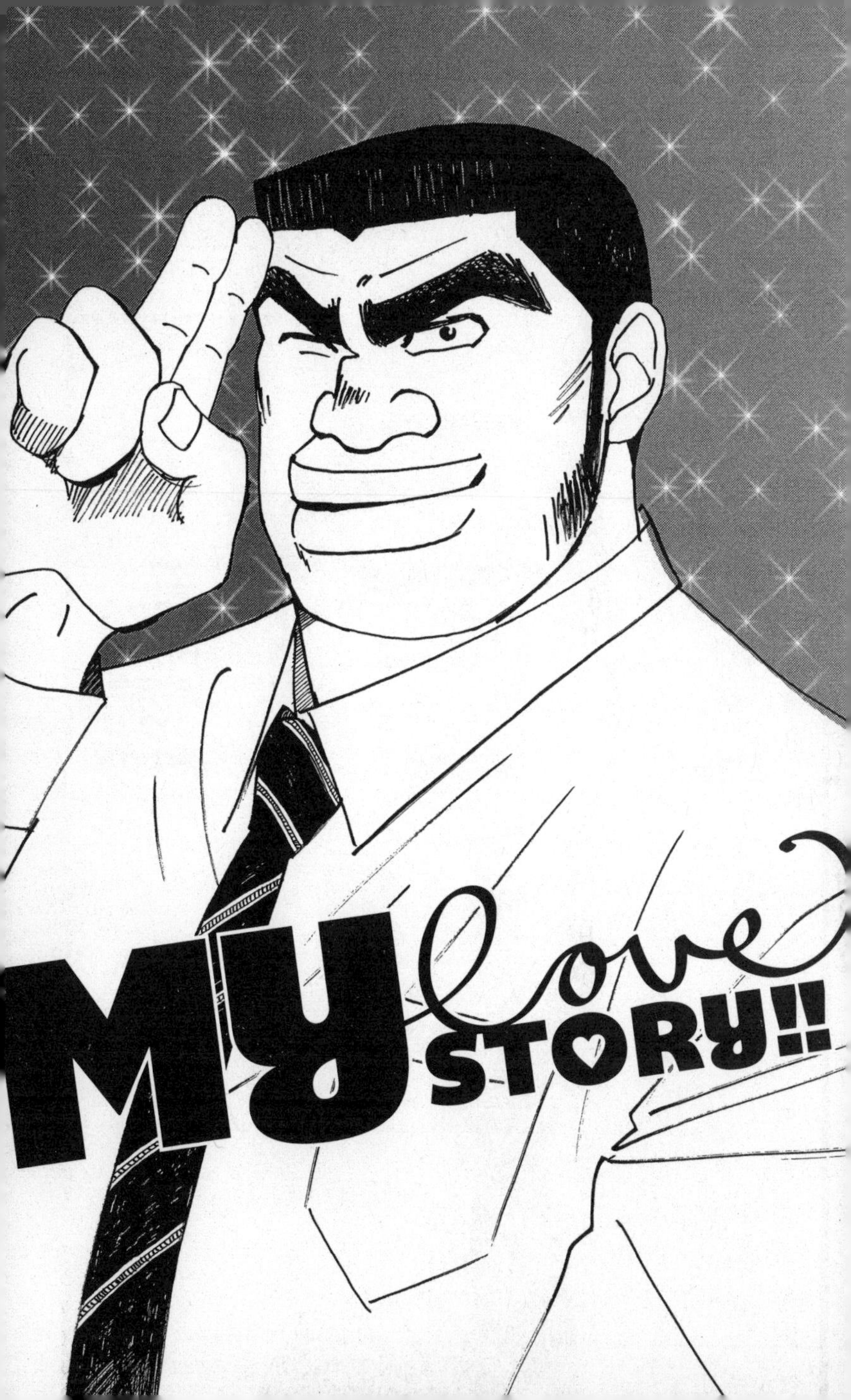
MY love STORY!!

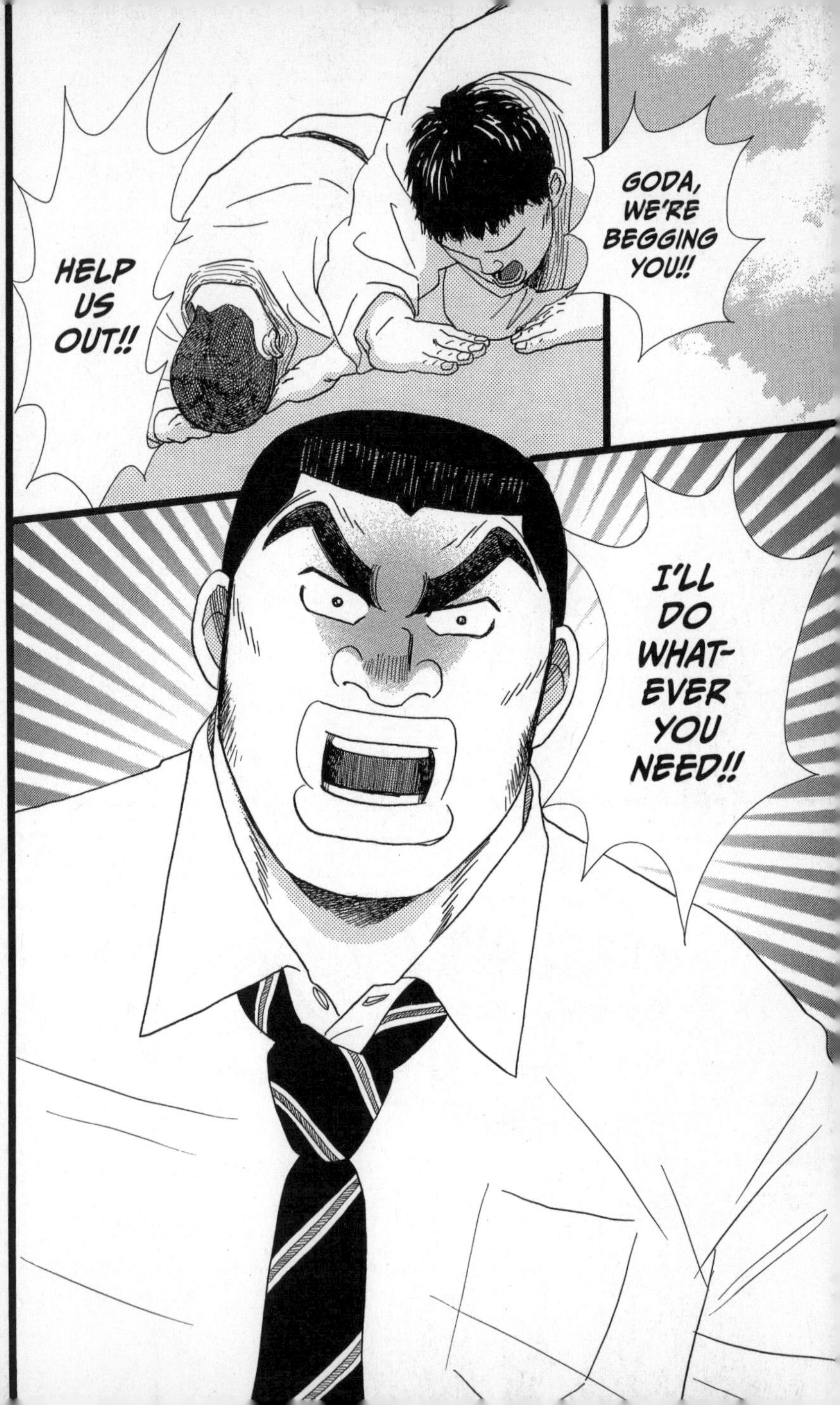
GODA, WE'RE BEGGING YOU!!
HELP US OUT!!
I'LL DO WHAT-EVER YOU NEED!!

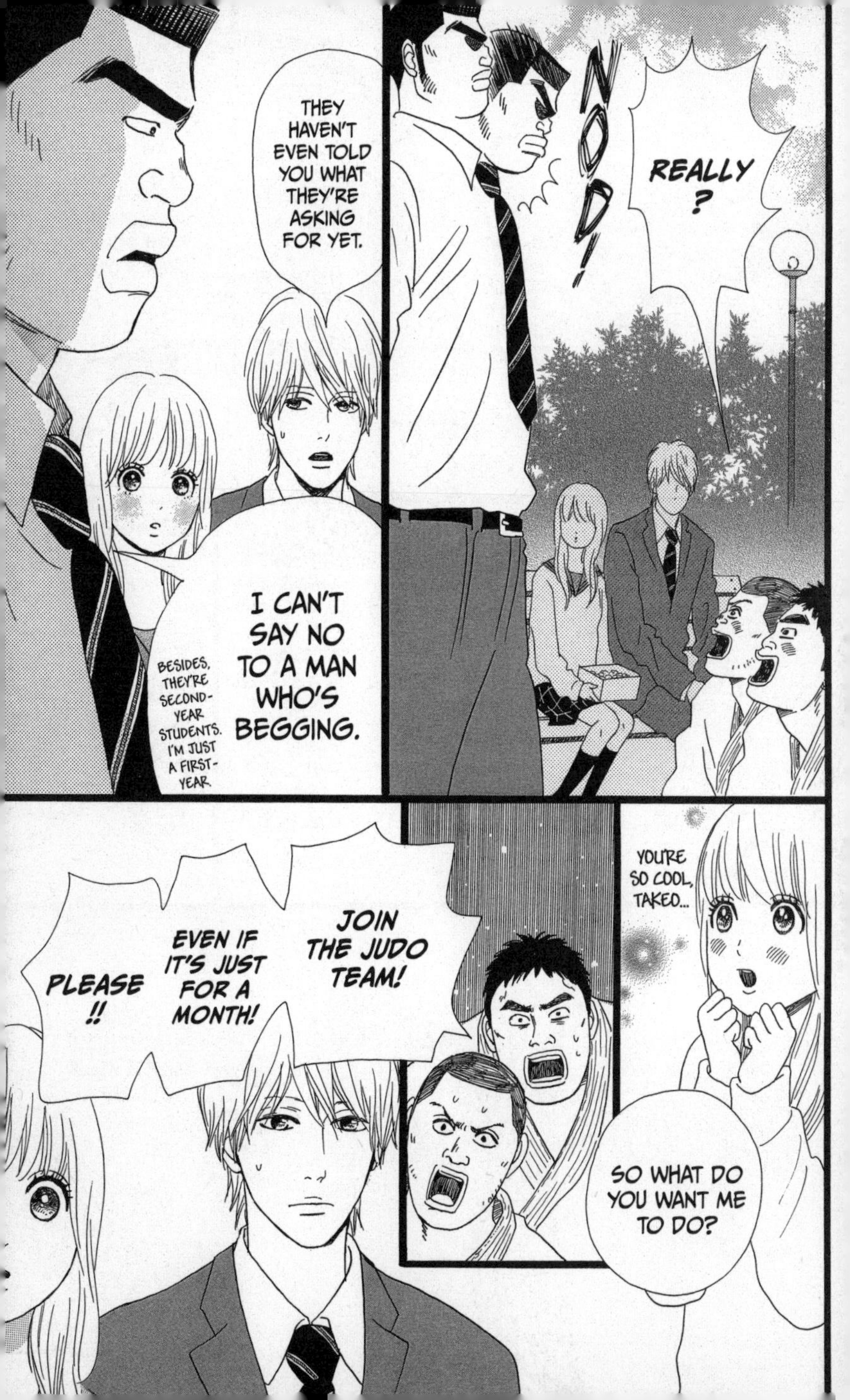
REALLY?
NOD!
THEY HAVEN'T EVEN TOLD YOU WHAT THEY'RE ASKING FOR YET.
I CAN'T SAY NO TO A MAN WHO'S BEGGING.
BESIDES, THEY'RE SECOND-YEAR STUDENTS. I'M JUST A FIRST-YEAR.
YOU'RE SO COOL, TAKEO...
SO WHAT DO YOU WANT ME TO DO?
JOIN THE JUDO TEAM!
EVEN IF IT'S JUST FOR A MONTH!
PLEASE!!

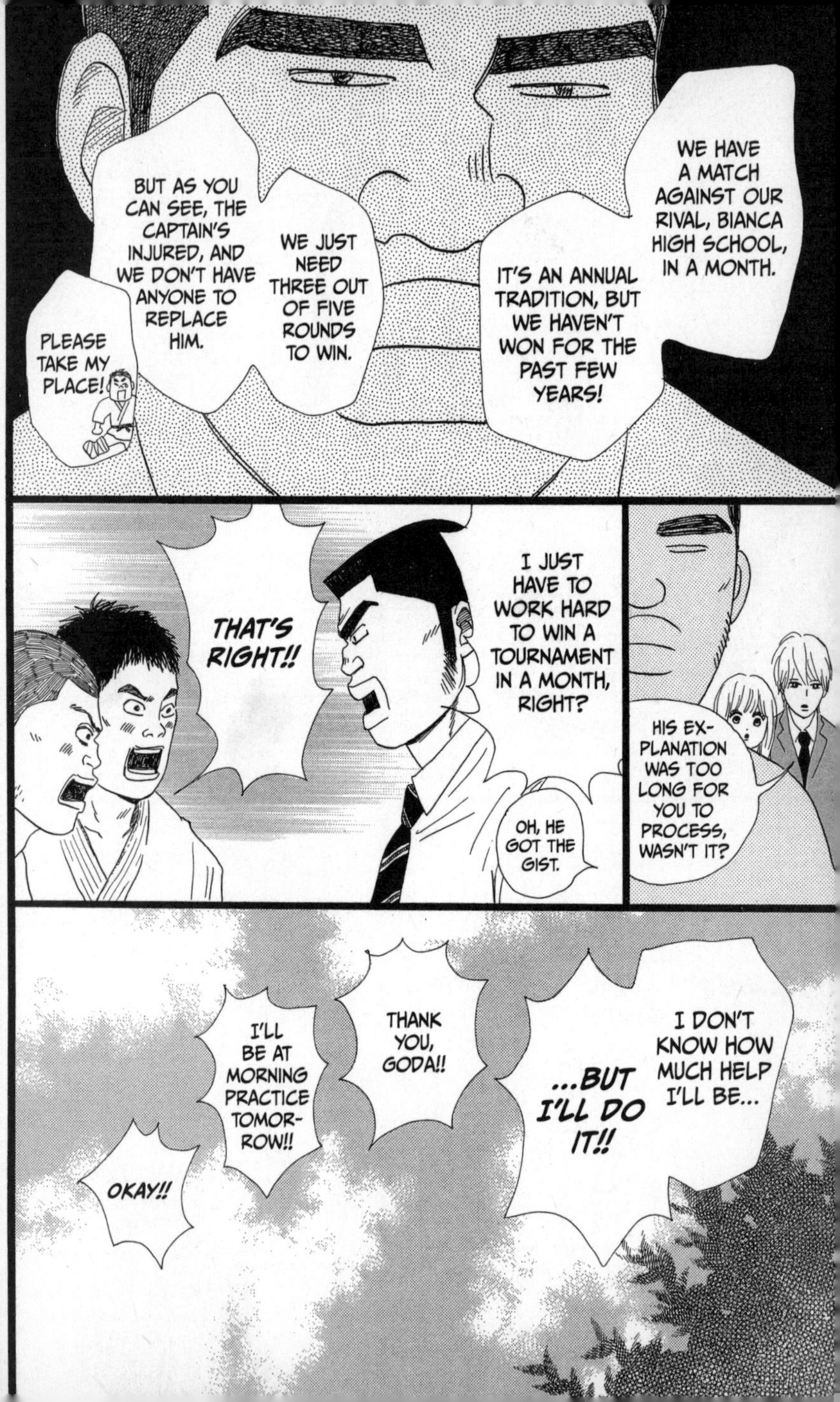
WE HAVE A MATCH AGAINST OUR RIVAL, BIANCA HIGH SCHOOL, IN A MONTH.
IT'S AN ANNUAL TRADITION, BUT WE HAVEN'T WON FOR THE PAST FEW YEARS!
WE JUST NEED THREE OUT OF FIVE ROUNDS TO WIN.
BUT AS YOU CAN SEE, THE CAPTAIN'S INJURED, AND WE DON'T HAVE ANYONE TO REPLACE HIM.
PLEASE TAKE MY PLACE!
HIS EX-PLANATION WAS TOO LONG FOR YOU TO PROCESS, WASN'T IT?
I JUST HAVE TO WORK HARD TO WIN A TOURNAMENT IN A MONTH, RIGHT?
OH, HE GOT THE GIST.
THAT'S RIGHT!!
I DON'T KNOW HOW MUCH HELP I'LL BE...
...BUT I'LL DO IT!!
THANK YOU, GODA!!
I'LL BE AT MORNING PRACTICE TOMOR-ROW!!
OKAY!!

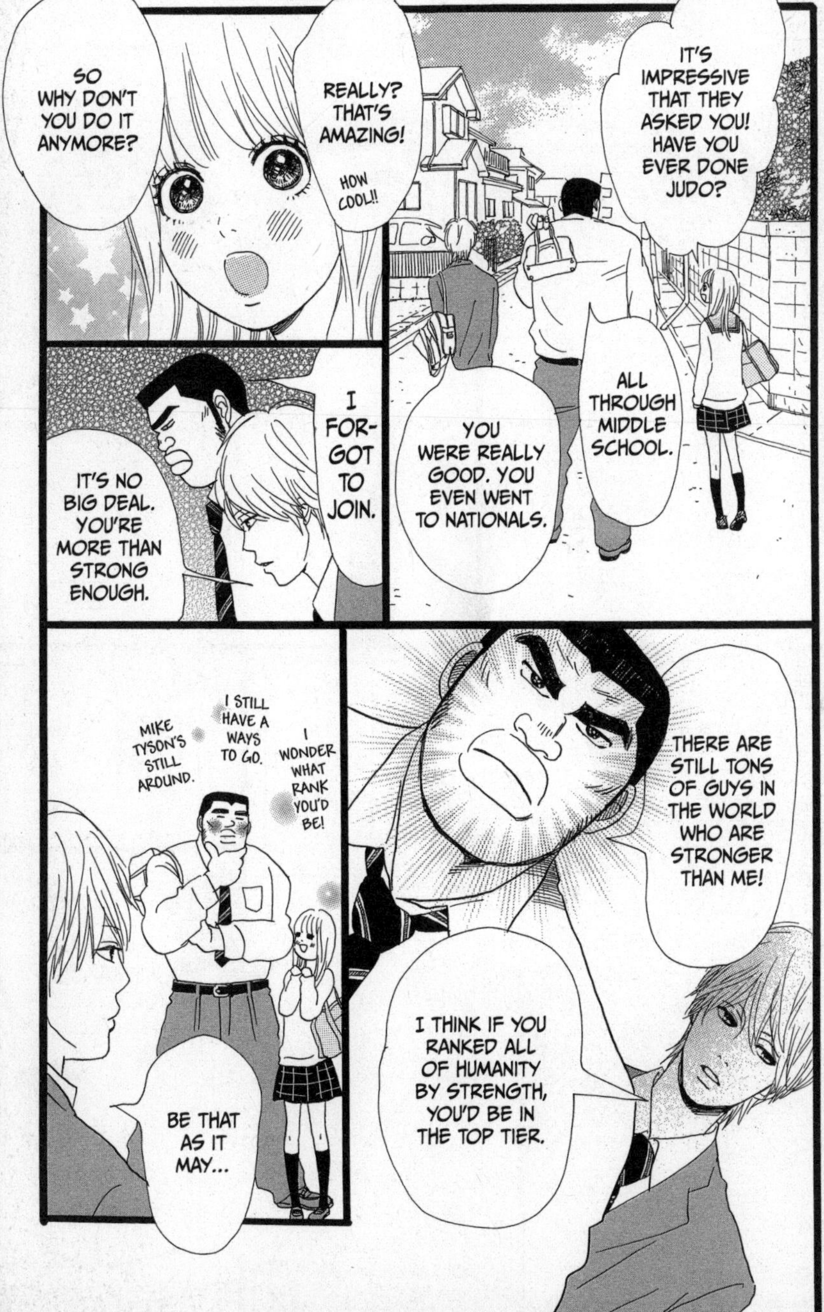
IT'S IMPRESSIVE THAT THEY ASKED YOU! HAVE YOU EVER DONE JUDO?
ALL THROUGH MIDDLE SCHOOL.
YOU WERE REALLY GOOD. YOU EVEN WENT TO NATIONALS.
REALLY? THAT'S AMAZING!
HOW COOL!!
SO WHY DON'T YOU DO IT ANYMORE?
I FOR-GOT TO JOIN.
IT'S NO BIG DEAL. YOU'RE MORE THAN STRONG ENOUGH.
THERE ARE STILL TONS OF GUYS IN THE WORLD WHO ARE STRONGER THAN ME!
I THINK IF YOU RANKED ALL OF HUMANITY BY STRENGTH, YOU'D BE IN THE TOP TIER.
I WONDER WHAT RANK YOU'D BE!
I STILL HAVE A WAYS TO GO.
MIKE TYSON'S STILL AROUND.
BE THAT AS IT MAY...

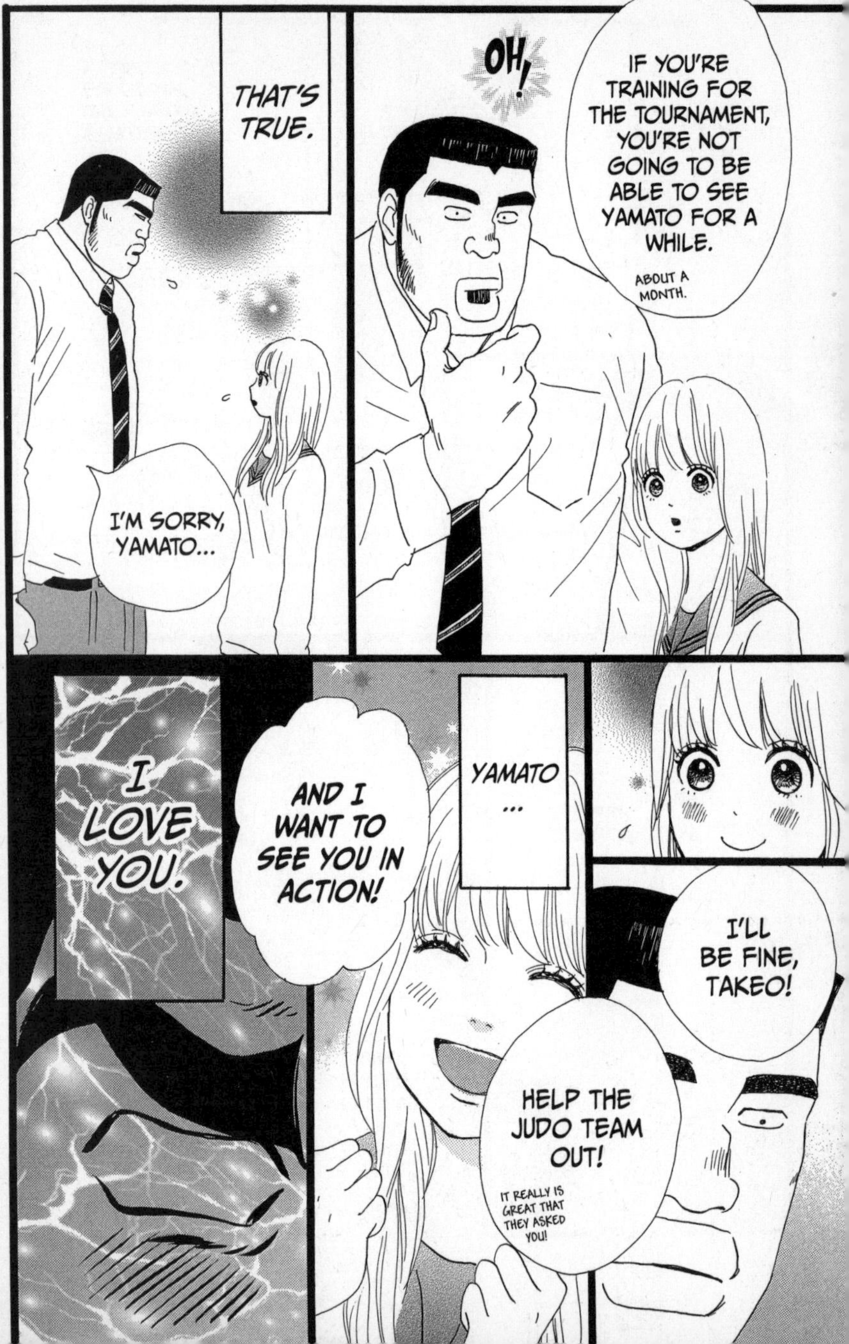
OH!
IF YOU'RE TRAINING FOR THE TOURNAMENT, YOU'RE NOT GOING TO BE ABLE TO SEE YAMATO FOR A WHILE.
ABOUT A MONTH.
THAT'S TRUE.
I'M SORRY, YAMATO...
I'LL BE FINE, TAKEO!
HELP THE JUDO TEAM OUT!
IT REALLY IS GREAT THAT THEY ASKED YOU!
YAMATO ...
AND I WANT TO SEE YOU IN ACTION!
I LOVE YOU.

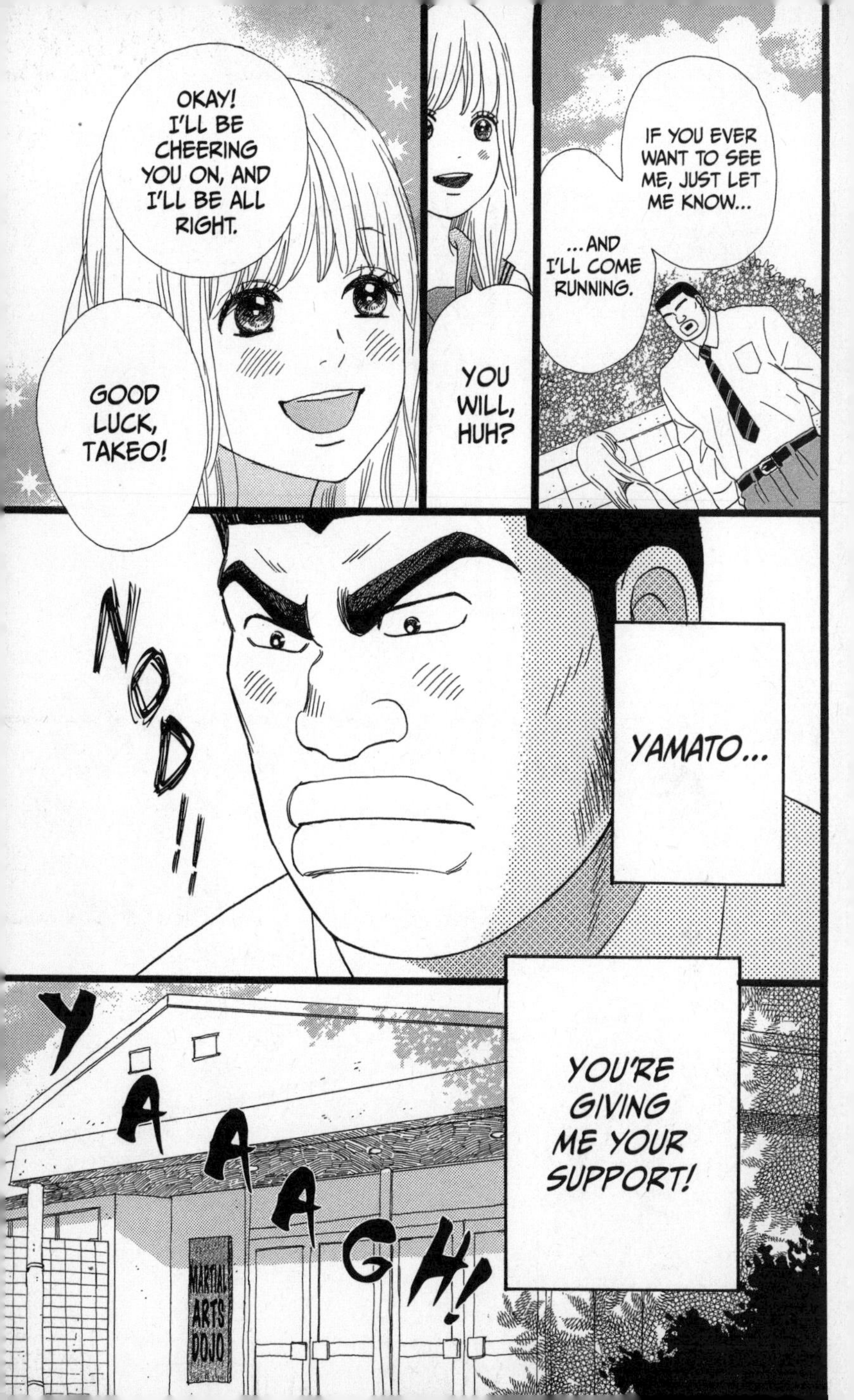
IF YOU EVER WANT TO SEE ME, JUST LET ME KNOW...
...AND I'LL COME RUNNING.
YOU WILL, HUH?
OKAY! I'LL BE CHEERING YOU ON, AND I'LL BE ALL RIGHT.
GOOD LUCK, TAKEO!
YAMATO...
NOD!!
YOU'RE GIVING ME YOUR SUPPORT!
YAAAAGH!
MARTIAL ARTS DOJO

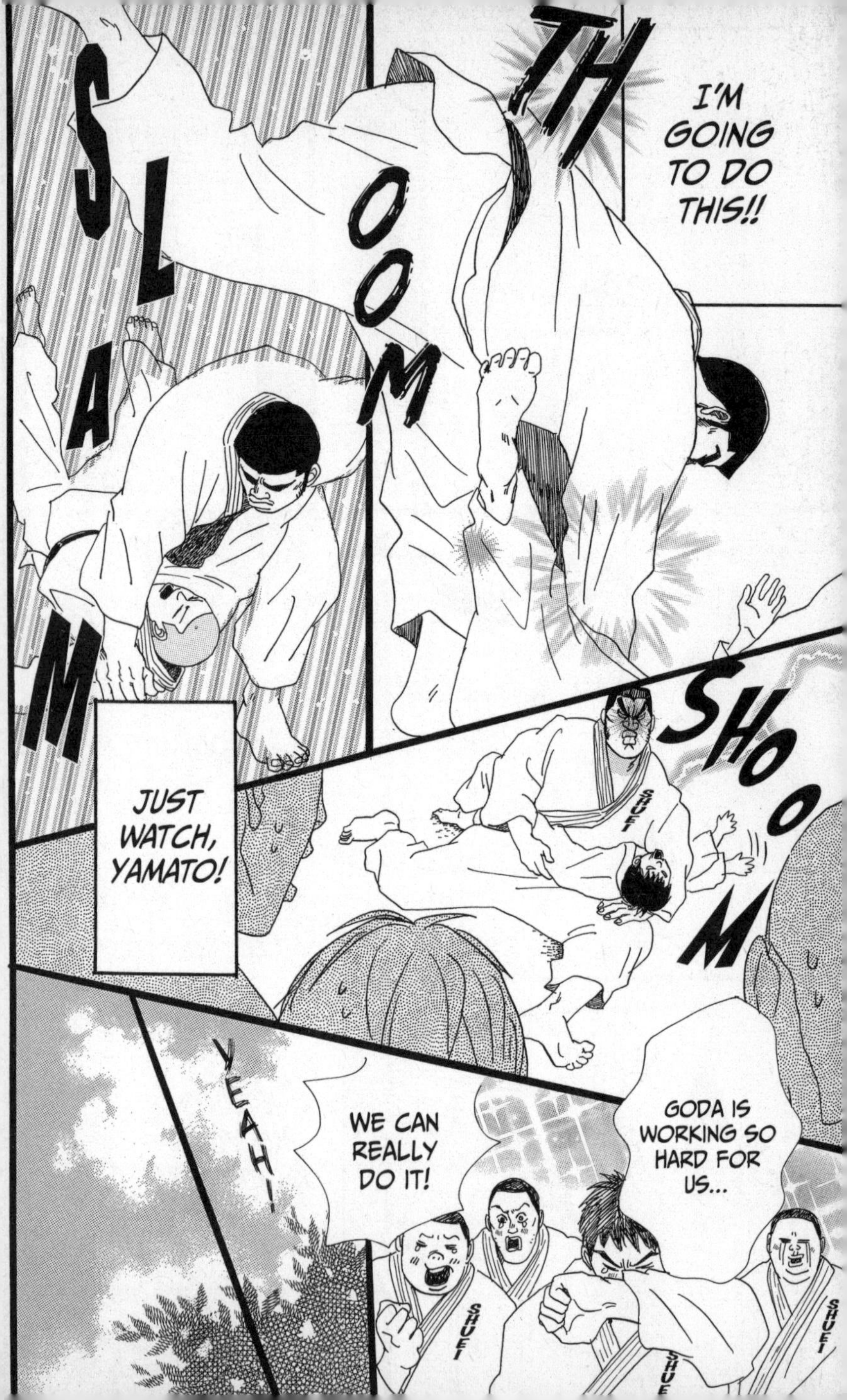
THOOM
I'M GOING TO DO THIS!!
SLAM
JUST WATCH, YAMATO!
SHOOM
SHUEI
GODA IS WORKING SO HARD FOR US...
WE CAN REALLY DO IT!
YEAH!
SHUEI
SHUEI
SHUEI

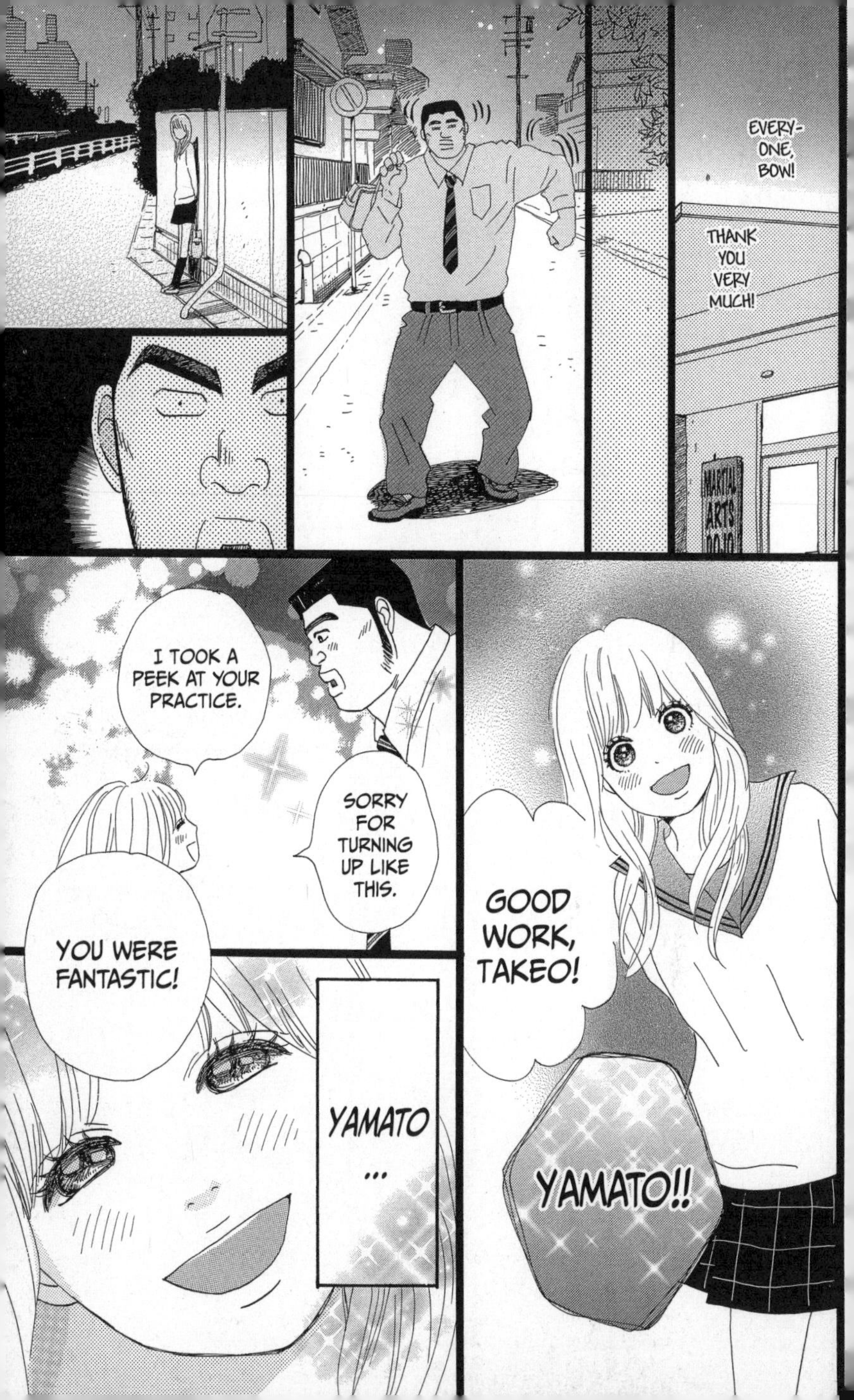
EVERY-ONE, BOW!
THANK YOU VERY MUCH!
MARTIAL ARTS
GOOD WORK, TAKEO!
YAMATO!!
I TOOK A PEEK AT YOUR PRACTICE.
SORRY FOR TURNING UP LIKE THIS.
YOU WERE FANTASTIC!
YAMATO ...

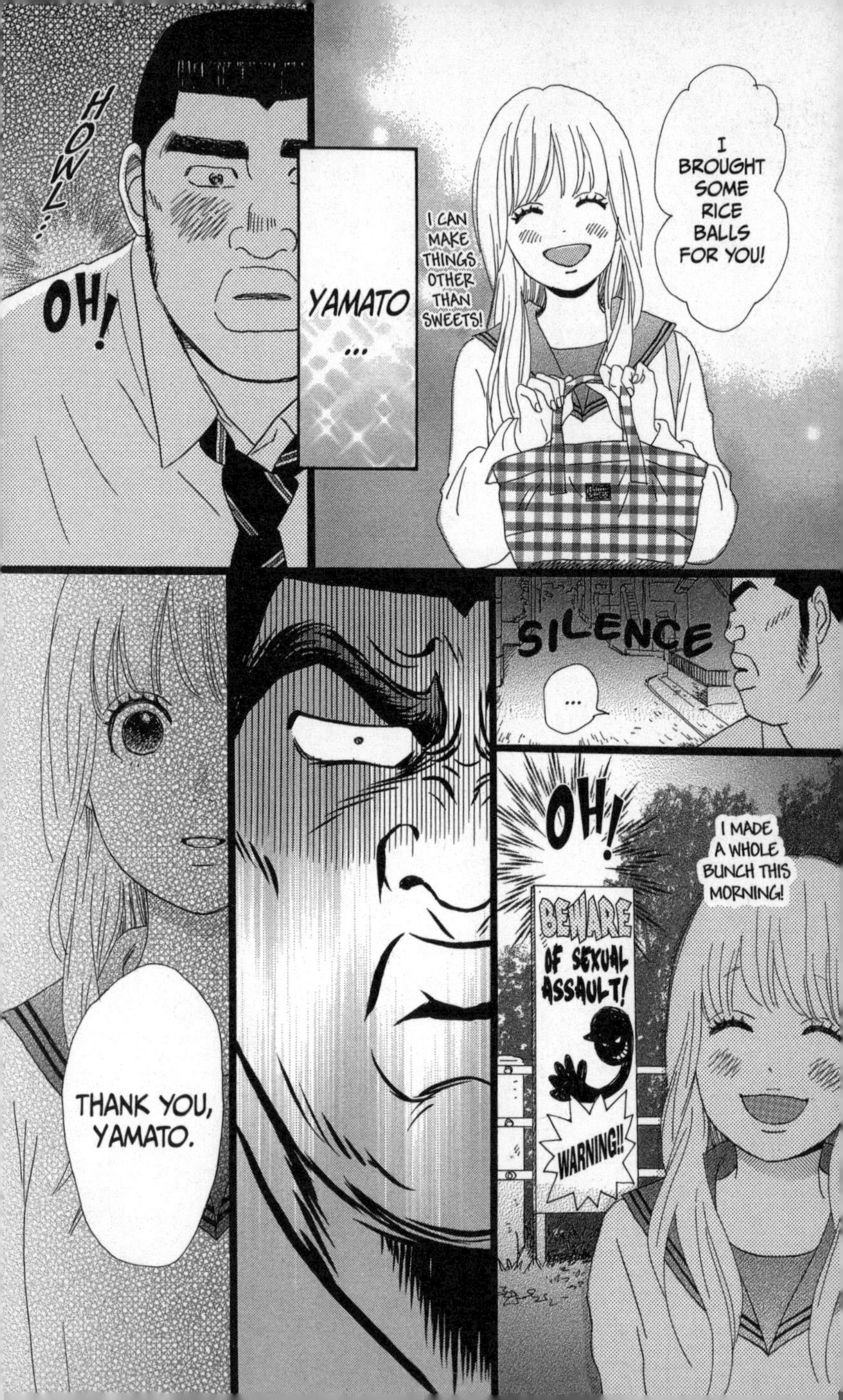
I BROUGHT SOME RICE BALLS FOR YOU!
I CAN MAKE THINGS OTHER THAN SWEETS!
YAMATO ...
HOWL...
OH!
SILENCE
...
I MADE A WHOLE BUNCH THIS MORNING!
OH!
BEWARE OF SEXUAL ASSAULT!
WARNING!!
THANK YOU, YAMATO.

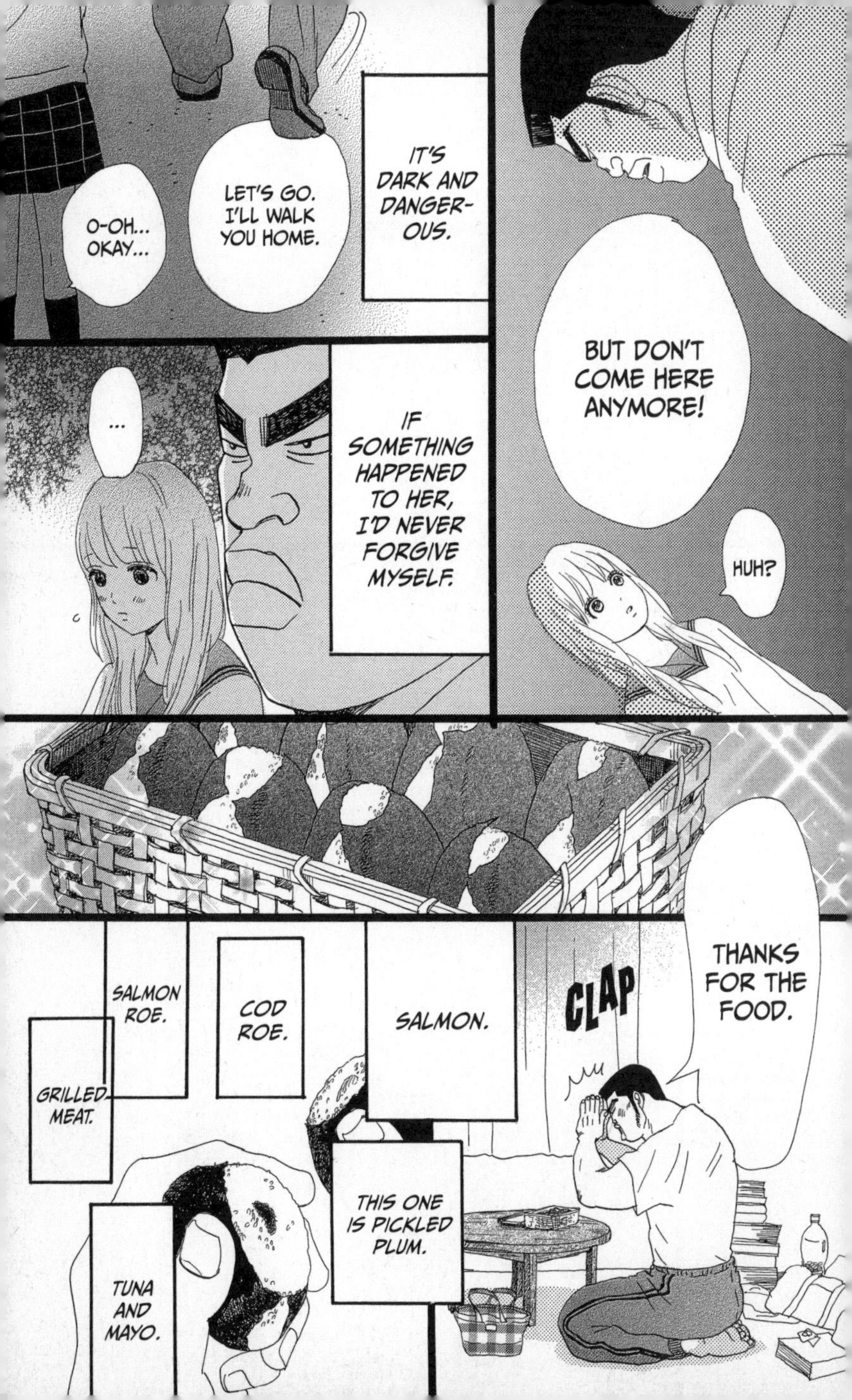
BUT DON'T COME HERE ANYMORE!
HUH?
IT'S DARK AND DANGER-OUS.
LET'S GO. I'LL WALK YOU HOME.
O-OH... OKAY...
IF SOMETHING HAPPENED TO HER, I'D NEVER FORGIVE MYSELF.
...
THANKS FOR THE FOOD.
CLAP
SALMON.
COD ROE.
SALMON ROE.
GRILLED MEAT.
THIS ONE IS PICKLED PLUM.
TUNA AND MAYO.

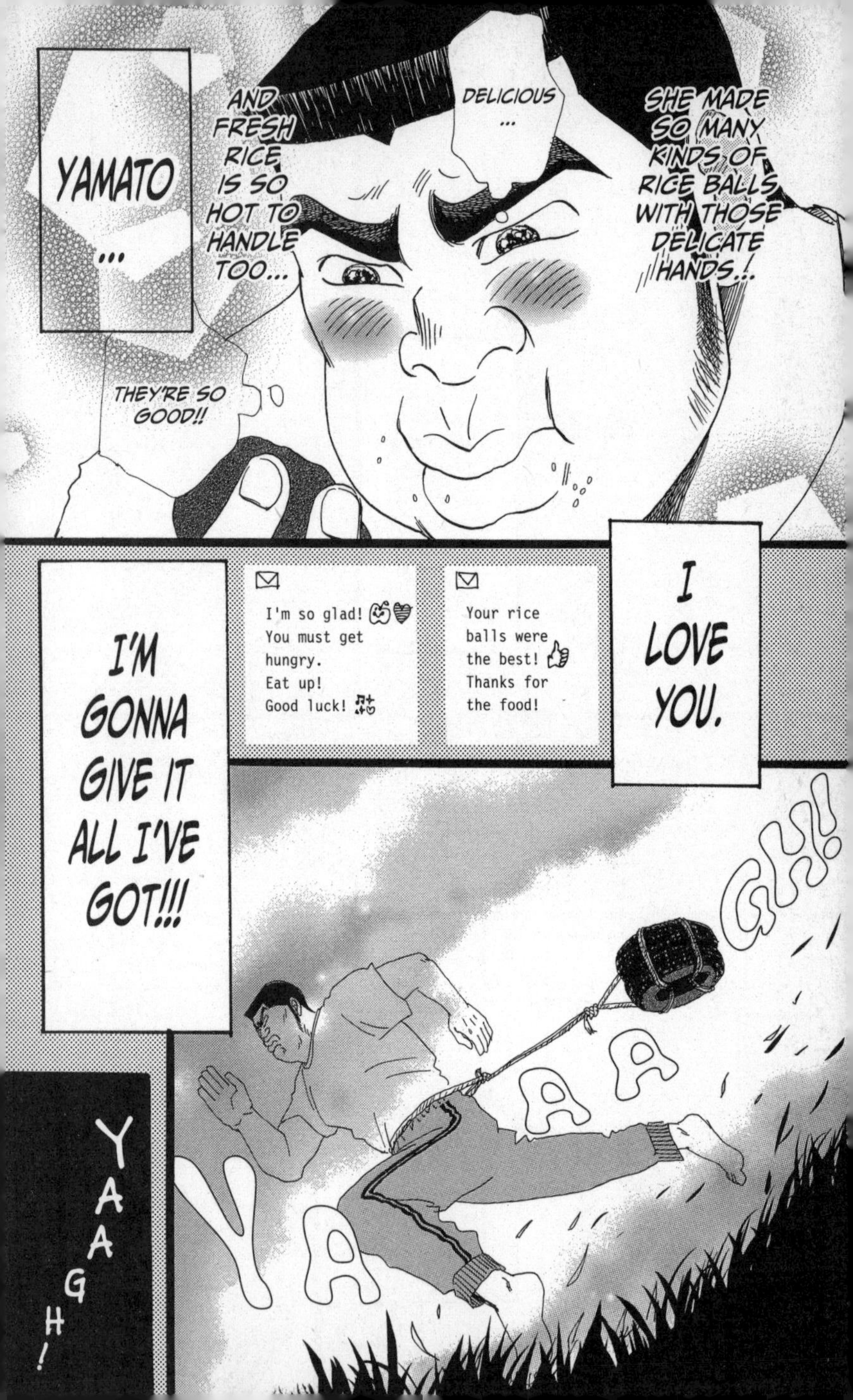
SHE MADE SO MANY KINDS OF RICE BALLS WITH THOSE DELICATE HANDS...
DELICIOUS ...
AND FRESH RICE IS SO HOT TO HANDLE TOO...
YAMATO ...
THEY'RE SO GOOD!!
I LOVE YOU.
Your rice balls were the best! Thanks for the food!
I'm so glad! You must get hungry. Eat up! Good luck!
I'M GONNA GIVE IT ALL I'VE GOT!!!
YAAAGH!!
YAAGH!

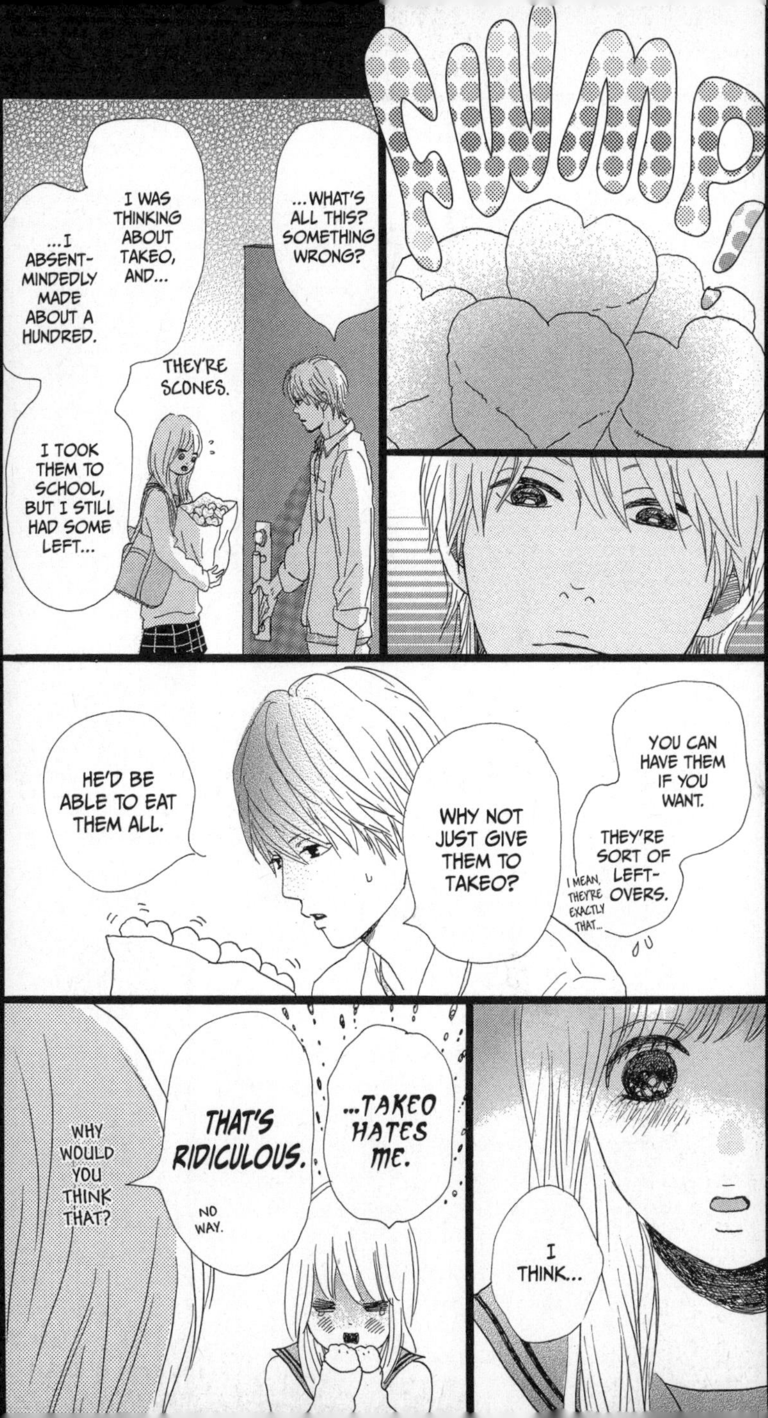
FWMP!
...WHAT'S ALL THIS? SOMETHING WRONG?
THEY'RE SCONES.
I WAS THINKING ABOUT TAKEO, AND...
...I ABSENT-MINDEDLY MADE ABOUT A HUNDRED.
I TOOK THEM TO SCHOOL, BUT I STILL HAD SOME LEFT...
YOU CAN HAVE THEM IF YOU WANT.
THEY'RE SORT OF LEFT-OVERS.
I MEAN, THEY'RE EXACTLY THAT...
WHY NOT JUST GIVE THEM TO TAKEO?
HE'D BE ABLE TO EAT THEM ALL.
I THINK...
...TAKEO HATES ME.
THAT'S RIDICULOUS.
NO WAY.
WHY WOULD YOU THINK THAT?

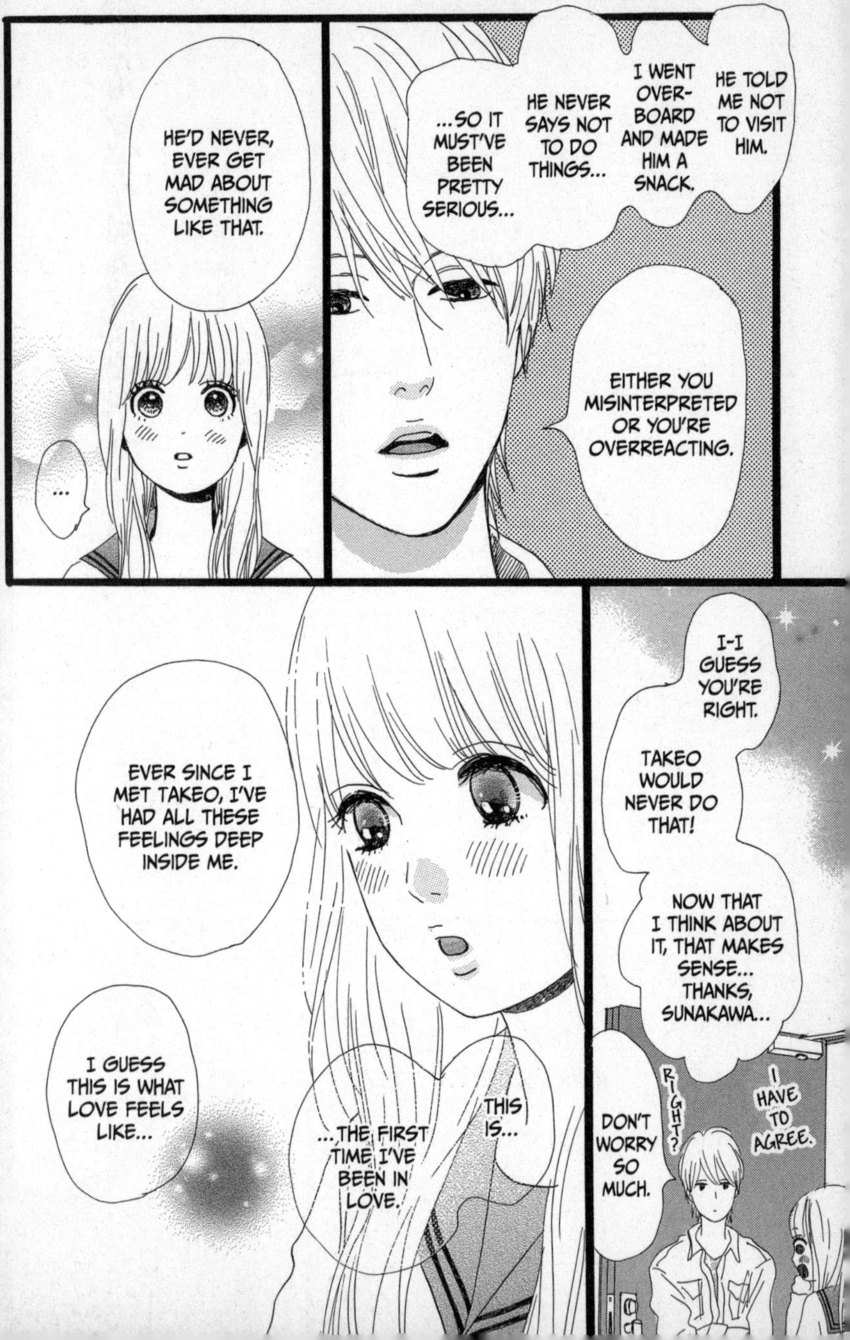
HE TOLD ME NOT TO VISIT HIM.
I WENT OVER-BOARD AND MADE HIM A SNACK.
HE NEVER SAYS NOT TO DO THINGS...
...SO IT MUST'VE BEEN PRETTY SERIOUS...
EITHER YOU MISINTERPRETED OR YOU'RE OVERREACTING.
HE'D NEVER, EVER GET MAD ABOUT SOMETHING LIKE THAT.
...
I-I GUESS YOU'RE RIGHT.
TAKEO WOULD NEVER DO THAT!
NOW THAT I THINK ABOUT IT, THAT MAKES SENSE... THANKS, SUNAKAWA...
I HAVE TO AGREE.
RIGHT?
DON'T WORRY SO MUCH.
EVER SINCE I MET TAKEO, I'VE HAD ALL THESE FEELINGS DEEP INSIDE ME.
THIS IS...
...THE FIRST TIME I'VE BEEN IN LOVE.
I GUESS THIS IS WHAT LOVE FEELS LIKE...

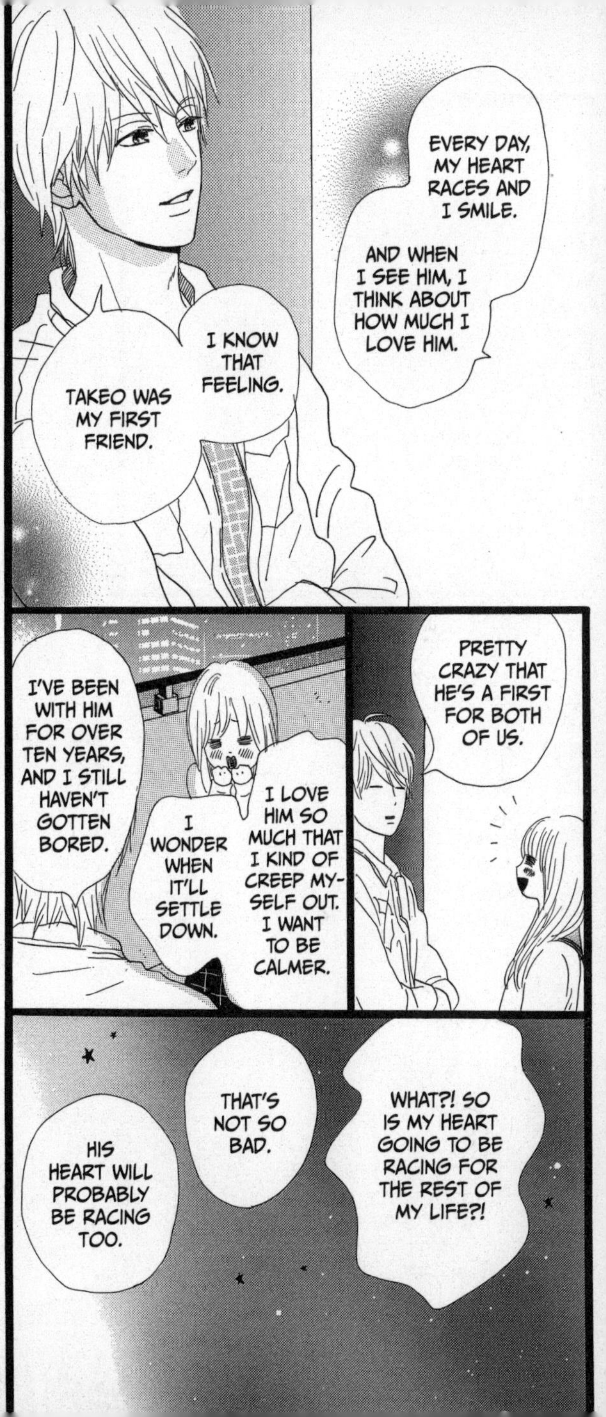
EVERY DAY, MY HEART RACES AND I SMILE.
AND WHEN I SEE HIM, I THINK ABOUT HOW MUCH I LOVE HIM.
I KNOW THAT FEELING.
TAKEO WAS MY FIRST FRIEND.
PRETTY CRAZY THAT HE'S A FIRST FOR BOTH OF US.
I LOVE HIM SO MUCH THAT I KIND OF CREEP MY-SELF OUT. I WANT TO BE CALMER.
I WONDER WHEN IT'LL SETTLE DOWN.
I'VE BEEN WITH HIM FOR OVER TEN YEARS, AND I STILL HAVEN'T GOTTEN BORED.
WHAT?! SO IS MY HEART GOING TO BE RACING FOR THE REST OF MY LIFE?!
THAT'S NOT SO BAD.
HIS HEART WILL PROBABLY BE RACING TOO.
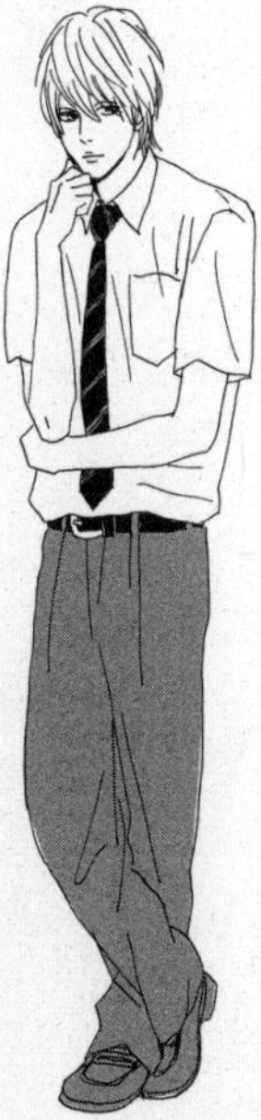

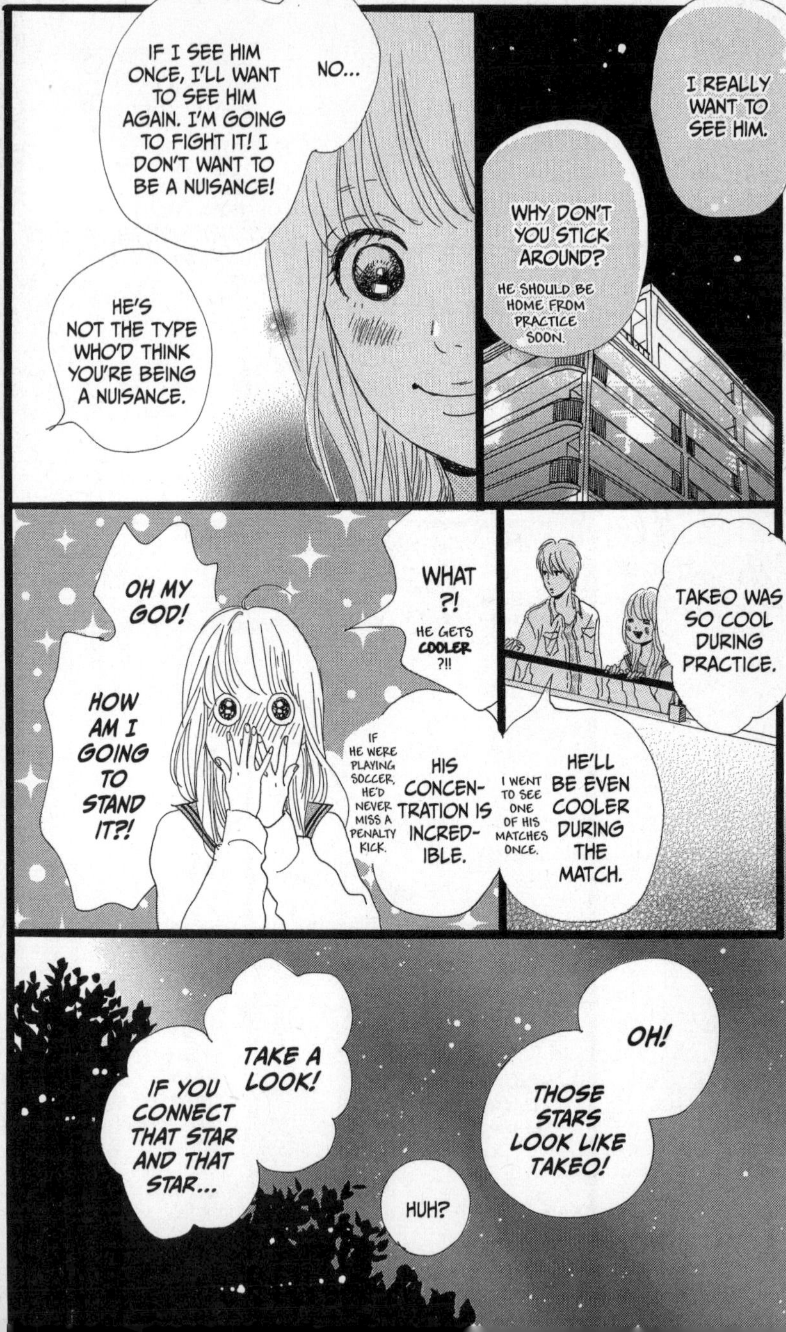
I REALLY WANT TO SEE HIM.
WHY DON'T YOU STICK AROUND?
HE SHOULD BE HOME FROM PRACTICE SOON.
NO...
IF I SEE HIM ONCE, I'LL WANT TO SEE HIM AGAIN. I'M GOING TO FIGHT IT! I DON'T WANT TO BE A NUISANCE!
HE'S NOT THE TYPE WHO'D THINK YOU'RE BEING A NUISANCE.
TAKEO WAS SO COOL DURING PRACTICE.
HE'LL BE EVEN COOLER DURING THE MATCH.
I WENT TO SEE ONE OF HIS MATCHES ONCE.
WHAT?!
HE GETS COOLER?!!
HIS CONCEN-TRATION IS INCRED-IBLE.
IF HE WERE PLAYING SOCCER, HE'D NEVER MISS A PENALTY KICK.
OH MY GOD!
HOW AM I GOING TO STAND IT?!
OH!
THOSE STARS LOOK LIKE TAKEO!
HUH?
TAKE A LOOK!
IF YOU CONNECT THAT STAR AND THAT STAR...

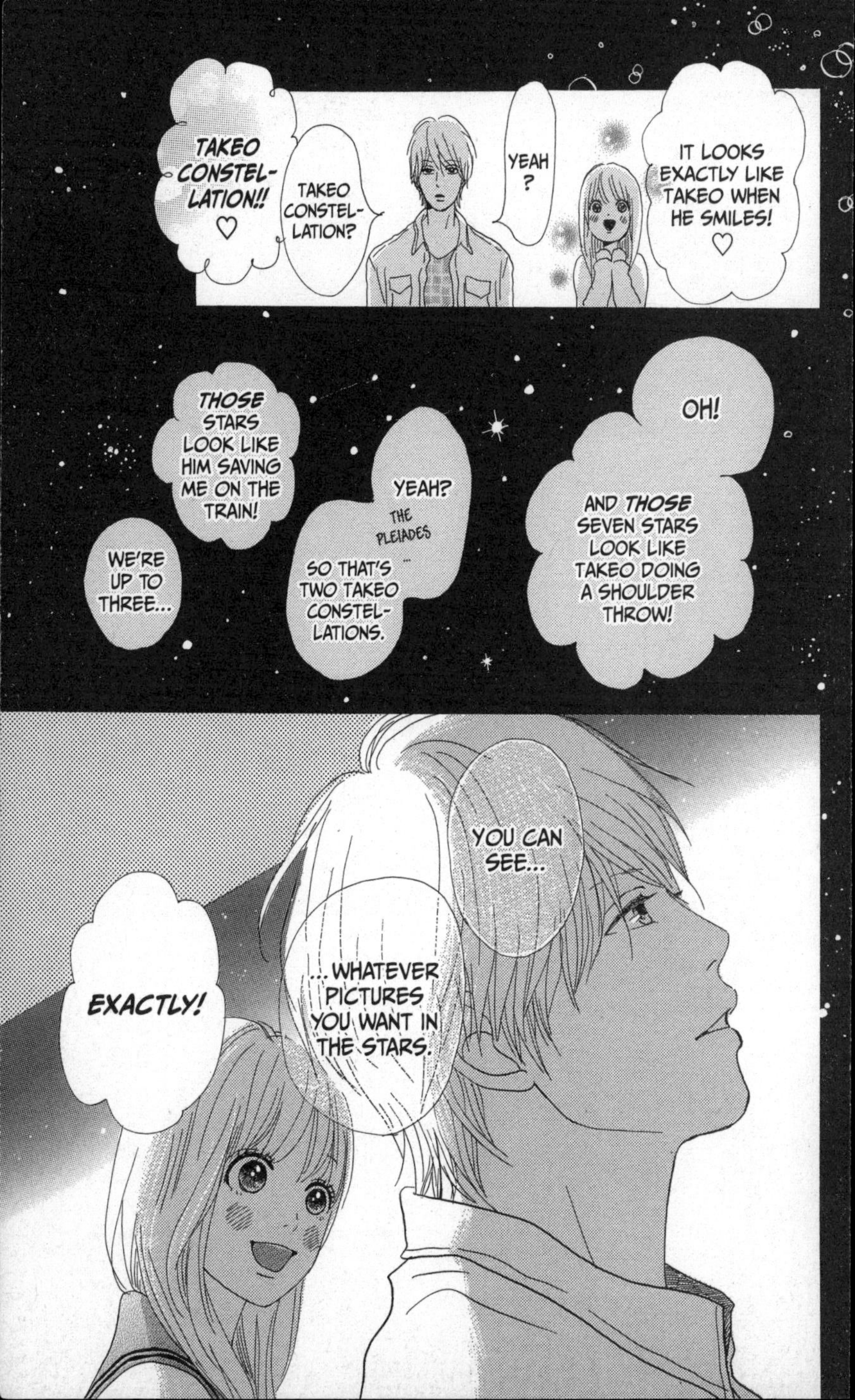
IT LOOKS EXACTLY LIKE TAKEO WHEN HE SMILES! ♡
YEAH?
TAKEO CONSTEL-LATION?
TAKEO CONSTEL-LATION!! ♡
OH!
AND THOSE SEVEN STARS LOOK LIKE TAKEO DOING A SHOULDER THROW!
THE PLEIADES...
YEAH?
SO THAT'S TWO TAKEO CONSTEL-LATIONS.
THOSE STARS LOOK LIKE HIM SAVING ME ON THE TRAIN!
WE'RE UP TO THREE...
YOU CAN SEE...
...WHATEVER PICTURES YOU WANT IN THE STARS.
EXACTLY!

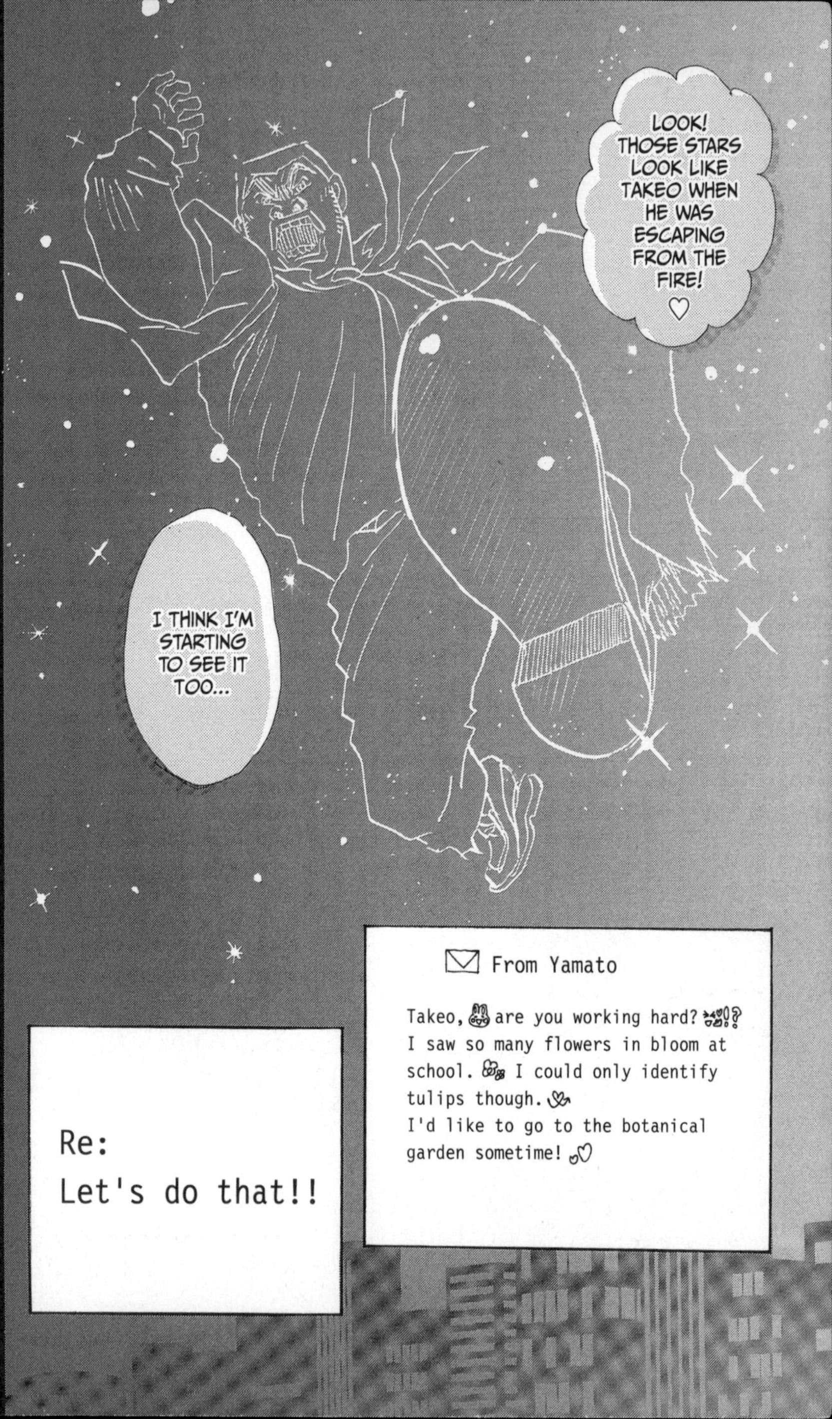
LOOK! THOSE STARS LOOK LIKE TAKEO WHEN HE WAS ESCAPING FROM THE FIRE! ♡
I THINK I'M STARTING TO SEE IT TOO...
From Yamato
Takeo, are you working hard?
I saw so many flowers in bloom at school. I could only identify tulips though.
I'd like to go to the botanical garden sometime!
Re:
Let's do that!!

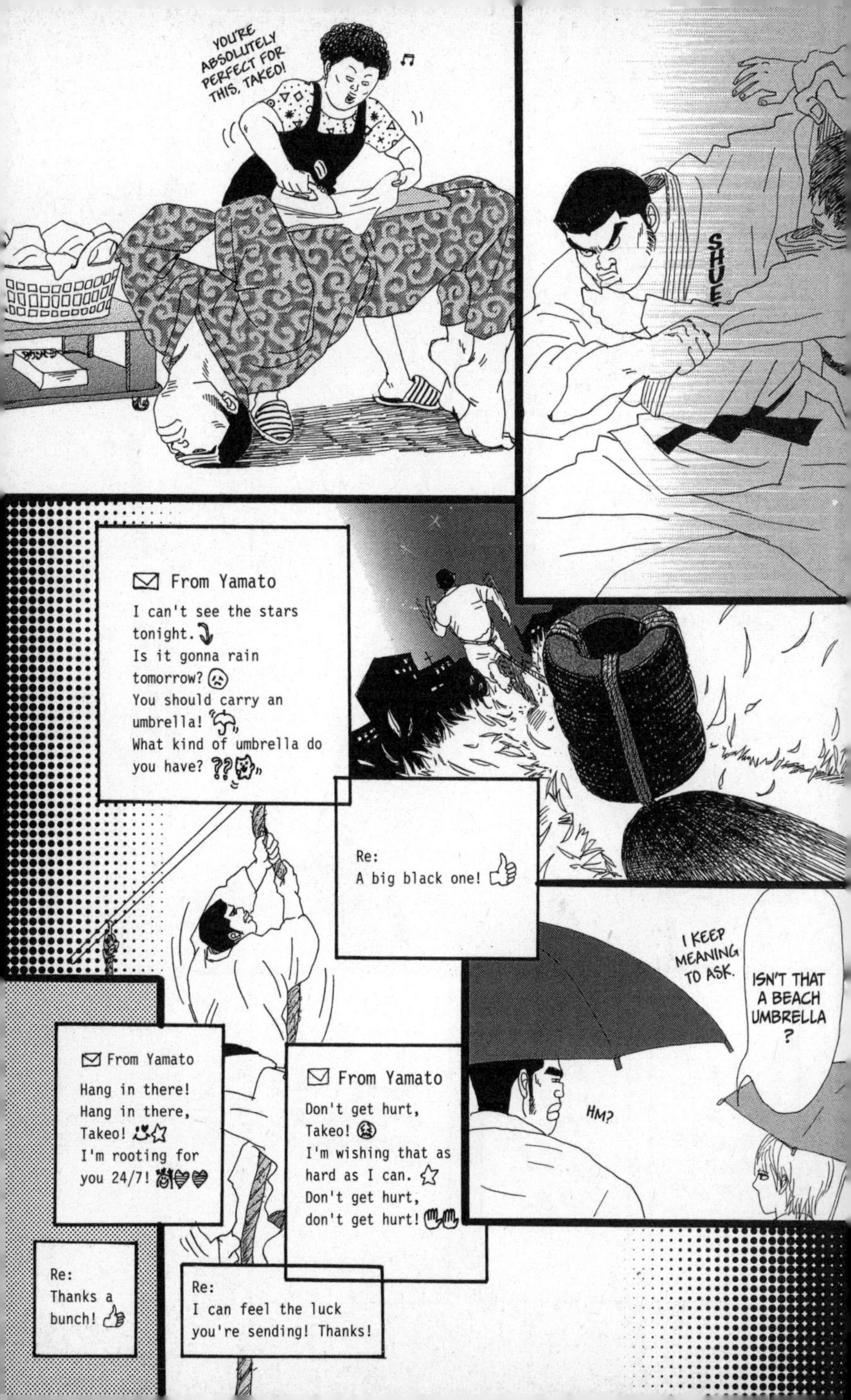
SHUE
YOU'RE ABSOLUTELY PERFECT FOR THIS, TAKEO!
From Yamato
I can't see the stars
tonight.
Is it gonna rain
tomorrow?
You should carry an
umbrella!
What kind of umbrella do
you have?
Re:
A big black one!
I KEEP MEANING TO ASK.
ISN'T THAT A BEACH UMBRELLA?
HM?
From Yamato
Don't get hurt,
Takeo!
I'm wishing that as
hard as I can.
Don't get hurt,
don't get hurt!
Re:
I can feel the luck
you're sending! Thanks!
From Yamato
Hang in there!
Hang in there,
Takeo!
I'm rooting for
you 24/7!
Re:
Thanks a
bunch!

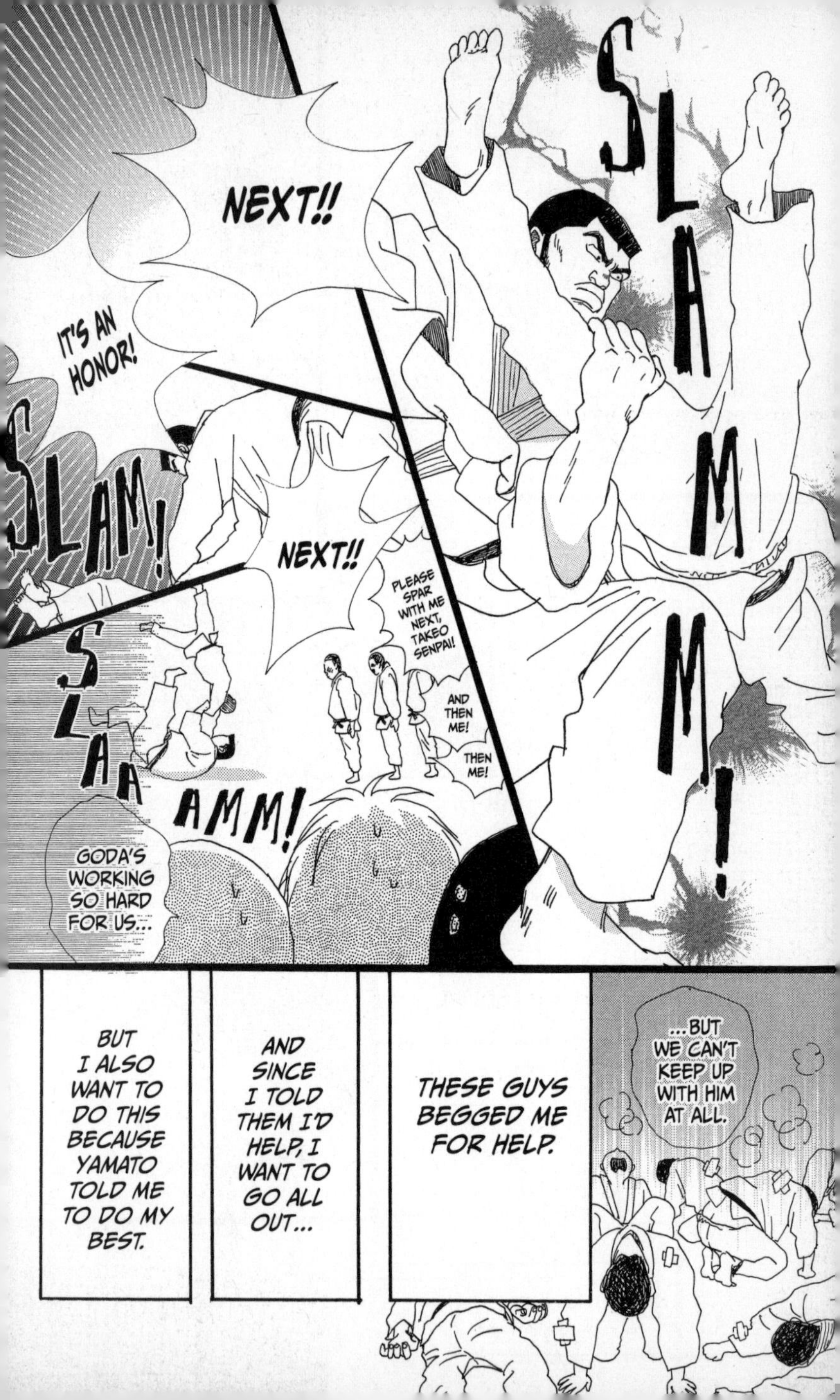
NEXT!!
SLAMM!
IT'S AN HONOR!
SLAM!
NEXT!!
PLEASE SPAR WITH ME NEXT, TAKEO SENPAI!
AND THEN ME!
THEN ME!
SLAAAMM!
GODA'S WORKING SO HARD FOR US...
...BUT WE CAN'T KEEP UP WITH HIM AT ALL.
THESE GUYS BEGGED ME FOR HELP.
AND SINCE I TOLD THEM I'D HELP, I WANT TO GO ALL OUT...
BUT I ALSO WANT TO DO THIS BECAUSE YAMATO TOLD ME TO DO MY BEST.

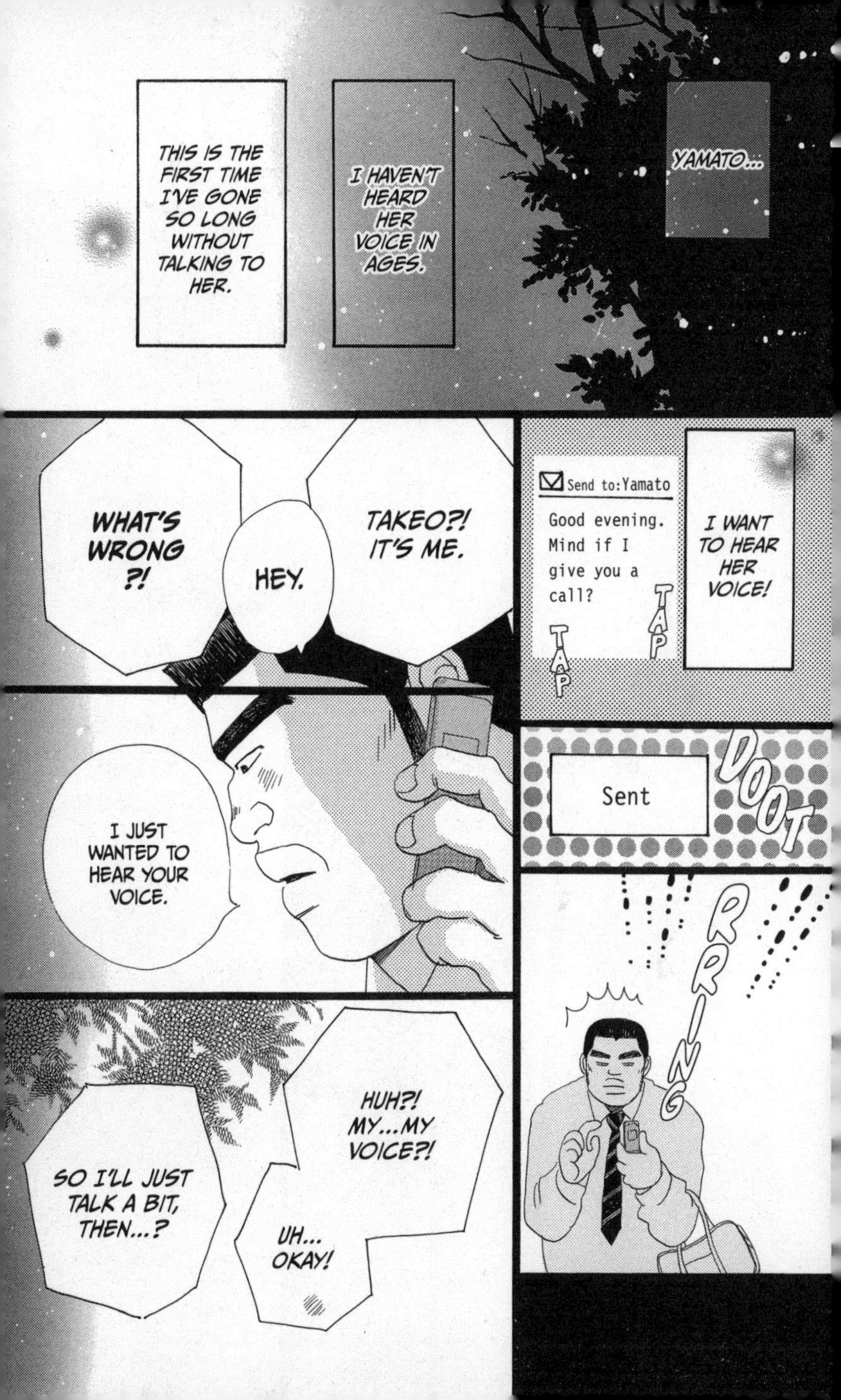
YAMATO...
I HAVEN'T HEARD HER VOICE IN AGES.
THIS IS THE FIRST TIME I'VE GONE SO LONG WITHOUT TALKING TO HER.
I WANT TO HEAR HER VOICE!
Send to:Yamato
Good evening. Mind if I give you a call?
TAP
TAP
DOOT
Sent
RRRING
TAKEO?! IT'S ME.
HEY.
WHAT'S WRONG ?!
I JUST WANTED TO HEAR YOUR VOICE.
HUH?! MY...MY VOICE?!
SO I'LL JUST TALK A BIT, THEN...?
UH... OKAY!

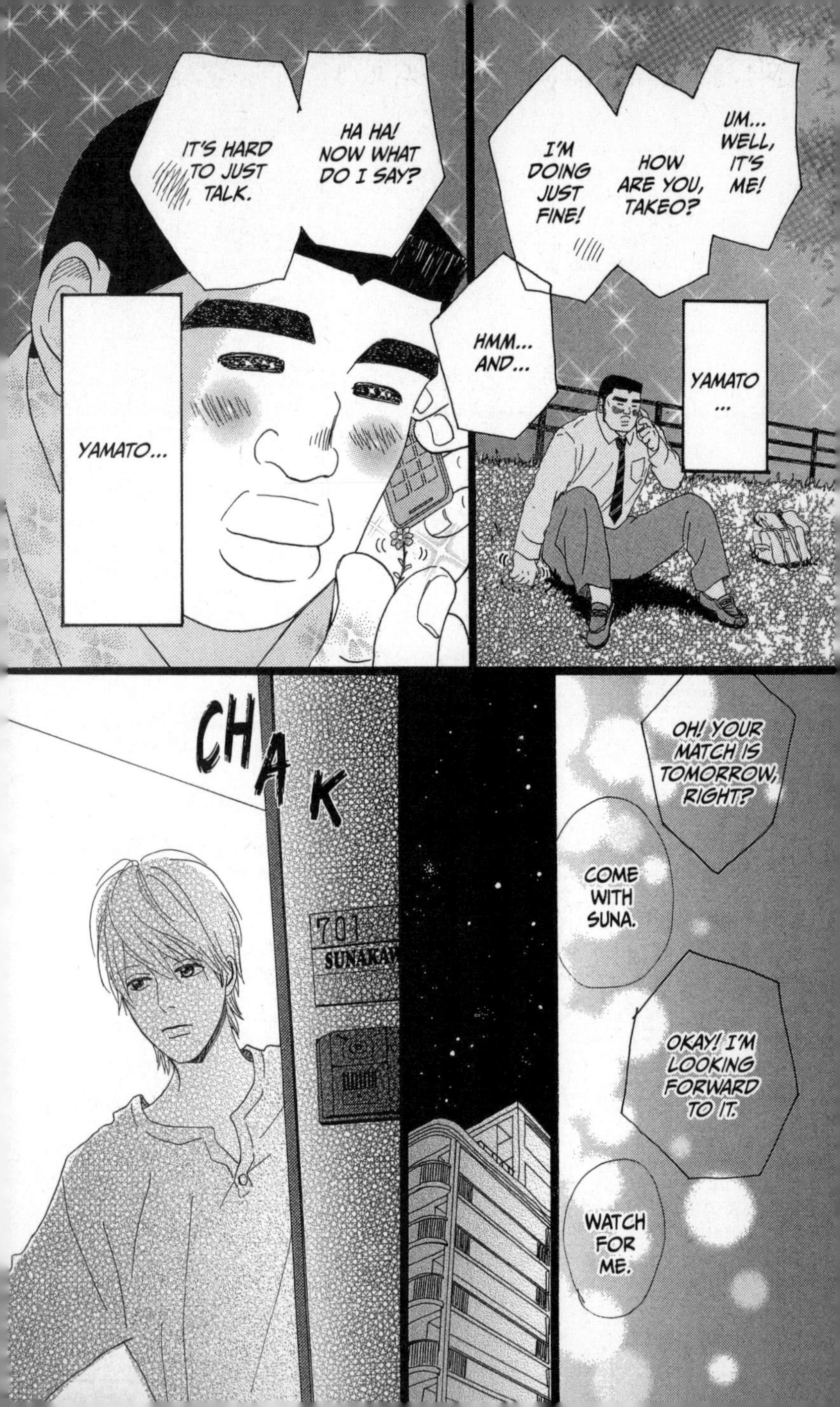
UM... WELL, IT'S ME!
HOW ARE YOU, TAKEO?
I'M DOING JUST FINE!
HMM... AND...
YAMATO ...
HA HA! NOW WHAT DO I SAY?
IT'S HARD TO JUST TALK.
YAMATO...
OH! YOUR MATCH IS TOMORROW, RIGHT?
COME WITH SUNA.
OKAY! I'M LOOKING FORWARD TO IT.
WATCH FOR ME.
CHAK
701

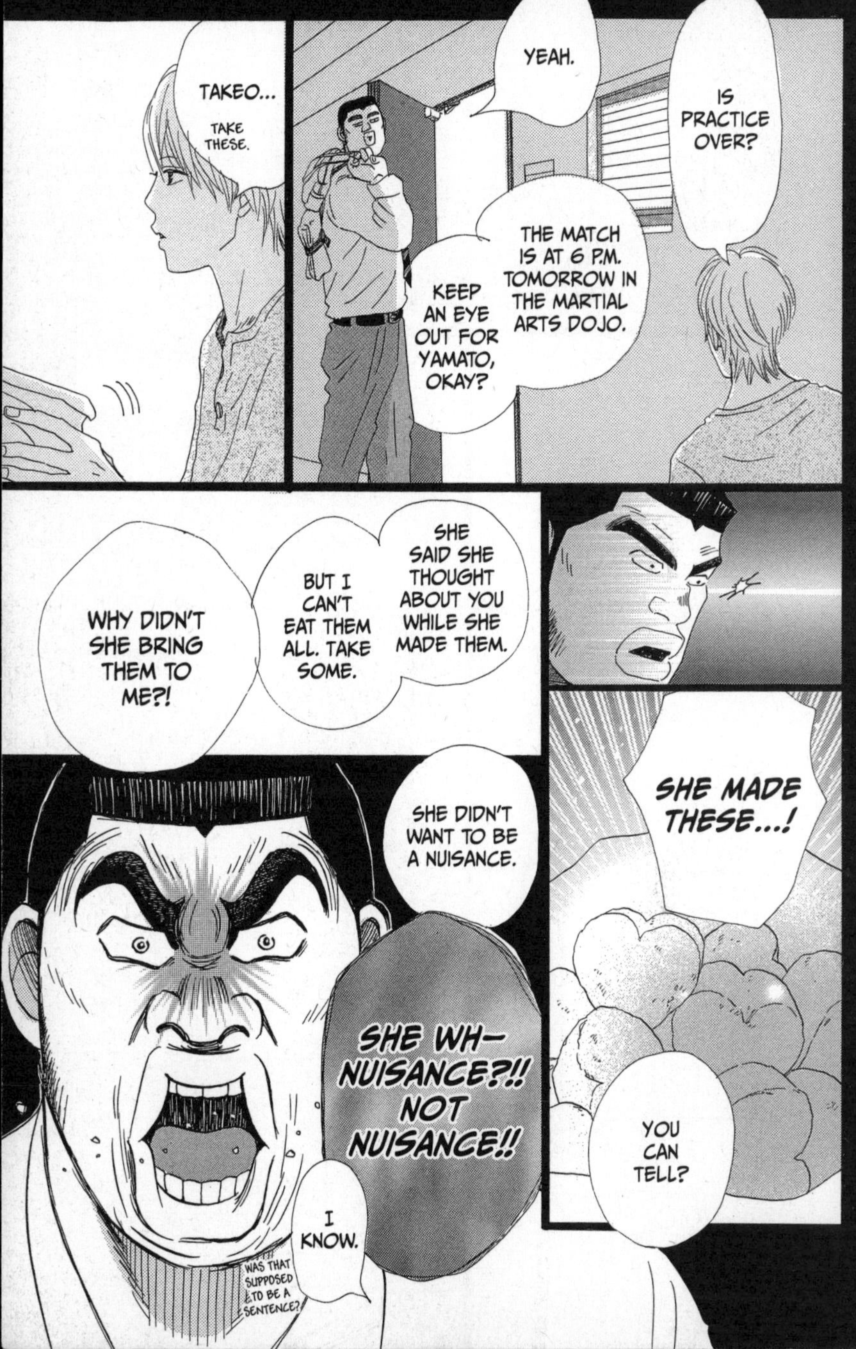
IS PRACTICE OVER?
YEAH.
THE MATCH IS AT 6 P.M. TOMORROW IN THE MARTIAL ARTS DOJO.
KEEP AN EYE OUT FOR YAMATO, OKAY?
TAKEO...
TAKE THESE.
SHE SAID SHE THOUGHT ABOUT YOU WHILE SHE MADE THEM.
BUT I CAN'T EAT THEM ALL. TAKE SOME.
WHY DIDN'T SHE BRING THEM TO ME?!
SHE MADE THESE...!
YOU CAN TELL?
SHE DIDN'T WANT TO BE A NUISANCE.
SHE WH— NUISANCE?!! NOT NUISANCE!!
I KNOW.
WAS THAT SUPPOSED TO BE A SENTENCE?

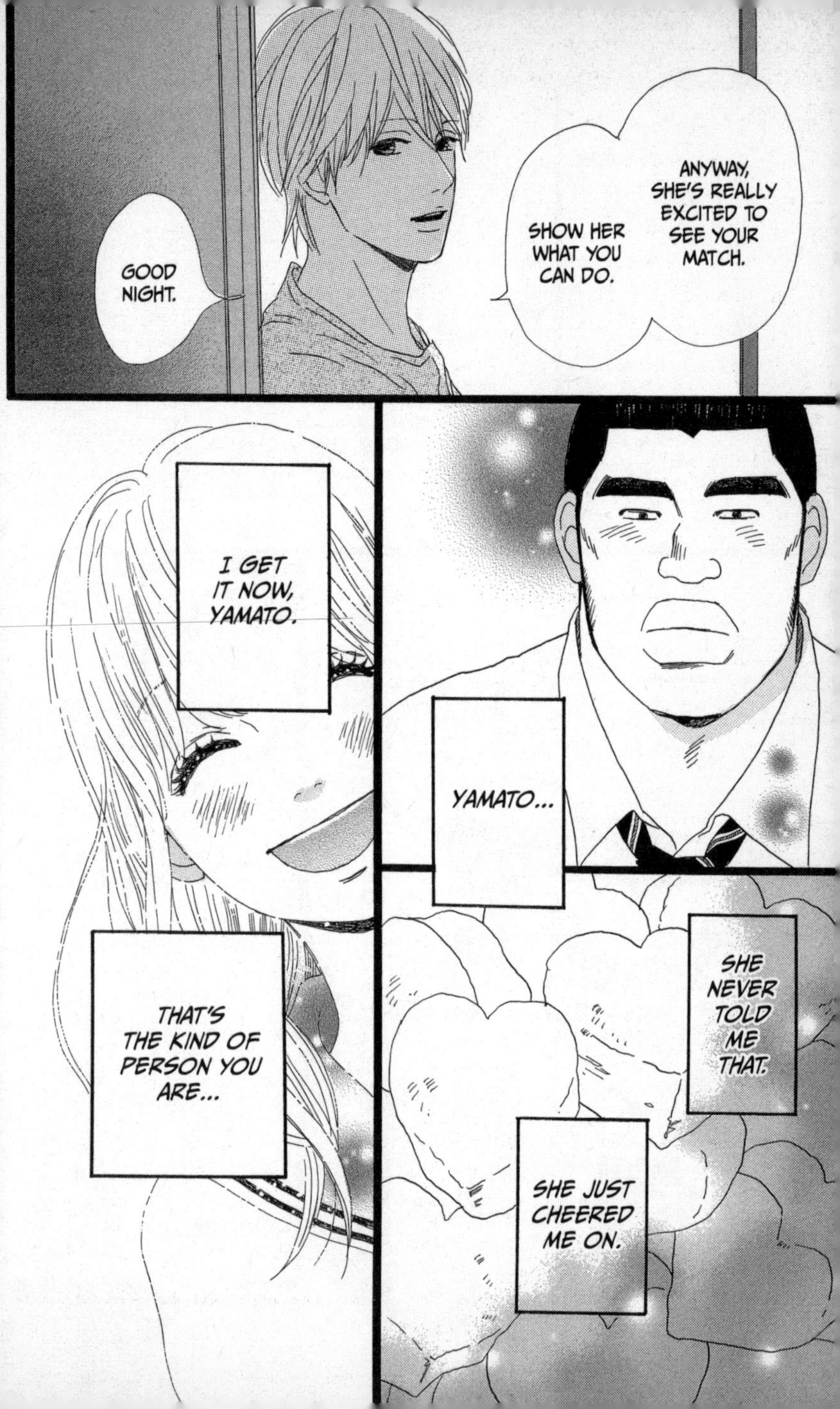
ANYWAY, SHE'S REALLY EXCITED TO SEE YOUR MATCH.
SHOW HER WHAT YOU CAN DO.
GOOD NIGHT.
YAMATO...
SHE NEVER TOLD ME THAT.
SHE JUST CHEERED ME ON.
I GET IT NOW, YAMATO.
THAT'S THE KIND OF PERSON YOU ARE...

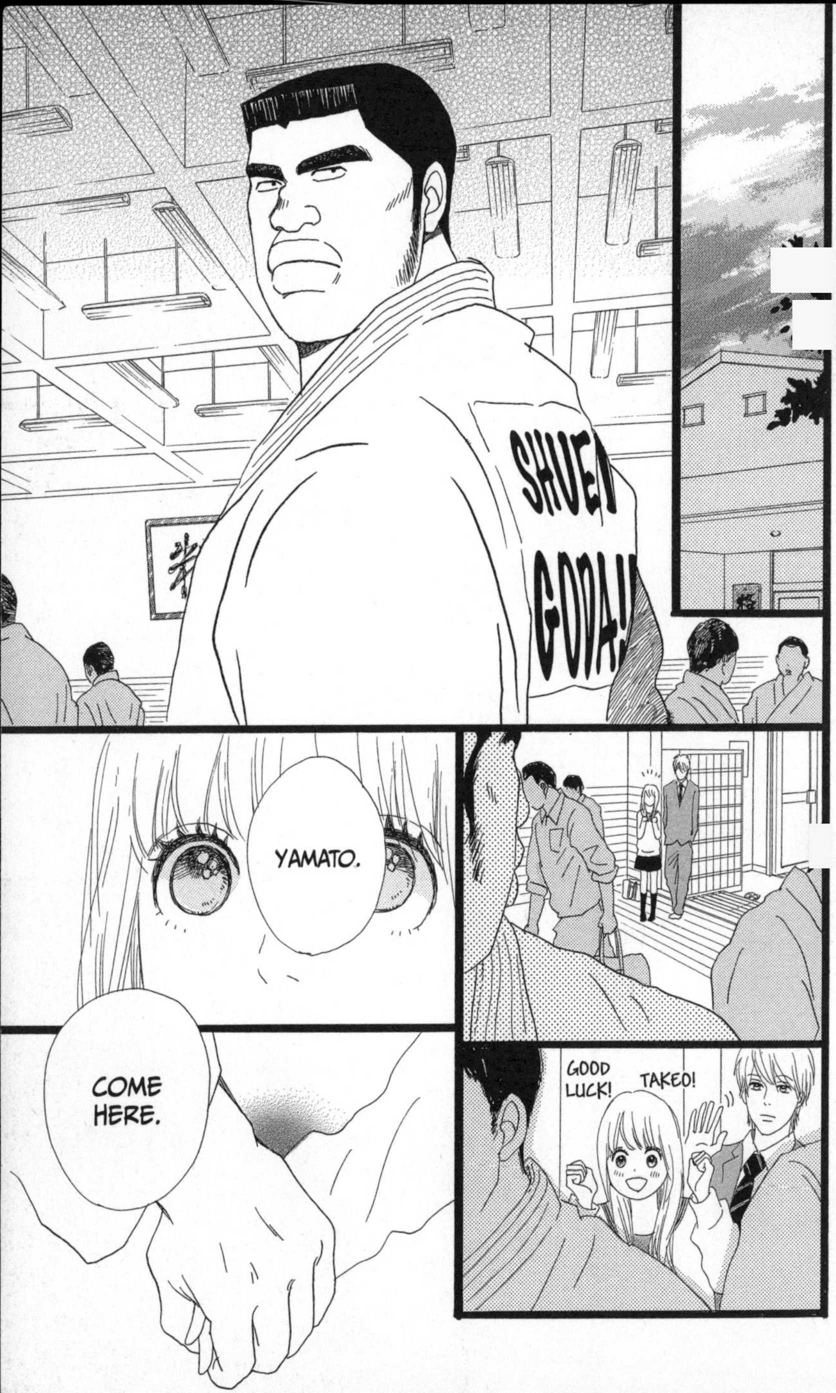
YAMATO.
TAKEO!
GOOD LUCK!
COME HERE.

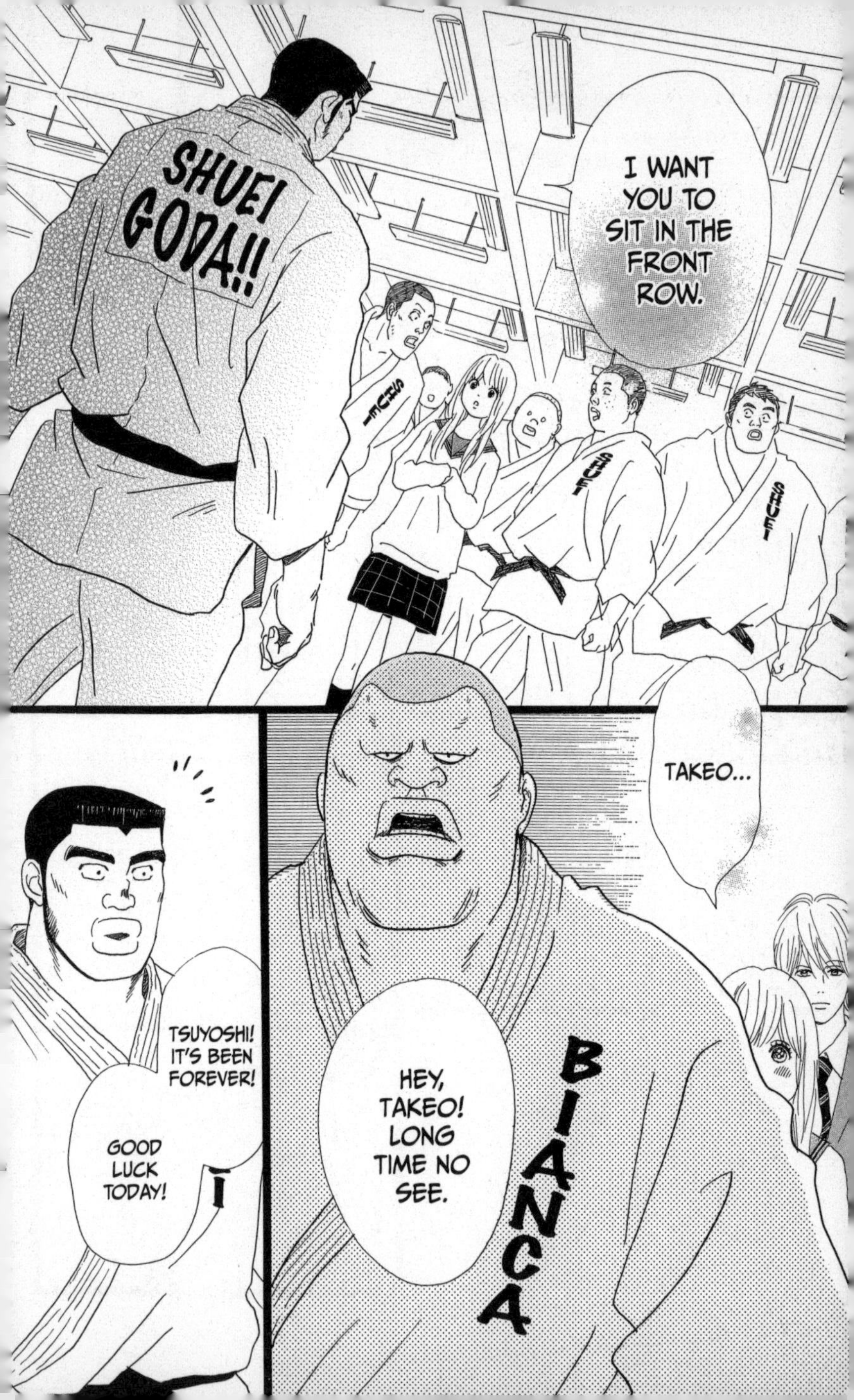
I WANT YOU TO SIT IN THE FRONT ROW.
SHUEI GODA!!
SHUEI
SHUEI
TAKEO...
HEY, TAKEO! LONG TIME NO SEE.
BIANCA
TSUYOSHI! IT'S BEEN FOREVER!
GOOD LUCK TODAY!

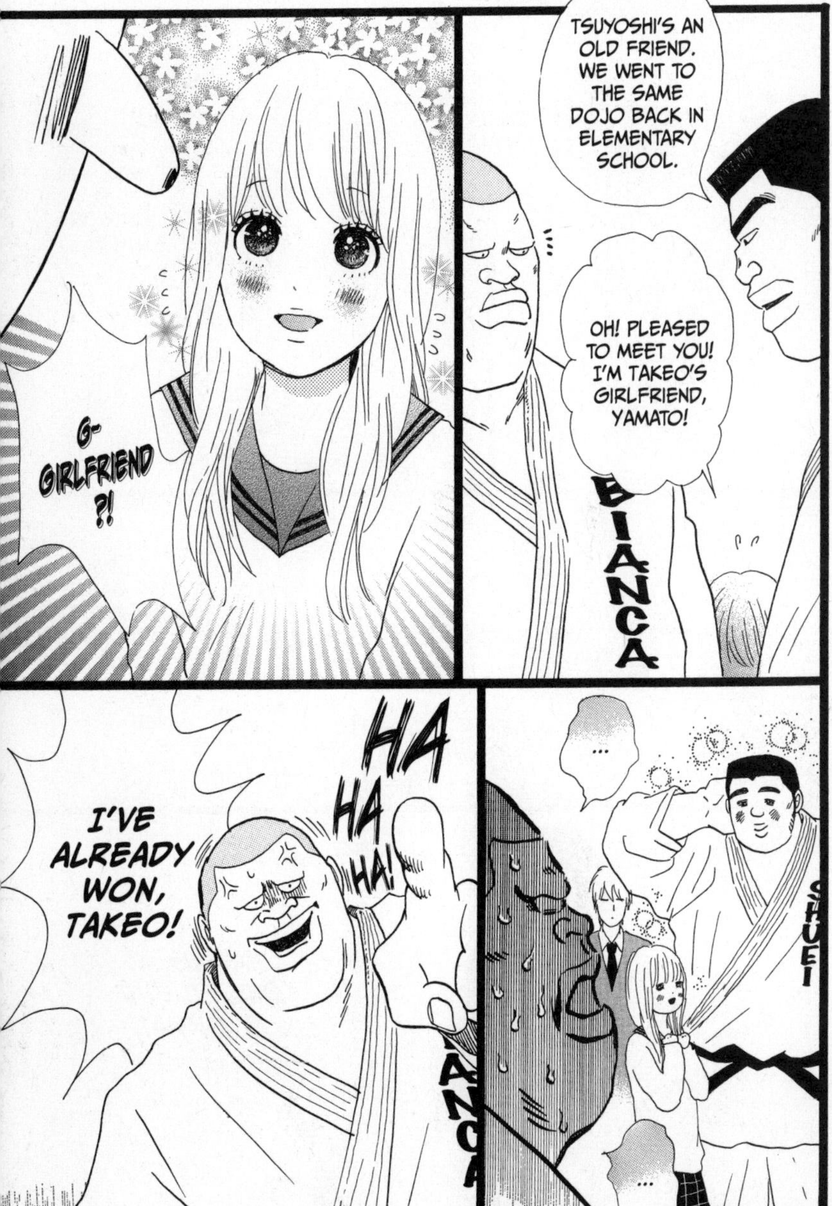
TSUYOSHI'S AN OLD FRIEND. WE WENT TO THE SAME DOJO BACK IN ELEMENTARY SCHOOL.
OH! PLEASED TO MEET YOU! I'M TAKEO'S GIRLFRIEND, YAMATO!
BIANCA
G-GIRLFRIEND?!
...
SHUEI
...
HA HA HA!
I'VE ALREADY WON, TAKEO!

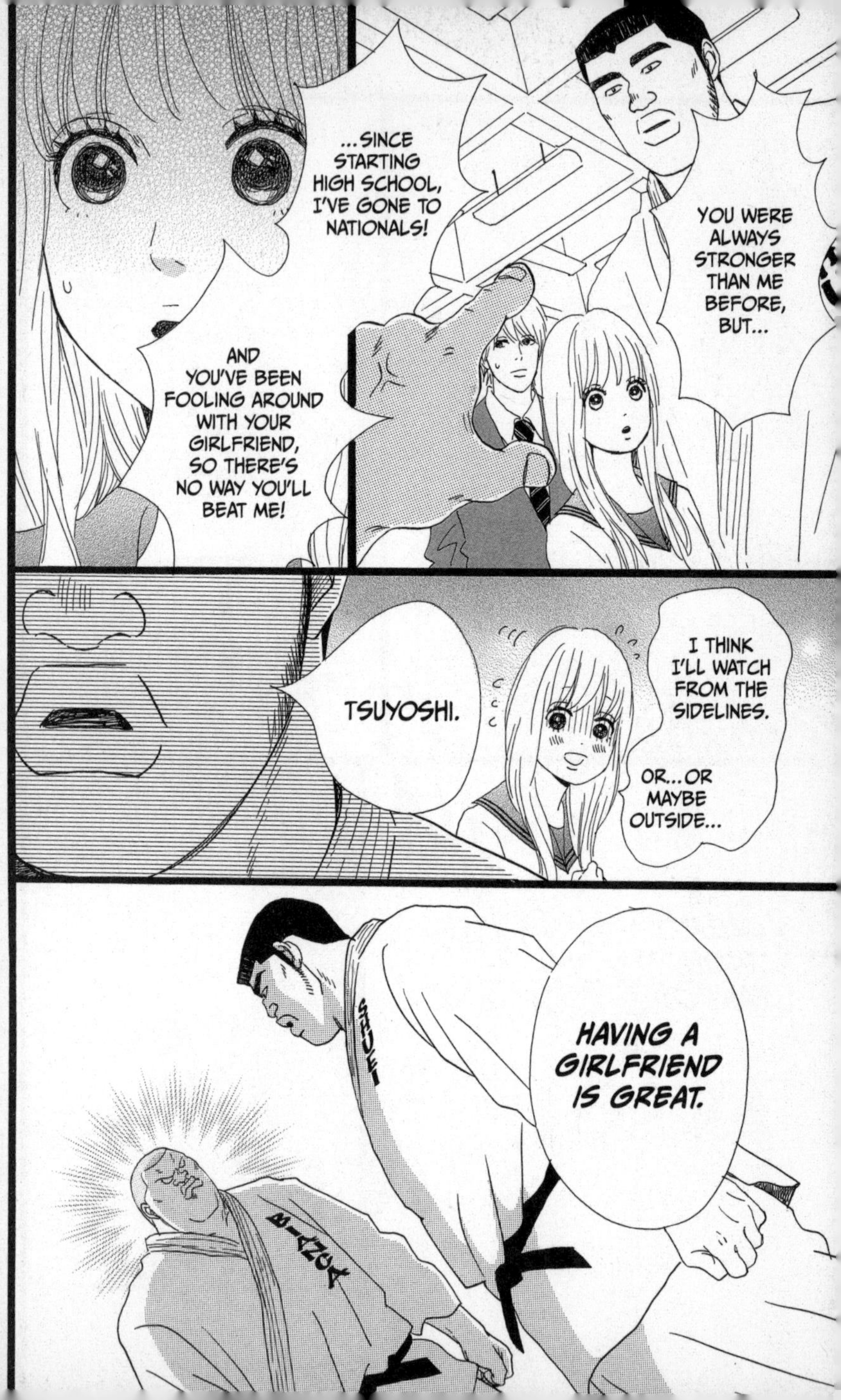
YOU WERE ALWAYS STRONGER THAN ME BEFORE, BUT...
...SINCE STARTING HIGH SCHOOL, I'VE GONE TO NATIONALS!
AND YOU'VE BEEN FOOLING AROUND WITH YOUR GIRLFRIEND, SO THERE'S NO WAY YOU'LL BEAT ME!
I THINK I'LL WATCH FROM THE SIDELINES.
OR...OR MAYBE OUTSIDE...
TSUYOSHI.
SHUEI
HAVING A GIRLFRIEND IS GREAT.

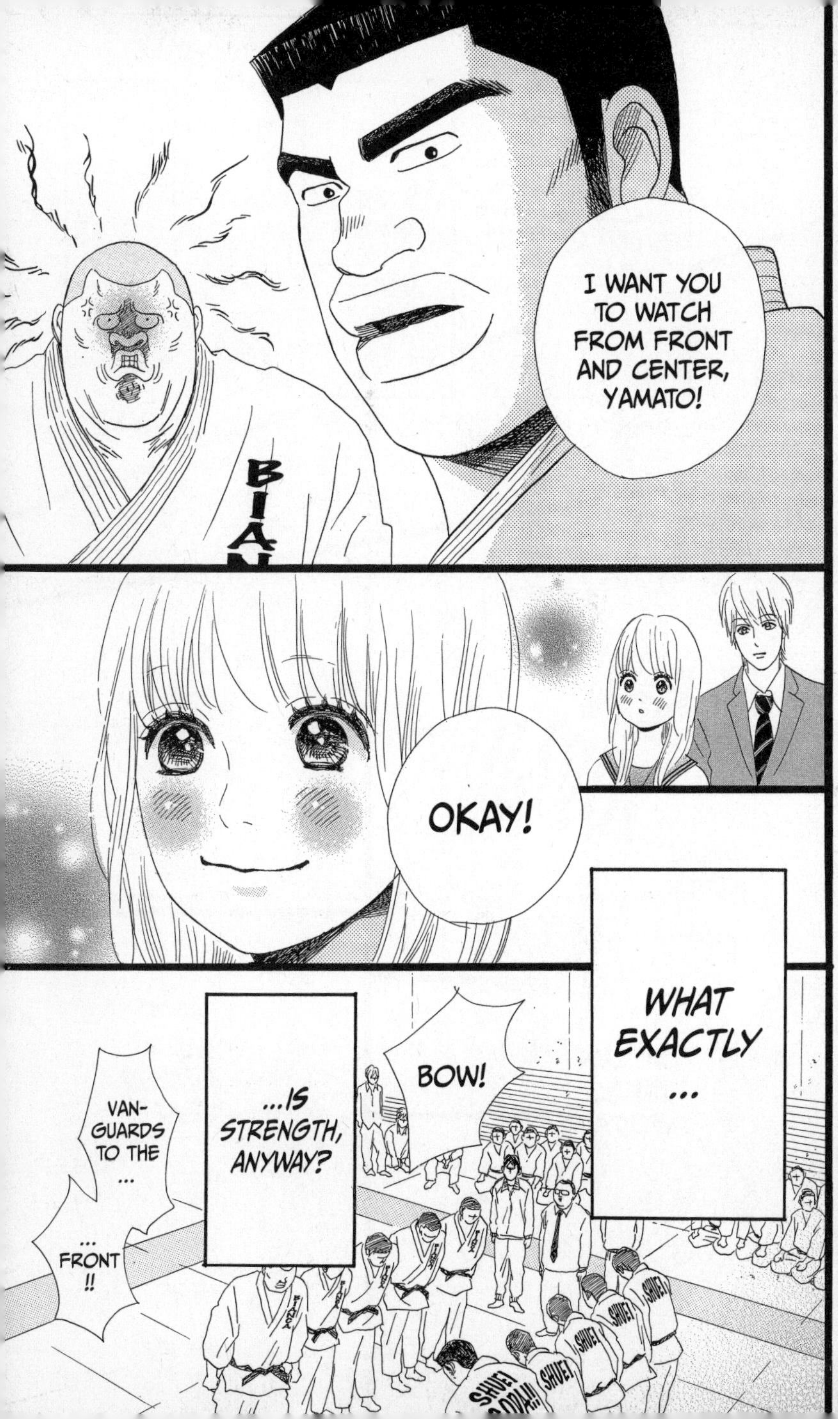
I WANT YOU TO WATCH FROM FRONT AND CENTER, YAMATO!
OKAY!
WHAT EXACTLY ...
BOW!
...IS STRENGTH, ANYWAY?
VAN-GUARDS TO THE ...
... FRONT !!

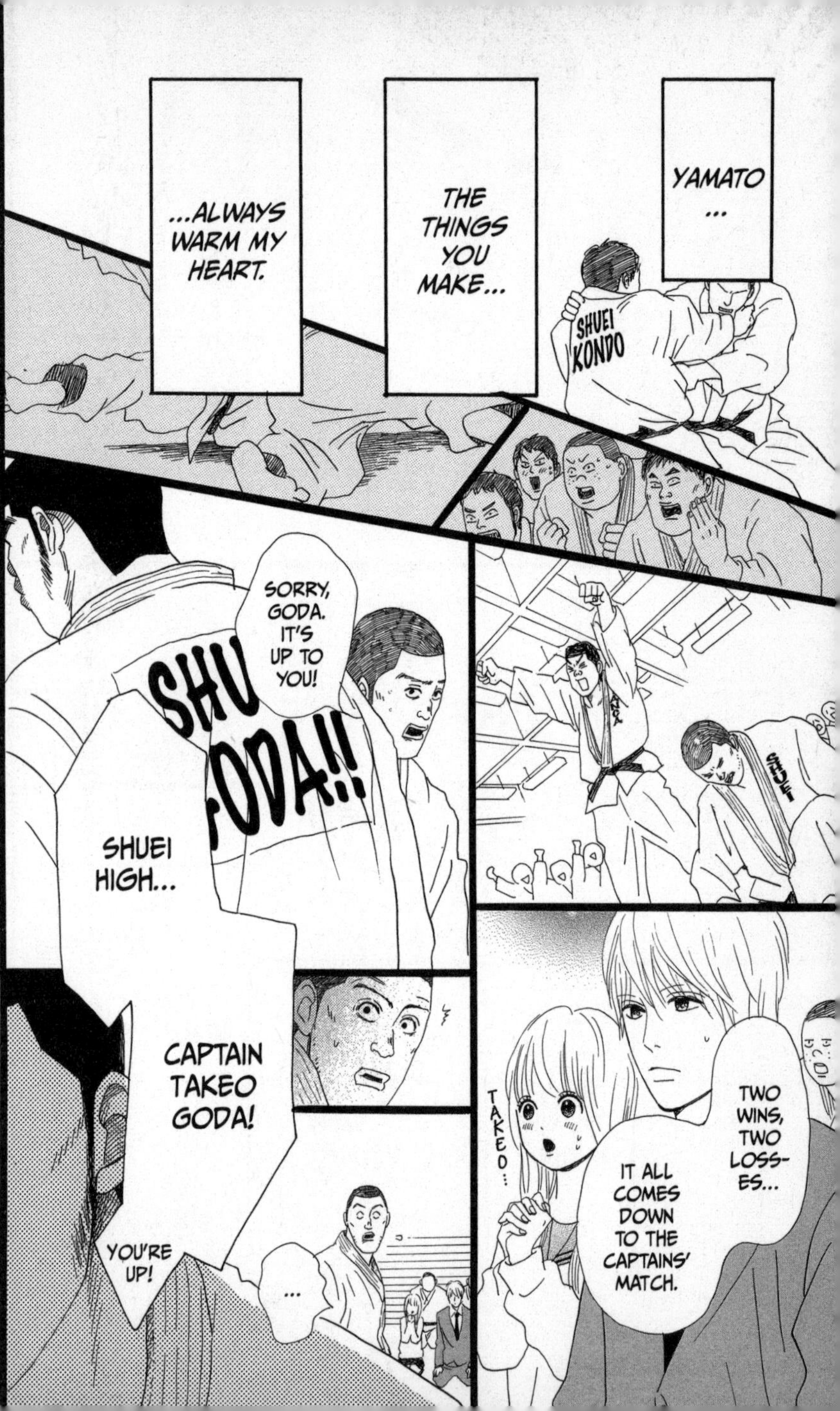
YAMATO ...
THE THINGS YOU MAKE...
...ALWAYS WARM MY HEART.
SHUEI KONDO
SHUEI
SORRY, GODA. IT'S UP TO YOU!
SHU
ODA!!
SHUEI HIGH...
CAPTAIN TAKEO GODA!
TWO WINS, TWO LOSS-ES...
IT ALL COMES DOWN TO THE CAPTAINS' MATCH.
TAKEO...
YOU'RE UP!
...

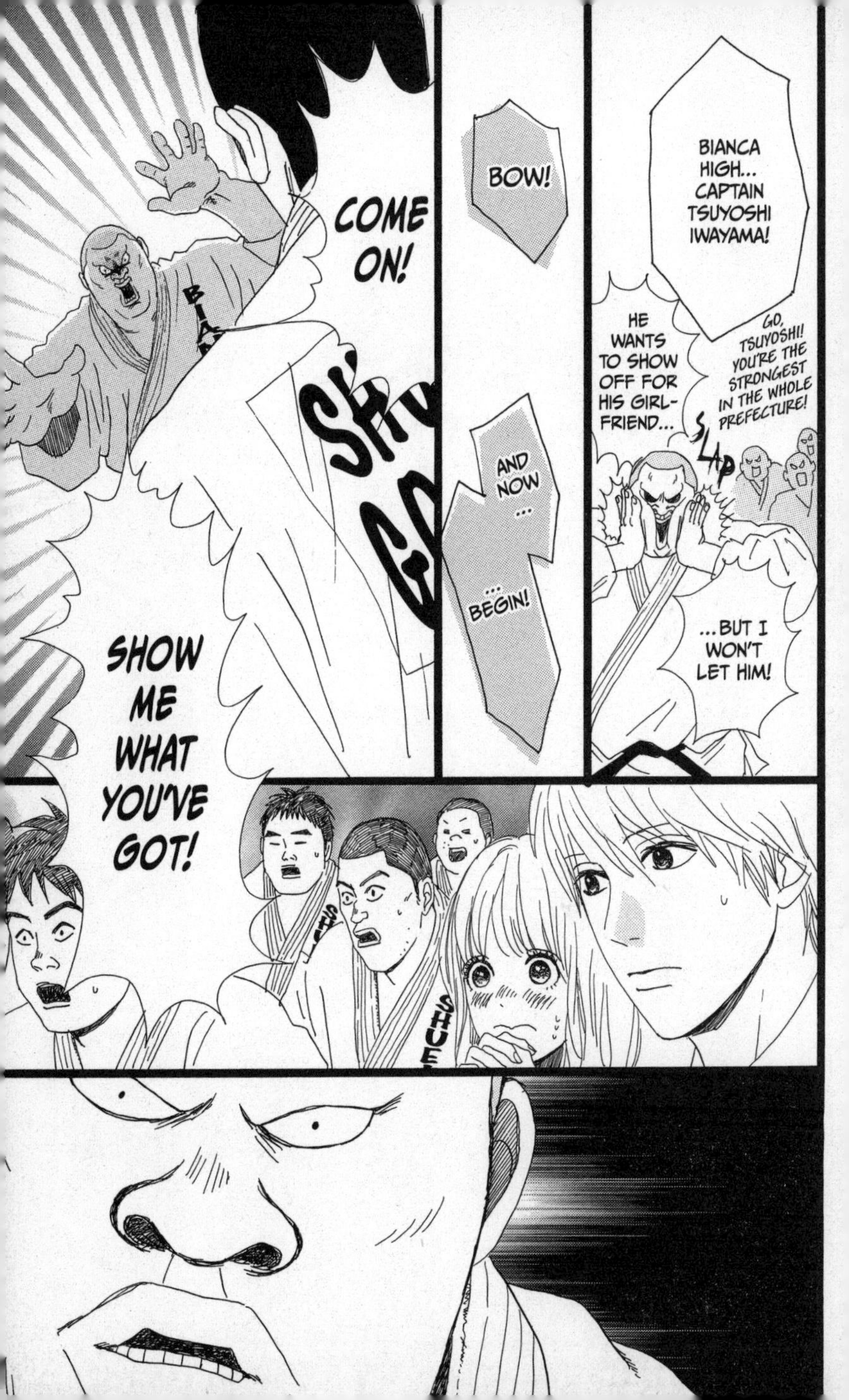
BIANCA HIGH... CAPTAIN TSUYOSHI IWAYAMA!
GO, TSUYOSHI! YOU'RE THE STRONGEST IN THE WHOLE PREFECTURE!
HE WANTS TO SHOW OFF FOR HIS GIRL-FRIEND...
SLAP
...BUT I WON'T LET HIM!
BOW!
AND NOW...
...BEGIN!
COME ON!
SHOW ME WHAT YOU'VE GOT!

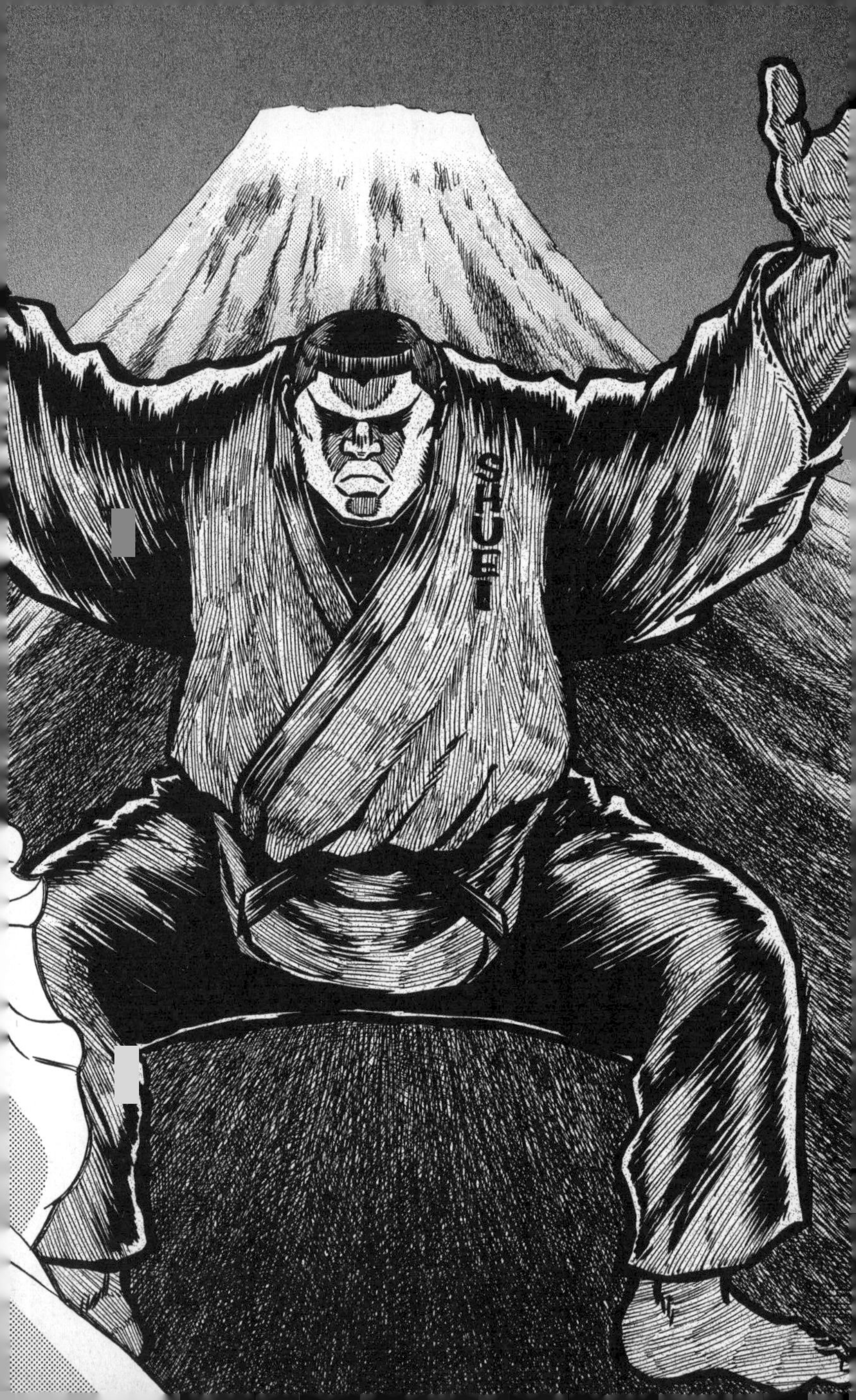
SHUEI

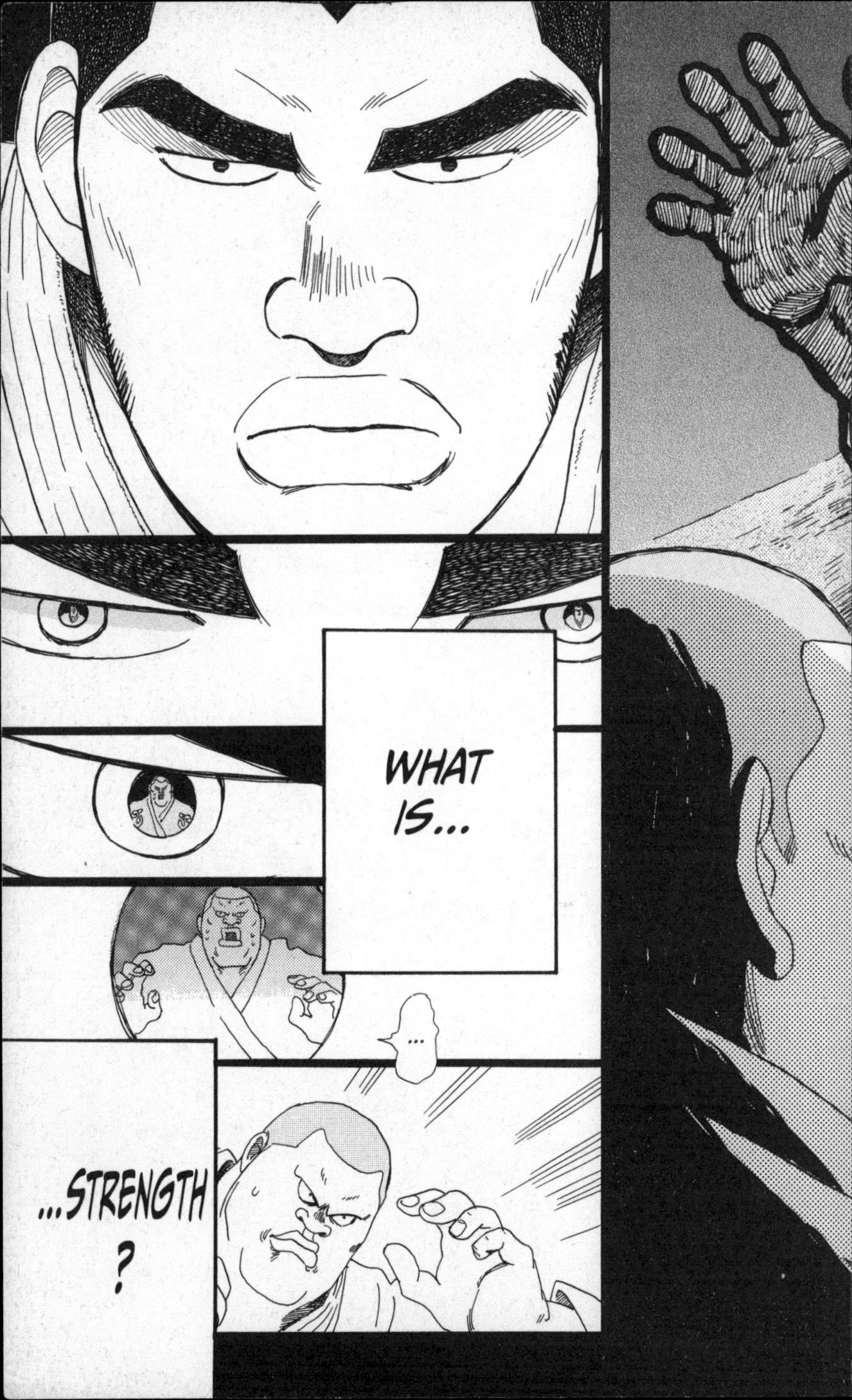
WHAT IS...
...
...STRENGTH ?

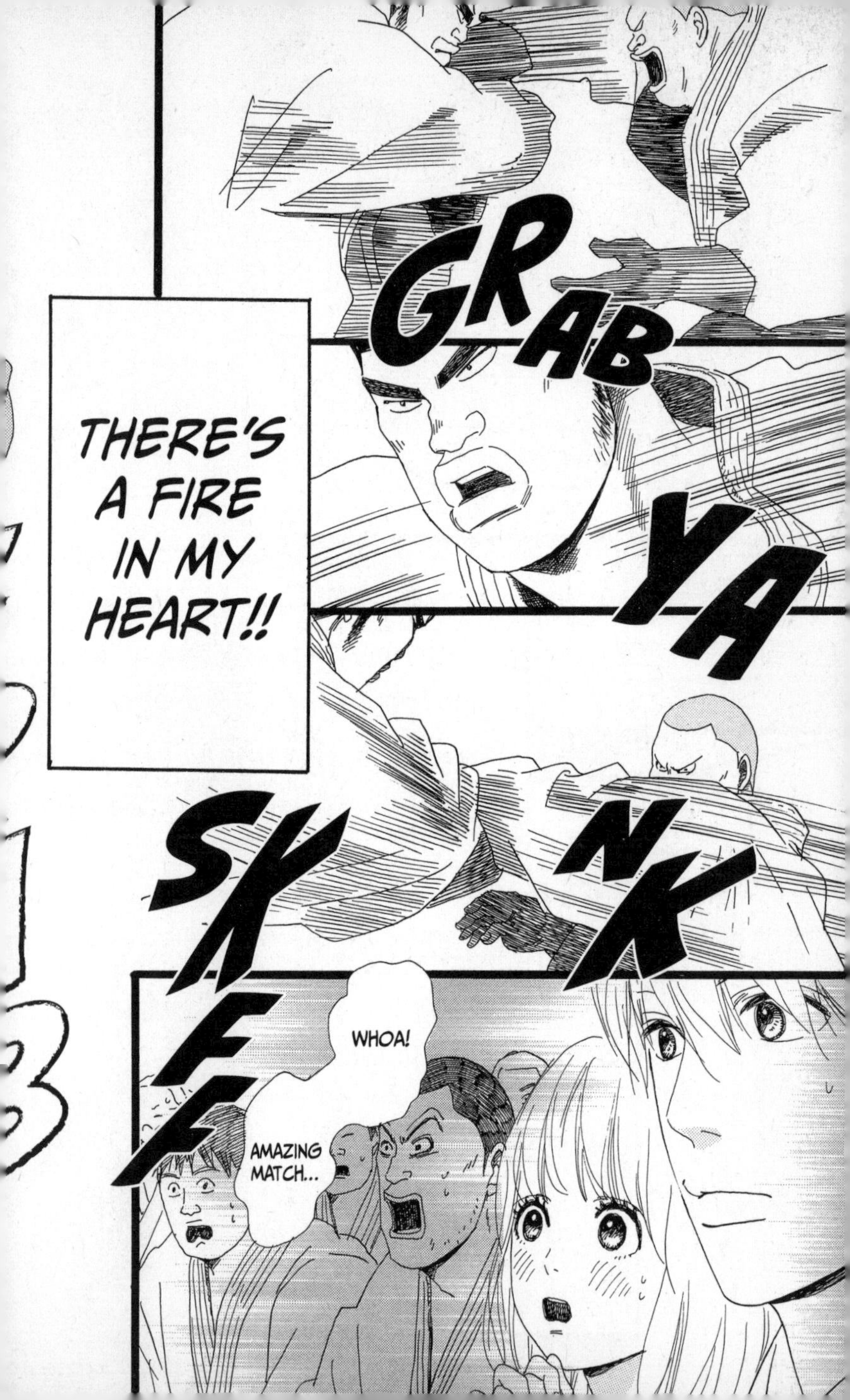
GRAB
YANK
THERE'S A FIRE IN MY HEART!!
SKFFF
WHOA!
AMAZING MATCH...

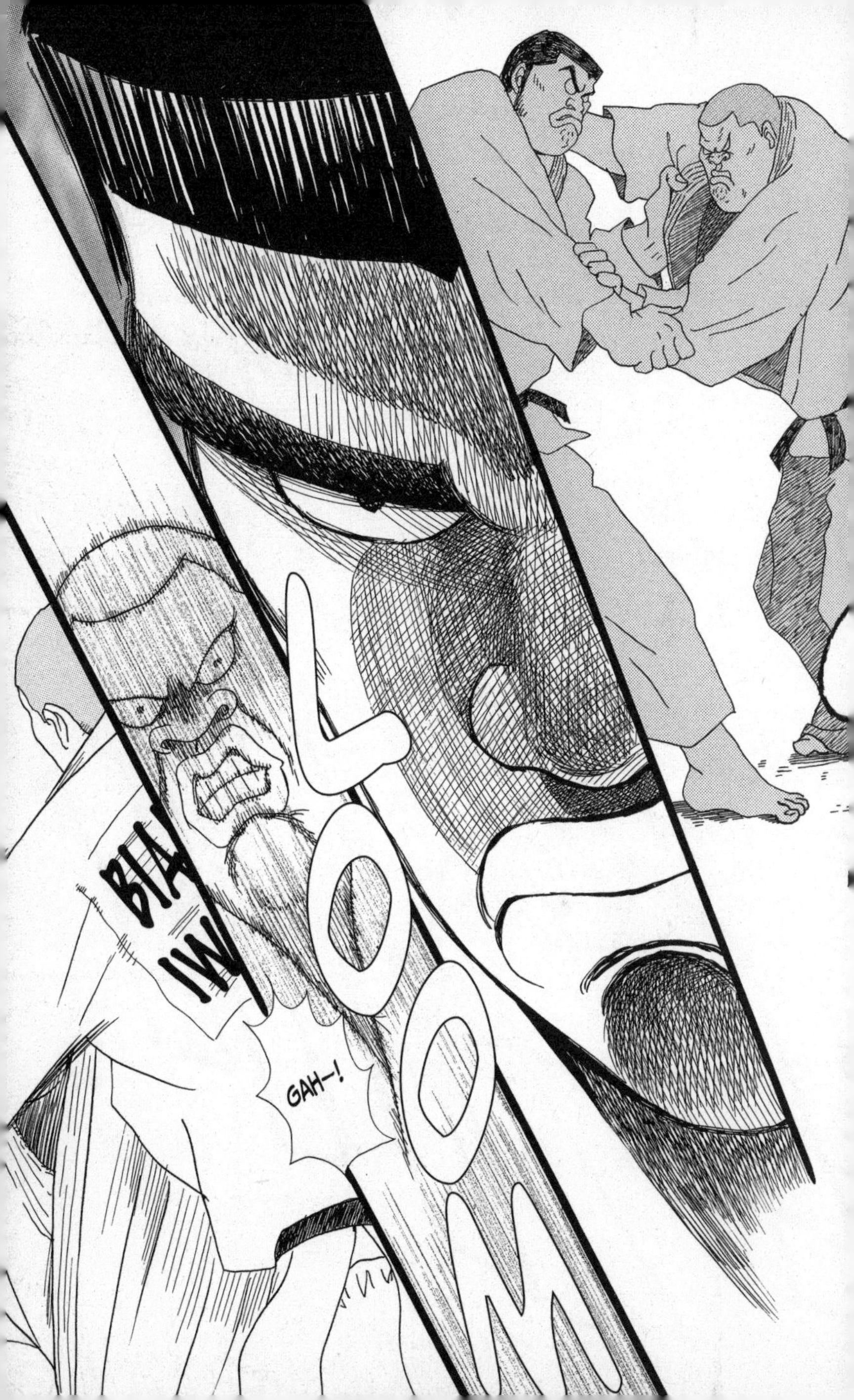
GAH–!

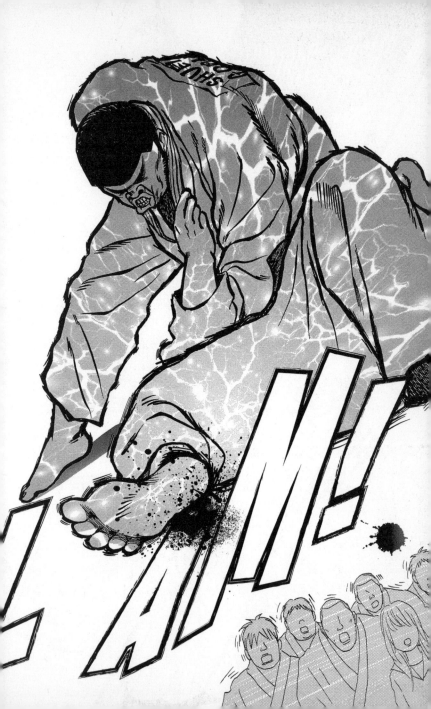

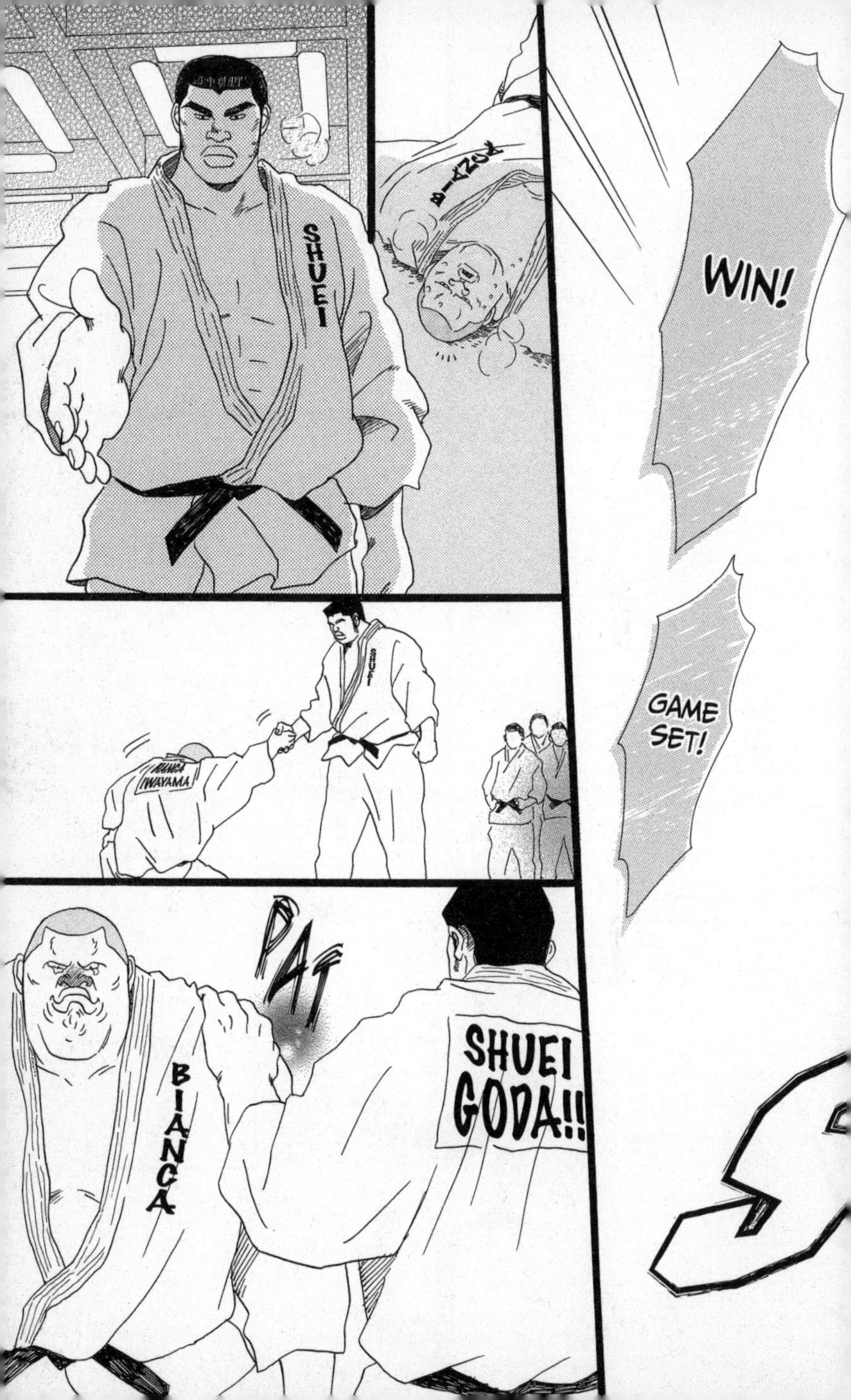
WIN!
GAME SET!
SHUEI
PAT
SHUEI GODA!!
BIANCA

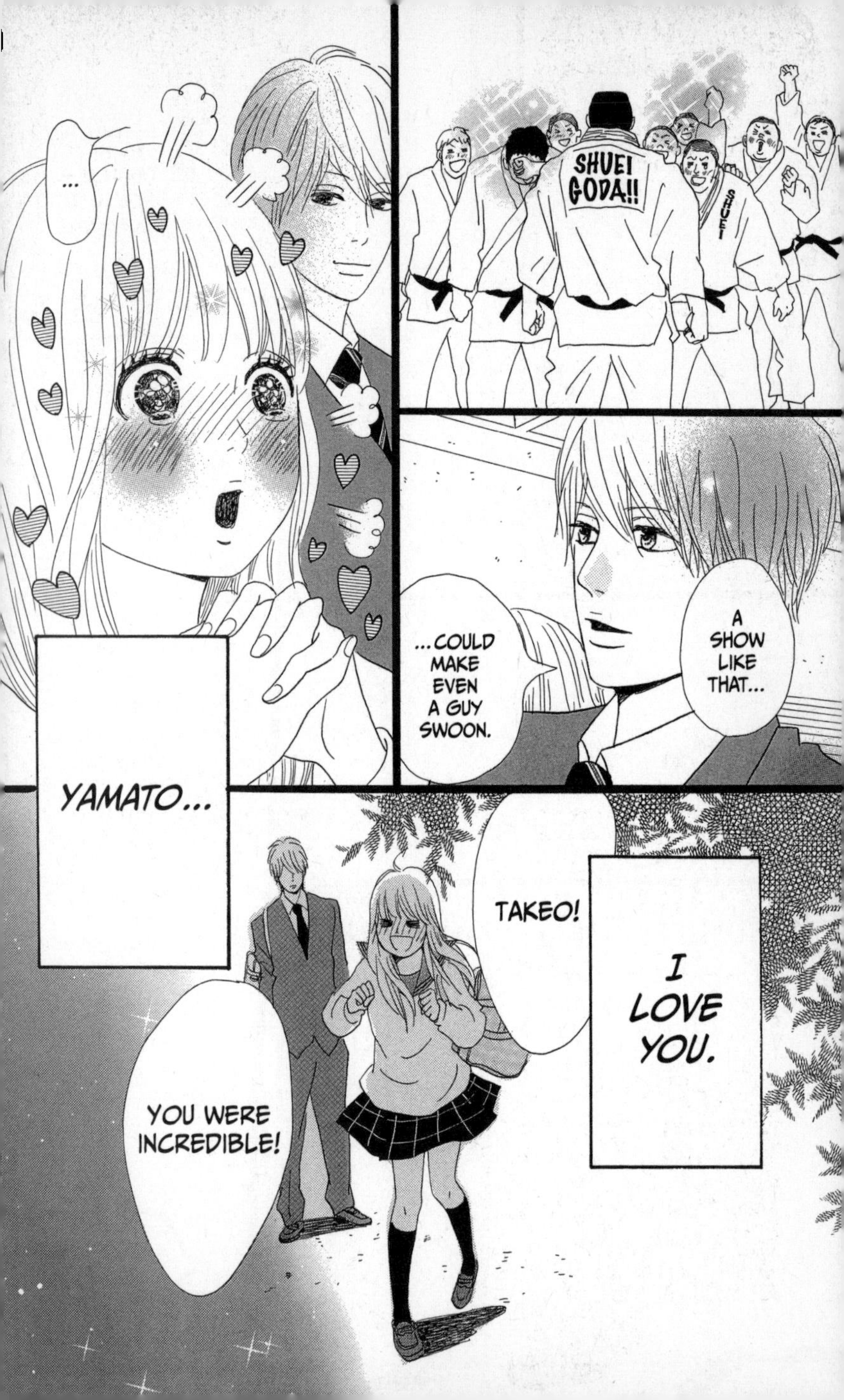
SHUEI GODA!!
SHUEI
A SHOW LIKE THAT...
...COULD MAKE EVEN A GUY SWOON.
...
YAMATO...
I LOVE YOU.
TAKEO!
YOU WERE INCREDIBLE!

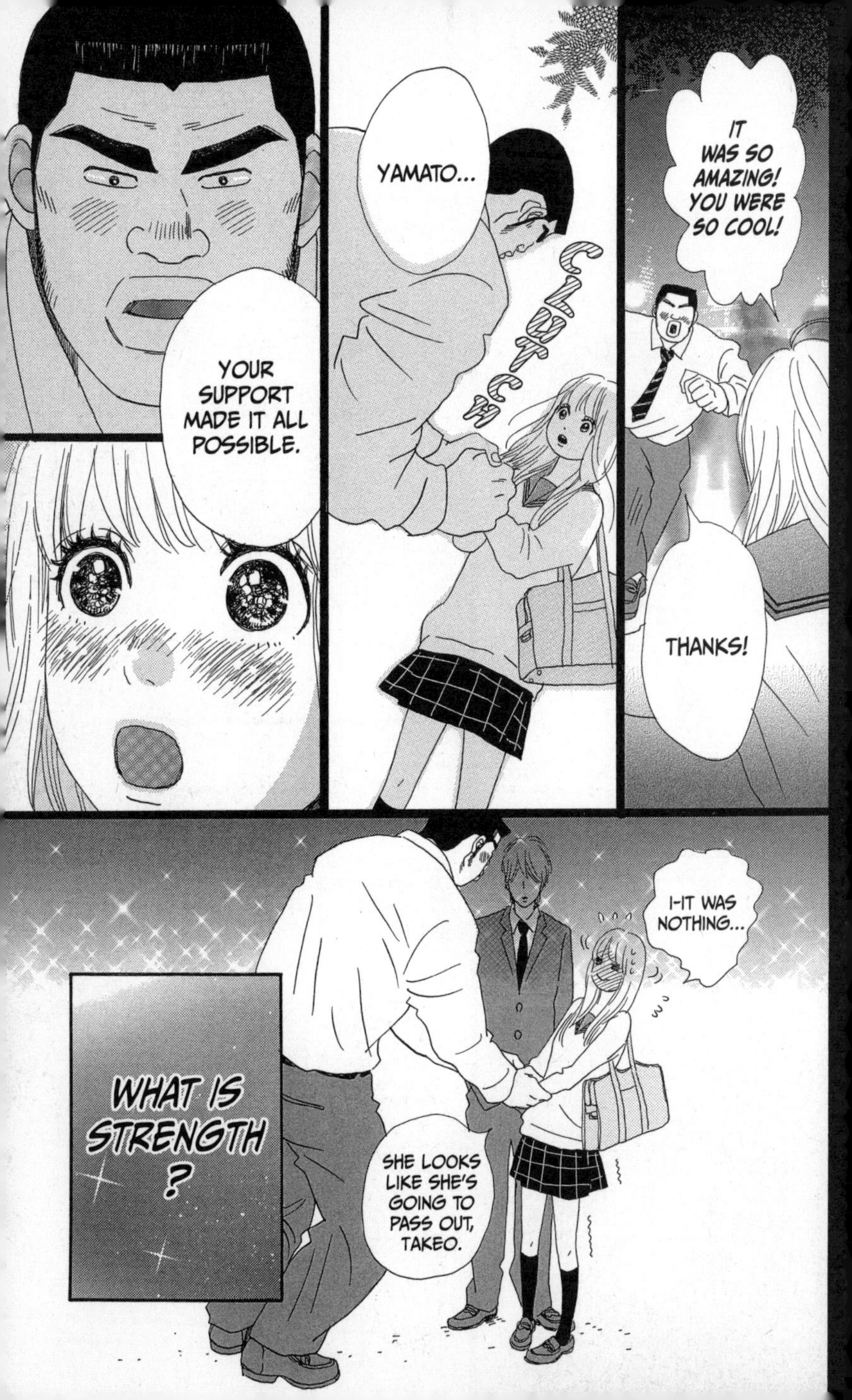
IT WAS SO AMAZING! YOU WERE SO COOL!
THANKS!
YAMATO...
CLUTCH
YOUR SUPPORT MADE IT ALL POSSIBLE.
I-IT WAS NOTHING...
SHE LOOKS LIKE SHE'S GOING TO PASS OUT, TAKEO.
WHAT IS STRENGTH ?

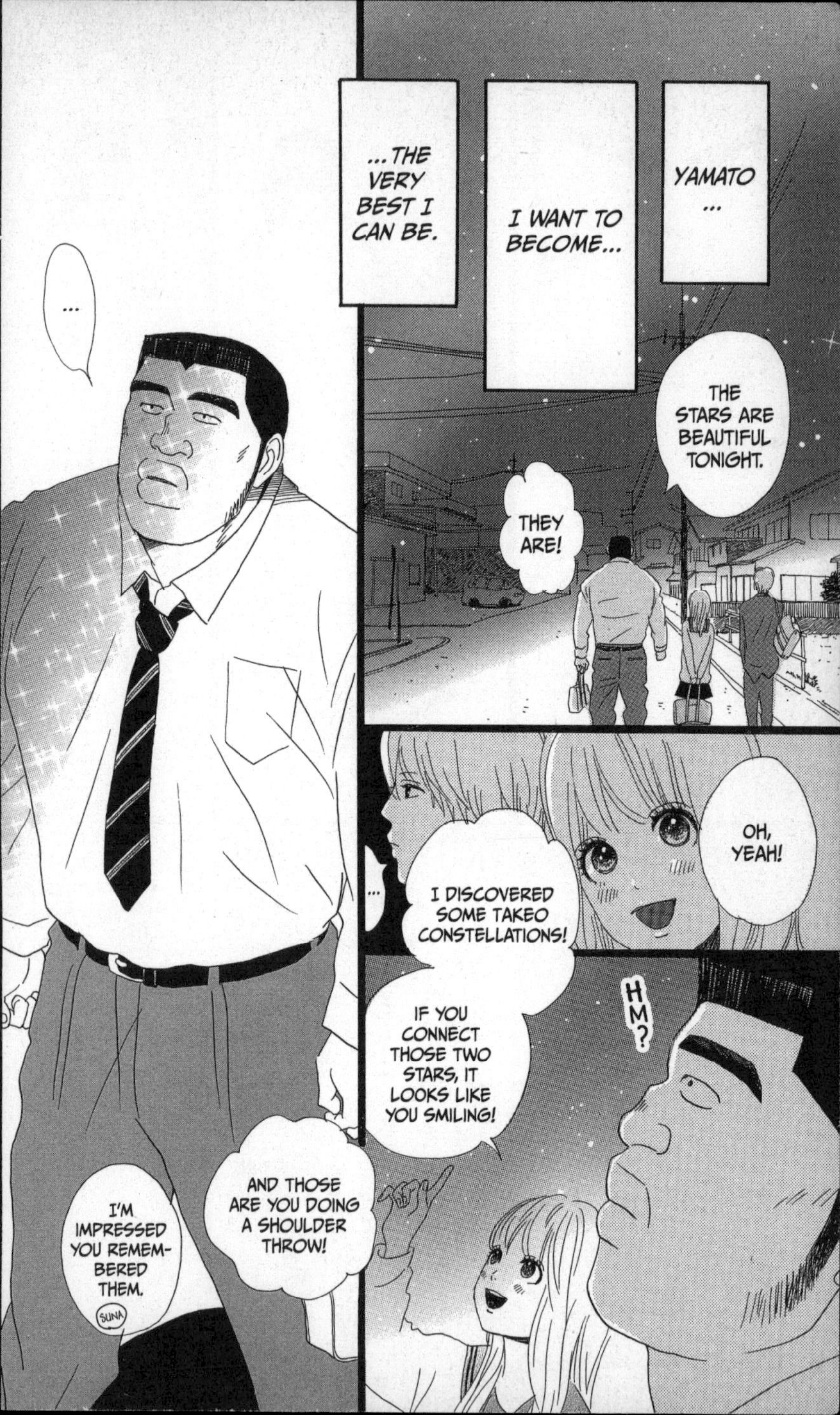
YAMATO ...
I WANT TO BECOME...
...THE VERY BEST I CAN BE.
THE STARS ARE BEAUTIFUL TONIGHT.
THEY ARE!
OH, YEAH!
I DISCOVERED SOME TAKEO CONSTELLATIONS!
...
HM?
IF YOU CONNECT THOSE TWO STARS, IT LOOKS LIKE YOU SMILING!
AND THOSE ARE YOU DOING A SHOULDER THROW!
...
I'M IMPRESSED YOU REMEM-BERED THEM.
SUNA

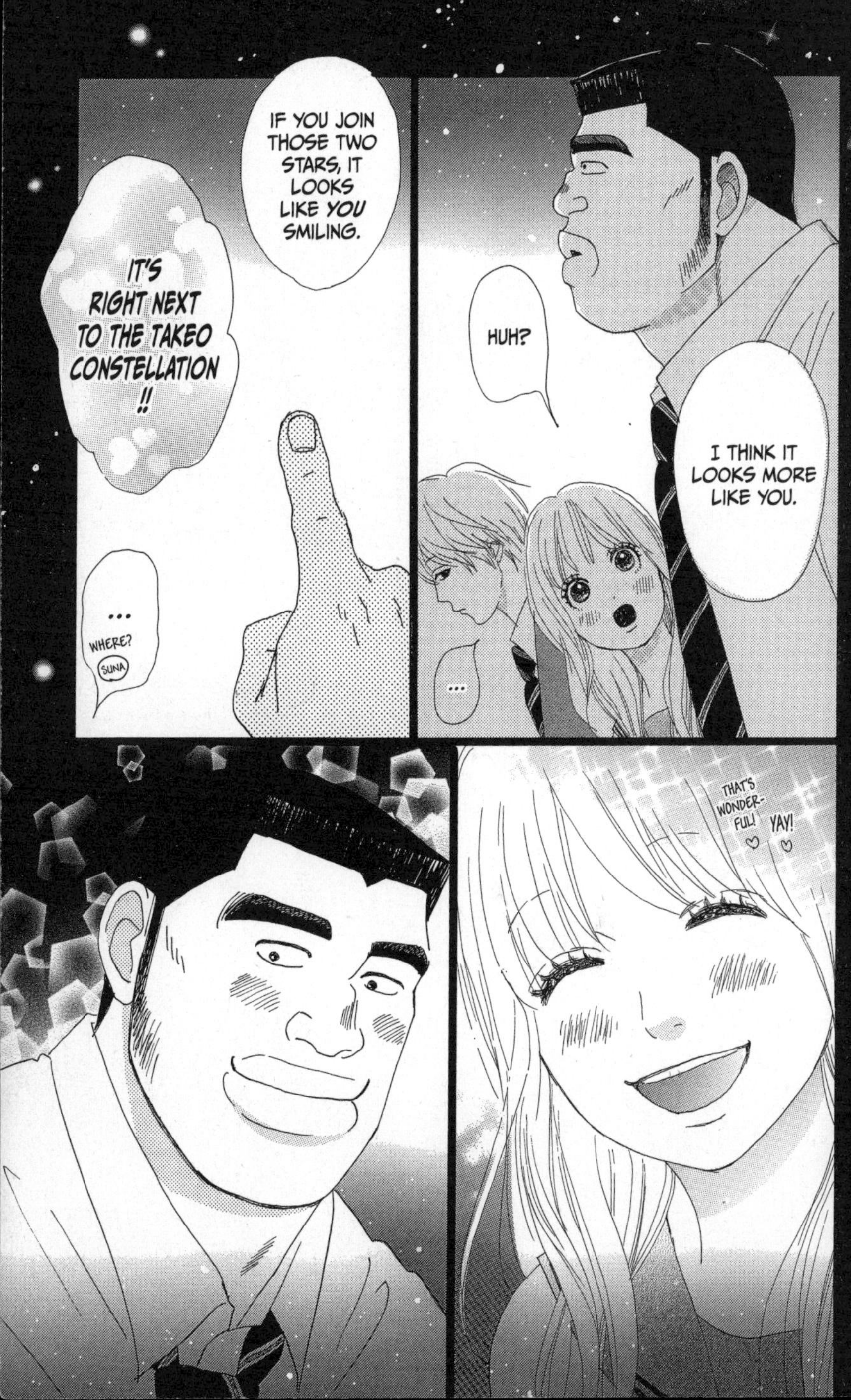
HUH?
I THINK IT LOOKS MORE LIKE YOU.
...
IF YOU JOIN THOSE TWO STARS, IT LOOKS LIKE YOU SMILING.
IT'S RIGHT NEXT TO THE TAKEO CONSTELLATION!!
... WHERE?
SUNA
THAT'S WONDER-FUL!
YAY!

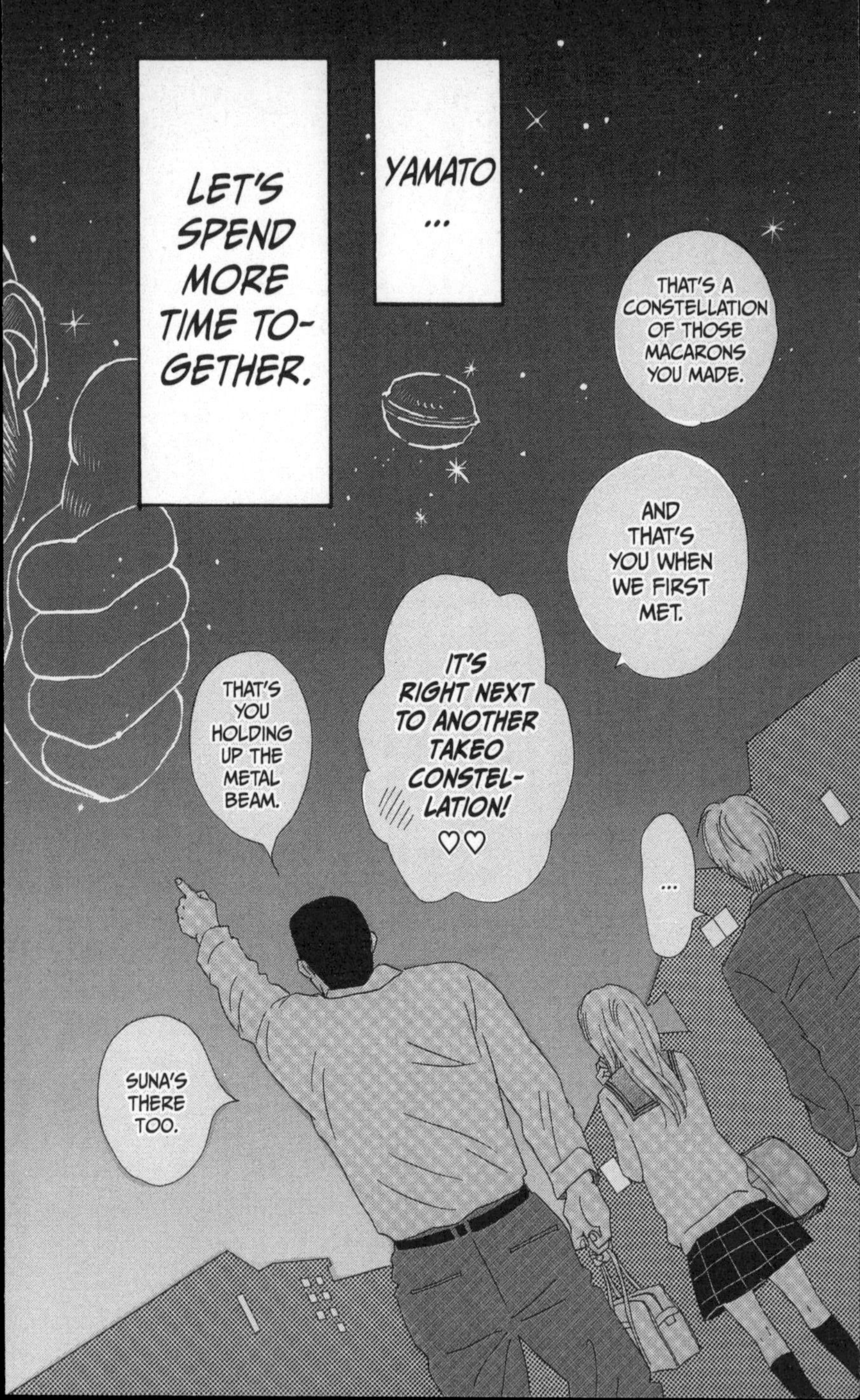
YAMATO ...
LET'S SPEND MORE TIME TO-GETHER.
THAT'S A CONSTELLATION OF THOSE MACARONS YOU MADE.
AND THAT'S YOU WHEN WE FIRST MET.
IT'S RIGHT NEXT TO ANOTHER TAKEO CONSTEL-LATION! ♡♡
THAT'S YOU HOLDING UP THE METAL BEAM.
...
SUNA'S THERE TOO.

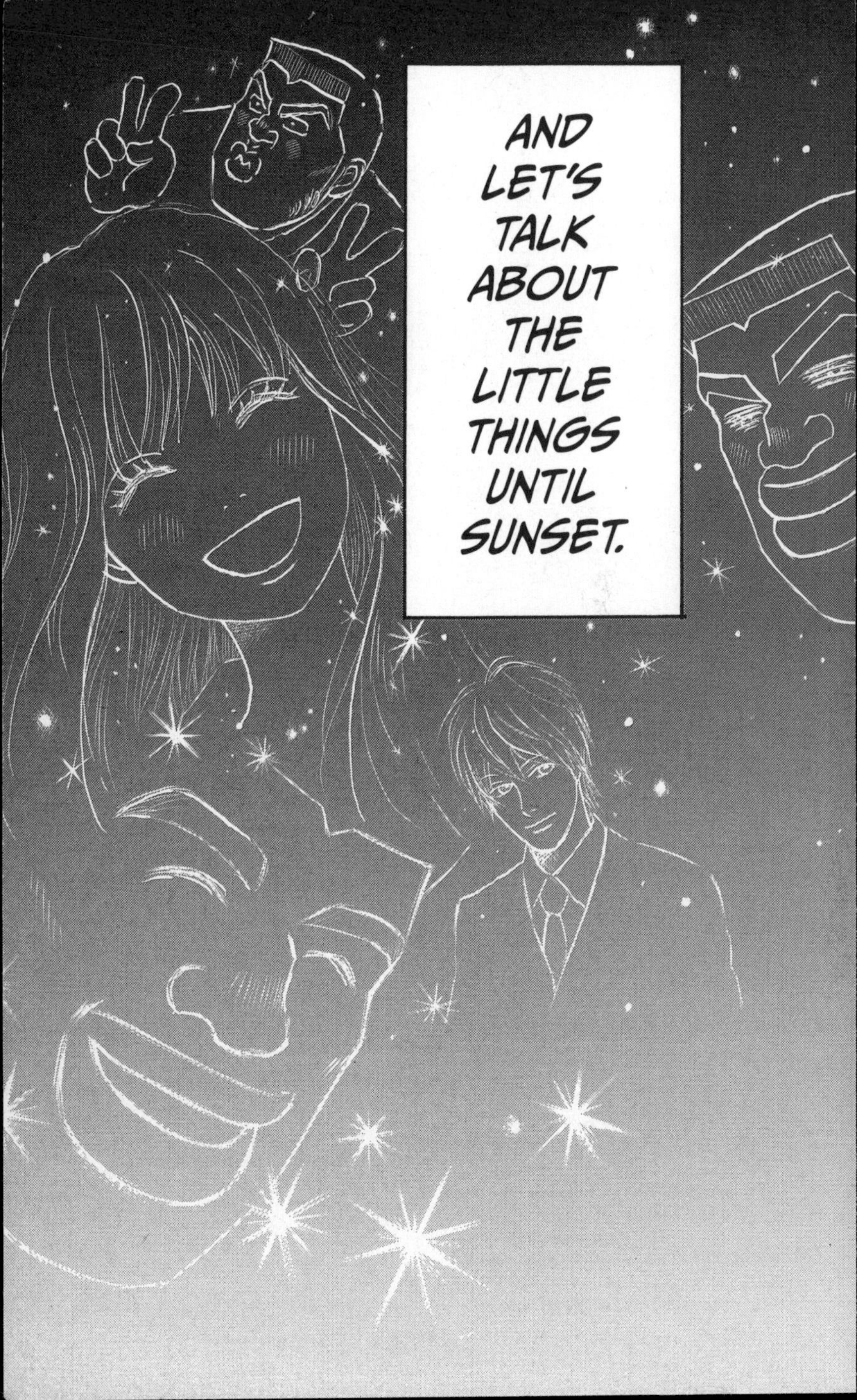
AND LET'S TALK ABOUT THE LITTLE THINGS UNTIL SUNSET.

My Love Story!!

SWEETS of LOVE RECIPE COLLECTION 2

SPRING FRUITS SAKURA RICE CAKES

Sweet No.3

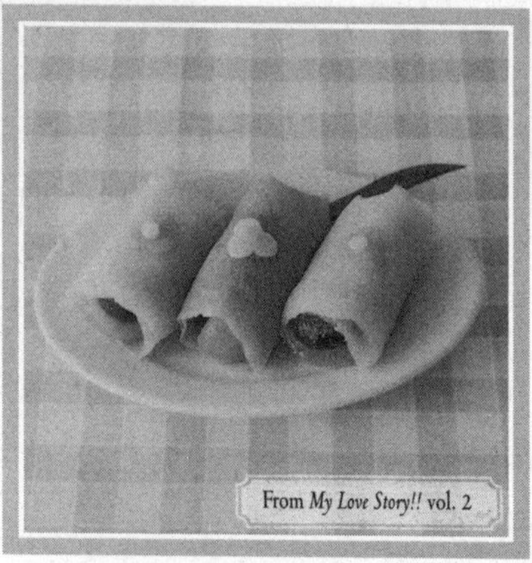

From *My Love Story!!* vol. 2

Ingredients (8 pieces):

70g [0.3 cup] cake flour
20g [1 1/3 tablespoon] rice flour
20g [1 1/3 tablespoon] sugar
130ml [0.55 cup] water
1/2 teaspoon powdered green tea
vegetable oil as needed
160g [5.64 oz] puréed sweet bean paste
apricot compote

INSTRUCTIONS

1 Sift the cake flour into a bowl and add the rice flour, sugar and water. Mix well with an egg beater until the lumps are gone.
2 Divide the resulting mixture in half. Set one half aside. Dissolve the green tea in 1 teaspoon of hot water, and add to the remaining half. Mix well.
3 Heat a frying pan on medium-low heat and coat it with vegetable oil. With a small ladle, pour in some of the batter from step 1 and 2, and spread it into a small circle using the back of the ladle. When the surface of the batter dries, carefully peel away the edges and flip it over. Cook it for about 30 seconds and remove it from the pan. Repeat with remaining batter.
4 Spread the puréed sweet bean paste and apricot on each sheet, then roll it up. If desired, you can cut some sheets into shapes to decorate the rolled ones.

WEDDING CAKE of LOVE for SUNAKAWA

Sweet No.4

Ingredients:

Large sponge cake (7-inch diameter) Small sponge cake (5-inch diameter)
(Each sliced horizontally in two)

A 40g [2 2/3 tbsp] sugar 100ml [0.4 cup] water

Remaining ingredients:

200ml [0.8 cup] + 200ml [0.8 cup] fresh cream
15g [1 tbsp] + 15g [1 tbsp] sugar
1 package of strawberries
1 orange
Marble chocolate, cookies, jellybeans, chocolate spray, chocolate decorations (as needed)

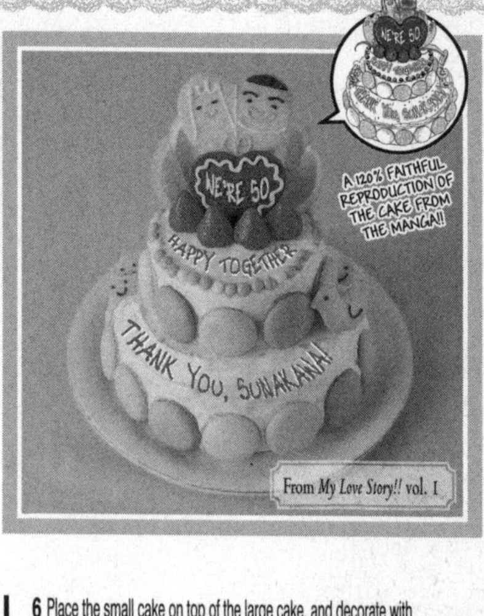
WE'RE 50
HAPPY TOGETHER
THANK YOU, SUNAKAWA!
A 120% FAITHFUL REPRODUCTION OF THE CAKE FROM THE MANGA!!

From *My Love Story!!* vol. 1

INSTRUCTIONS

1 Combine the first two ingredients (A) in a small pot and bring to a boil. Stir until the sugar is completely dissolved.
2 Spread the syrup resulting from step 1 onto the cut areas of the two sponge cakes.
3 Place 200ml of fresh cream and 1 tbsp of sugar into a bowl. Chill the bowl with ice water and beat with an egg beater for 8 minutes.
4 Take one each of the small and large sponge cake slices and spread the cream from step 3 onto them. Place thinly-sliced strawberries on top, and then place the remaining sponge cake slices on top.
5 Repeat step 3, and beat the fresh cream. Spread onto the surface of the cakes.
6 Place the small cake on top of the large cake, and decorate with candy or fruit.

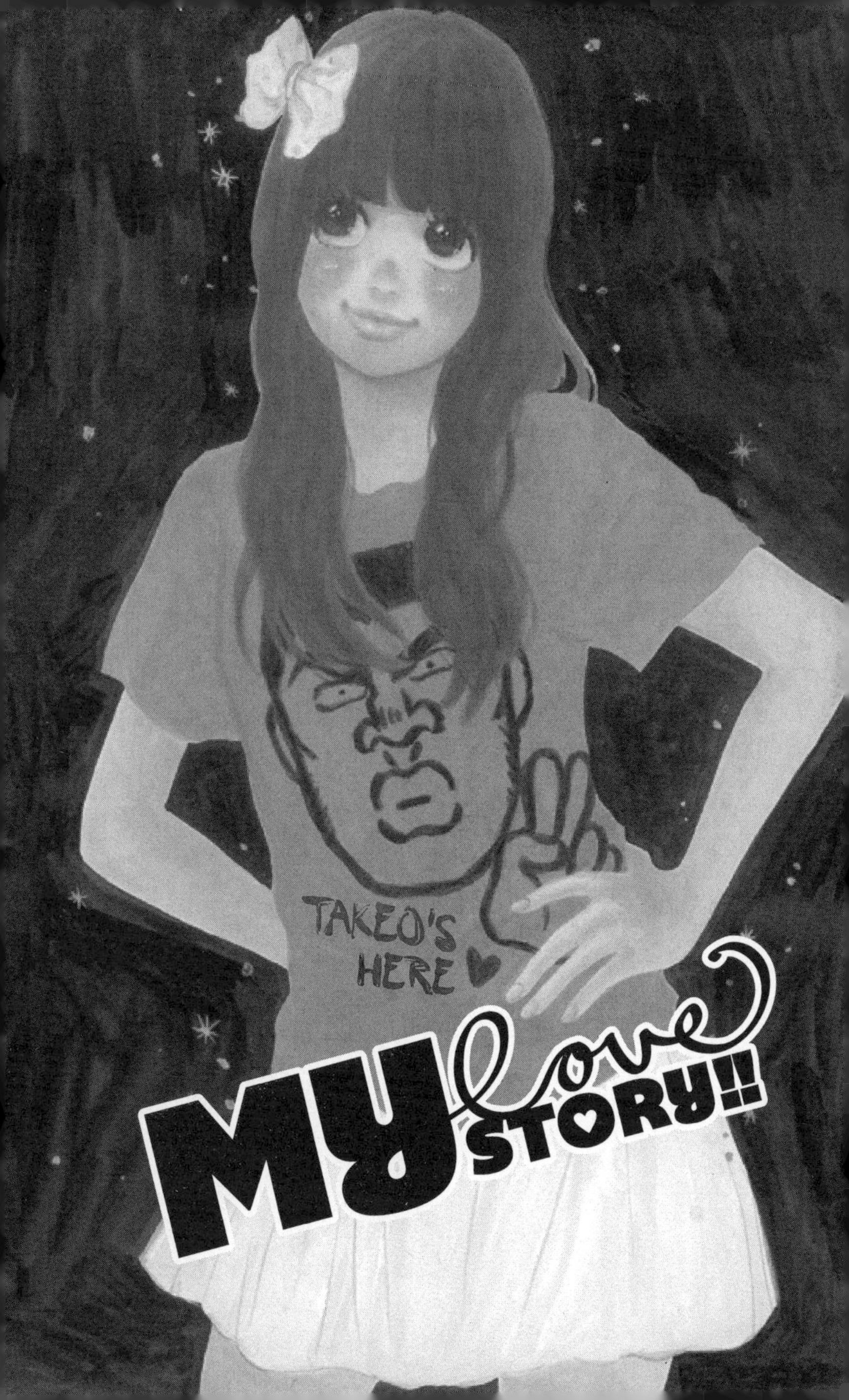
TAKEO'S HERE
MY love STORY!!

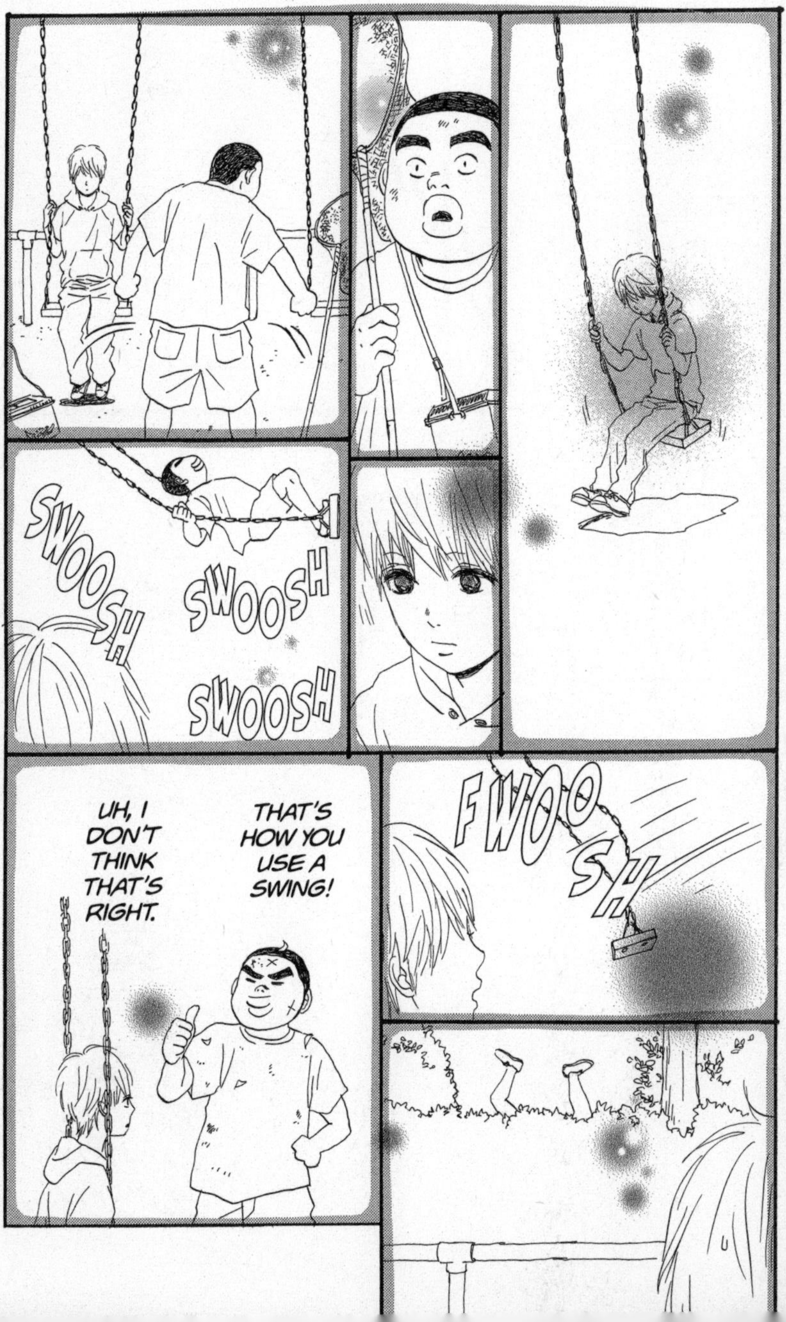
SWOOSH
SWOOSH
SWOOSH
FWOOSH
THAT'S HOW YOU USE A SWING!
UH, I DON'T THINK THAT'S RIGHT.

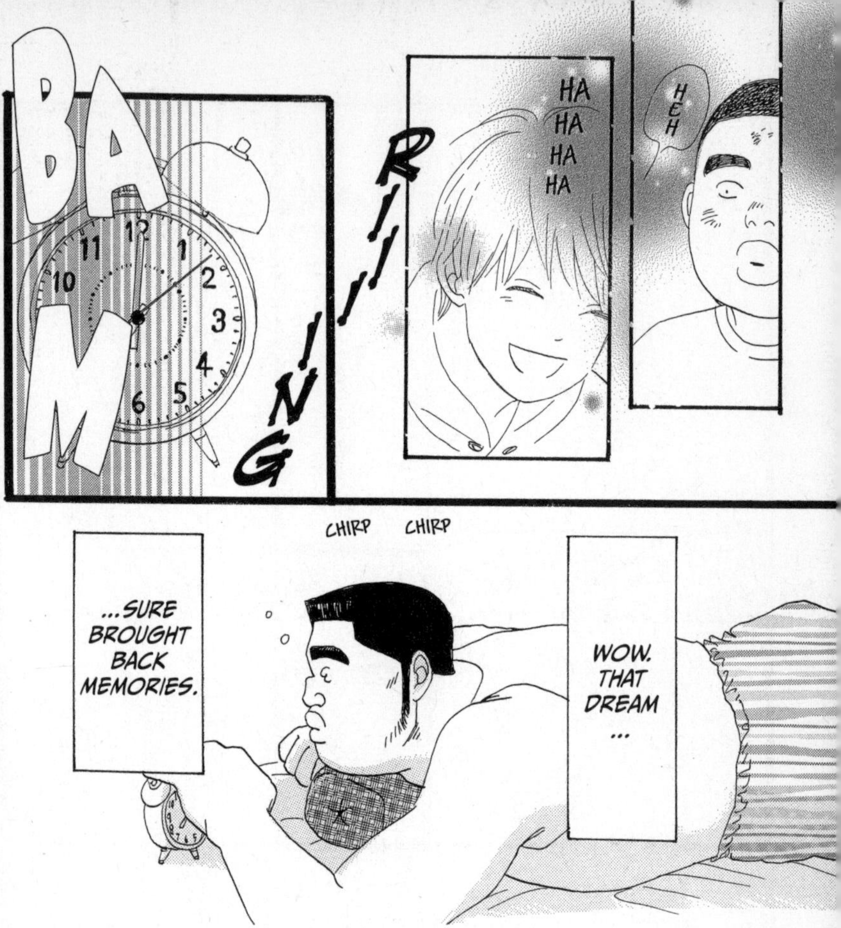
HEH
HA HA HA HA
BAM
RIIIING
CHIRP CHIRP
WOW. THAT DREAM ...
...SURE BROUGHT BACK MEMORIES.

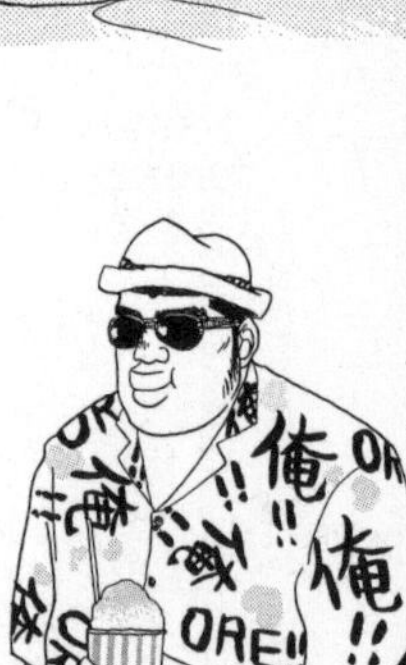

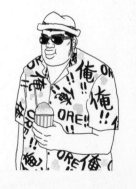

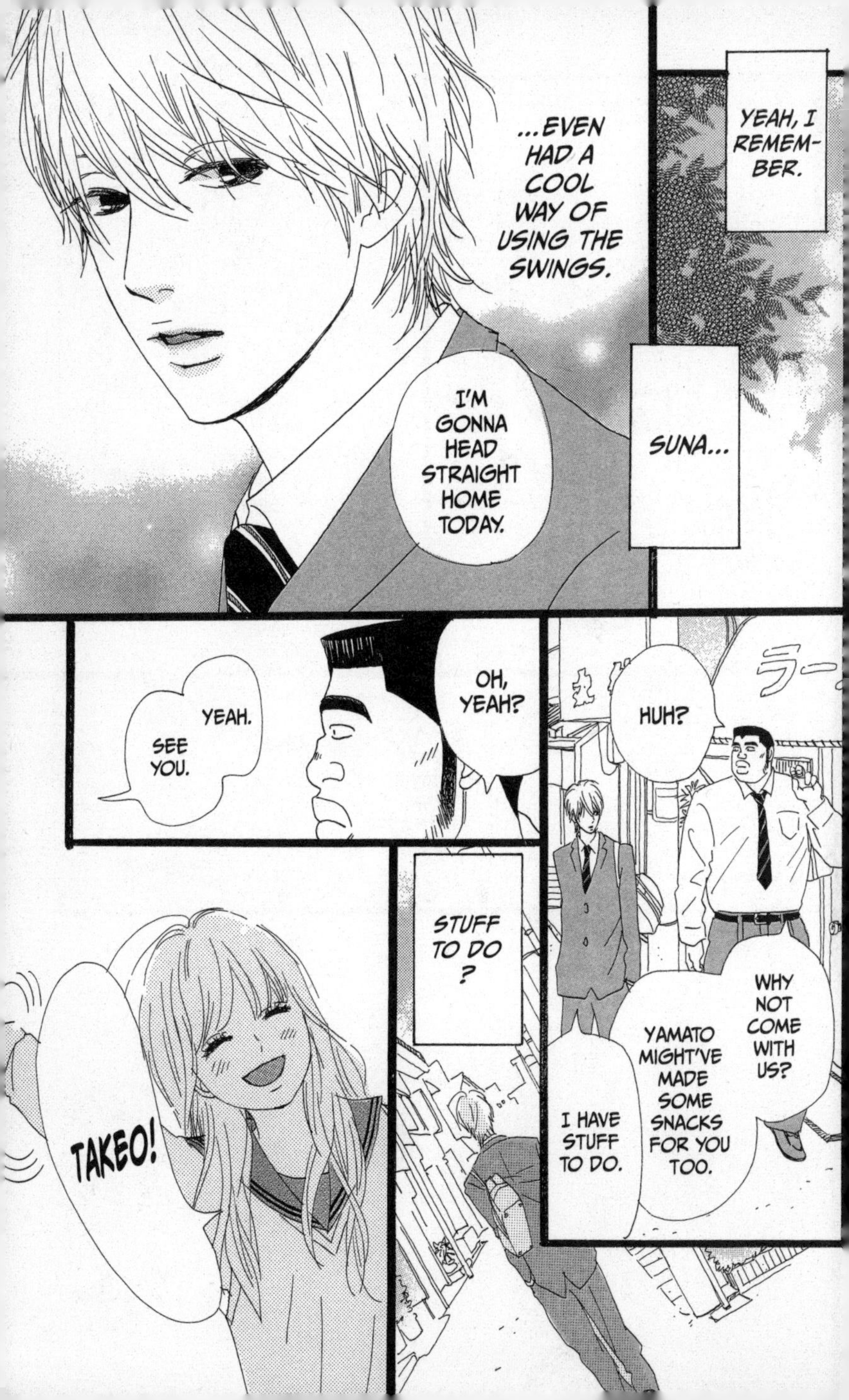
...EVEN HAD A COOL WAY OF USING THE SWINGS.
YEAH, I REMEMBER.
SUNA...
I'M GONNA HEAD STRAIGHT HOME TODAY.
HUH?
WHY NOT COME WITH US?
YAMATO MIGHT'VE MADE SOME SNACKS FOR YOU TOO.
I HAVE STUFF TO DO.
OH, YEAH?
YEAH.
SEE YOU.
STUFF TO DO ?
TAKEO!

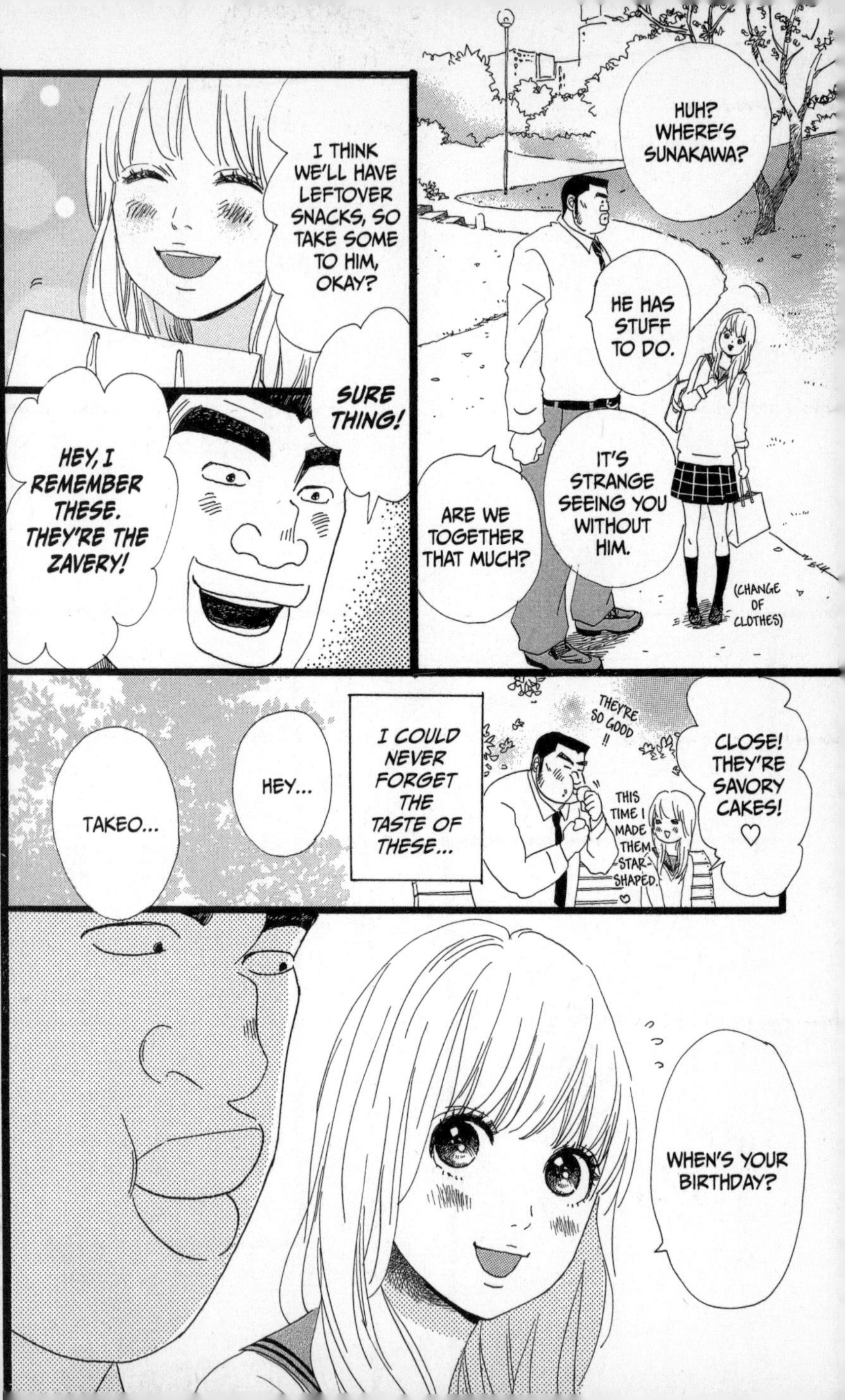
HUH? WHERE'S SUNAKAWA?
HE HAS STUFF TO DO.
IT'S STRANGE SEEING YOU WITHOUT HIM.
ARE WE TOGETHER THAT MUCH?
(CHANGE OF CLOTHES)
I THINK WE'LL HAVE LEFTOVER SNACKS, SO TAKE SOME TO HIM, OKAY?
SURE THING!
HEY, I REMEMBER THESE. THEY'RE THE ZAVERY!
CLOSE! THEY'RE SAVORY CAKES! ♡
THIS TIME I MADE THEM STAR-SHAPED. ♡
THEY'RE SO GOOD !!
I COULD NEVER FORGET THE TASTE OF THESE...
HEY...
TAKEO...
WHEN'S YOUR BIRTHDAY?

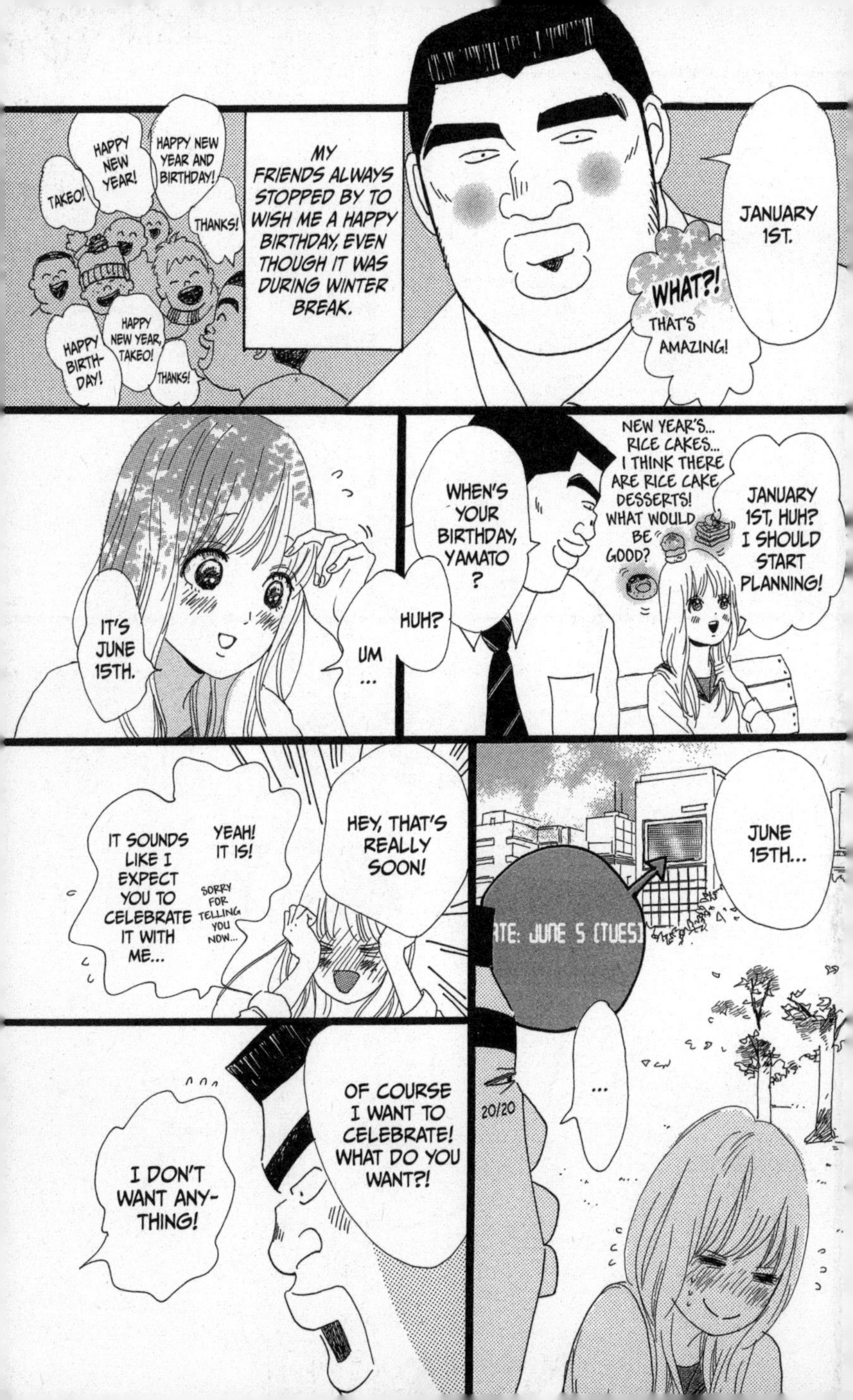
JANUARY 1ST.
WHAT?! THAT'S AMAZING!
MY FRIENDS ALWAYS STOPPED BY TO WISH ME A HAPPY BIRTHDAY, EVEN THOUGH IT WAS DURING WINTER BREAK.
HAPPY NEW YEAR AND BIRTHDAY!
HAPPY NEW YEAR!
TAKEO!
THANKS!
HAPPY NEW YEAR, TAKEO!
HAPPY BIRTH-DAY!
THANKS!
JANUARY 1ST, HUH? I SHOULD START PLANNING!
NEW YEAR'S... RICE CAKES... I THINK THERE ARE RICE CAKE DESSERTS! WHAT WOULD BE GOOD?
WHEN'S YOUR BIRTHDAY, YAMATO?
HUH?
UM...
IT'S JUNE 15TH.
JUNE 15TH...
ATE: JUNE 5 (TUES)
HEY, THAT'S REALLY SOON!
YEAH! IT IS!
SORRY FOR TELLING YOU NOW...
IT SOUNDS LIKE I EXPECT YOU TO CELEBRATE IT WITH ME...
20/20
...
OF COURSE I WANT TO CELEBRATE! WHAT DO YOU WANT?!
I DON'T WANT ANY-THING!

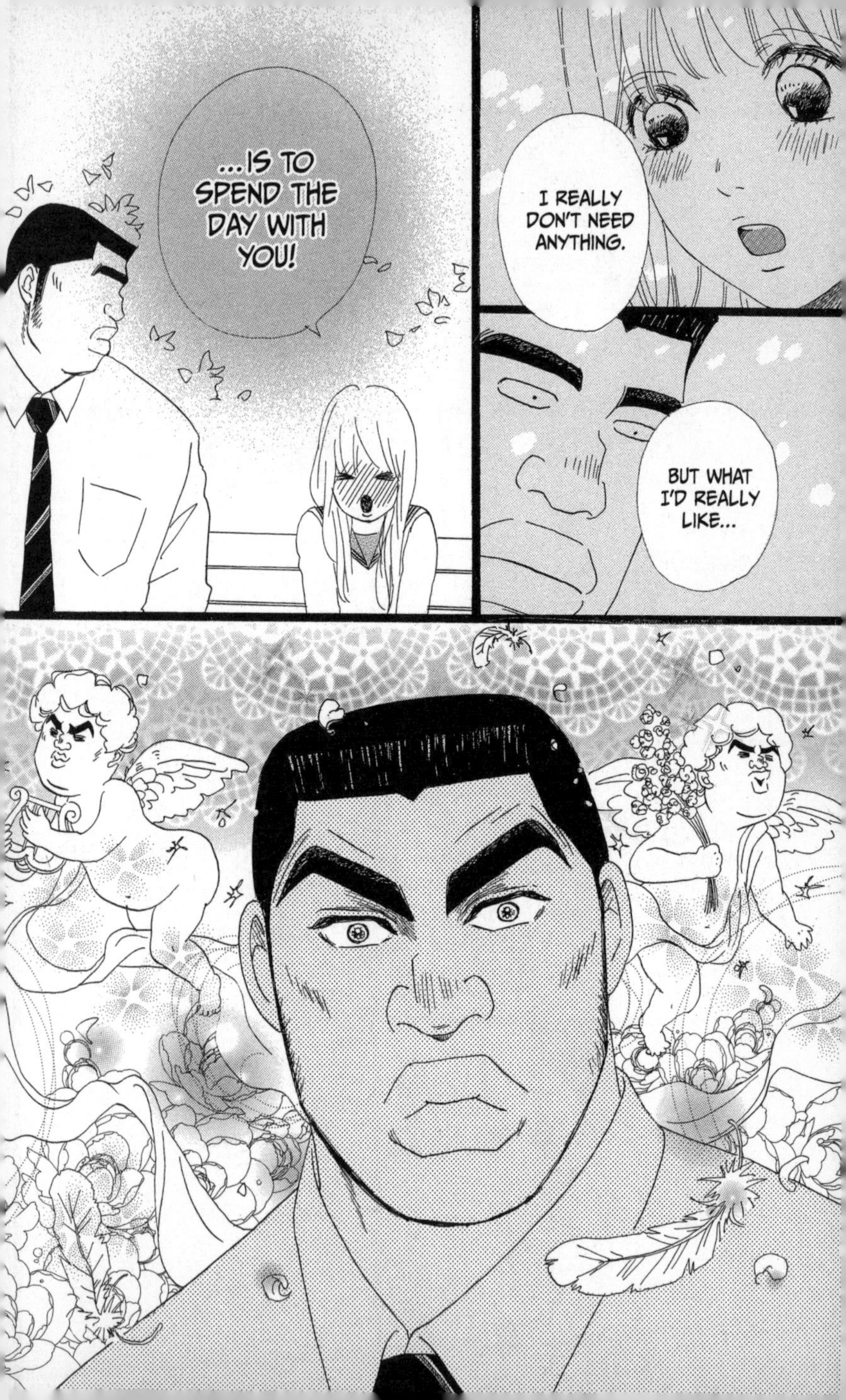
I REALLY DON'T NEED ANYTHING.
BUT WHAT I'D REALLY LIKE...
...IS TO SPEND THE DAY WITH YOU!

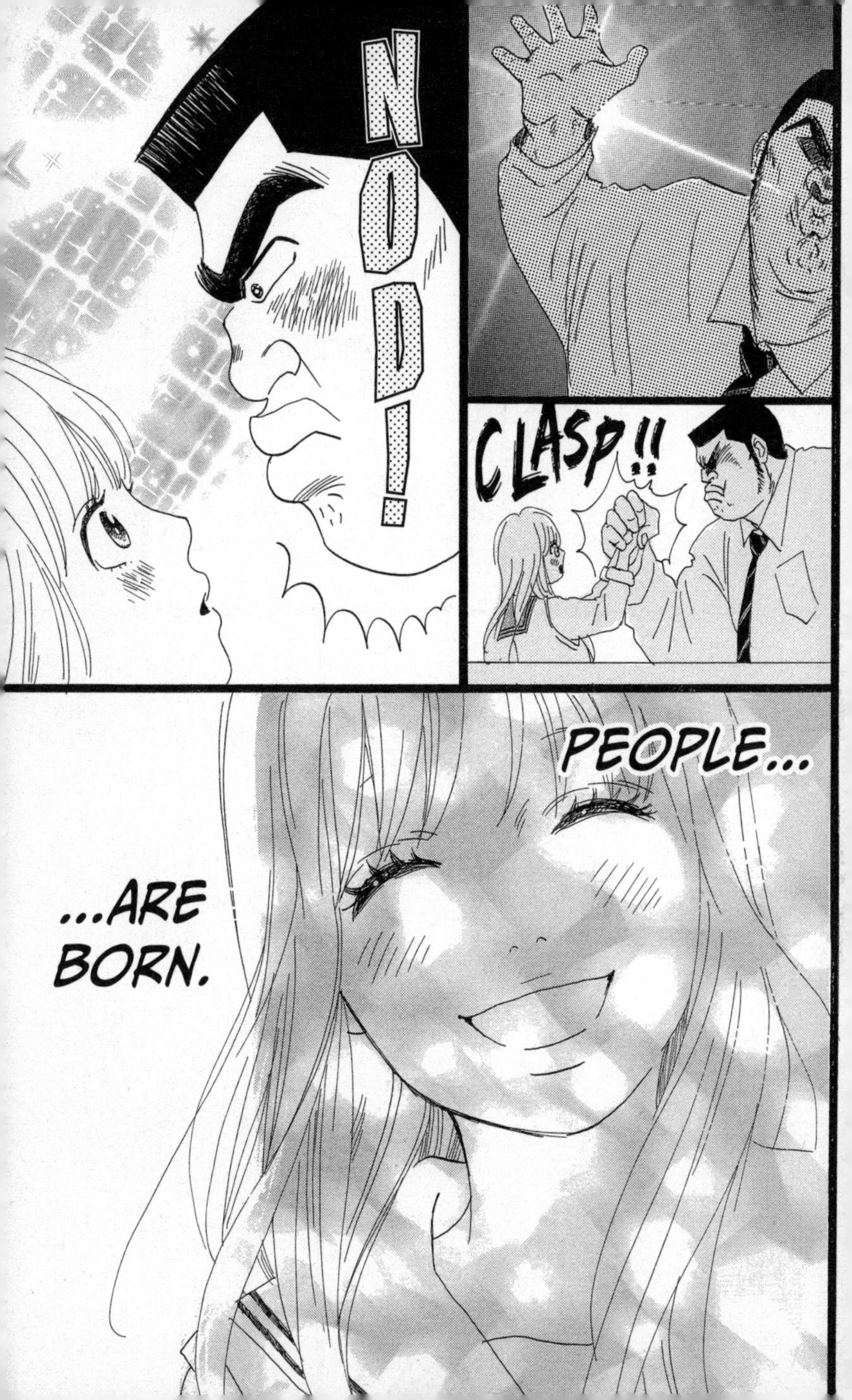
CLASP!!
NOD!
PEOPLE...
...ARE BORN.

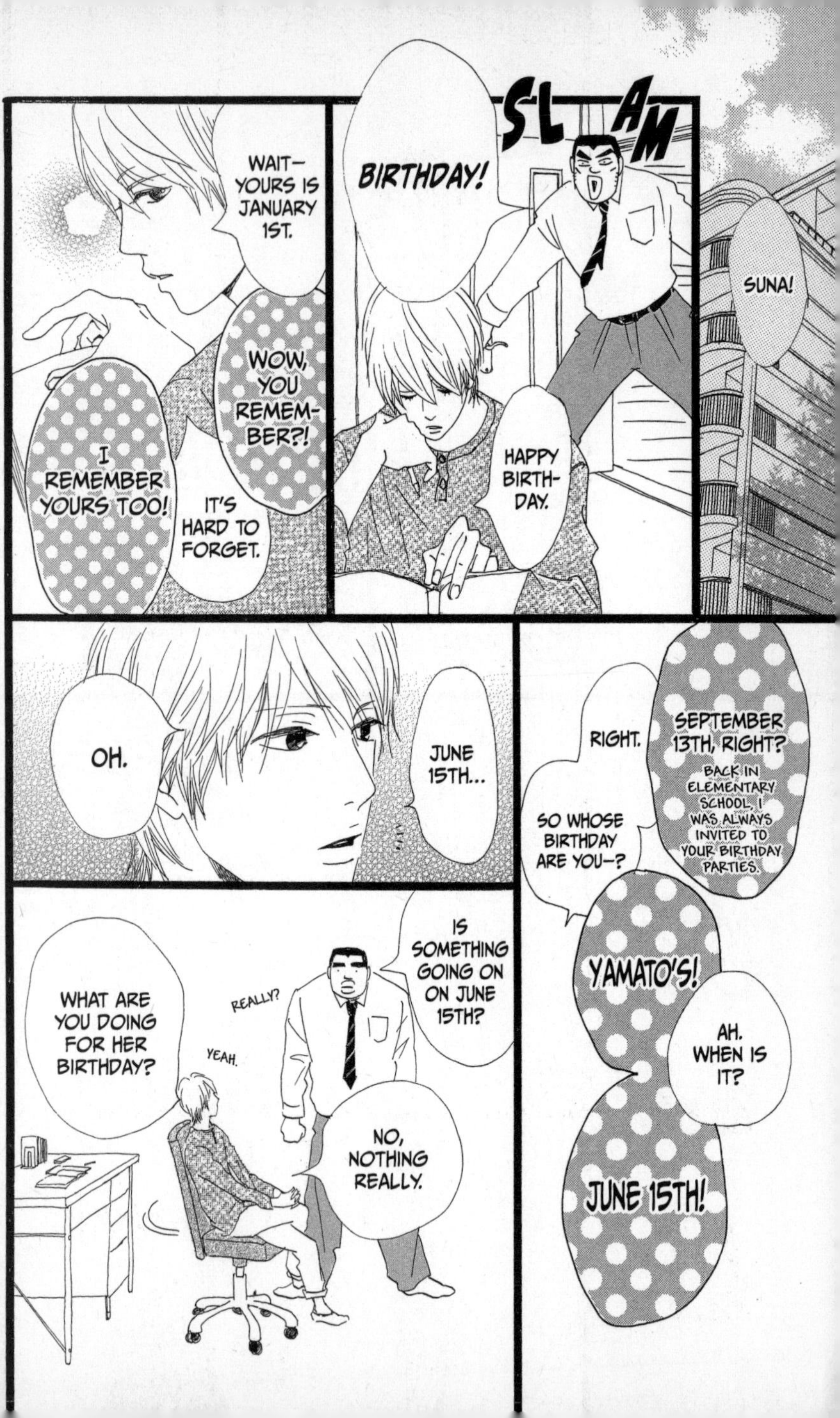
SUNA!
SLAM
BIRTHDAY!
HAPPY BIRTHDAY.
WAIT— YOURS IS JANUARY 1ST.
WOW, YOU REMEMBER?!
I REMEMBER YOURS TOO!
IT'S HARD TO FORGET.
SEPTEMBER 13TH, RIGHT?
BACK IN ELEMENTARY SCHOOL, I WAS ALWAYS INVITED TO YOUR BIRTHDAY PARTIES.
RIGHT.
SO WHOSE BIRTHDAY ARE YOU—?
YAMATO'S!
AH. WHEN IS IT?
JUNE 15TH!
JUNE 15TH...
OH.
IS SOMETHING GOING ON ON JUNE 15TH?
NO, NOTHING REALLY.
REALLY?
YEAH.
WHAT ARE YOU DOING FOR HER BIRTHDAY?

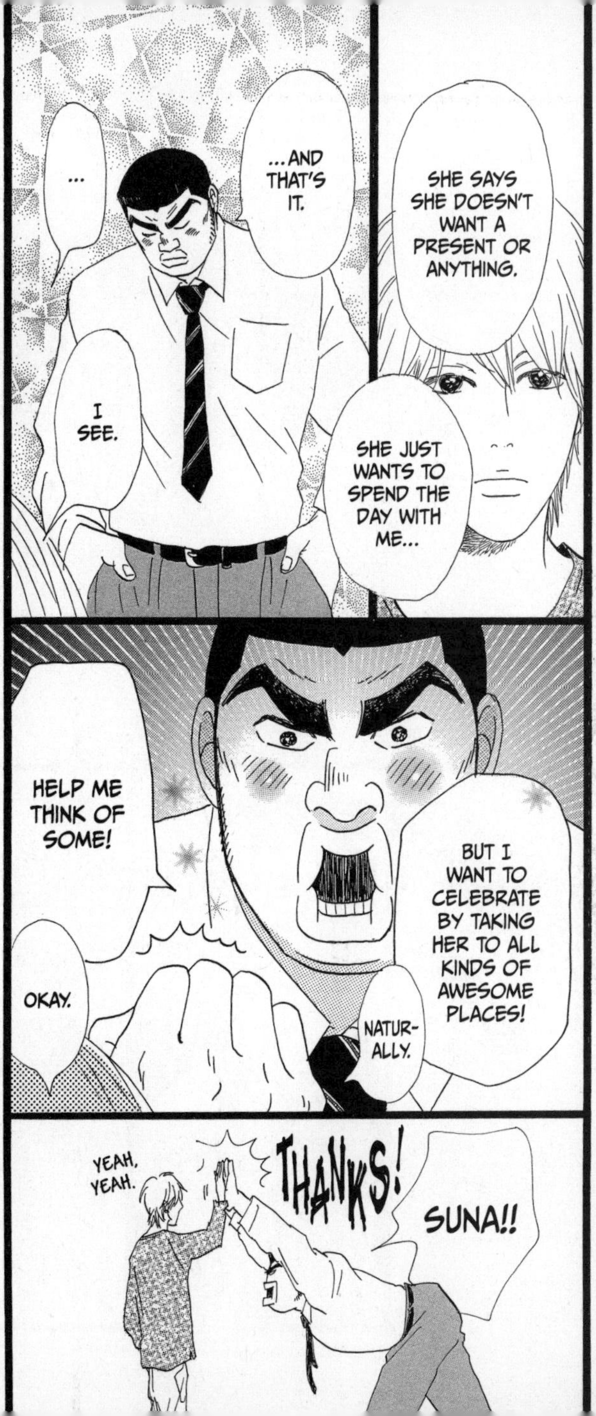
SHE SAYS SHE DOESN'T WANT A PRESENT OR ANYTHING.
SHE JUST WANTS TO SPEND THE DAY WITH ME...
...AND THAT'S IT.
...
I SEE.
BUT I WANT TO CELEBRATE BY TAKING HER TO ALL KINDS OF AWESOME PLACES!
NATUR-ALLY.
HELP ME THINK OF SOME!
OKAY.
SUNA!!
THANKS!
YEAH, YEAH.

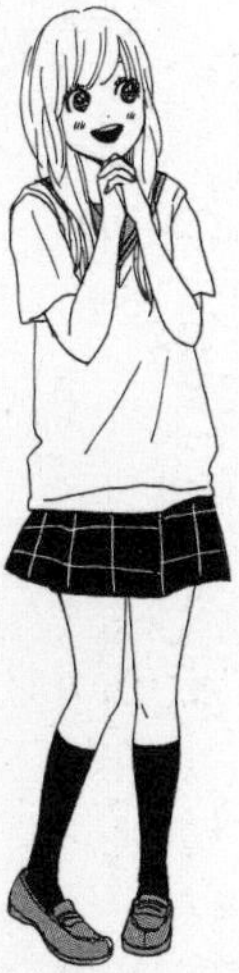

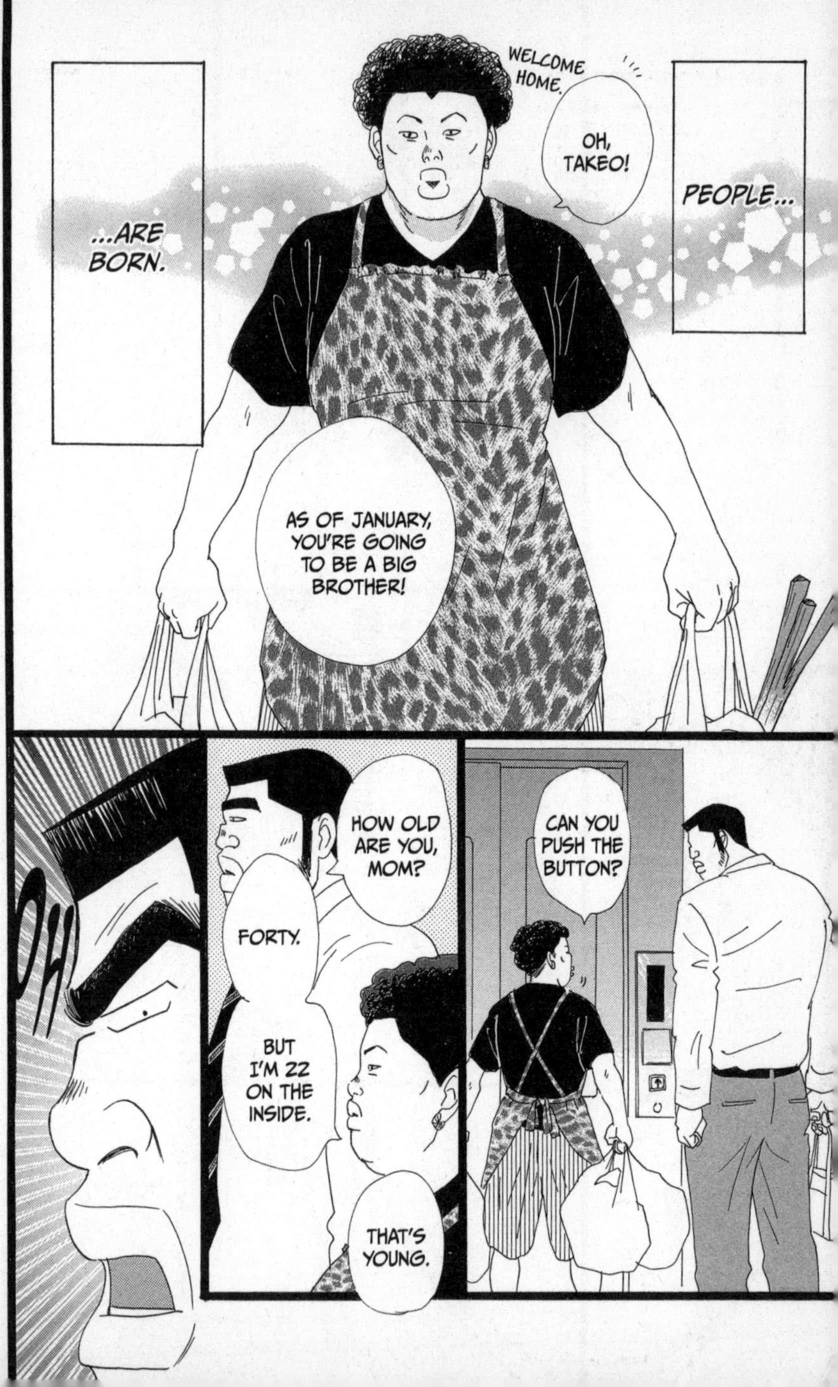
PEOPLE...
OH, TAKEO!
WELCOME HOME.
...ARE BORN.
AS OF JANUARY, YOU'RE GOING TO BE A BIG BROTHER!
CAN YOU PUSH THE BUTTON?
HOW OLD ARE YOU, MOM?
FORTY.
BUT I'M 22 ON THE INSIDE.
THAT'S YOUNG.
OH!

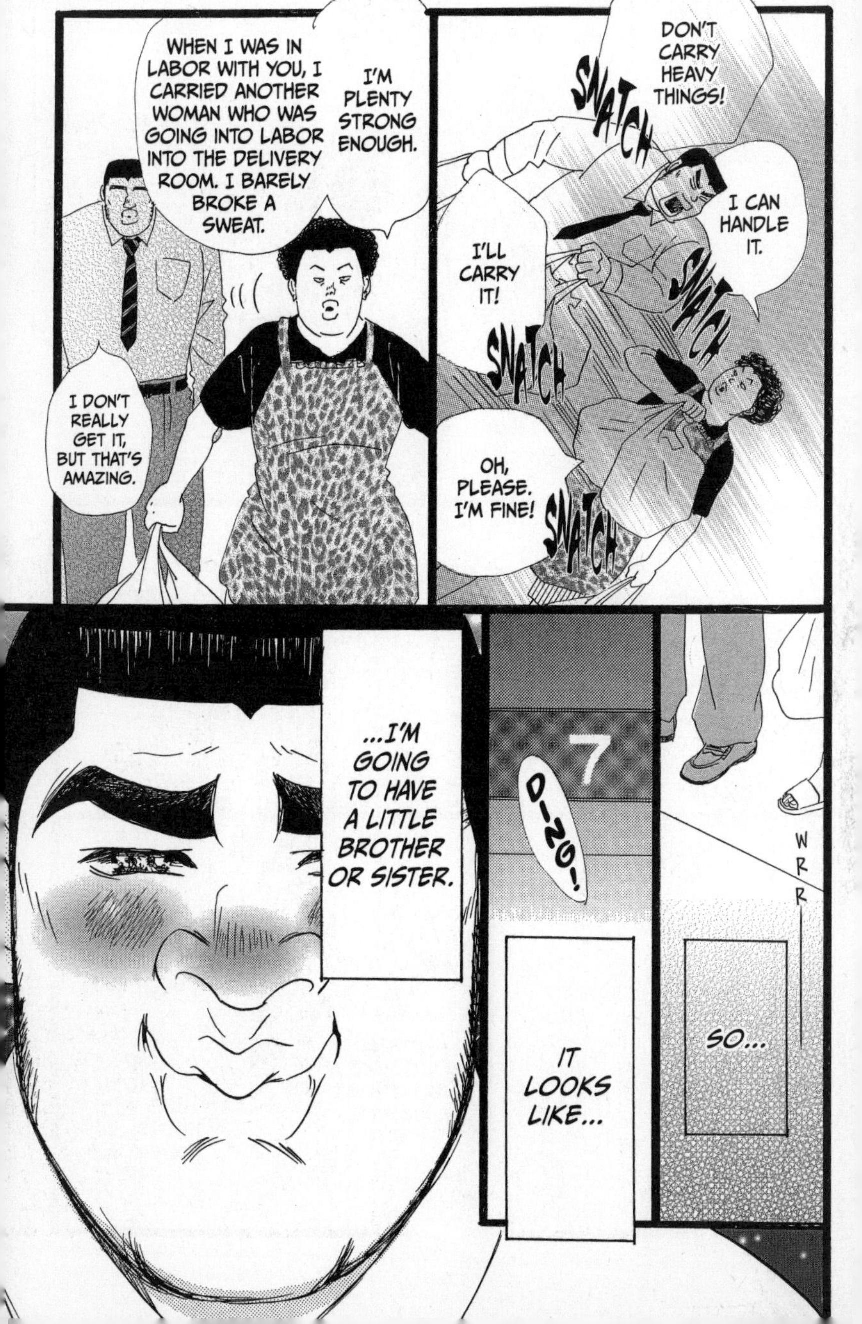
DON'T CARRY HEAVY THINGS!
SNATCH
I CAN HANDLE IT.
SNATCH
I'LL CARRY IT!
SNATCH
OH, PLEASE. I'M FINE!
SNATCH
I'M PLENTY STRONG ENOUGH.
WHEN I WAS IN LABOR WITH YOU, I CARRIED ANOTHER WOMAN WHO WAS GOING INTO LABOR INTO THE DELIVERY ROOM. I BARELY BROKE A SWEAT.
I DON'T REALLY GET IT, BUT THAT'S AMAZING.
WRR
SO...
7
DING!
IT LOOKS LIKE...
...I'M GOING TO HAVE A LITTLE BROTHER OR SISTER.

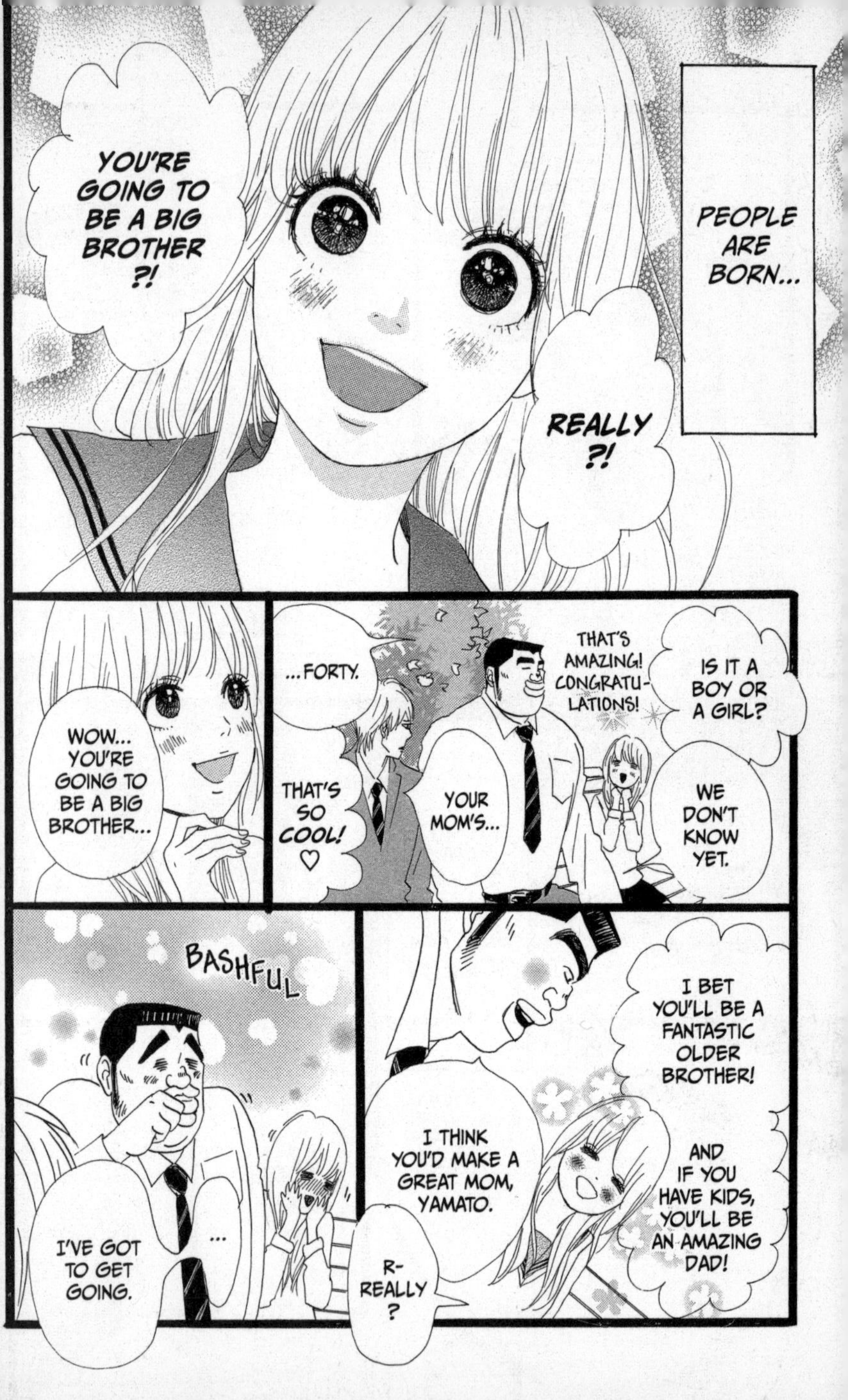
PEOPLE ARE BORN...
YOU'RE GOING TO BE A BIG BROTHER ?!
REALLY ?!
IS IT A BOY OR A GIRL?
THAT'S AMAZING! CONGRATU-LATIONS!
WE DON'T KNOW YET.
YOUR MOM'S...
...FORTY.
THAT'S SO COOL! ♡
WOW... YOU'RE GOING TO BE A BIG BROTHER...
I BET YOU'LL BE A FANTASTIC OLDER BROTHER!
AND IF YOU HAVE KIDS, YOU'LL BE AN AMAZING DAD!
I THINK YOU'D MAKE A GREAT MOM, YAMATO.
R-REALLY ?
BASHFUL
...
I'VE GOT TO GET GOING.

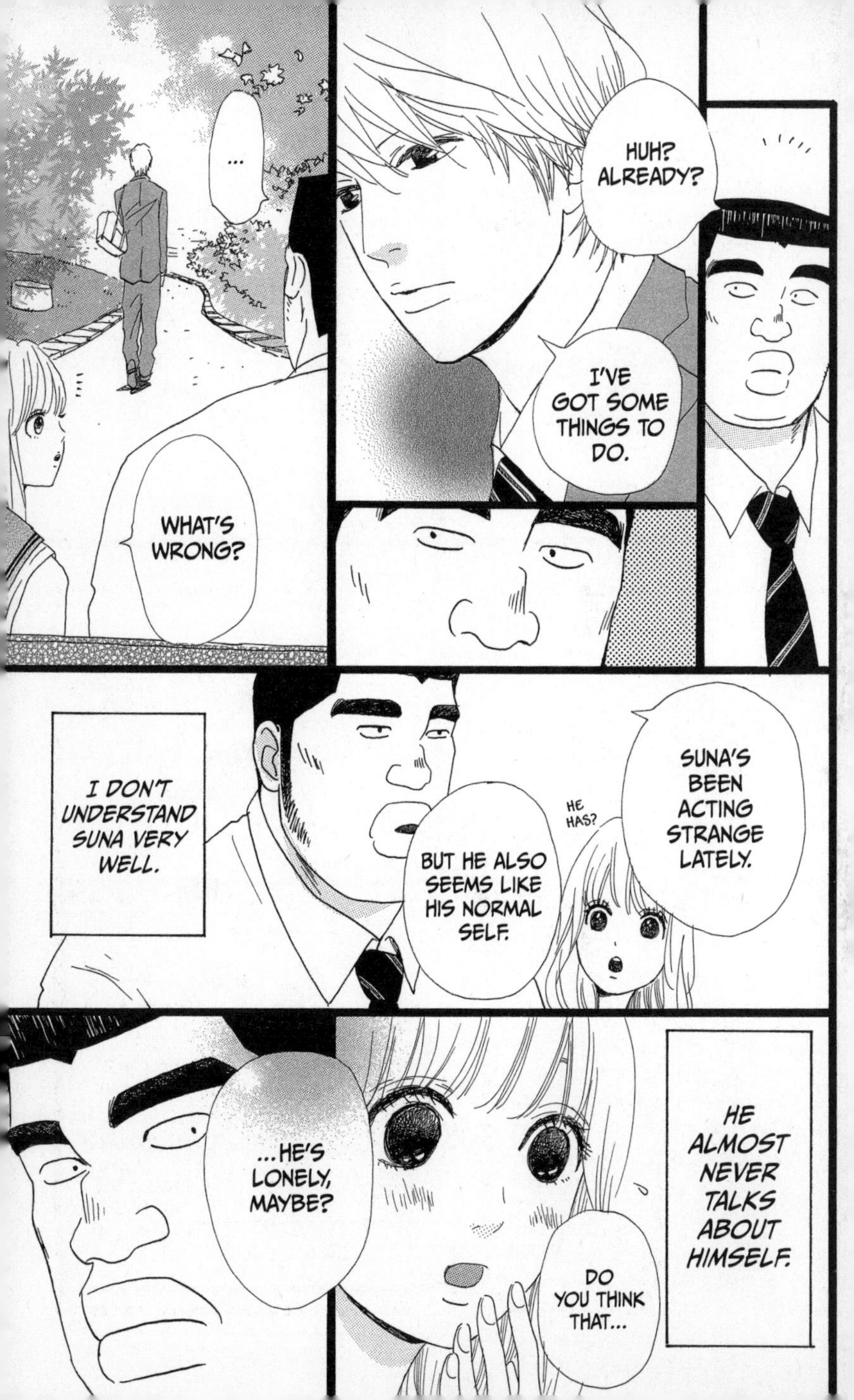
HUH? ALREADY?
I'VE GOT SOME THINGS TO DO.
...
WHAT'S WRONG?
SUNA'S BEEN ACTING STRANGE LATELY.
HE HAS?
BUT HE ALSO SEEMS LIKE HIS NORMAL SELF.
I DON'T UNDERSTAND SUNA VERY WELL.
HE ALMOST NEVER TALKS ABOUT HIMSELF.
DO YOU THINK THAT...
...HE'S LONELY, MAYBE?

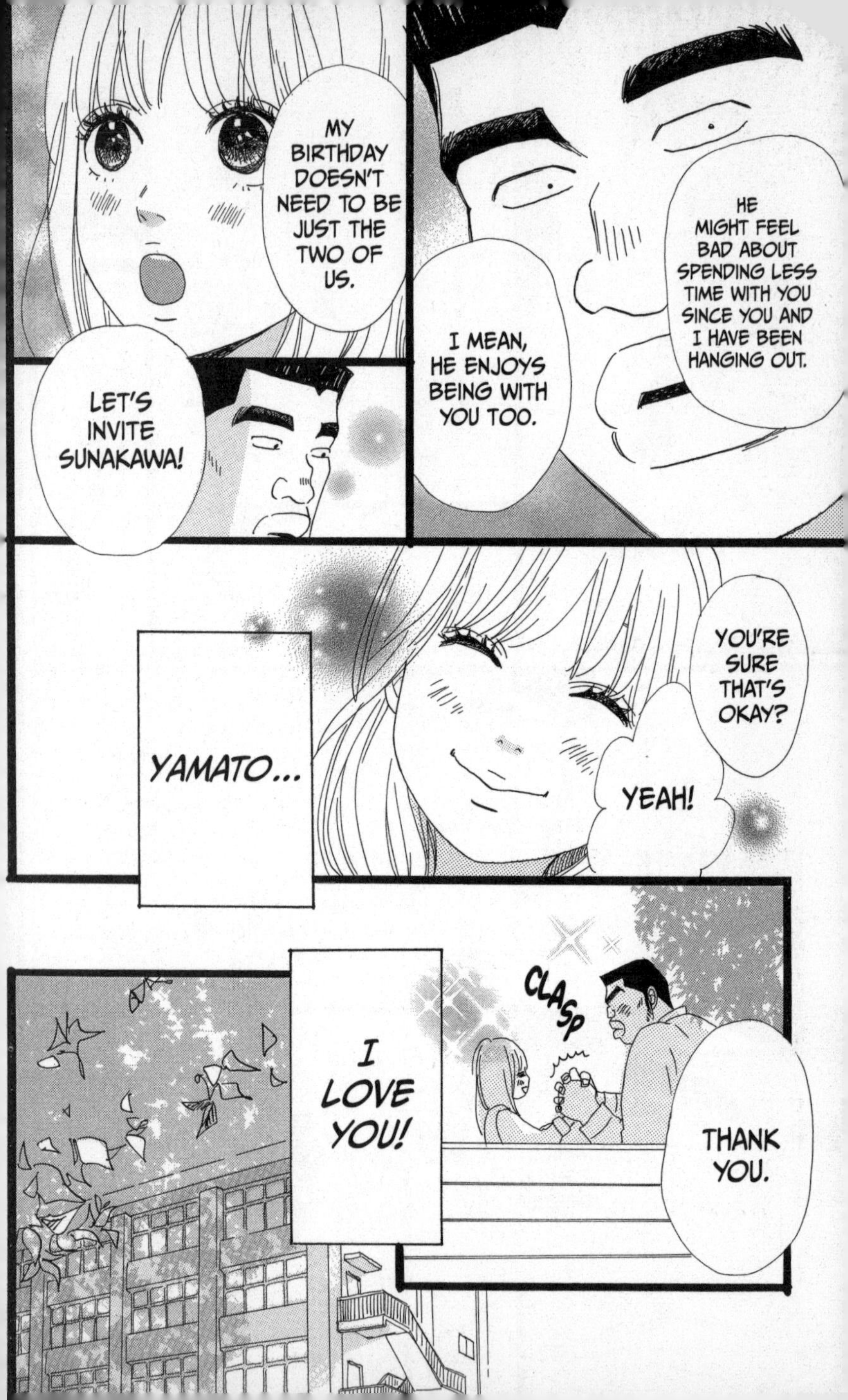
HE MIGHT FEEL BAD ABOUT SPENDING LESS TIME WITH YOU SINCE YOU AND I HAVE BEEN HANGING OUT.
I MEAN, HE ENJOYS BEING WITH YOU TOO.
MY BIRTHDAY DOESN'T NEED TO BE JUST THE TWO OF US.
LET'S INVITE SUNAKAWA!
YOU'RE SURE THAT'S OKAY?
YEAH!
YAMATO...
THANK YOU.
CLASP
I LOVE YOU!

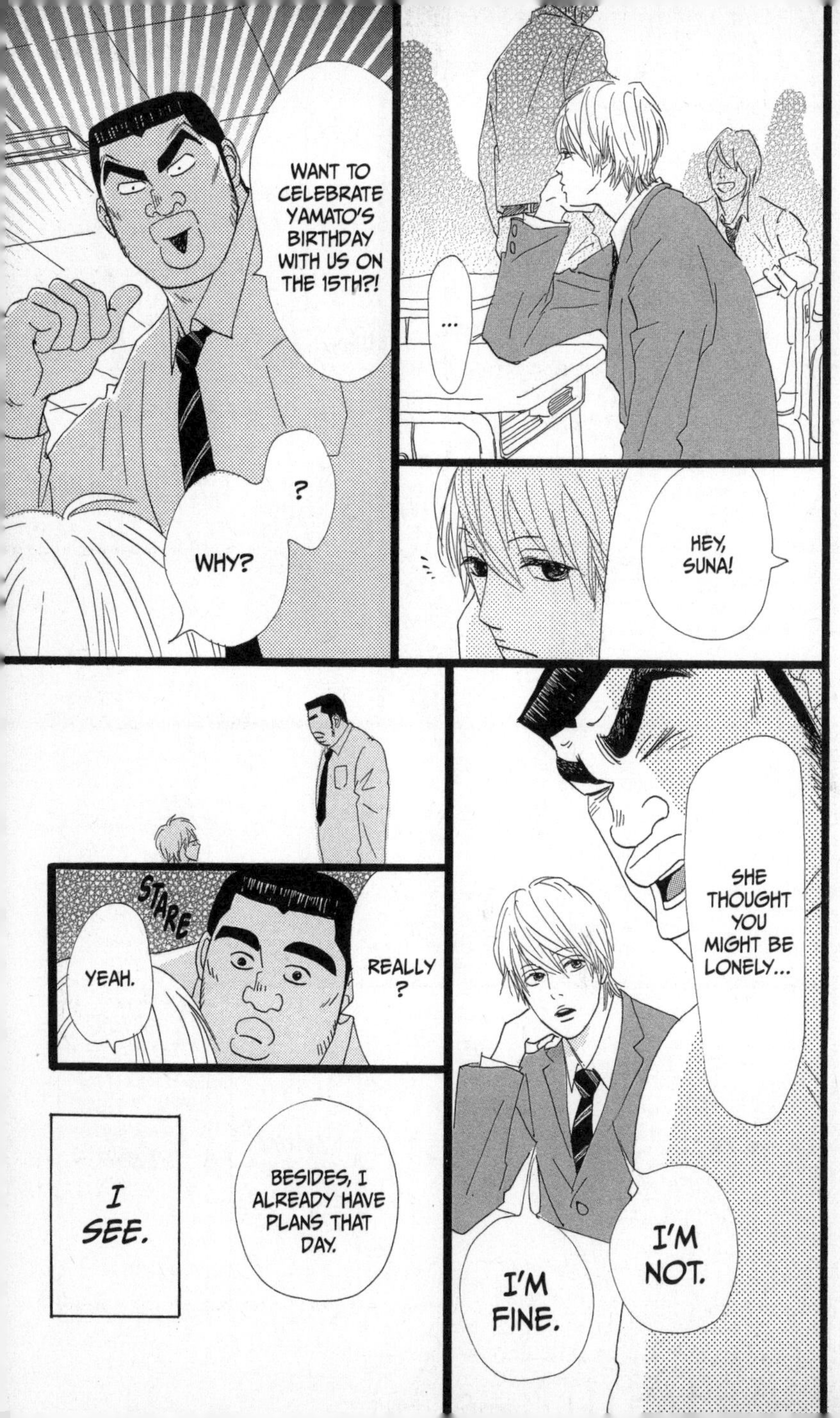
...
HEY, SUNA!
WANT TO CELEBRATE YAMATO'S BIRTHDAY WITH US ON THE 15TH?!
? WHY?
SHE THOUGHT YOU MIGHT BE LONELY...
I'M NOT.
I'M FINE.
REALLY?
STARE
YEAH.
BESIDES, I ALREADY HAVE PLANS THAT DAY.
I SEE.

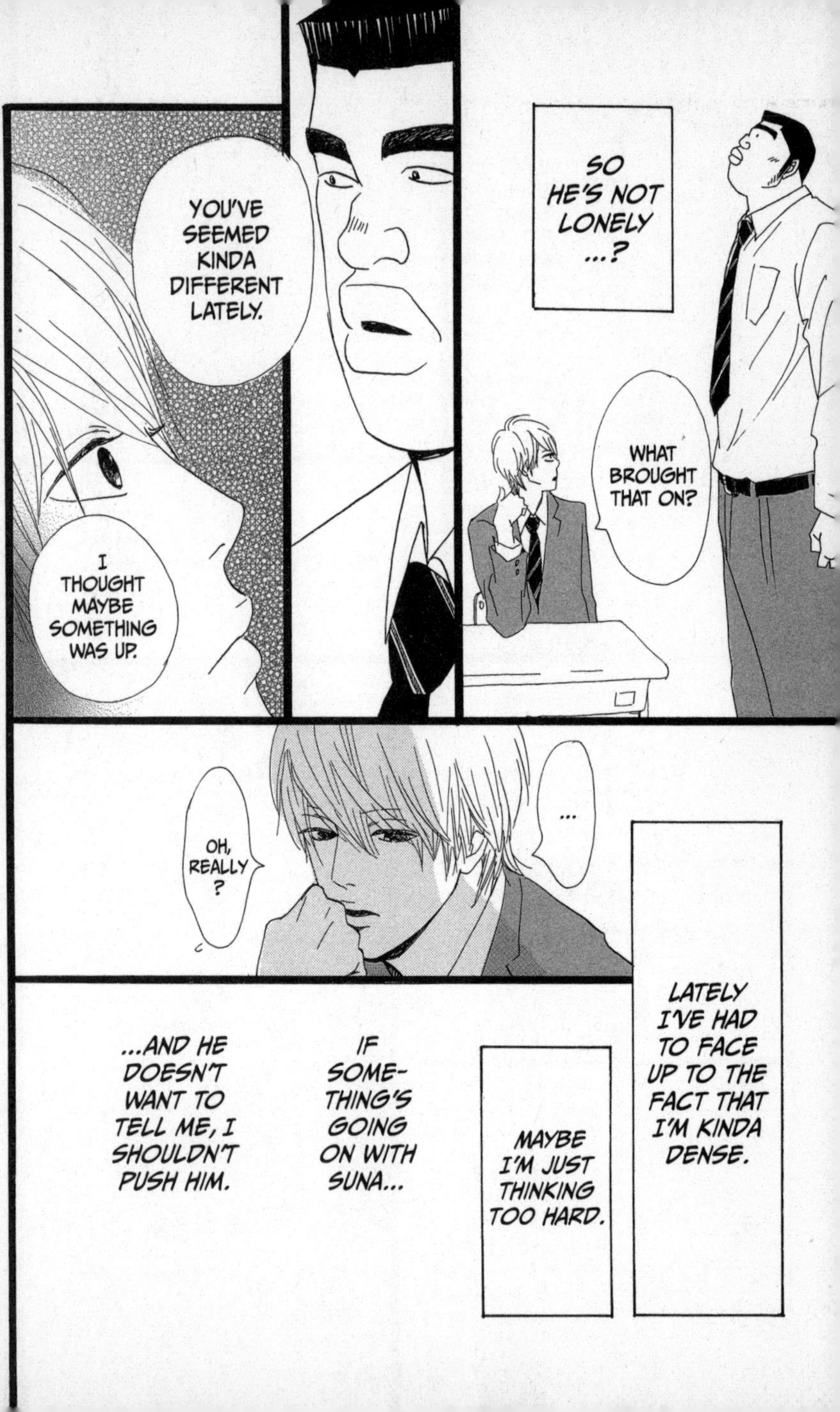
SO HE'S NOT LONELY ...?
WHAT BROUGHT THAT ON?
YOU'VE SEEMED KINDA DIFFERENT LATELY.
I THOUGHT MAYBE SOMETHING WAS UP.
...
OH, REALLY?
LATELY I'VE HAD TO FACE UP TO THE FACT THAT I'M KINDA DENSE.
MAYBE I'M JUST THINKING TOO HARD.
IF SOME-THING'S GOING ON WITH SUNA...
...AND HE DOESN'T WANT TO TELL ME, I SHOULDN'T PUSH HIM.

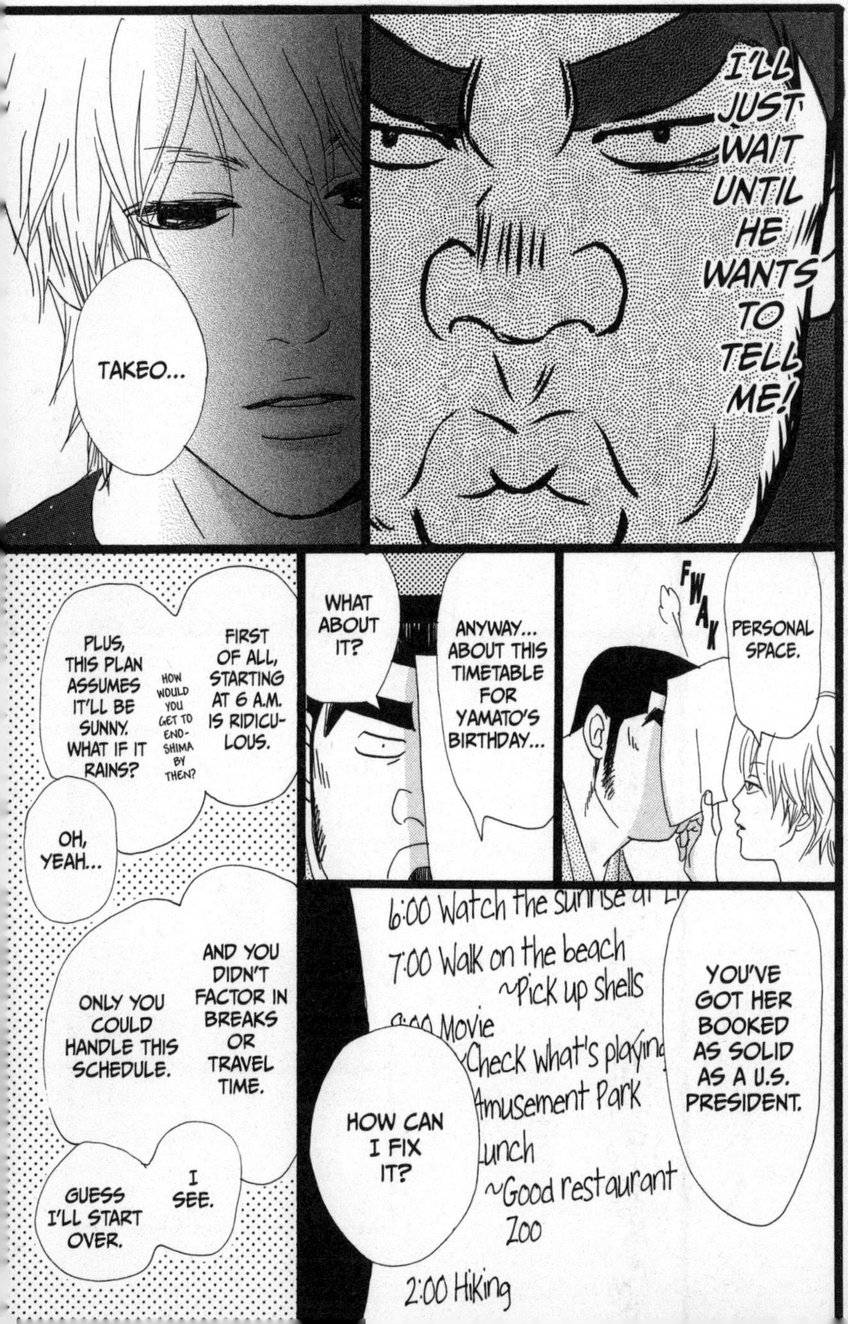
I'LL JUST WAIT UNTIL HE WANTS TO TELL ME!
TAKEO...
FWAK
PERSONAL SPACE.
ANYWAY... ABOUT THIS TIMETABLE FOR YAMATO'S BIRTHDAY...
WHAT ABOUT IT?
YOU'VE GOT HER BOOKED AS SOLID AS A U.S. PRESIDENT.
HOW CAN I FIX IT?
6:00 Watch the sunrise
7:00 Walk on the beach
~Pick up shells
Movie
Check what's playing
Amusement Park
unch
~Good restaurant
Zoo
2:00 Hiking
FIRST OF ALL, STARTING AT 6 A.M. IS RIDICULOUS.
HOW WOULD YOU GET TO ENOSHIMA BY THEN?
PLUS, THIS PLAN ASSUMES IT'LL BE SUNNY. WHAT IF IT RAINS?
OH, YEAH...
AND YOU DIDN'T FACTOR IN BREAKS OR TRAVEL TIME.
ONLY YOU COULD HANDLE THIS SCHEDULE.
I SEE.
GUESS I'LL START OVER.

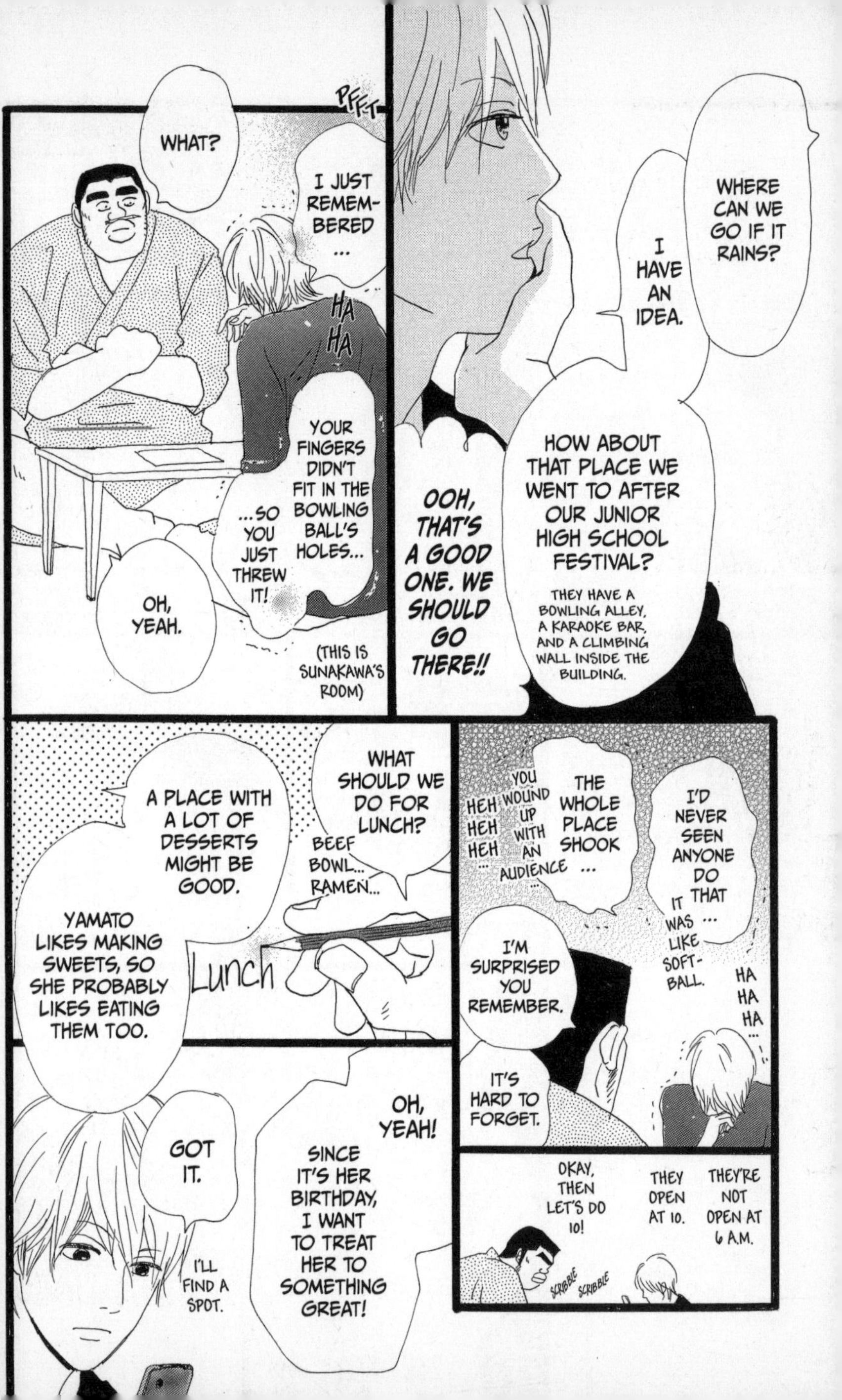
WHERE CAN WE GO IF IT RAINS?
I HAVE AN IDEA.
HOW ABOUT THAT PLACE WE WENT TO AFTER OUR JUNIOR HIGH SCHOOL FESTIVAL?
THEY HAVE A BOWLING ALLEY, A KARAOKE BAR, AND A CLIMBING WALL INSIDE THE BUILDING.
OOH, THAT'S A GOOD ONE. WE SHOULD GO THERE!!
PFFFT
I JUST REMEMBERED...
WHAT?
HA HA
YOUR FINGERS DIDN'T FIT IN THE BOWLING BALL'S HOLES...
...SO YOU JUST THREW IT!
OH, YEAH.
(THIS IS SUNAKAWA'S ROOM)
I'D NEVER SEEN ANYONE DO THAT...
THE WHOLE PLACE SHOOK...
YOU WOUND UP WITH AN AUDIENCE...
HEH HEH HEH...
IT WAS LIKE SOFT-BALL.
HA HA HA...
I'M SURPRISED YOU REMEMBER.
IT'S HARD TO FORGET.
THEY'RE NOT OPEN AT 6 A.M.
THEY OPEN AT 10.
OKAY, THEN LET'S DO 10!
SCRIBBLE SCRIBBLE
WHAT SHOULD WE DO FOR LUNCH?
BEEF BOWL... RAMEN...
A PLACE WITH A LOT OF DESSERTS MIGHT BE GOOD.
Lunch
YAMATO LIKES MAKING SWEETS, SO SHE PROBABLY LIKES EATING THEM TOO.
OH, YEAH!
SINCE IT'S HER BIRTHDAY, I WANT TO TREAT HER TO SOMETHING GREAT!
GOT IT.
I'LL FIND A SPOT.

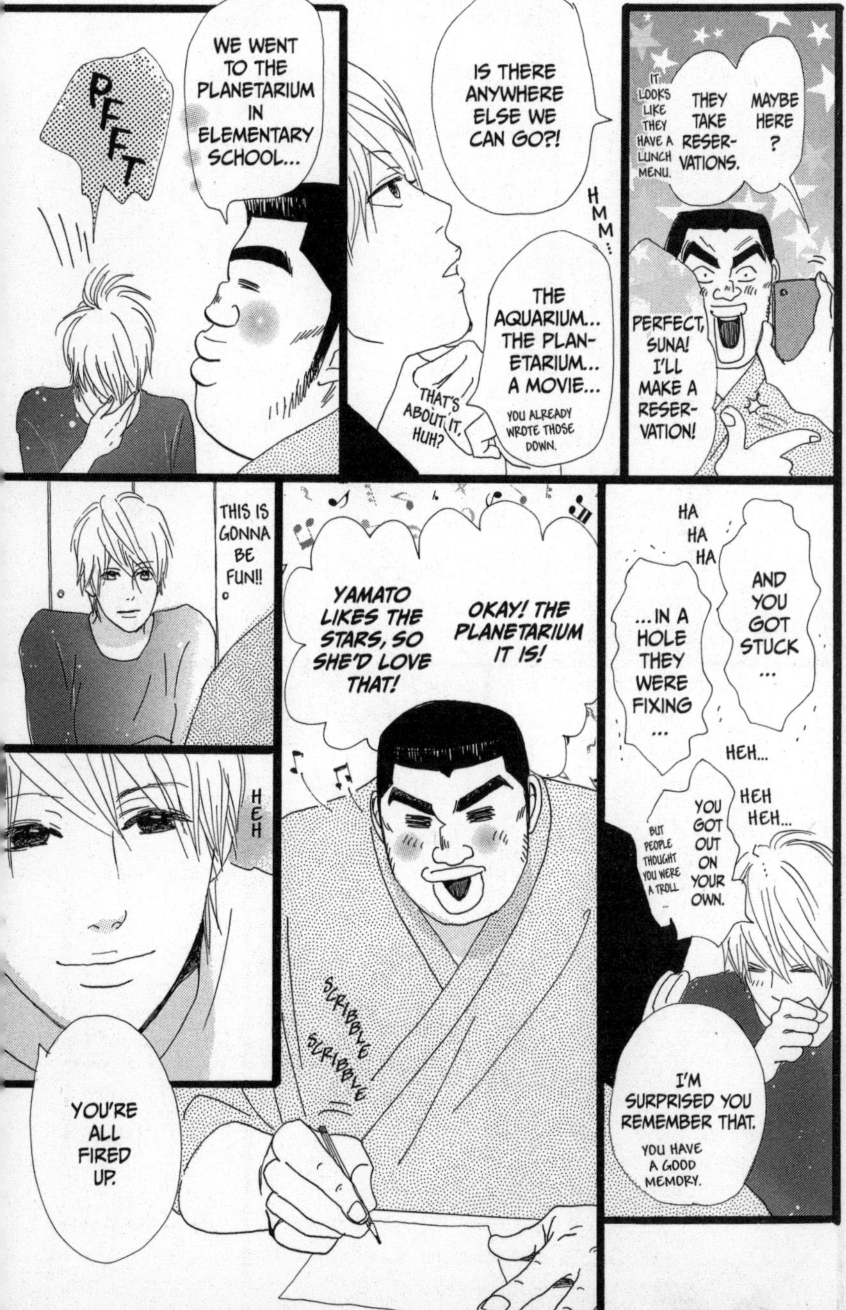
MAYBE HERE?
THEY TAKE RESERVATIONS.
IT LOOKS LIKE THEY HAVE A LUNCH MENU.
PERFECT, SUNA! I'LL MAKE A RESERVATION!
IS THERE ANYWHERE ELSE WE CAN GO?!
HMM...
THE AQUARIUM... THE PLANETARIUM... A MOVIE...
YOU ALREADY WROTE THOSE DOWN.
THAT'S ABOUT IT, HUH?
WE WENT TO THE PLANETARIUM IN ELEMENTARY SCHOOL...
PFFT
AND YOU GOT STUCK...
HA HA HA
...IN A HOLE THEY WERE FIXING...
HEH...
HEH HEH...
YOU GOT OUT ON YOUR OWN.
BUT PEOPLE THOUGHT YOU WERE A TROLL...
I'M SURPRISED YOU REMEMBER THAT.
YOU HAVE A GOOD MEMORY.
OKAY! THE PLANETARIUM IT IS!
YAMATO LIKES THE STARS, SO SHE'D LOVE THAT!
SCRIBBLE
SCRIBBLE
THIS IS GONNA BE FUN!!
HEH
YOU'RE ALL FIRED UP.

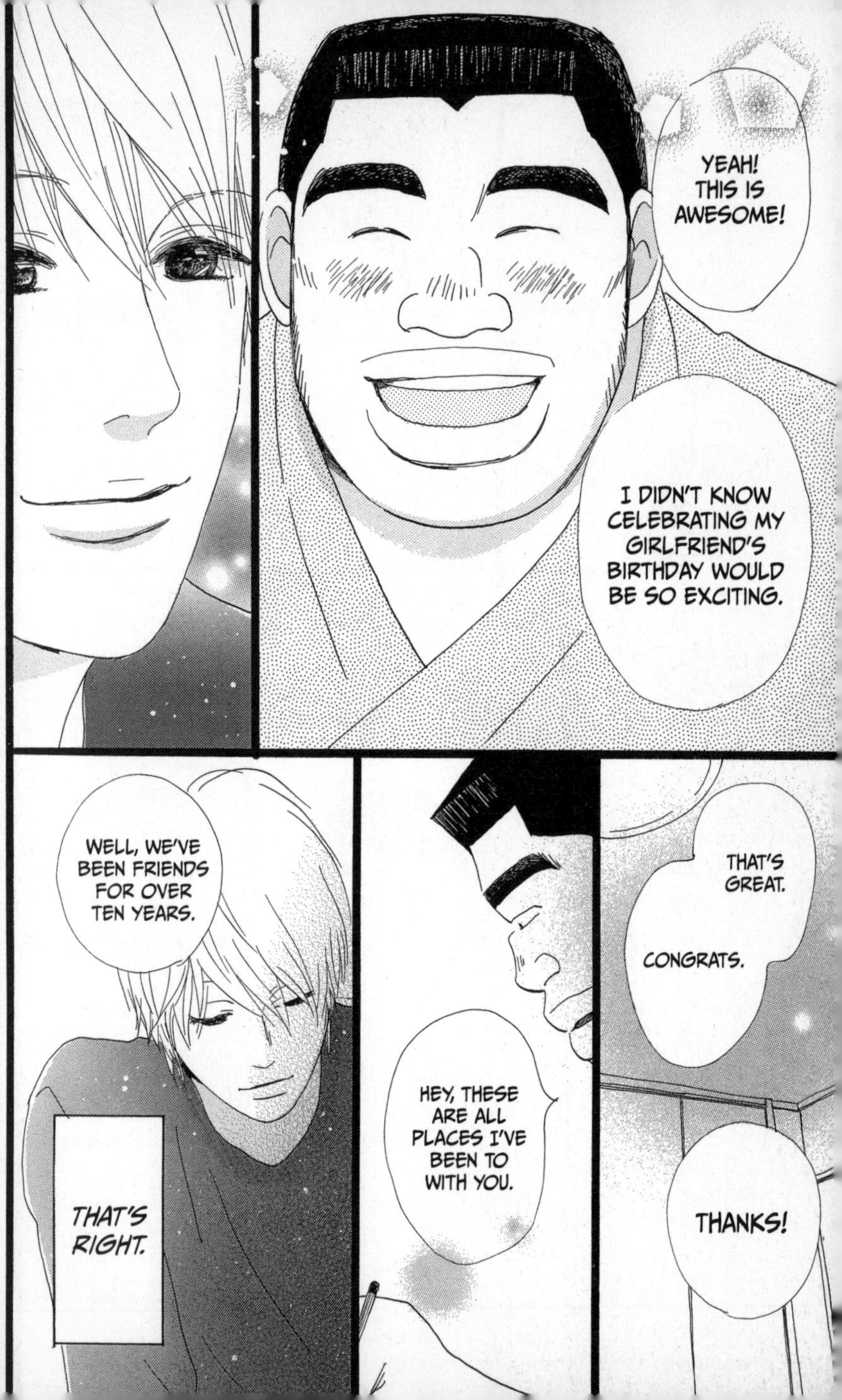
YEAH! THIS IS AWESOME!
I DIDN'T KNOW CELEBRATING MY GIRLFRIEND'S BIRTHDAY WOULD BE SO EXCITING.
THAT'S GREAT.
CONGRATS.
THANKS!
HEY, THESE ARE ALL PLACES I'VE BEEN TO WITH YOU.
WELL, WE'VE BEEN FRIENDS FOR OVER TEN YEARS.
THAT'S RIGHT.

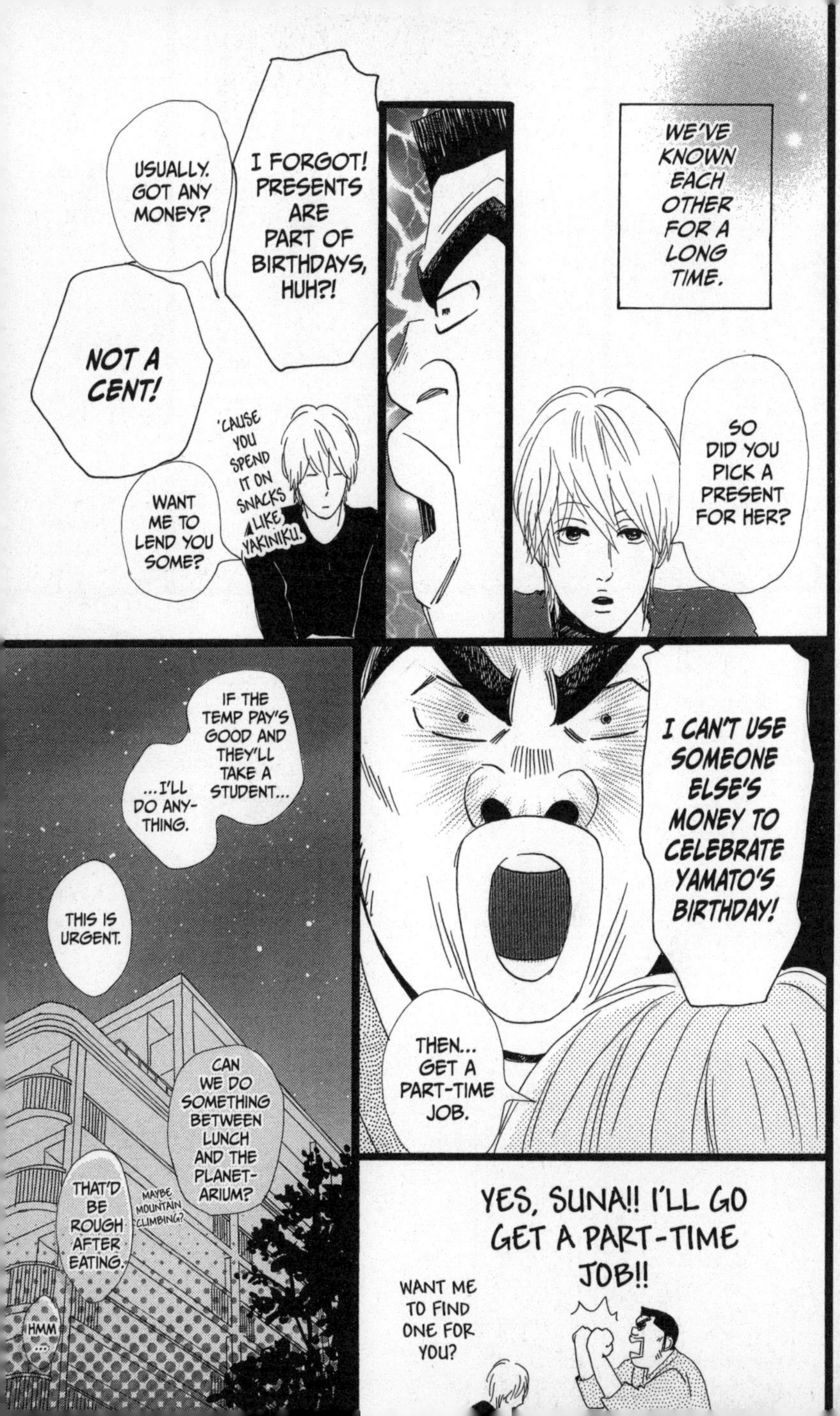
WE'VE KNOWN EACH OTHER FOR A LONG TIME.
SO DID YOU PICK A PRESENT FOR HER?
I FORGOT! PRESENTS ARE PART OF BIRTHDAYS, HUH?!
USUALLY. GOT ANY MONEY?
NOT A CENT!
'CAUSE YOU SPEND IT ON SNACKS LIKE YAKINIKU.
WANT ME TO LEND YOU SOME?
I CAN'T USE SOMEONE ELSE'S MONEY TO CELEBRATE YAMATO'S BIRTHDAY!
THEN... GET A PART-TIME JOB.
YES, SUNA!! I'LL GO GET A PART-TIME JOB!!
WANT ME TO FIND ONE FOR YOU?
IF THE TEMP PAY'S GOOD AND THEY'LL TAKE A STUDENT...
...I'LL DO ANY-THING.
THIS IS URGENT.
CAN WE DO SOMETHING BETWEEN LUNCH AND THE PLANET-ARIUM?
MAYBE MOUNTAIN CLIMBING?
THAT'D BE ROUGH AFTER EATING.
HMM...

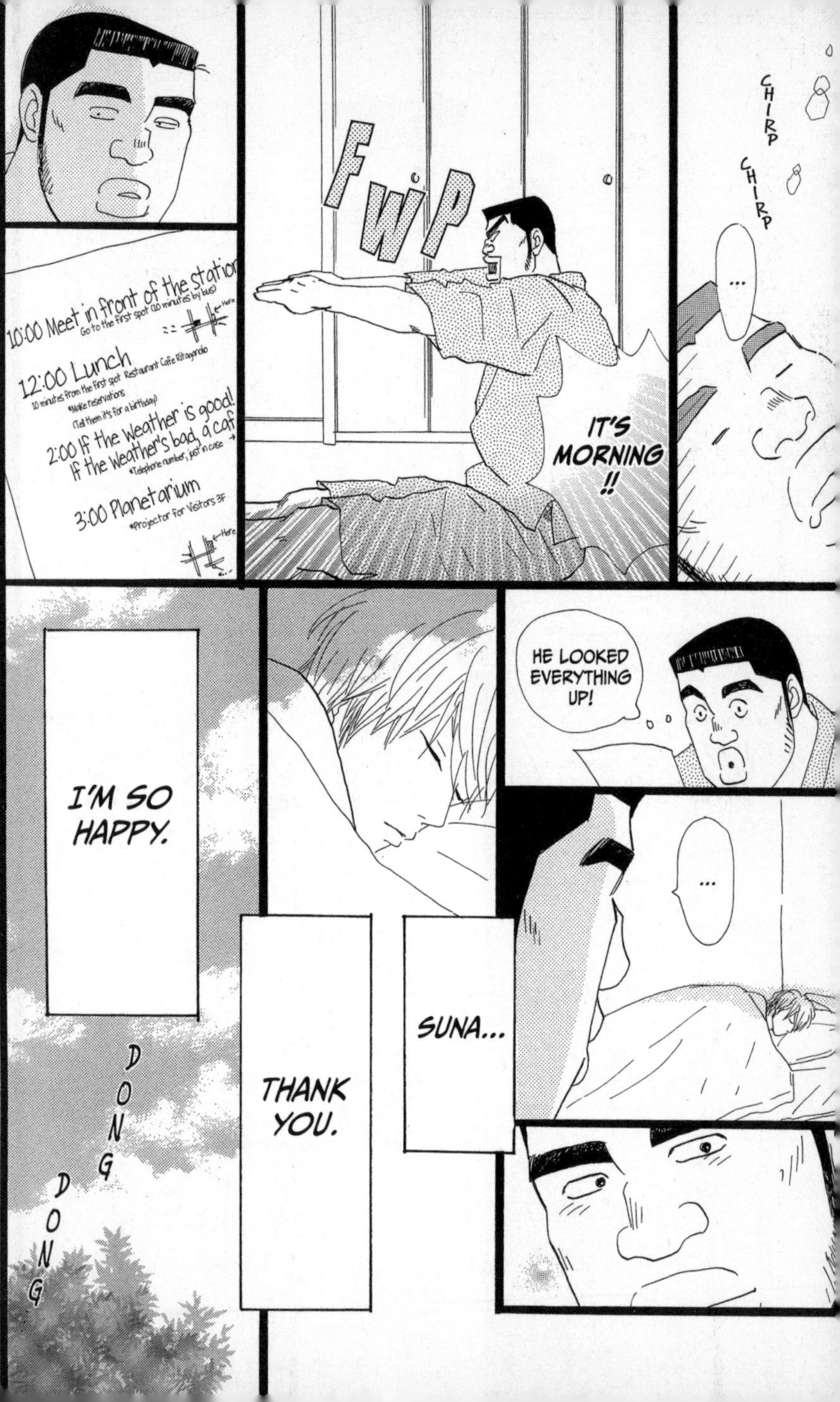
CHIRP
CHIRP
...
FWP
IT'S MORNING!!
10:00 Meet in front of the station
Go to the first spot (10 minutes by bus)
Here
12:00 Lunch
10 minutes from the first spot Restaurant Cafe Ritagnolo
*Make reservations
(Tell them it's for a birthday)
2:00 If the weather is good!
If the weather's bad, a caf
*Telephone number, just in case →
3:00 Planetarium
*Projector for Visitors 3F
Here
HE LOOKED EVERYTHING UP!
...
SUNA...
THANK YOU.
I'M SO HAPPY.
DONG
DONG

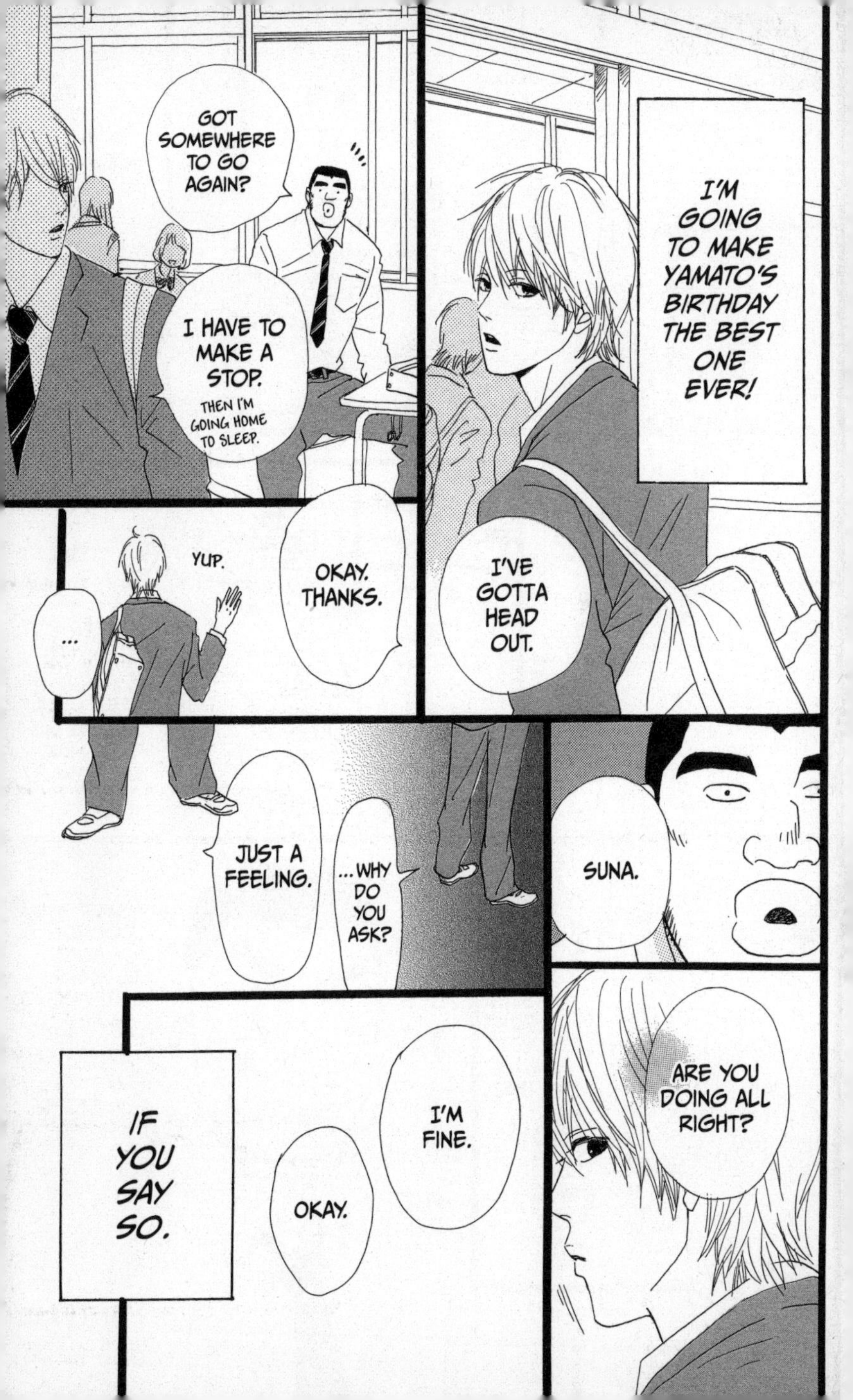
I'M GOING TO MAKE YAMATO'S BIRTHDAY THE BEST ONE EVER!
I'VE GOTTA HEAD OUT.
GOT SOMEWHERE TO GO AGAIN?
I HAVE TO MAKE A STOP.
THEN I'M GOING HOME TO SLEEP.
OKAY. THANKS.
YUP.
...
SUNA.
ARE YOU DOING ALL RIGHT?
...WHY DO YOU ASK?
JUST A FEELING.
I'M FINE.
OKAY.
IF YOU SAY SO.

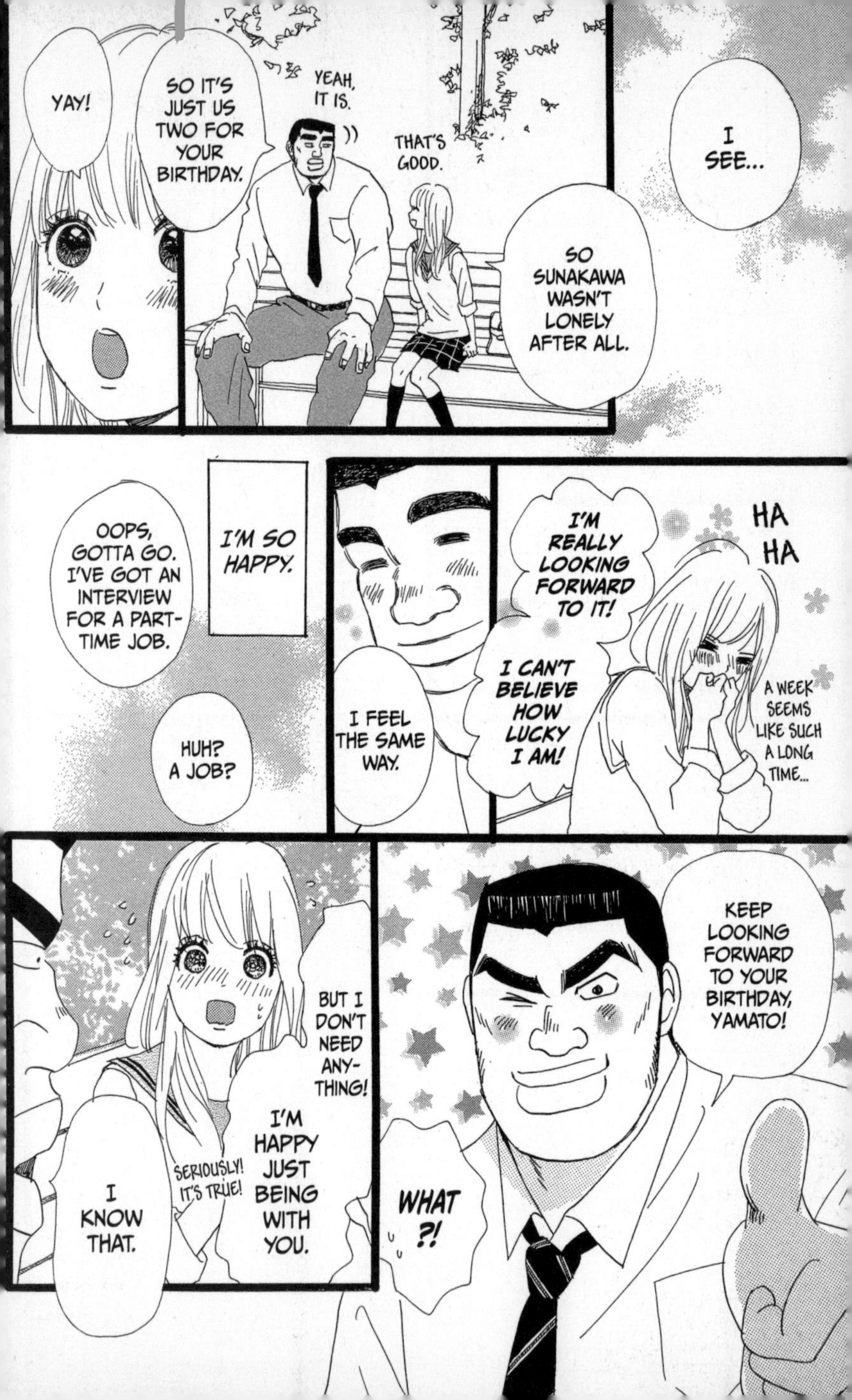
I SEE...
SO SUNAKAWA WASN'T LONELY AFTER ALL.
THAT'S GOOD.
YEAH, IT IS.
SO IT'S JUST US TWO FOR YOUR BIRTHDAY.
YAY!
HA HA
I'M REALLY LOOKING FORWARD TO IT!
A WEEK SEEMS LIKE SUCH A LONG TIME...
I CAN'T BELIEVE HOW LUCKY I AM!
I FEEL THE SAME WAY.
I'M SO HAPPY.
OOPS, GOTTA GO. I'VE GOT AN INTERVIEW FOR A PART-TIME JOB.
HUH? A JOB?
KEEP LOOKING FORWARD TO YOUR BIRTHDAY, YAMATO!
WHAT?!
BUT I DON'T NEED ANYTHING!
I'M HAPPY JUST BEING WITH YOU.
SERIOUSLY! IT'S TRUE!
I KNOW THAT.

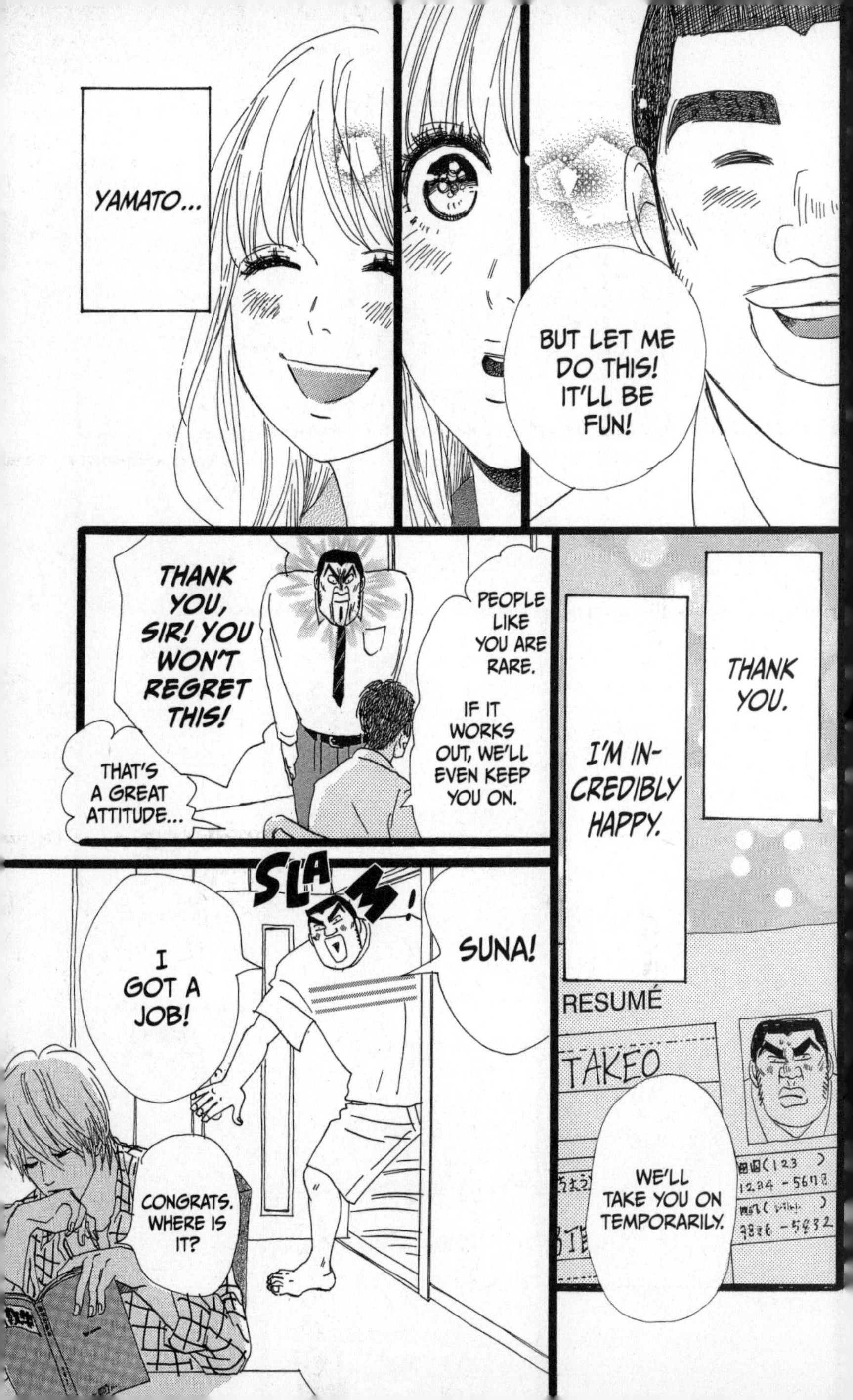
BUT LET ME DO THIS! IT'LL BE FUN!
YAMATO...
THANK YOU.
I'M IN-CREDIBLY HAPPY.
RESUMÉ
TAKEO
WE'LL TAKE YOU ON TEMPORARILY.
PEOPLE LIKE YOU ARE RARE.
IF IT WORKS OUT, WE'LL EVEN KEEP YOU ON.
THANK YOU, SIR! YOU WON'T REGRET THIS!
THAT'S A GREAT ATTITUDE...
SLAM!
SUNA!
I GOT A JOB!
CONGRATS. WHERE IS IT?

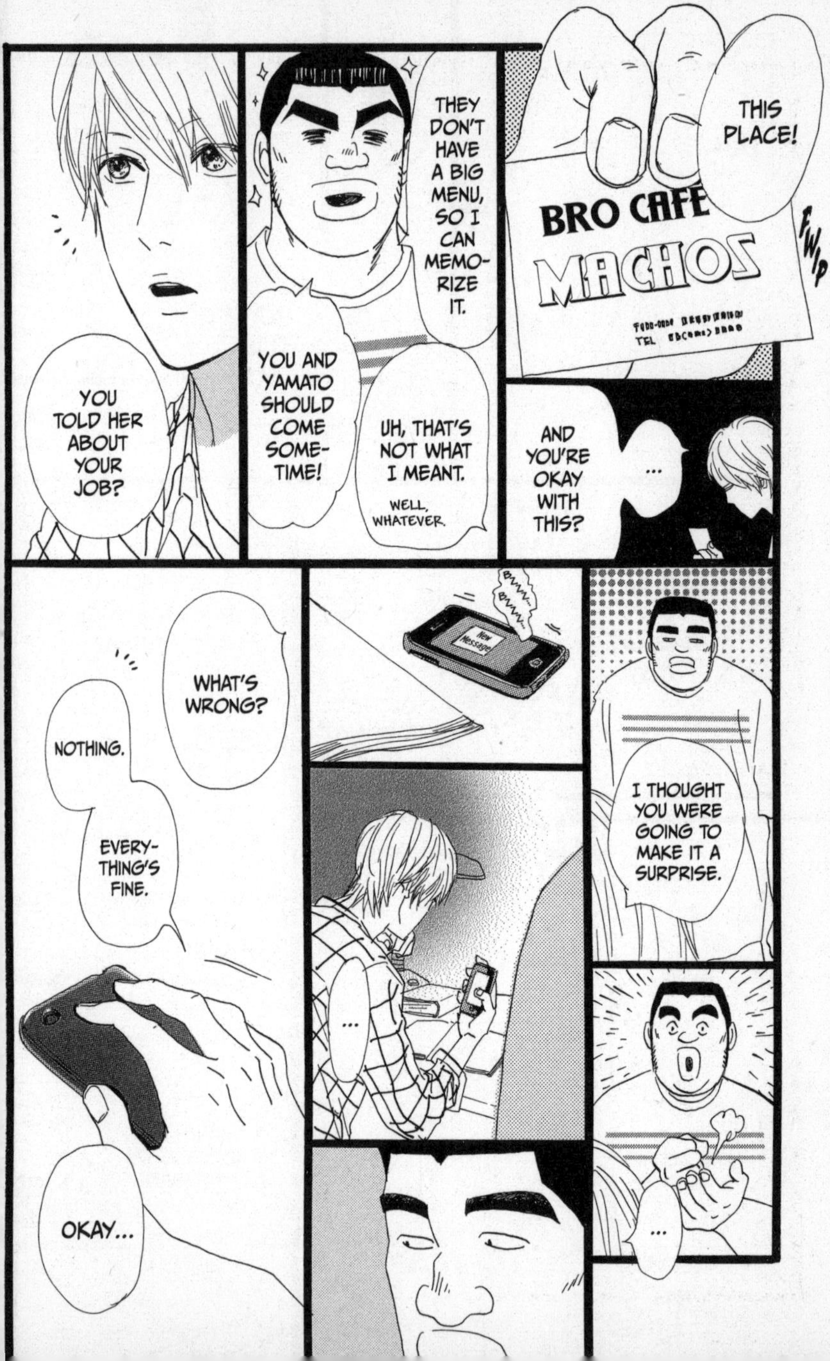
THIS PLACE!
BRO CAFÉ
MACHOS
FWIP
AND YOU'RE OKAY WITH THIS?
...
THEY DON'T HAVE A BIG MENU, SO I CAN MEMORIZE IT.
YOU AND YAMATO SHOULD COME SOMETIME!
UH, THAT'S NOT WHAT I MEANT.
WELL, WHATEVER.
YOU TOLD HER ABOUT YOUR JOB?
I THOUGHT YOU WERE GOING TO MAKE IT A SURPRISE.
...
New Message
...
WHAT'S WRONG?
NOTHING.
EVERYTHING'S FINE.
OKAY...

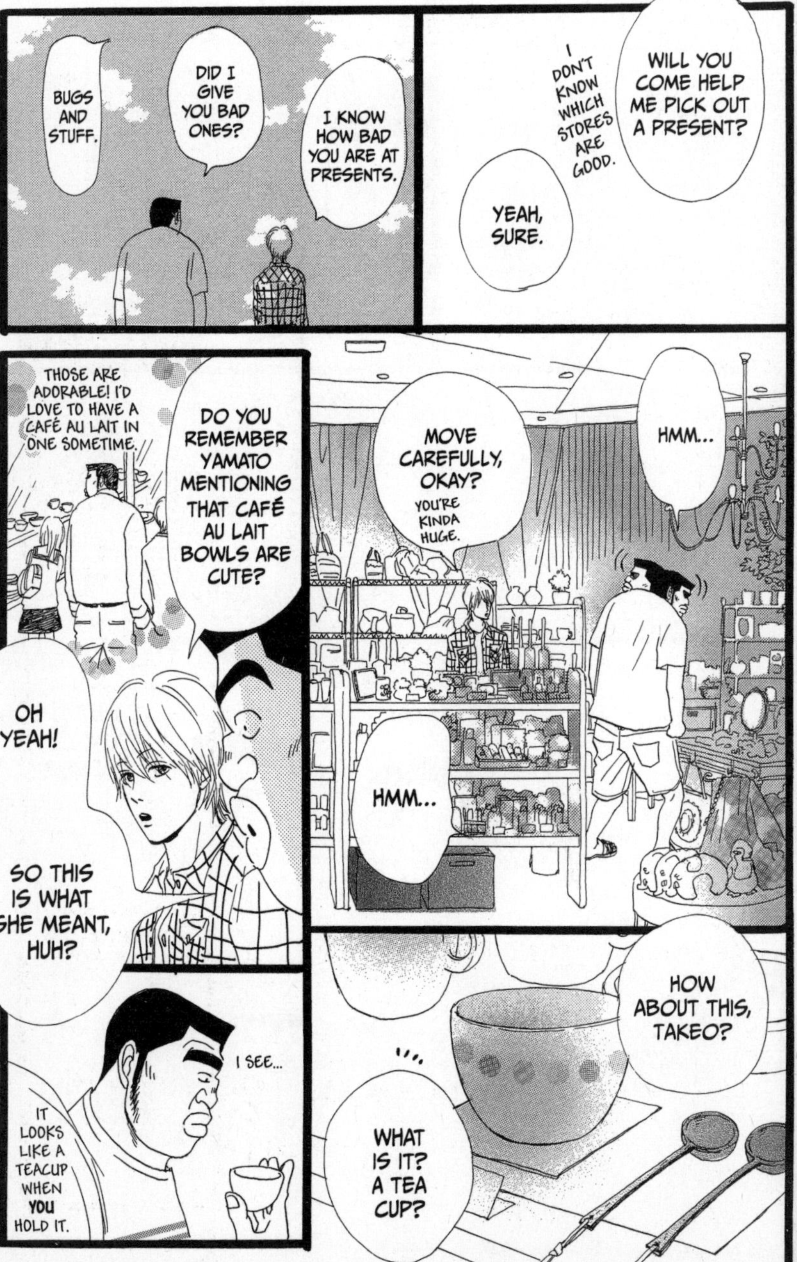
WILL YOU COME HELP ME PICK OUT A PRESENT?
I DON'T KNOW WHICH STORES ARE GOOD.
YEAH, SURE.
I KNOW HOW BAD YOU ARE AT PRESENTS.
DID I GIVE YOU BAD ONES?
BUGS AND STUFF.
HMM...
MOVE CAREFULLY, OKAY? YOU'RE KINDA HUGE.
HMM...
DO YOU REMEMBER YAMATO MENTIONING THAT CAFÉ AU LAIT BOWLS ARE CUTE?
THOSE ARE ADORABLE! I'D LOVE TO HAVE A CAFÉ AU LAIT IN ONE SOMETIME.
OH YEAH!
SO THIS IS WHAT SHE MEANT, HUH?
HOW ABOUT THIS, TAKEO?
WHAT IS IT? A TEA CUP?
I SEE...
IT LOOKS LIKE A TEACUP WHEN YOU HOLD IT.

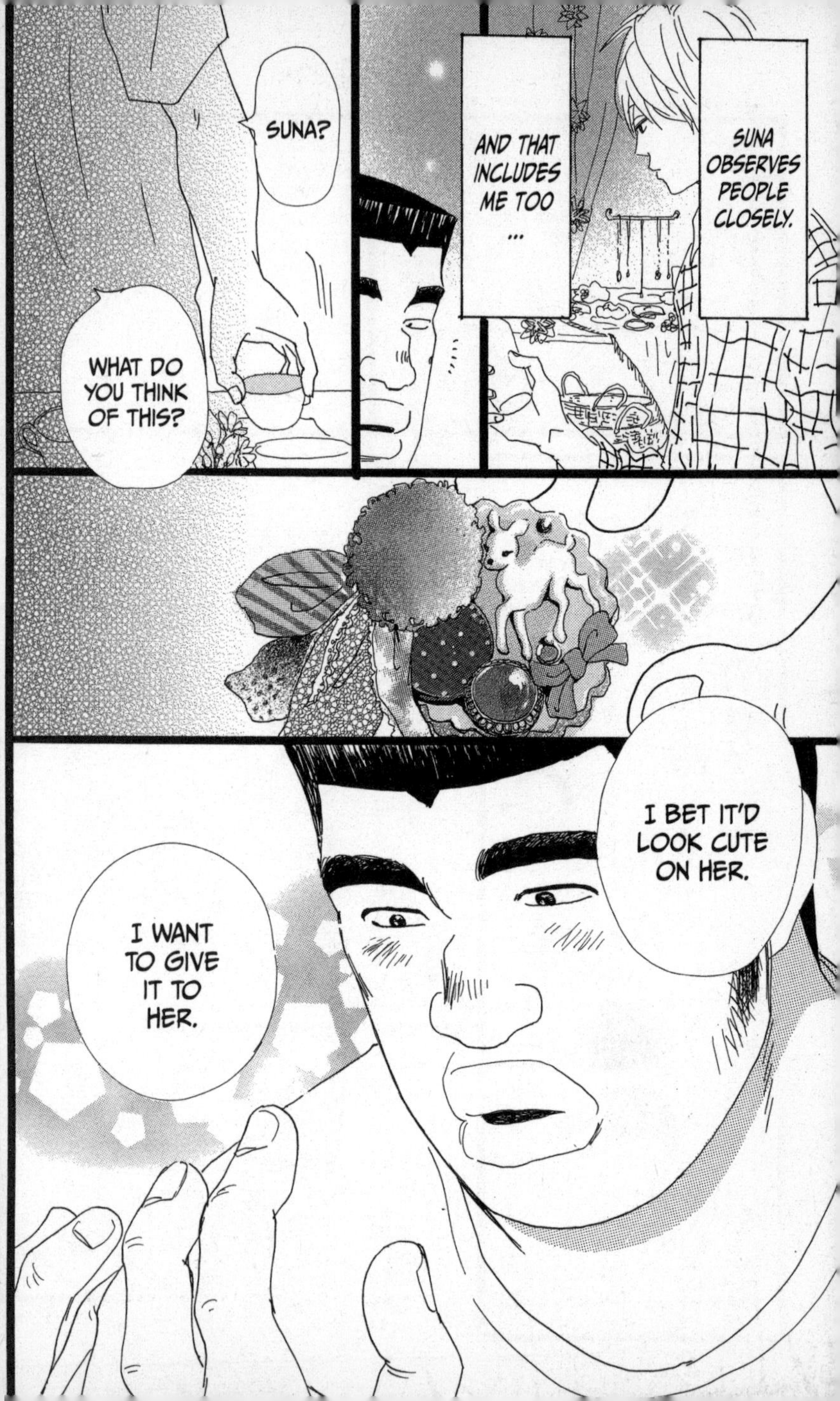
SUNA OBSERVES PEOPLE CLOSELY.
AND THAT INCLUDES ME TOO ...
SUNA?
WHAT DO YOU THINK OF THIS?
I BET IT'D LOOK CUTE ON HER.
I WANT TO GIVE IT TO HER.

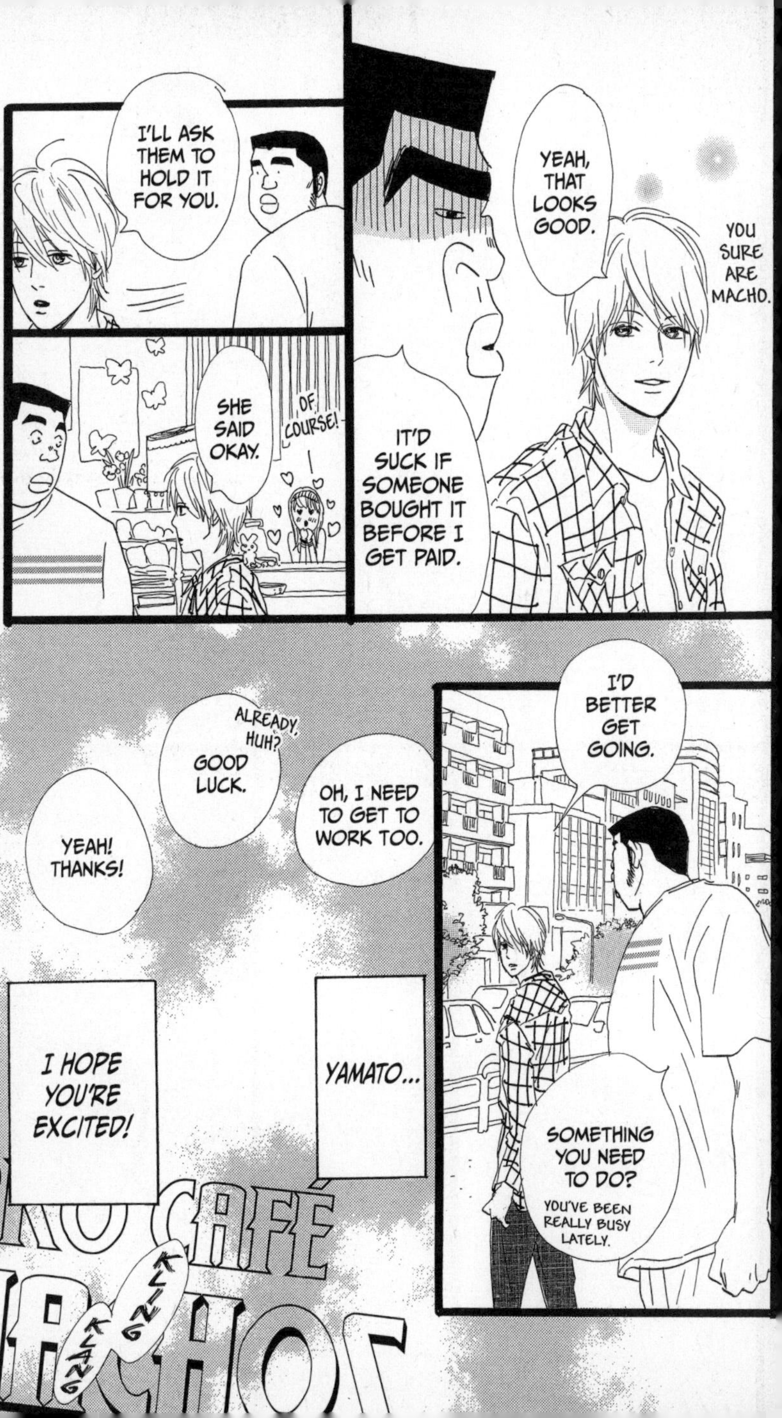
YEAH, THAT LOOKS GOOD.
YOU SURE ARE MACHO.
IT'D SUCK IF SOMEONE BOUGHT IT BEFORE I GET PAID.
I'LL ASK THEM TO HOLD IT FOR YOU.
SHE SAID OKAY.
OF COURSE!
I'D BETTER GET GOING.
SOMETHING YOU NEED TO DO?
YOU'VE BEEN REALLY BUSY LATELY.
OH, I NEED TO GET TO WORK TOO.
ALREADY, HUH?
GOOD LUCK.
YEAH! THANKS!
YAMATO...
I HOPE YOU'RE EXCITED!
BRO CAFÉ MACHO
KLING KLING
KLANG

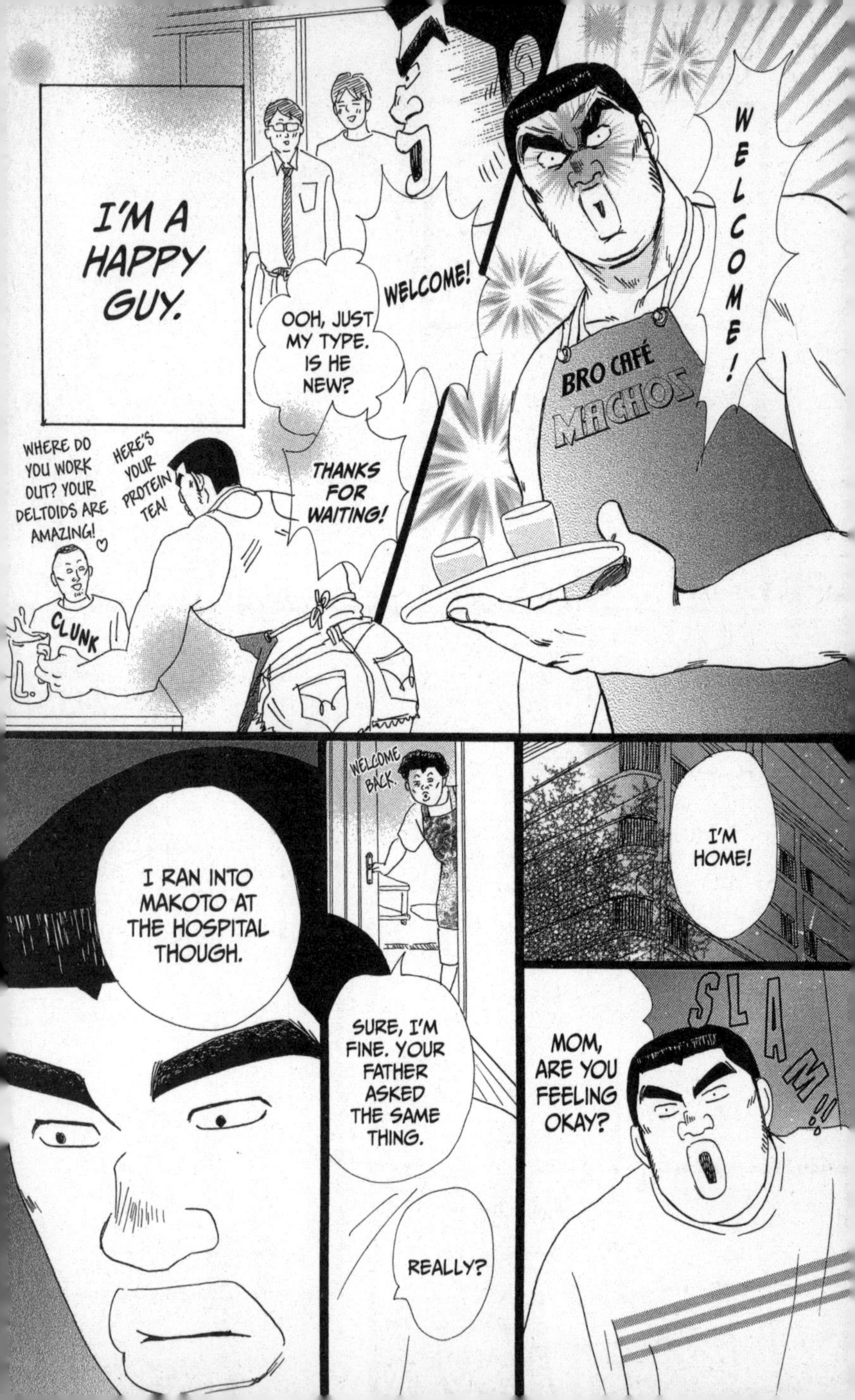
WELCOME!
WELCOME!
BRO CAFÉ
MACHOS
OOH, JUST MY TYPE. IS HE NEW?
I'M A HAPPY GUY.
THANKS FOR WAITING!
HERE'S YOUR PROTEIN TEA!
WHERE DO YOU WORK OUT? YOUR DELTOIDS ARE AMAZING!
CLUNK
I'M HOME!
SLAM!!
MOM, ARE YOU FEELING OKAY?
WELCOME BACK.
SURE, I'M FINE. YOUR FATHER ASKED THE SAME THING.
REALLY?
I RAN INTO MAKOTO AT THE HOSPITAL THOUGH.

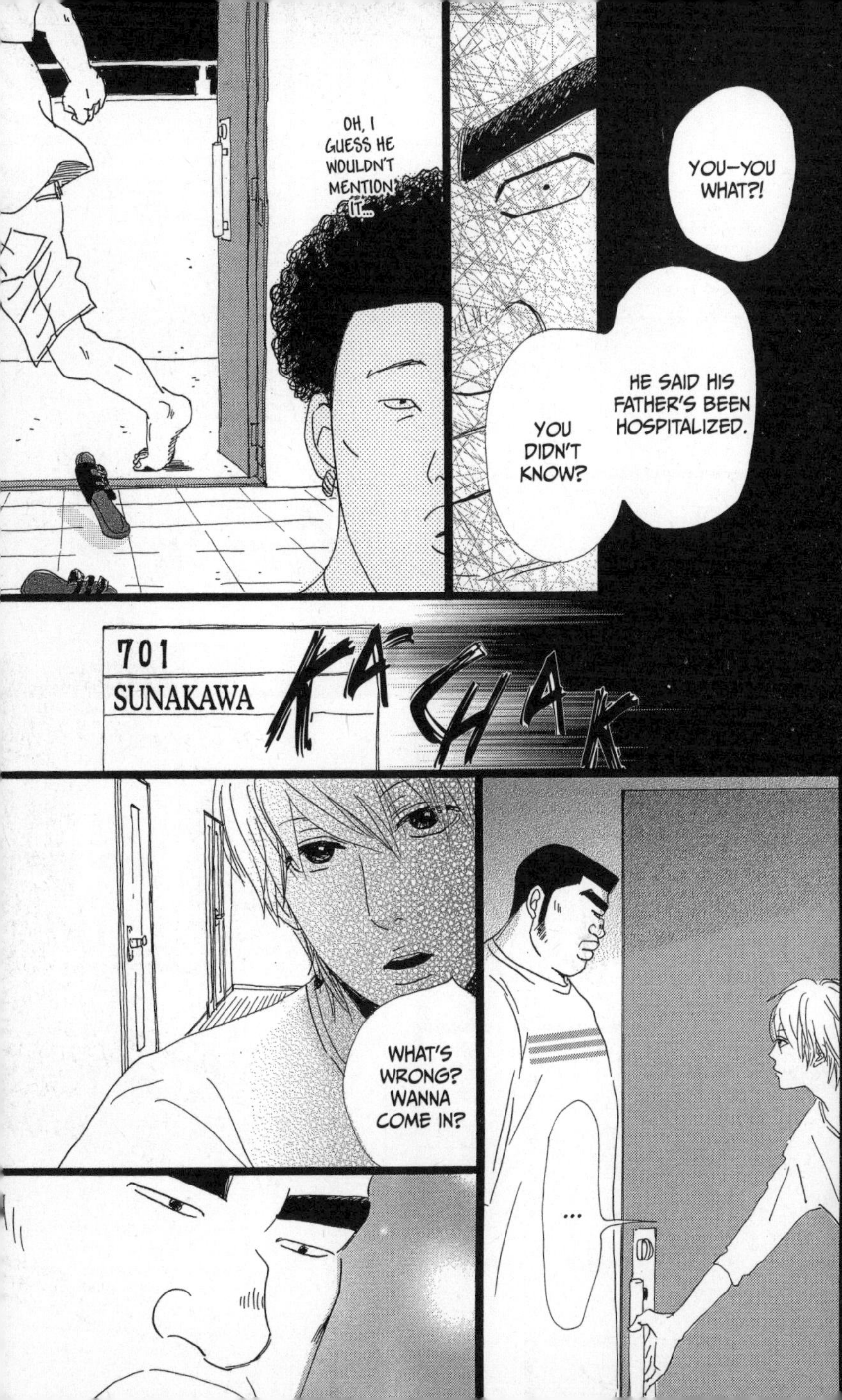
YOU—YOU WHAT?!
HE SAID HIS FATHER'S BEEN HOSPITALIZED.
YOU DIDN'T KNOW?
OH, I GUESS HE WOULDN'T MENTION IT...
KACHAK
701
SUNAKAWA
...
WHAT'S WRONG? WANNA COME IN?

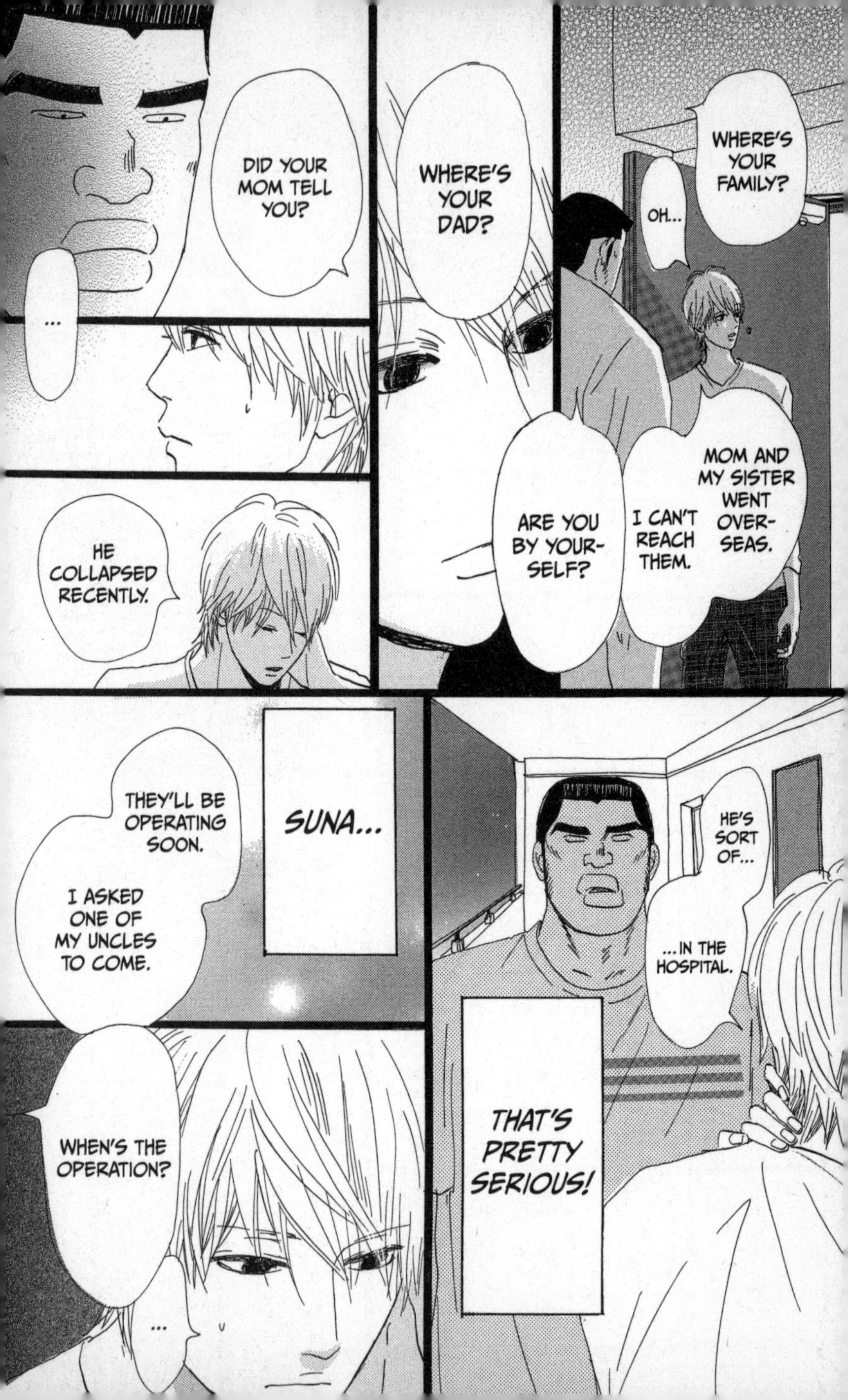

WHERE'S YOUR FAMILY?
OH...
MOM AND MY SISTER WENT OVER-SEAS.
I CAN'T REACH THEM.
ARE YOU BY YOUR-SELF?
WHERE'S YOUR DAD?
DID YOUR MOM TELL YOU?
...
HE COLLAPSED RECENTLY.
HE'S SORT OF...
...IN THE HOSPITAL.
THAT'S PRETTY SERIOUS!
SUNA...
THEY'LL BE OPERATING SOON.
I ASKED ONE OF MY UNCLES TO COME.
WHEN'S THE OPERATION?
...

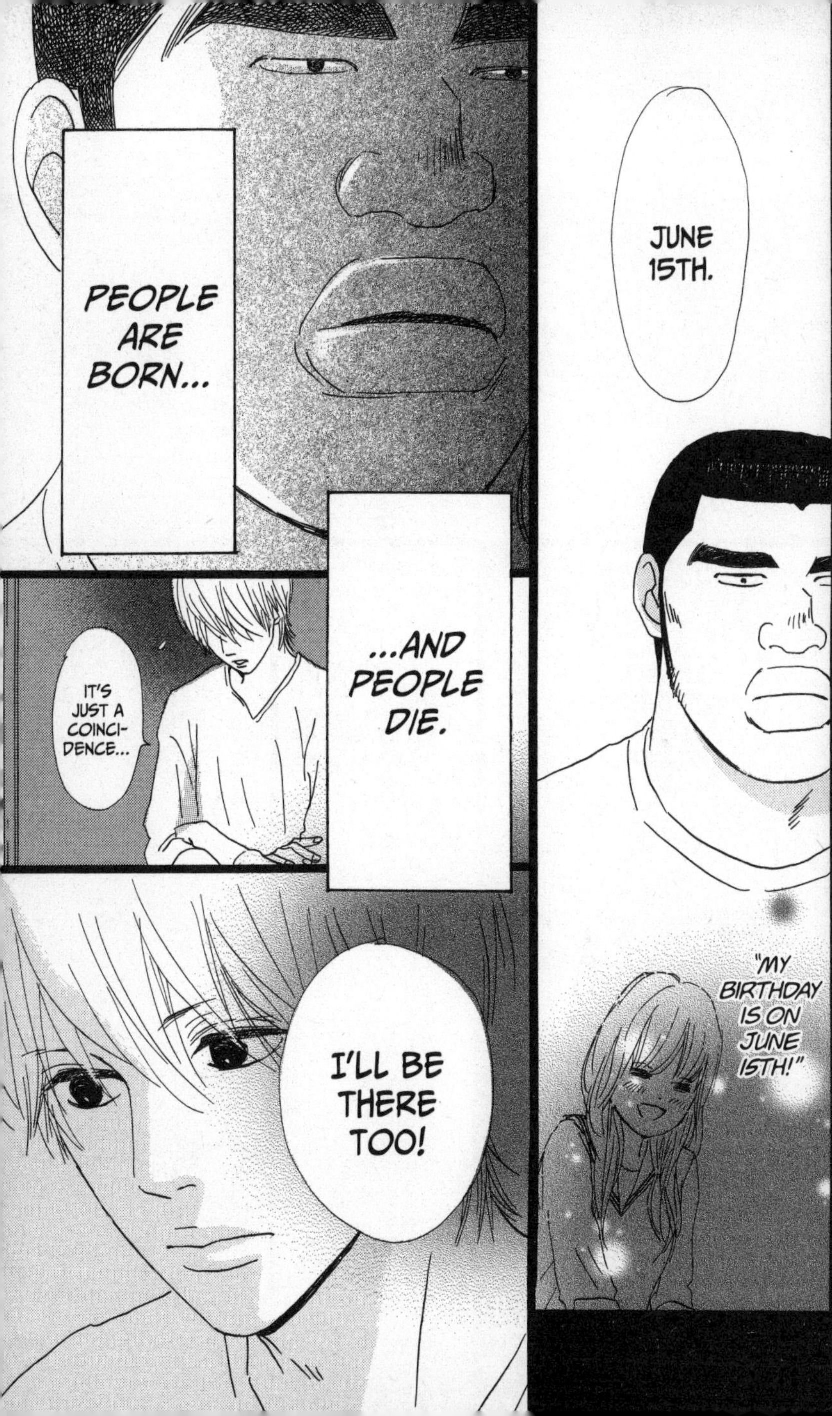
JUNE 15TH.
"MY BIRTHDAY IS ON JUNE 15TH!"
PEOPLE ARE BORN...
...AND PEOPLE DIE.
IT'S JUST A COINCI-DENCE...
I'LL BE THERE TOO!

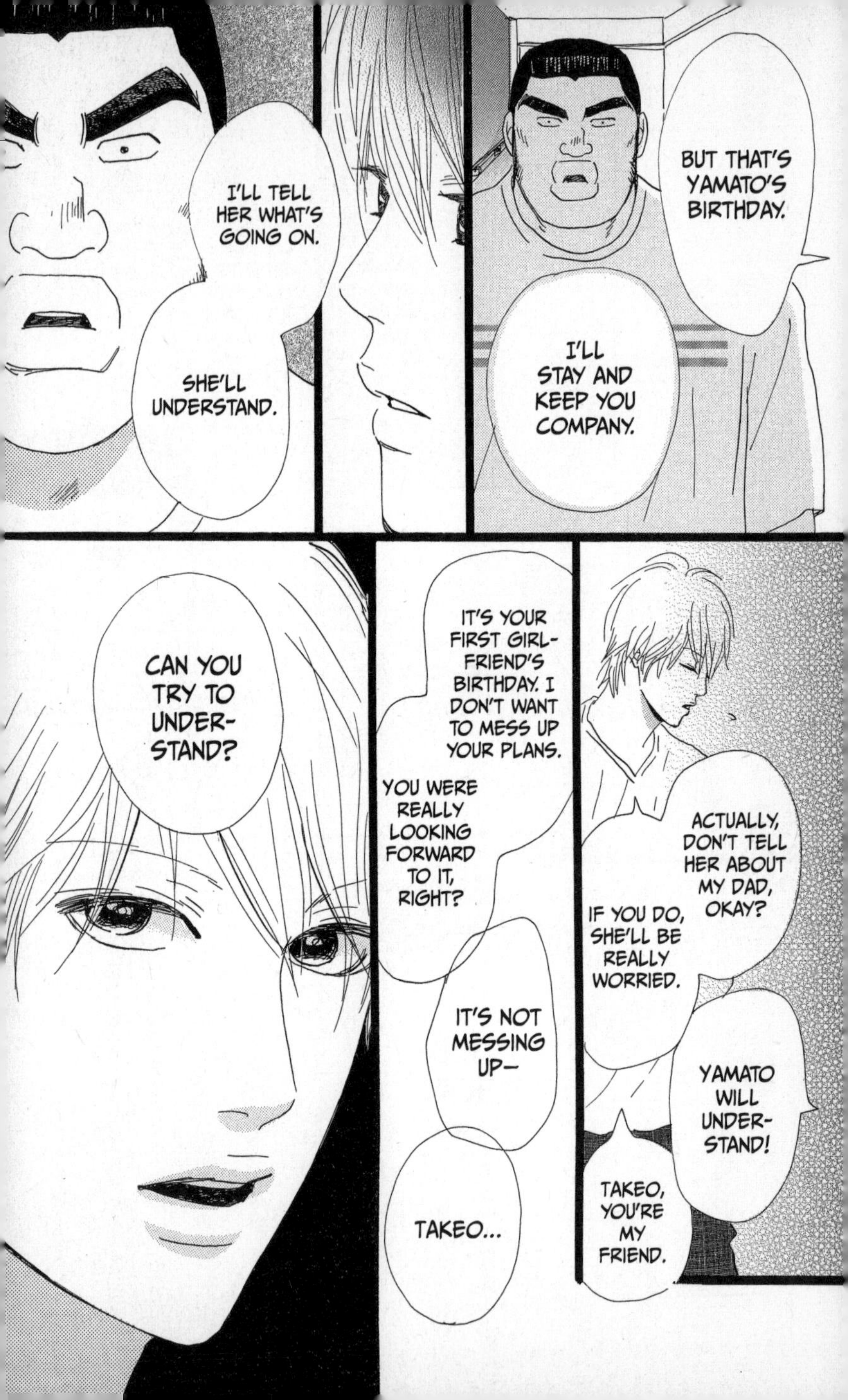
BUT THAT'S YAMATO'S BIRTHDAY.
I'LL STAY AND KEEP YOU COMPANY.
I'LL TELL HER WHAT'S GOING ON.
SHE'LL UNDERSTAND.
ACTUALLY, DON'T TELL HER ABOUT MY DAD, OKAY?
IF YOU DO, SHE'LL BE REALLY WORRIED.
YAMATO WILL UNDERSTAND!
TAKEO, YOU'RE MY FRIEND.
IT'S YOUR FIRST GIRL-FRIEND'S BIRTHDAY. I DON'T WANT TO MESS UP YOUR PLANS.
YOU WERE REALLY LOOKING FORWARD TO IT, RIGHT?
IT'S NOT MESSING UP—
TAKEO...
CAN YOU TRY TO UNDER-STAND?

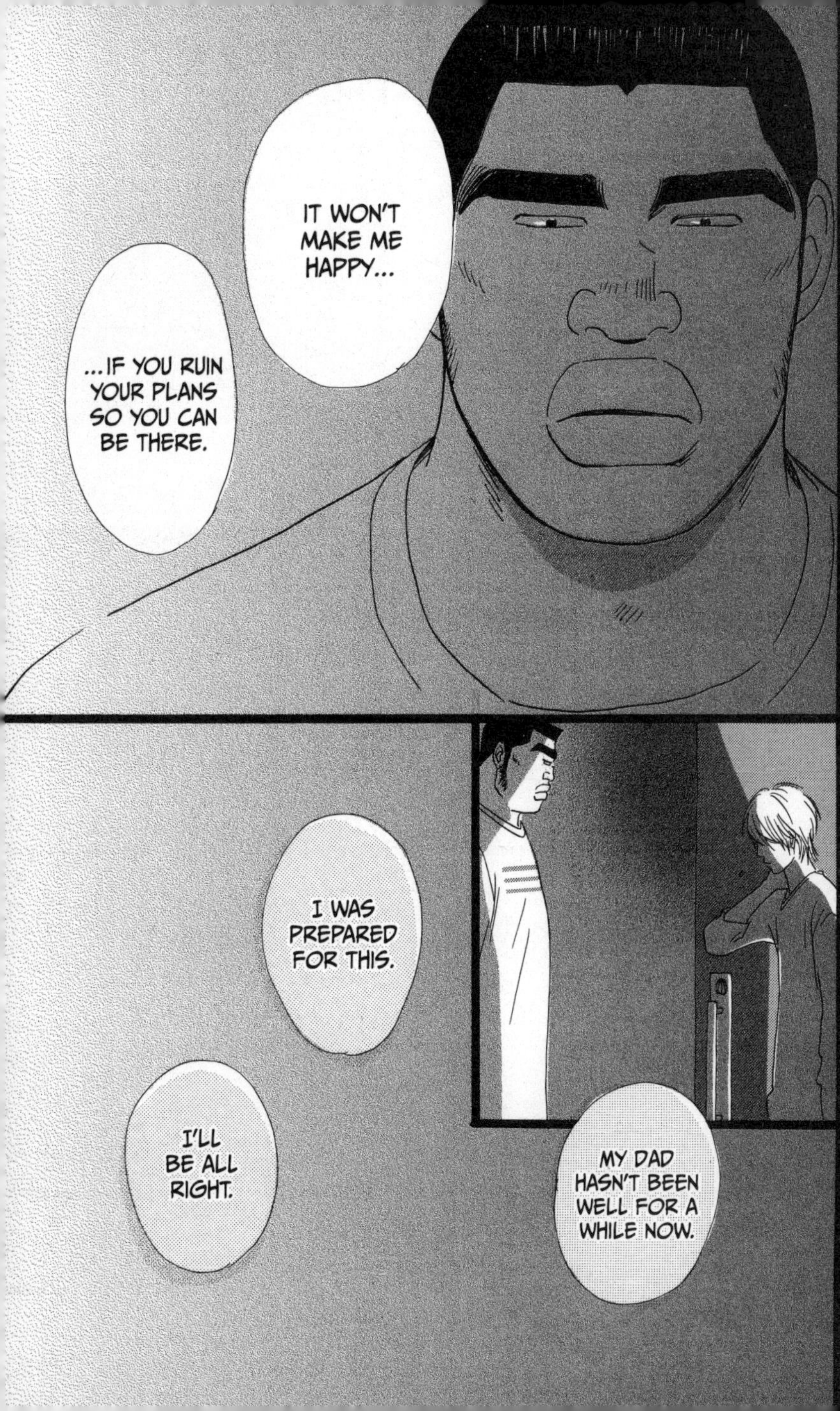
IT WON'T MAKE ME HAPPY...
...IF YOU RUIN YOUR PLANS SO YOU CAN BE THERE.
MY DAD HASN'T BEEN WELL FOR A WHILE NOW.
I WAS PREPARED FOR THIS.
I'LL BE ALL RIGHT.

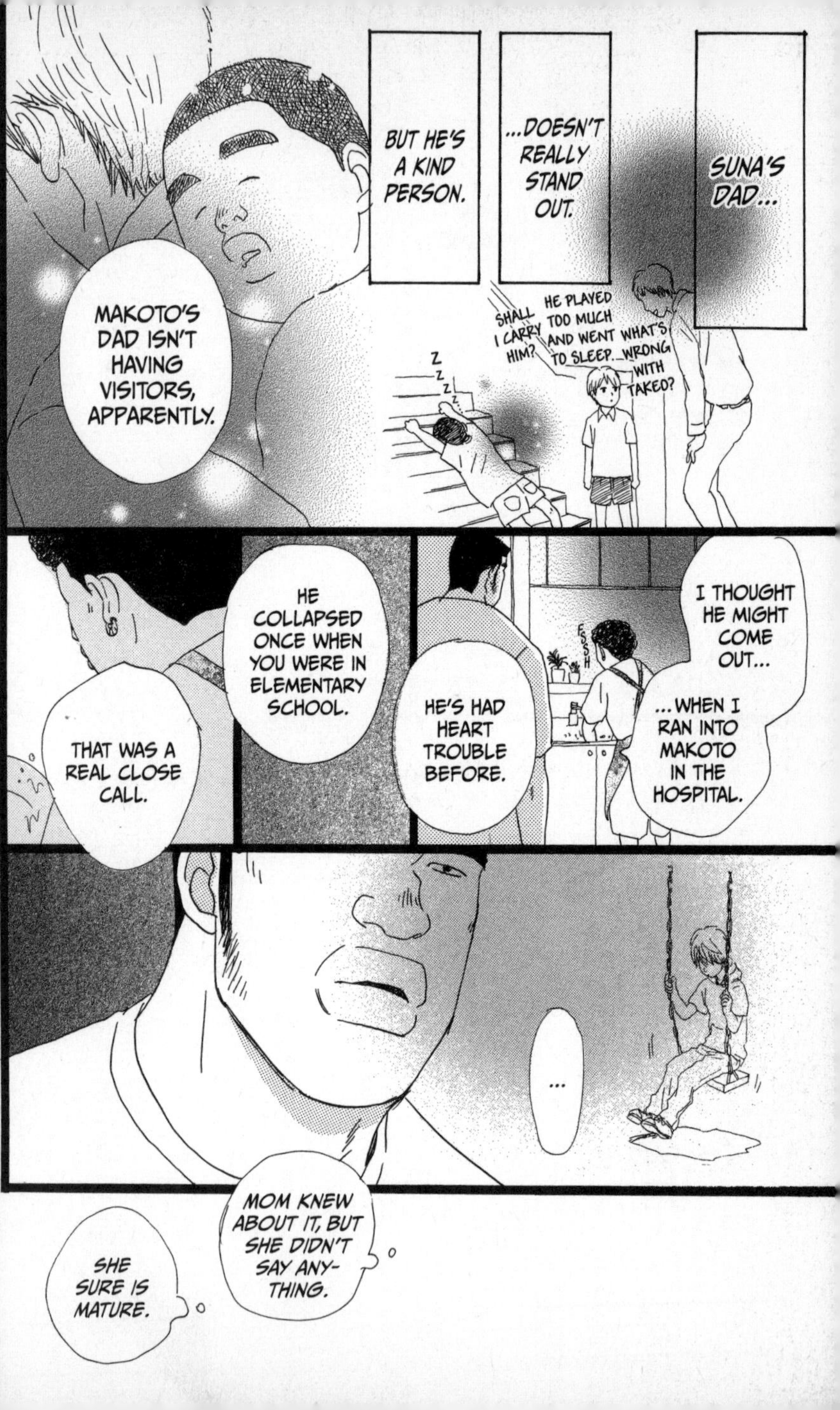
SUNA'S DAD...
...DOESN'T REALLY STAND OUT.
BUT HE'S A KIND PERSON.
WHAT'S WRONG WITH TAKEO?
HE PLAYED TOO MUCH AND WENT TO SLEEP.
SHALL I CARRY HIM?
Z Z Z Z
MAKOTO'S DAD ISN'T HAVING VISITORS, APPARENTLY.
I THOUGHT HE MIGHT COME OUT...
...WHEN I RAN INTO MAKOTO IN THE HOSPITAL.
FSSH
HE'S HAD HEART TROUBLE BEFORE.
HE COLLAPSED ONCE WHEN YOU WERE IN ELEMENTARY SCHOOL.
THAT WAS A REAL CLOSE CALL.
...
MOM KNEW ABOUT IT, BUT SHE DIDN'T SAY ANY-THING.
SHE SURE IS MATURE.

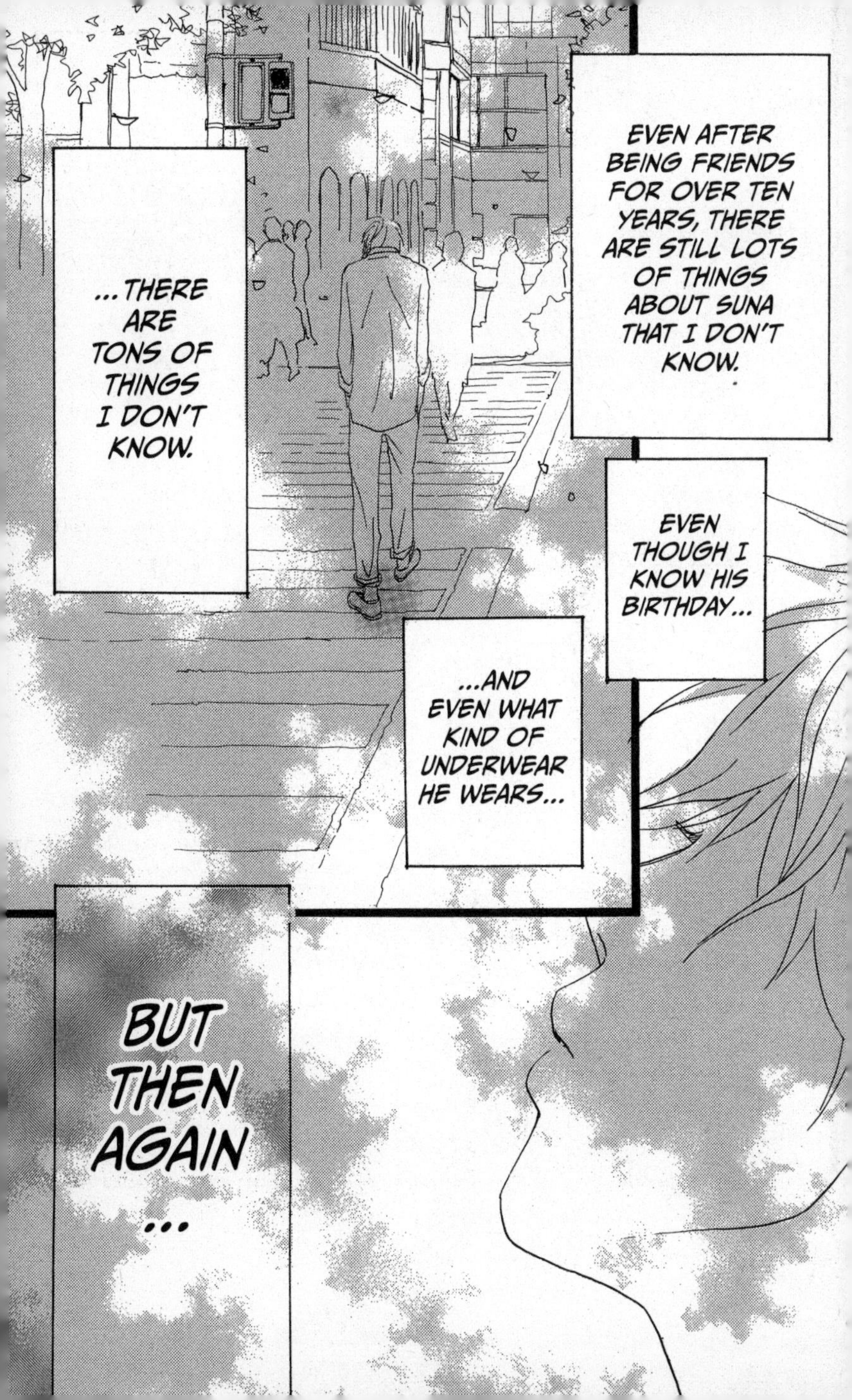
EVEN AFTER BEING FRIENDS FOR OVER TEN YEARS, THERE ARE STILL LOTS OF THINGS ABOUT SUNA THAT I DON'T KNOW.
EVEN THOUGH I KNOW HIS BIRTHDAY...
...AND EVEN WHAT KIND OF UNDERWEAR HE WEARS...
...THERE ARE TONS OF THINGS I DON'T KNOW.
BUT THEN AGAIN...

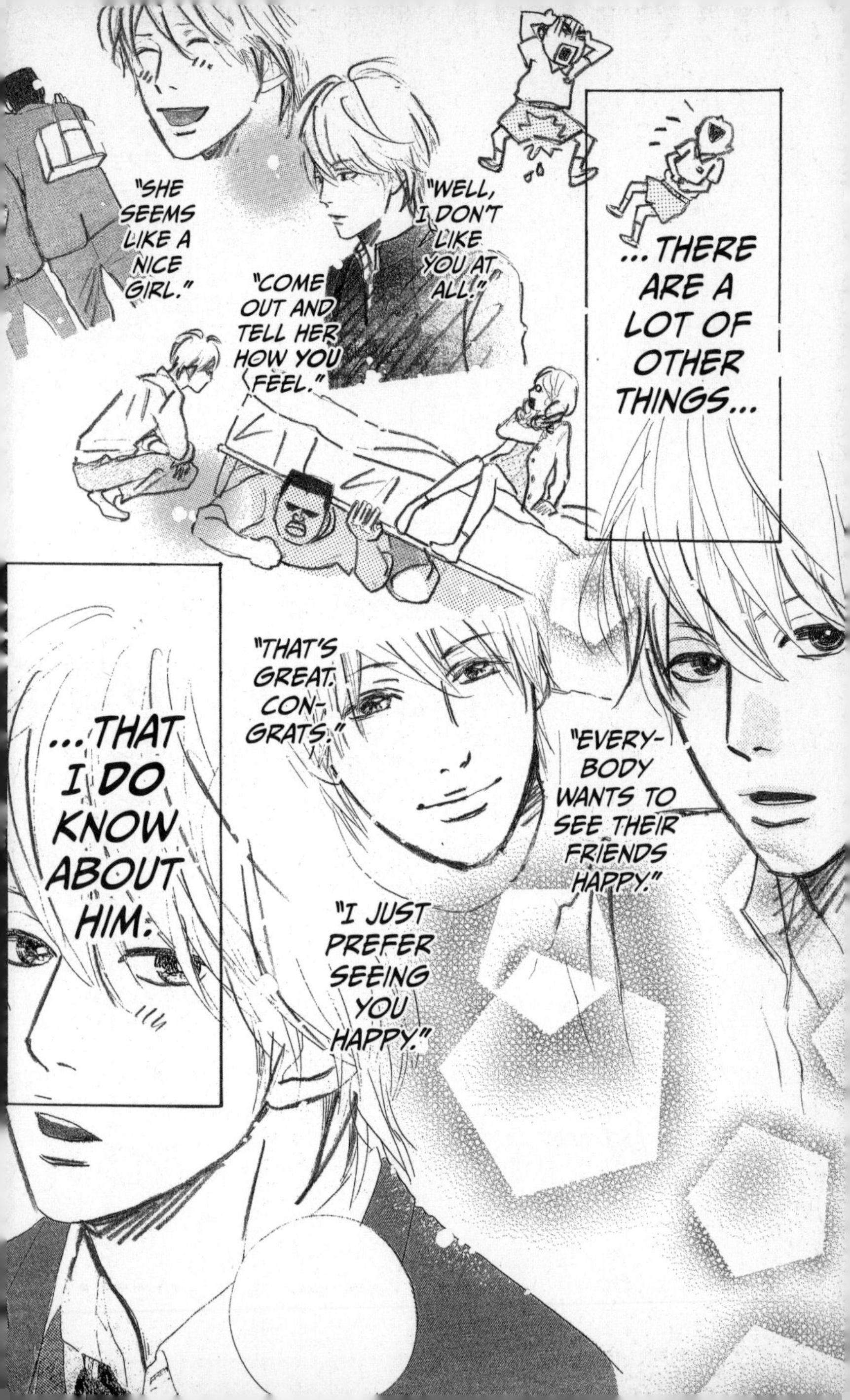
...THERE ARE A LOT OF OTHER THINGS...
"WELL, I DON'T LIKE YOU AT ALL!"
"SHE SEEMS LIKE A NICE GIRL."
"COME OUT AND TELL HER HOW YOU FEEL."
"EVERY-BODY WANTS TO SEE THEIR FRIENDS HAPPY."
"THAT'S GREAT. CON-GRATS."
"I JUST PREFER SEEING YOU HAPPY."
...THAT I DO KNOW ABOUT HIM.

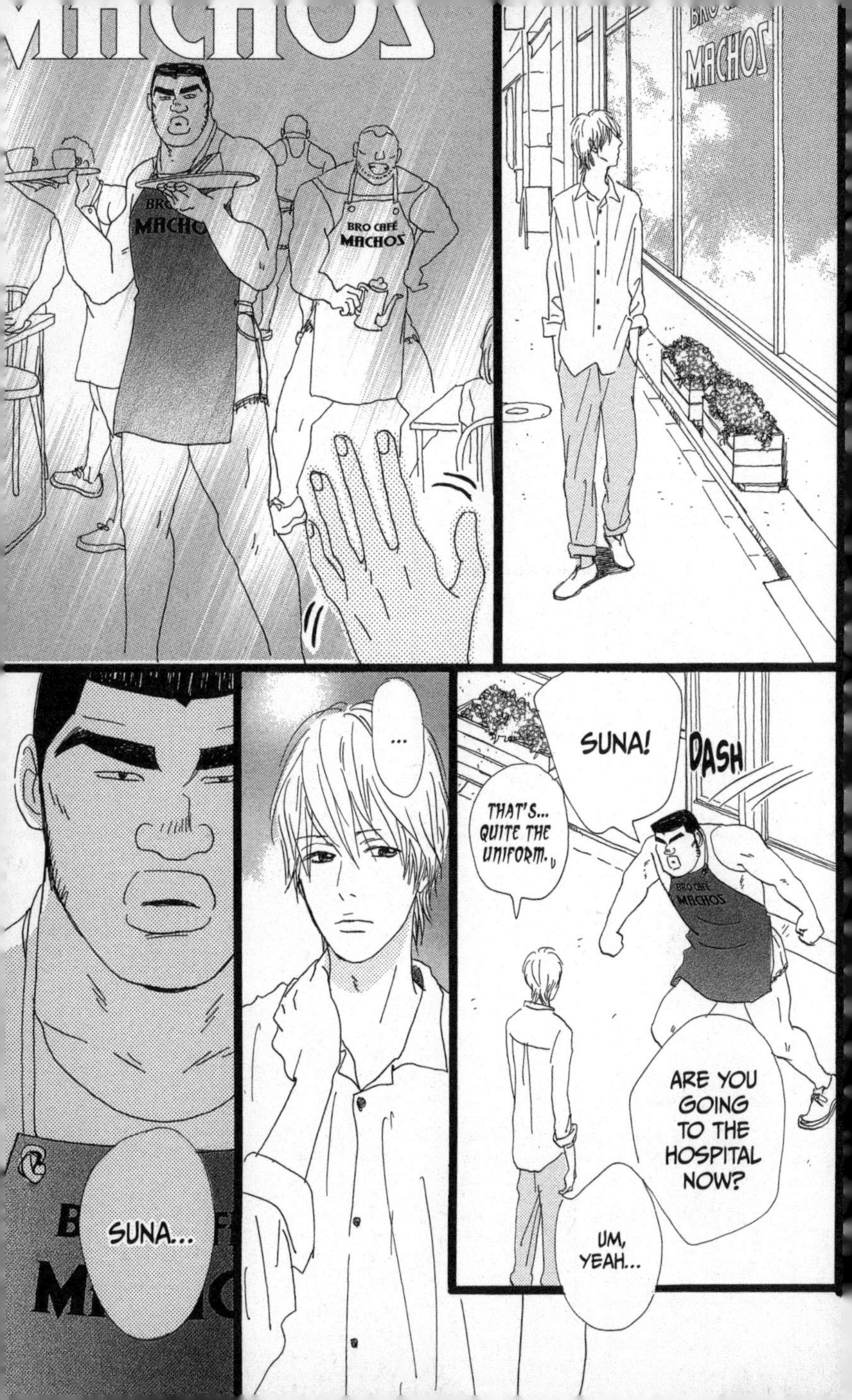
MACHOS
BRO CAFÉ MACHOS
SUNA!
DASH
THAT'S... QUITE THE UNIFORM.
ARE YOU GOING TO THE HOSPITAL NOW?
UM, YEAH...
...
SUNA...

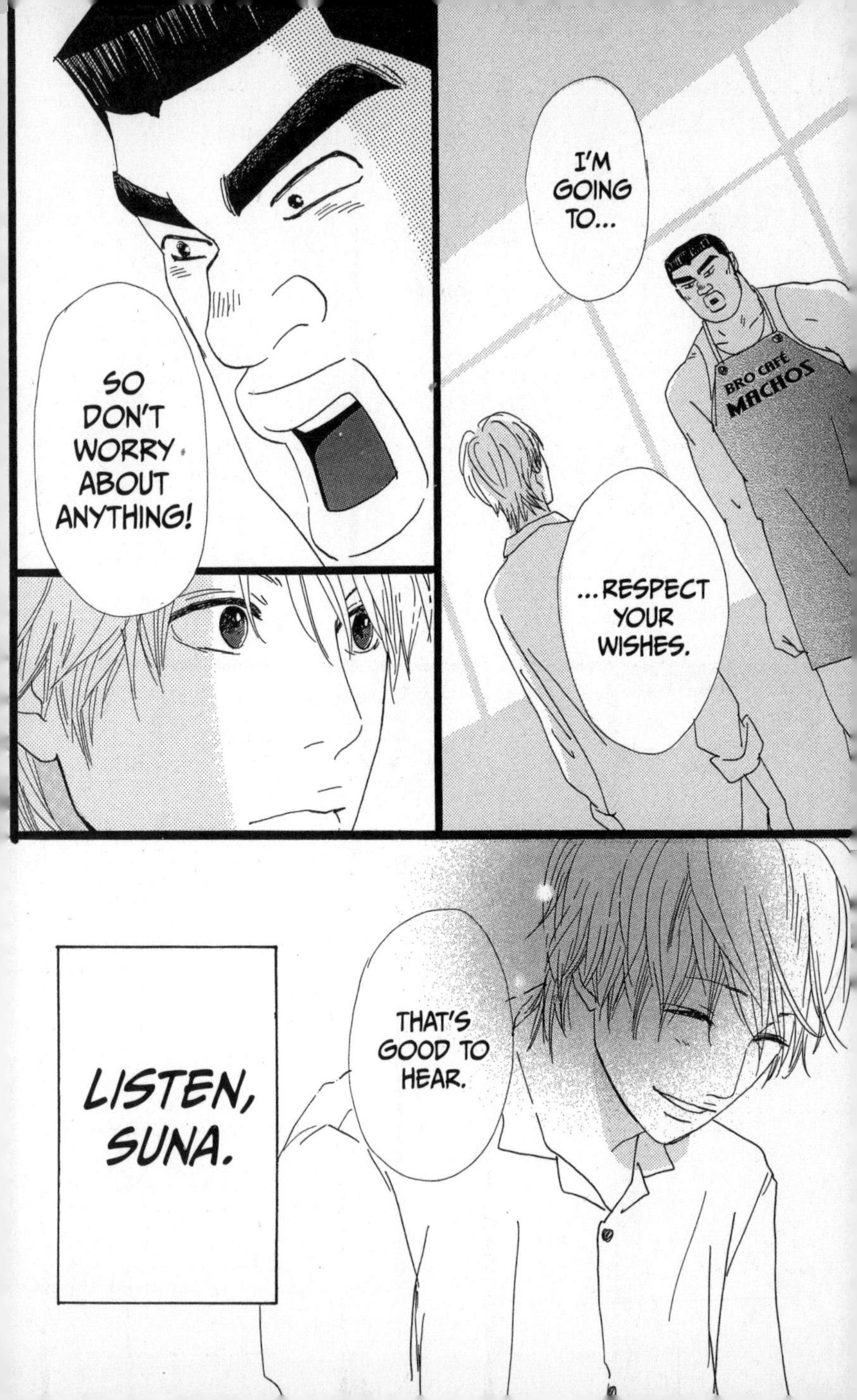
I'M GOING TO...
BRO CAFÉ
MACHOS
...RESPECT YOUR WISHES.
SO DON'T WORRY ABOUT ANYTHING!
THAT'S GOOD TO HEAR.
LISTEN, SUNA.

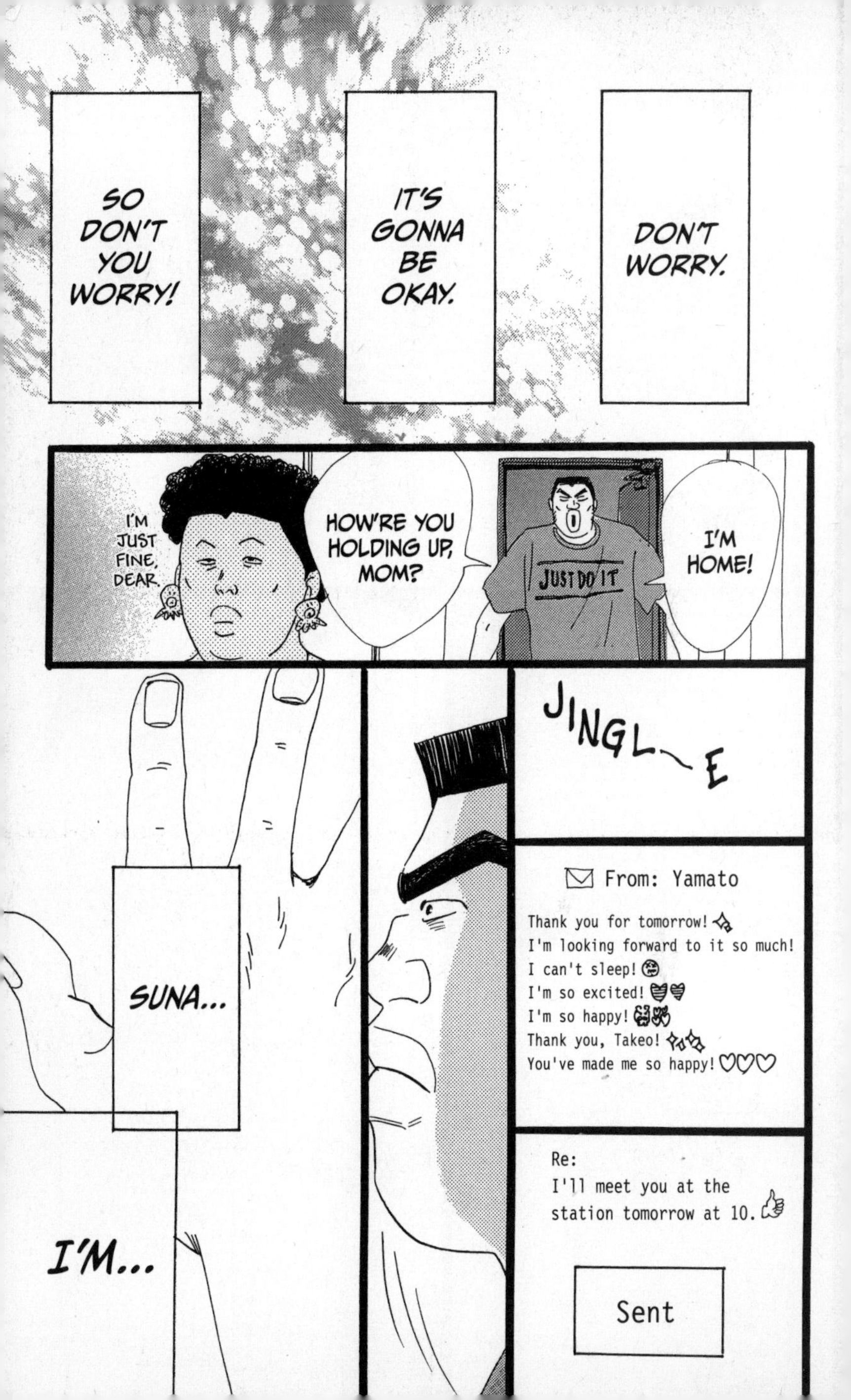
DON'T WORRY.
IT'S GONNA BE OKAY.
SO DON'T YOU WORRY!
I'M HOME!
JUST DO IT
HOW'RE YOU HOLDING UP, MOM?
I'M JUST FINE, DEAR.
JINGLE
From: Yamato
Thank you for tomorrow!
I'm looking forward to it so much!
I can't sleep!
I'm so excited!
I'm so happy!
Thank you, Takeo!
You've made me so happy!
Re:
I'll meet you at the station tomorrow at 10.
Sent
SUNA...
I'M...

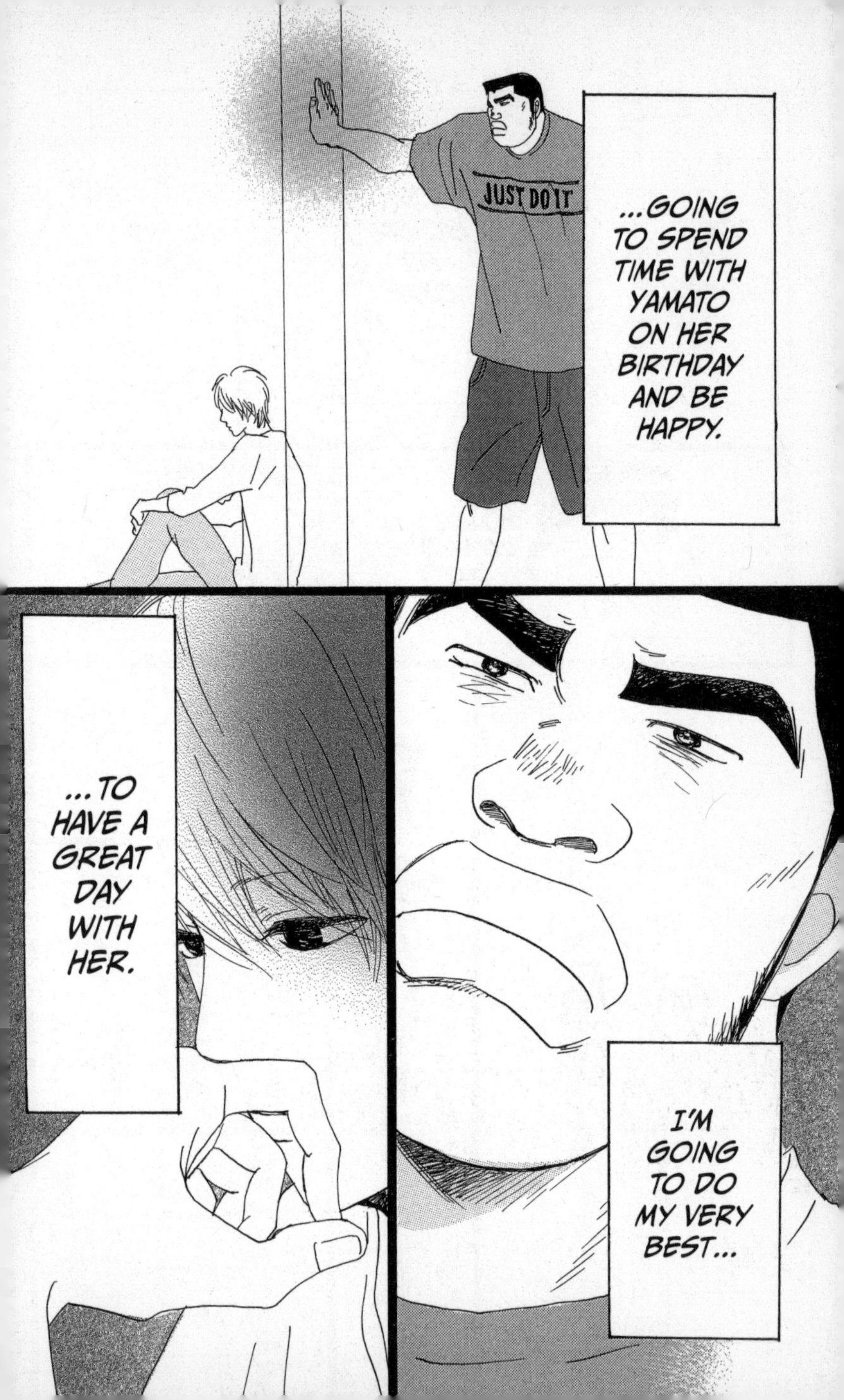
JUST DO IT
...GOING TO SPEND TIME WITH YAMATO ON HER BIRTHDAY AND BE HAPPY.
I'M GOING TO DO MY VERY BEST...
...TO HAVE A GREAT DAY WITH HER.

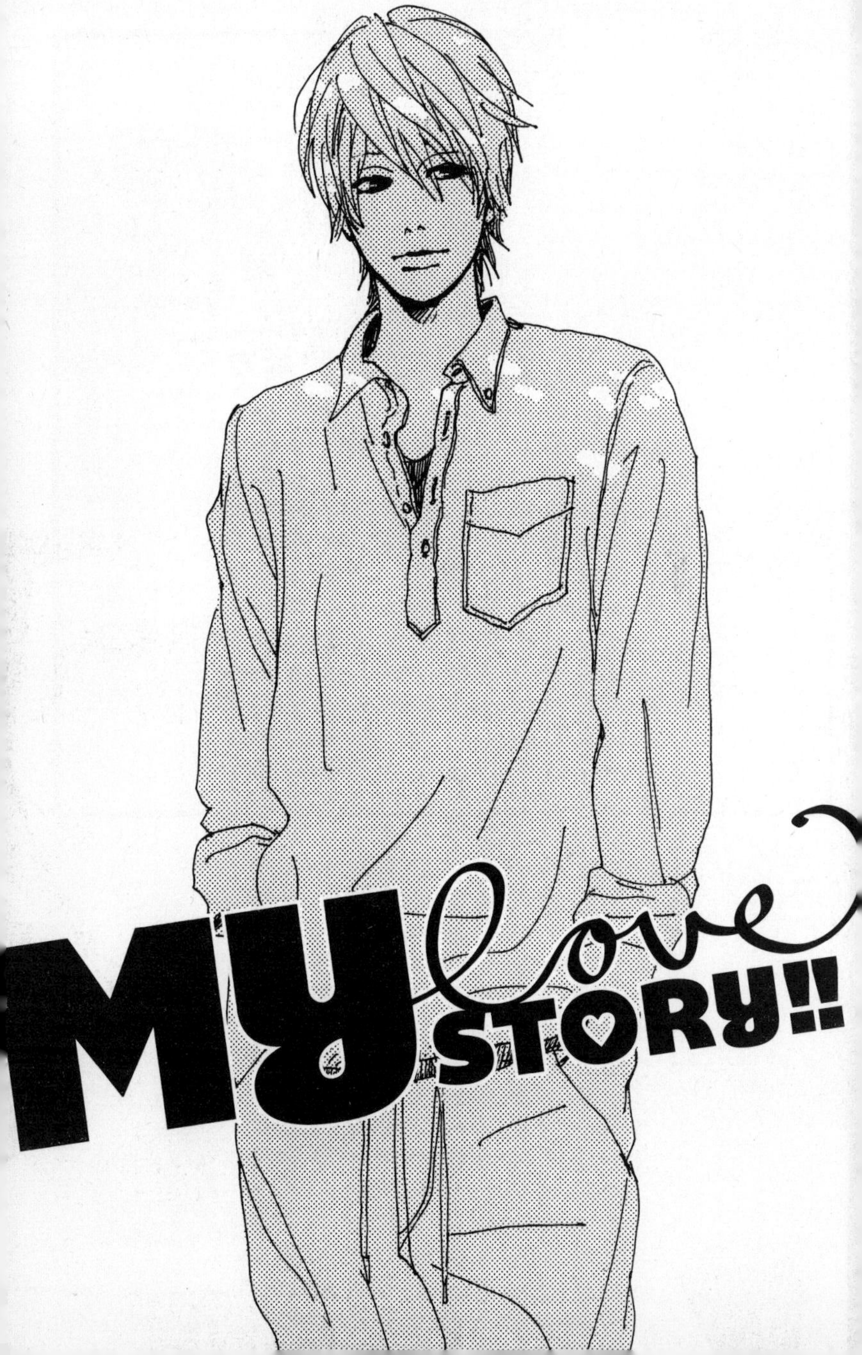
MY love STORY!!

AND...

FLASH

...GOING TO SPEND TIME WITH YAMATO ON HER BIRTHDAY AND BE HAPPY.

...TO HAVE A

...IT'S THE DAY SUNA'S DAD IS HAVING SURGERY.

TODAY IS YAMATO'S BIRTHDAY.

I'M GOING TO DO MY VERY BEST...

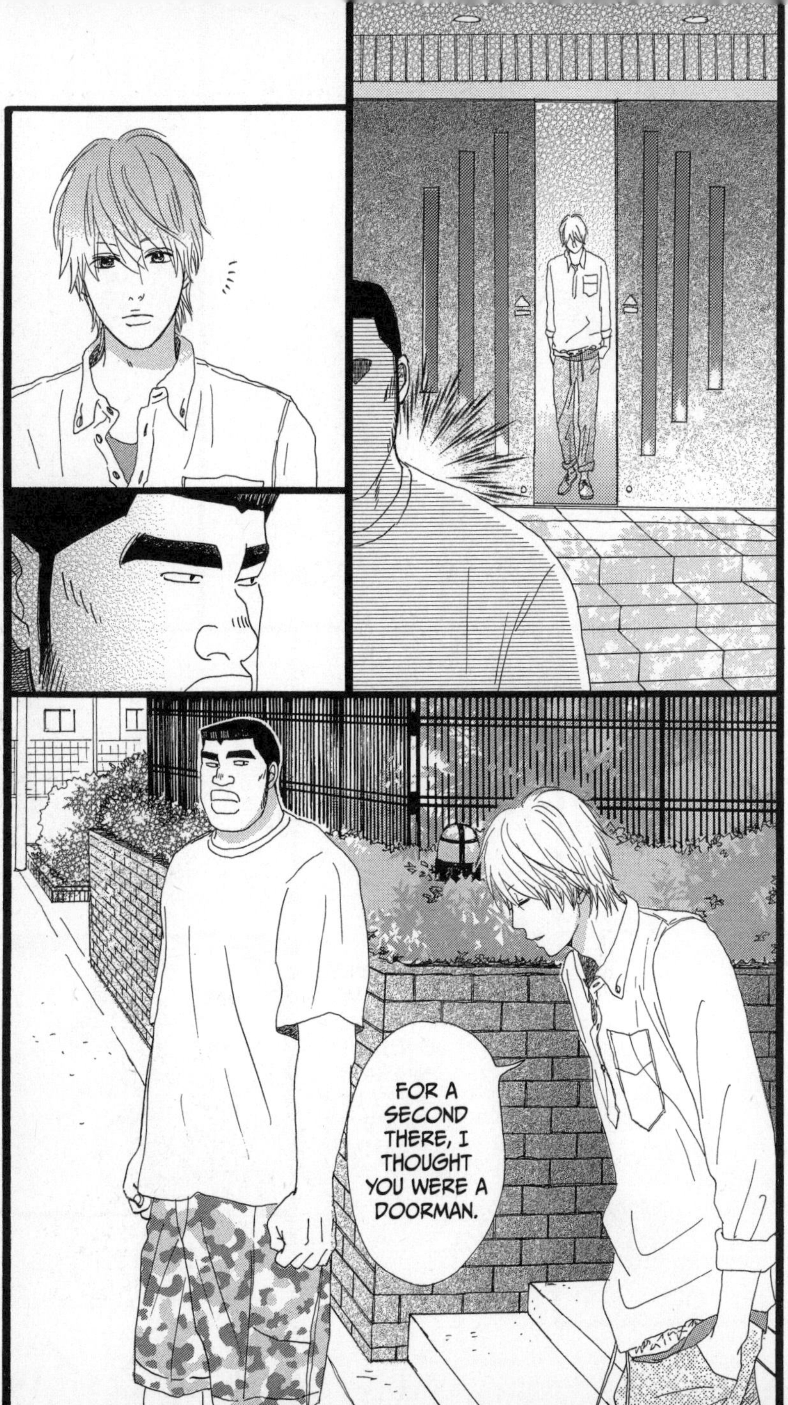
FOR A SECOND THERE, I THOUGHT YOU WERE A DOORMAN.

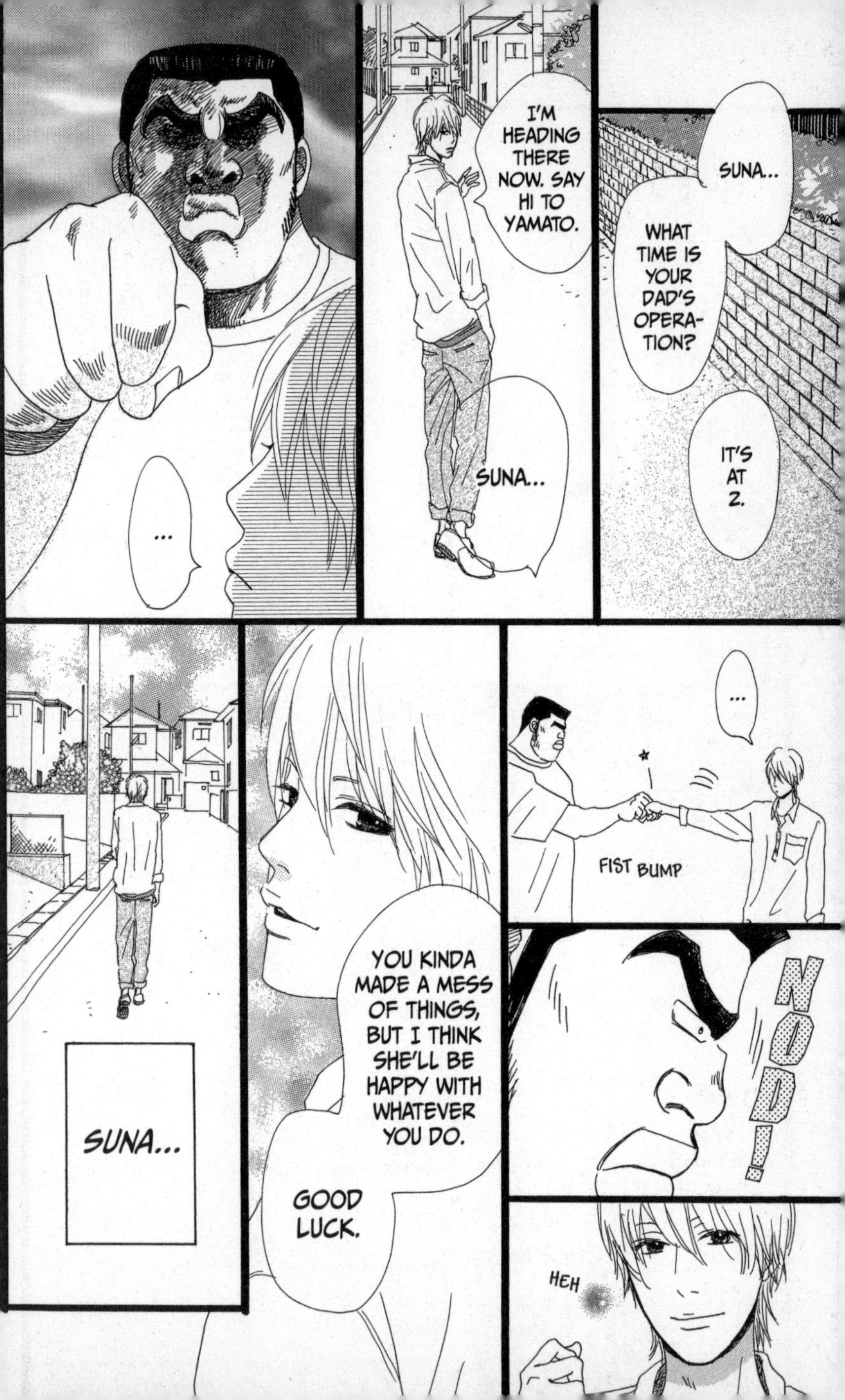
SUNA...
WHAT TIME IS YOUR DAD'S OPERATION?
IT'S AT 2.
I'M HEADING THERE NOW. SAY HI TO YAMATO.
SUNA...
...
...
FIST BUMP
NOD!
HEH
YOU KINDA MADE A MESS OF THINGS, BUT I THINK SHE'LL BE HAPPY WITH WHATEVER YOU DO.
GOOD LUCK.
SUNA...

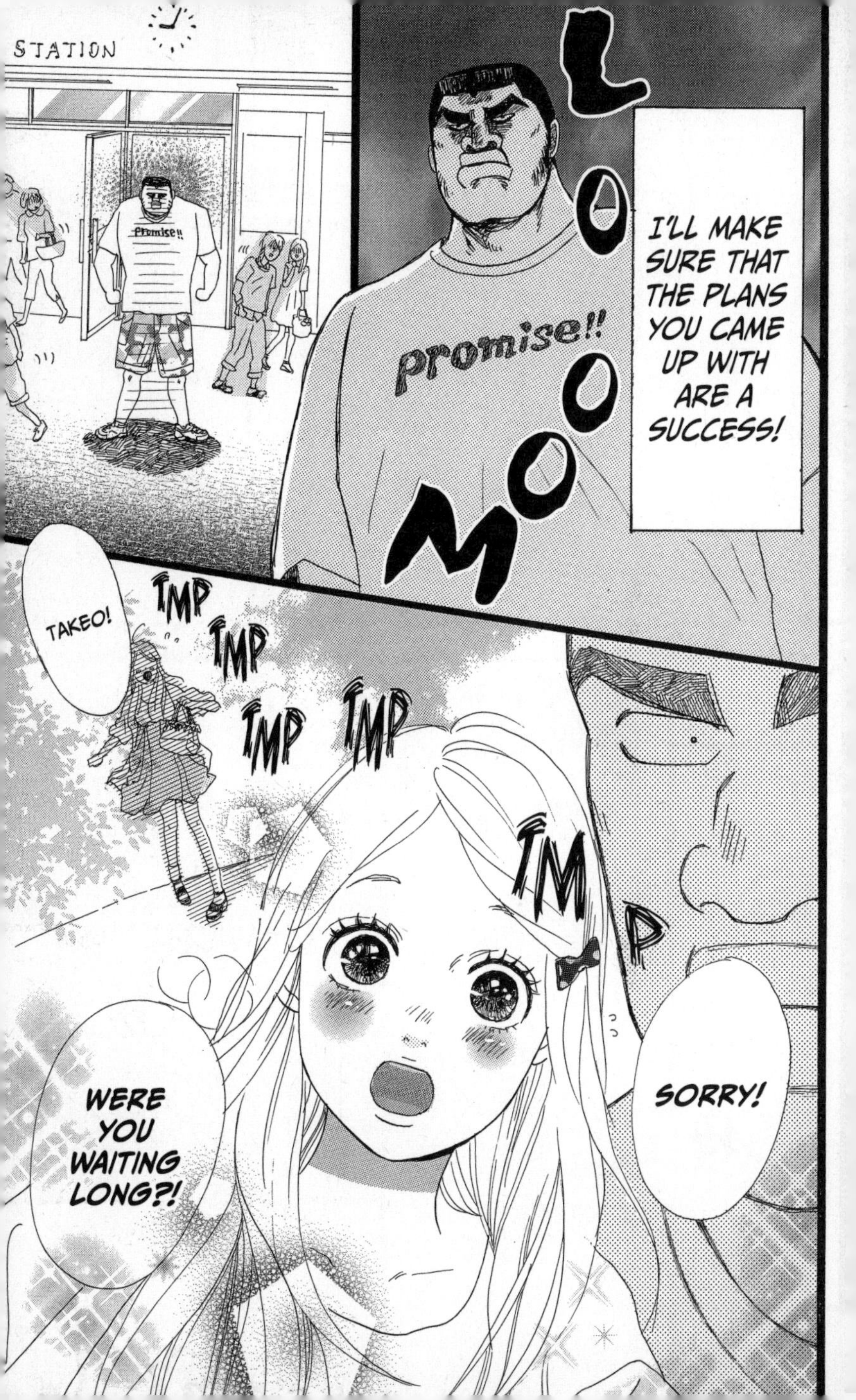
LOOOM
I'LL MAKE SURE THAT THE PLANS YOU CAME UP WITH ARE A SUCCESS!
STATION
promise!!
TMP TMP TMP TMP TMP
TAKEO!
SORRY!
WERE YOU WAITING LONG?!

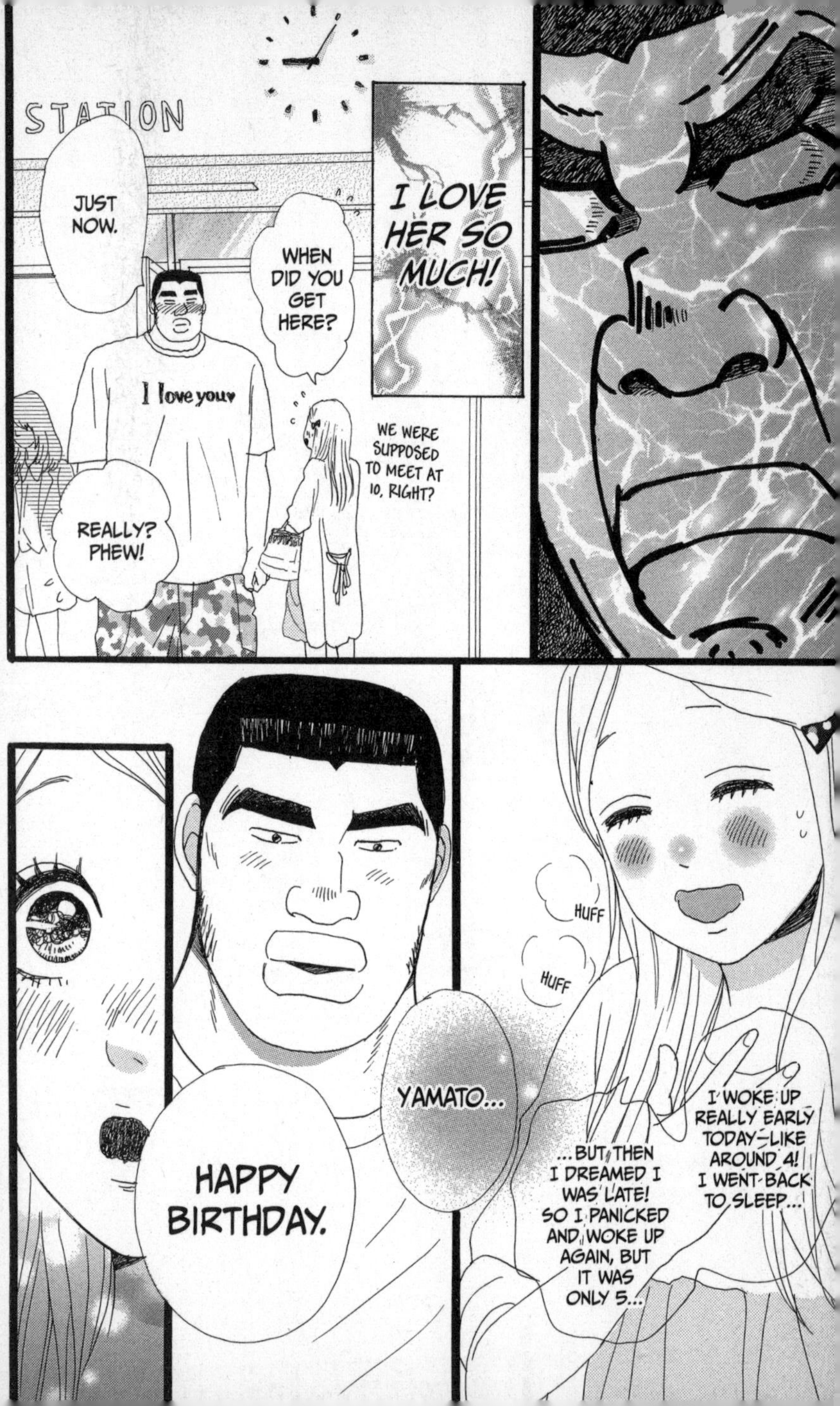
I LOVE HER SO MUCH!
STATION
WHEN DID YOU GET HERE?
JUST NOW.
I love you♥
WE WERE SUPPOSED TO MEET AT 10, RIGHT?
REALLY? PHEW!
HUFF
HUFF
I WOKE UP REALLY EARLY TODAY—LIKE AROUND 4! I WENT BACK TO SLEEP...
...BUT THEN I DREAMED I WAS LATE! SO I PANICKED AND WOKE UP AGAIN, BUT IT WAS ONLY 5...
YAMATO...
HAPPY BIRTHDAY.

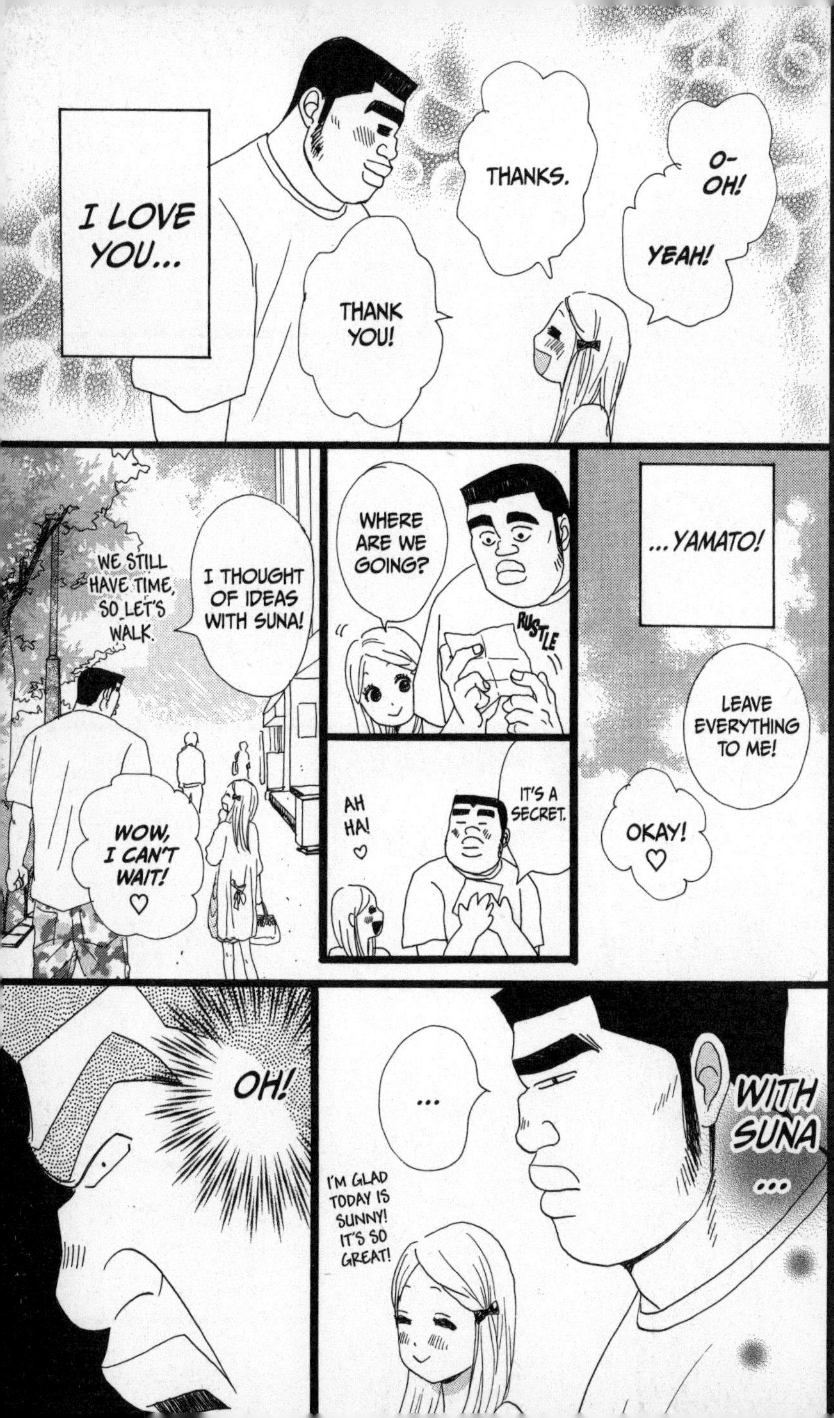
O-OH! YEAH!
THANKS.
I LOVE YOU...
THANK YOU!
...YAMATO!
LEAVE EVERYTHING TO ME!
OKAY! ♡
WHERE ARE WE GOING?
RUSTLE
IT'S A SECRET.
AH HA! ♡
I THOUGHT OF IDEAS WITH SUNA!
WE STILL HAVE TIME, SO LET'S WALK.
WOW, I CAN'T WAIT! ♡
WITH SUNA...
...
I'M GLAD TODAY IS SUNNY! IT'S SO GREAT!
OH!

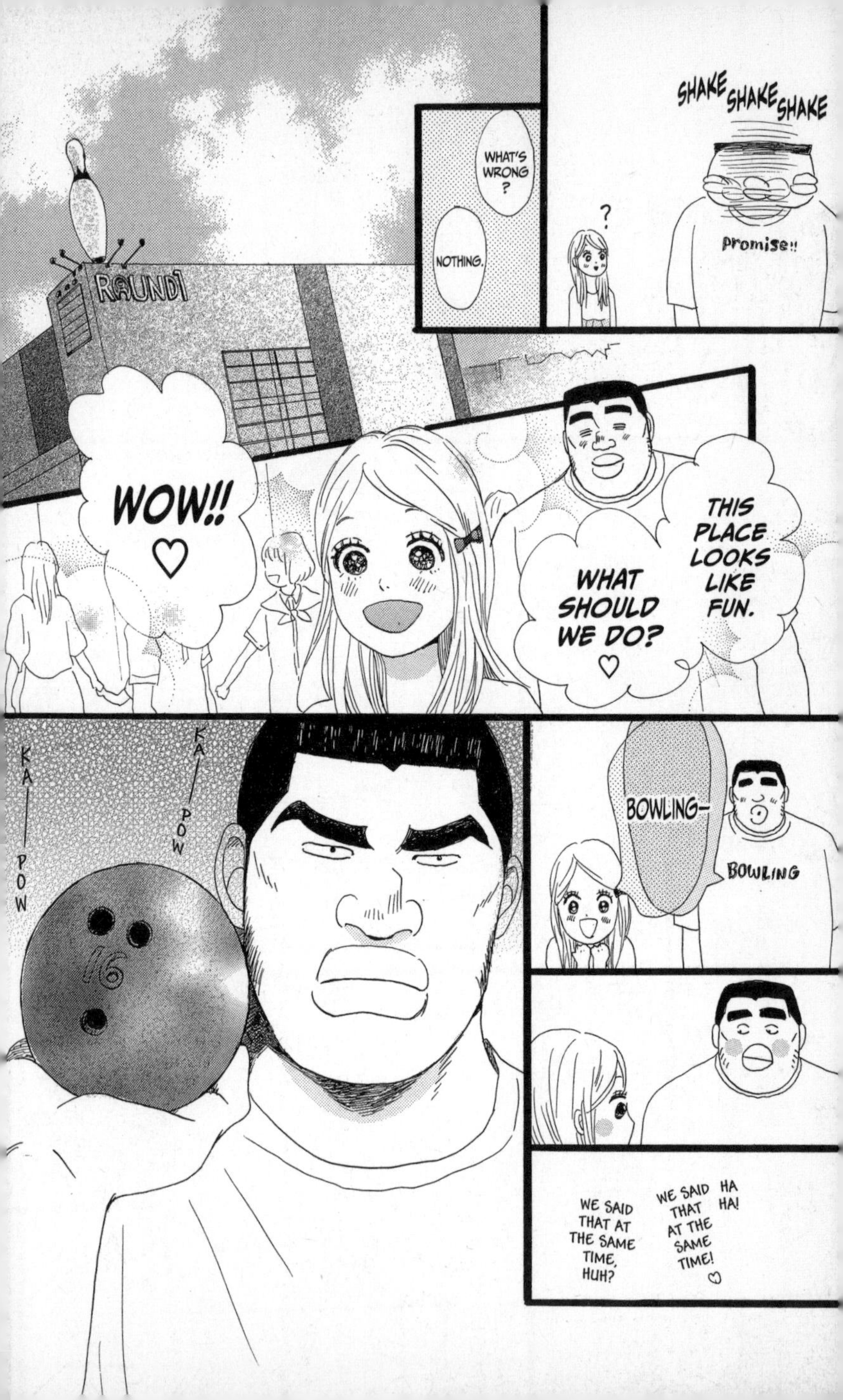

SHAKE SHAKE SHAKE
promise!!
WHAT'S WRONG?
NOTHING.
?
RAUND1
THIS PLACE LOOKS LIKE FUN.
WHAT SHOULD WE DO? ♡
WOW!! ♡
BOWLING—
BOWLING
HA HA!
WE SAID THAT AT THE SAME TIME! ♡
WE SAID THAT AT THE SAME TIME, HUH?
KA-POW
KA-POW

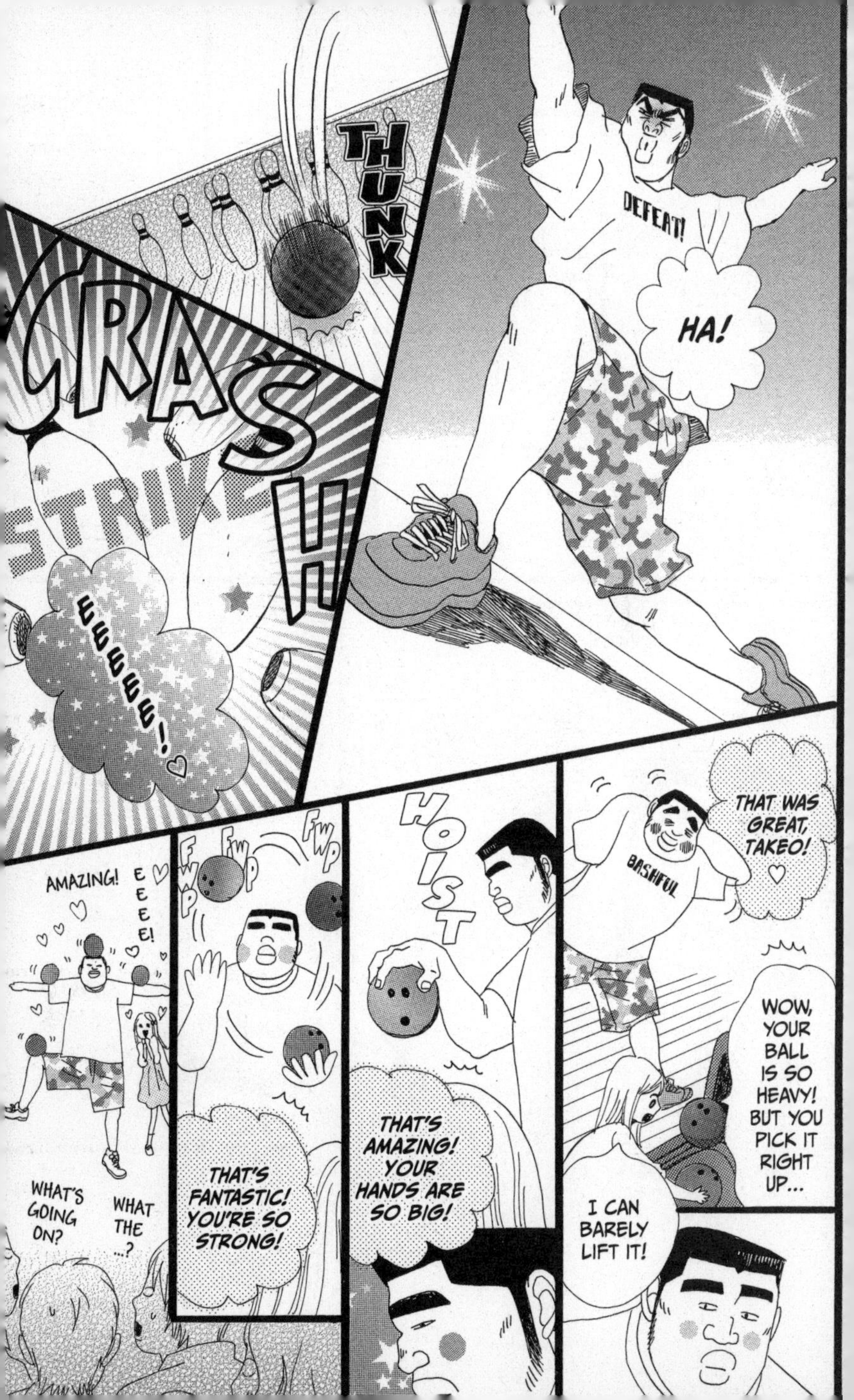
DEFEAT!
HA!
THUNK
CRASH
STRIKE
EEEEEE! ♡
BASHFUL
THAT WAS GREAT, TAKEO! ♡
WOW, YOUR BALL IS SO HEAVY! BUT YOU PICK IT RIGHT UP...
I CAN BARELY LIFT IT!
HOIST
THAT'S AMAZING! YOUR HANDS ARE SO BIG!
FWP
FWP
FWP
FWP
THAT'S FANTASTIC! YOU'RE SO STRONG!
EEEE! ♡
AMAZING! ♡
WHAT THE ...?
WHAT'S GOING ON?

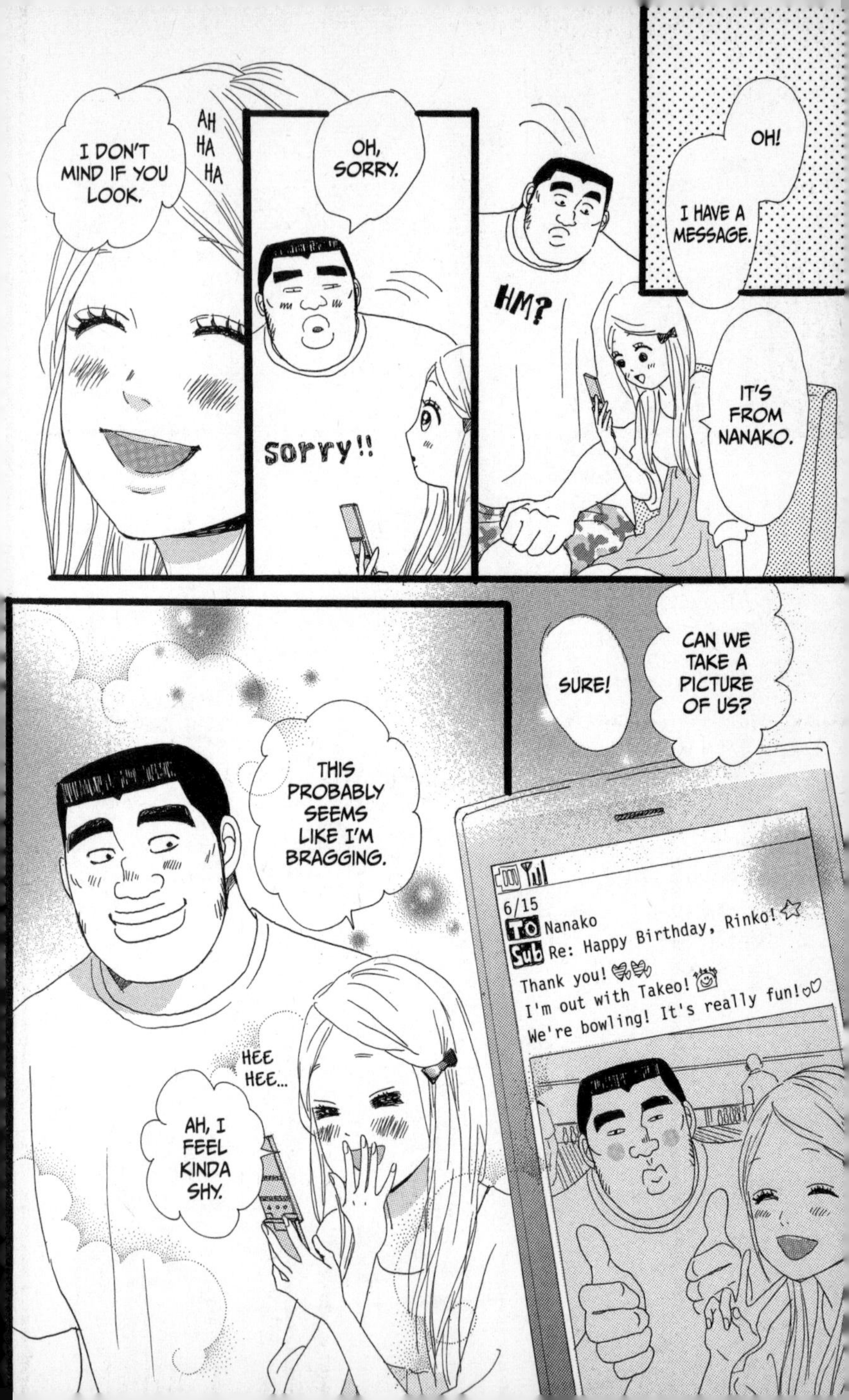
OH!
I HAVE A MESSAGE.
HM?
IT'S FROM NANAKO.
OH, SORRY.
SORRY!!
AH HA HA
I DON'T MIND IF YOU LOOK.
CAN WE TAKE A PICTURE OF US?
SURE!
6/15
To Nanako
Sub Re: Happy Birthday, Rinko!
Thank you!
I'm out with Takeo!
We're bowling! It's really fun!
THIS PROBABLY SEEMS LIKE I'M BRAGGING.
HEE HEE...
AH, I FEEL KINDA SHY.

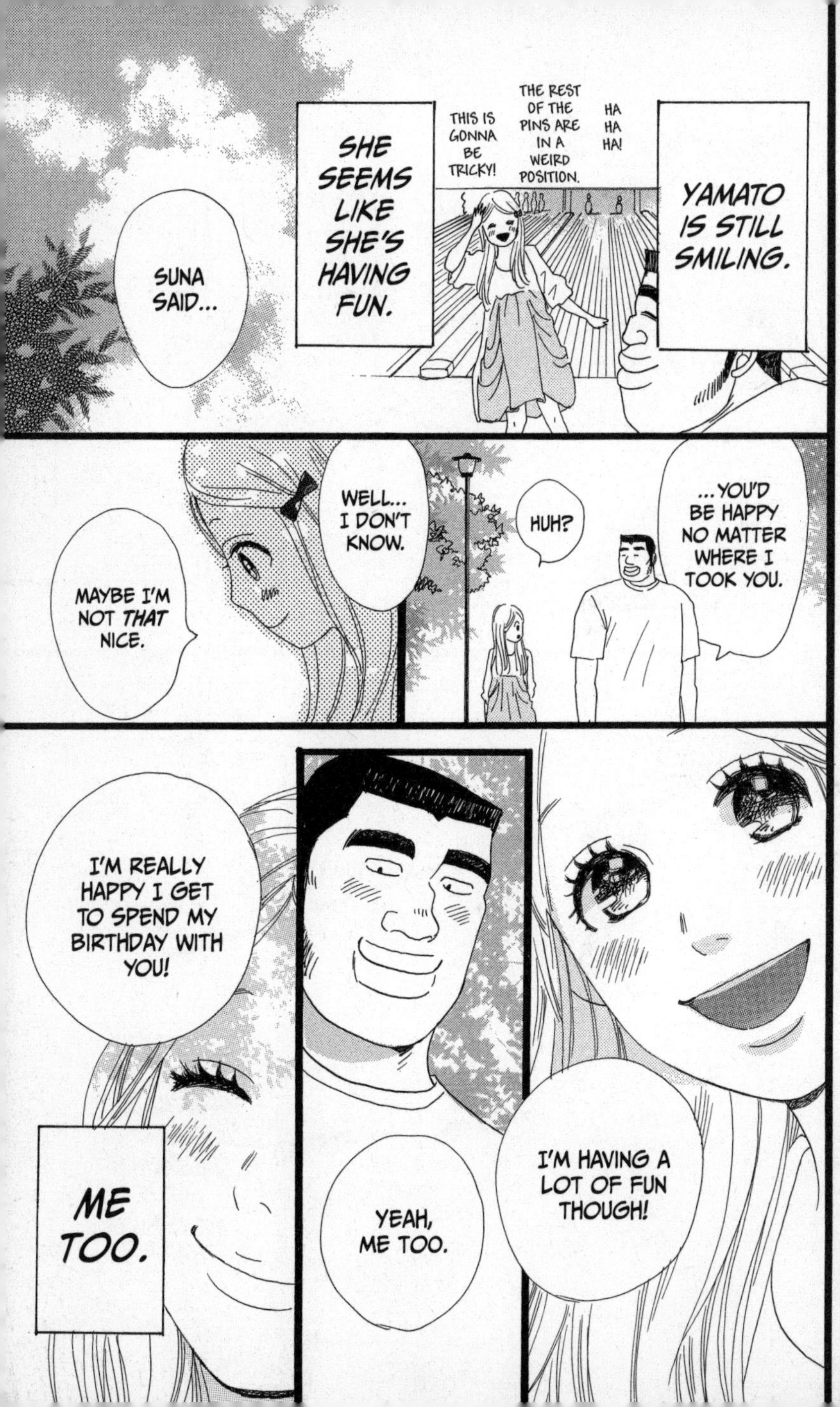
YAMATO IS STILL SMILING.
HA HA HA!
THE REST OF THE PINS ARE IN A WEIRD POSITION.
THIS IS GONNA BE TRICKY!
SHE SEEMS LIKE SHE'S HAVING FUN.
SUNA SAID...
...YOU'D BE HAPPY NO MATTER WHERE I TOOK YOU.
HUH?
WELL... I DON'T KNOW.
MAYBE I'M NOT *THAT* NICE.
I'M HAVING A LOT OF FUN THOUGH!
YEAH, ME TOO.
I'M REALLY HAPPY I GET TO SPEND MY BIRTHDAY WITH YOU!
ME TOO.

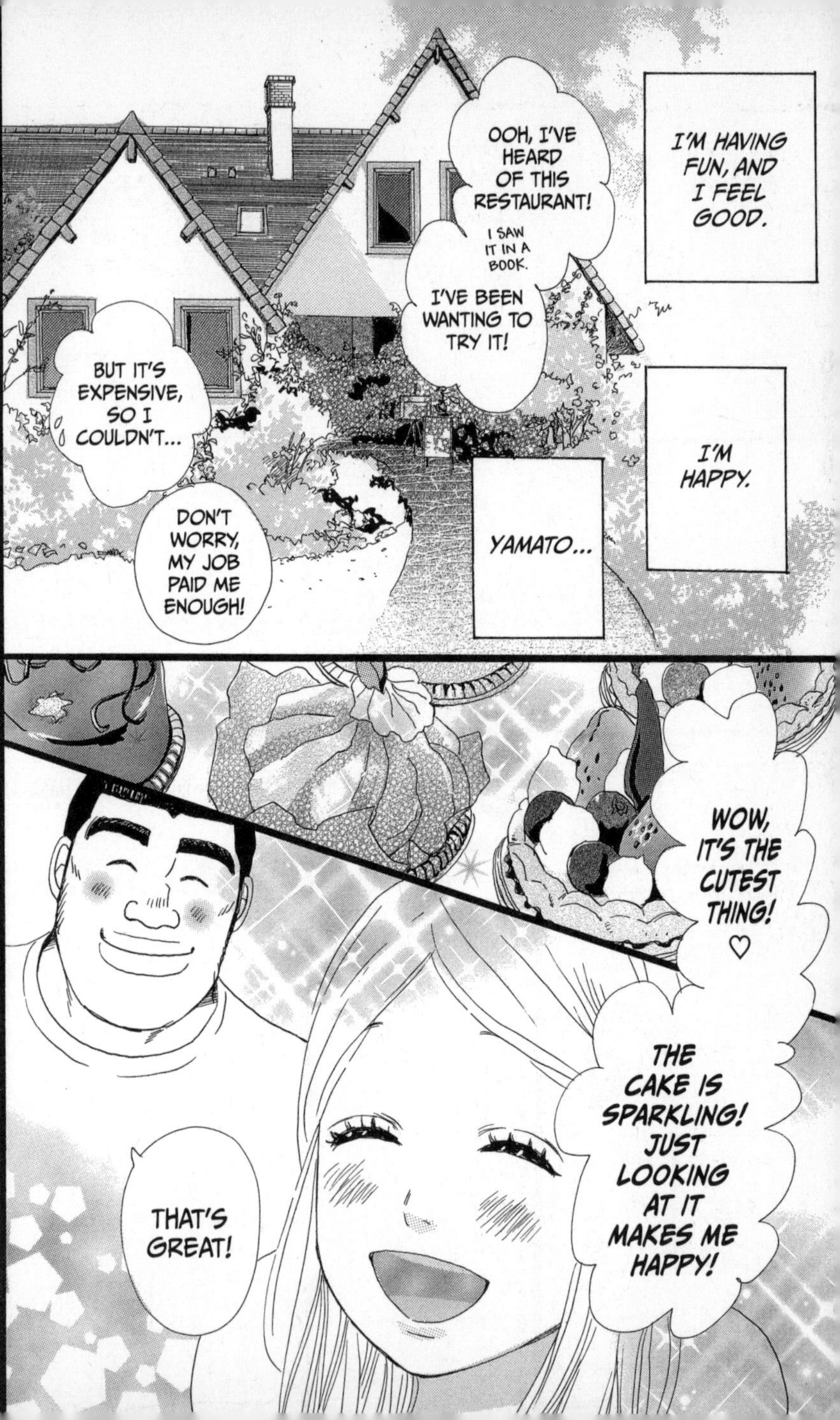
I'M HAVING FUN, AND I FEEL GOOD.
OOH, I'VE HEARD OF THIS RESTAURANT!
I SAW IT IN A BOOK.
I'VE BEEN WANTING TO TRY IT!
I'M HAPPY.
YAMATO...
BUT IT'S EXPENSIVE, SO I COULDN'T...
DON'T WORRY, MY JOB PAID ME ENOUGH!
WOW, IT'S THE CUTEST THING! ♡
THE CAKE IS SPARKLING! JUST LOOKING AT IT MAKES ME HAPPY!
THAT'S GREAT!

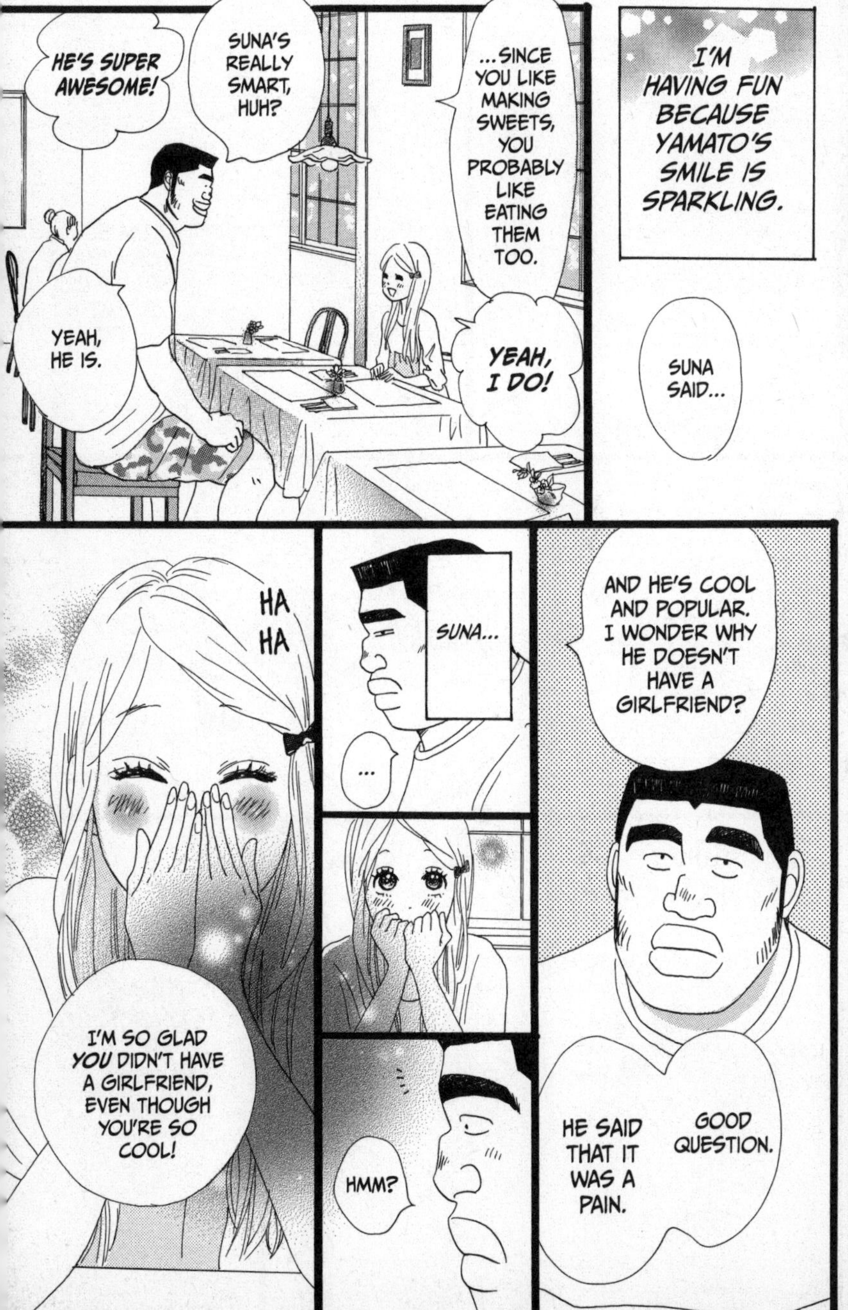
I'M HAVING FUN BECAUSE YAMATO'S SMILE IS SPARKLING.
SUNA SAID...
...SINCE YOU LIKE MAKING SWEETS, YOU PROBABLY LIKE EATING THEM TOO.
YEAH, I DO!
SUNA'S REALLY SMART, HUH?
HE'S SUPER AWESOME!
YEAH, HE IS.
AND HE'S COOL AND POPULAR. I WONDER WHY HE DOESN'T HAVE A GIRLFRIEND?
GOOD QUESTION.
HE SAID THAT IT WAS A PAIN.
SUNA...
...
HMM?
HA HA
I'M SO GLAD *YOU* DIDN'T HAVE A GIRLFRIEND, EVEN THOUGH YOU'RE SO COOL!

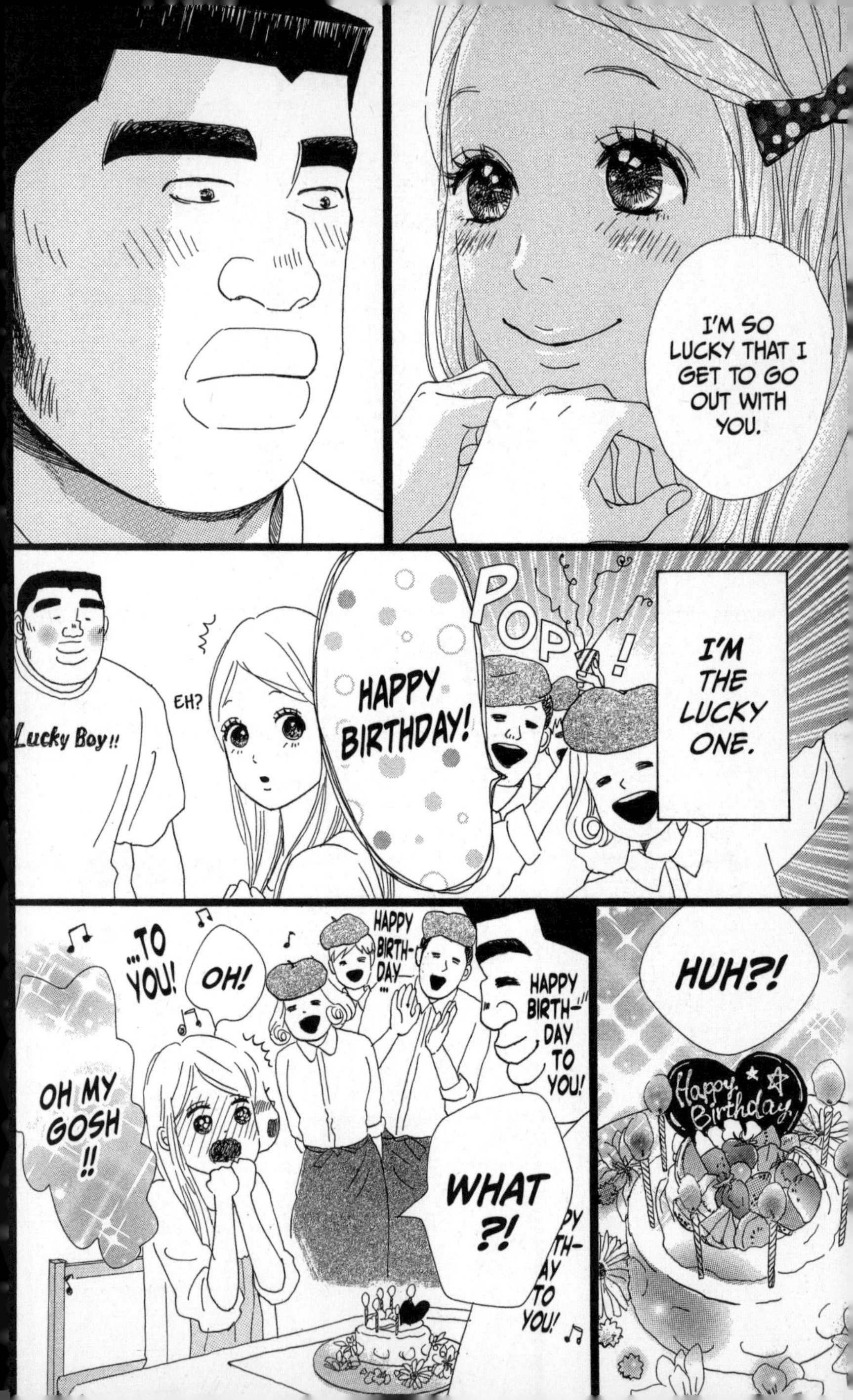
I'M SO LUCKY THAT I GET TO GO OUT WITH YOU.
I'M THE LUCKY ONE.
POP!
HAPPY BIRTHDAY!
EH?
Lucky Boy!!
HUH?!
Happy Birthday
HAPPY BIRTH-DAY TO YOU!
HAPPY BIRTH-DAY...
OH!
...TO YOU!
WHAT?!
TO YOU!
OH MY GOSH!!

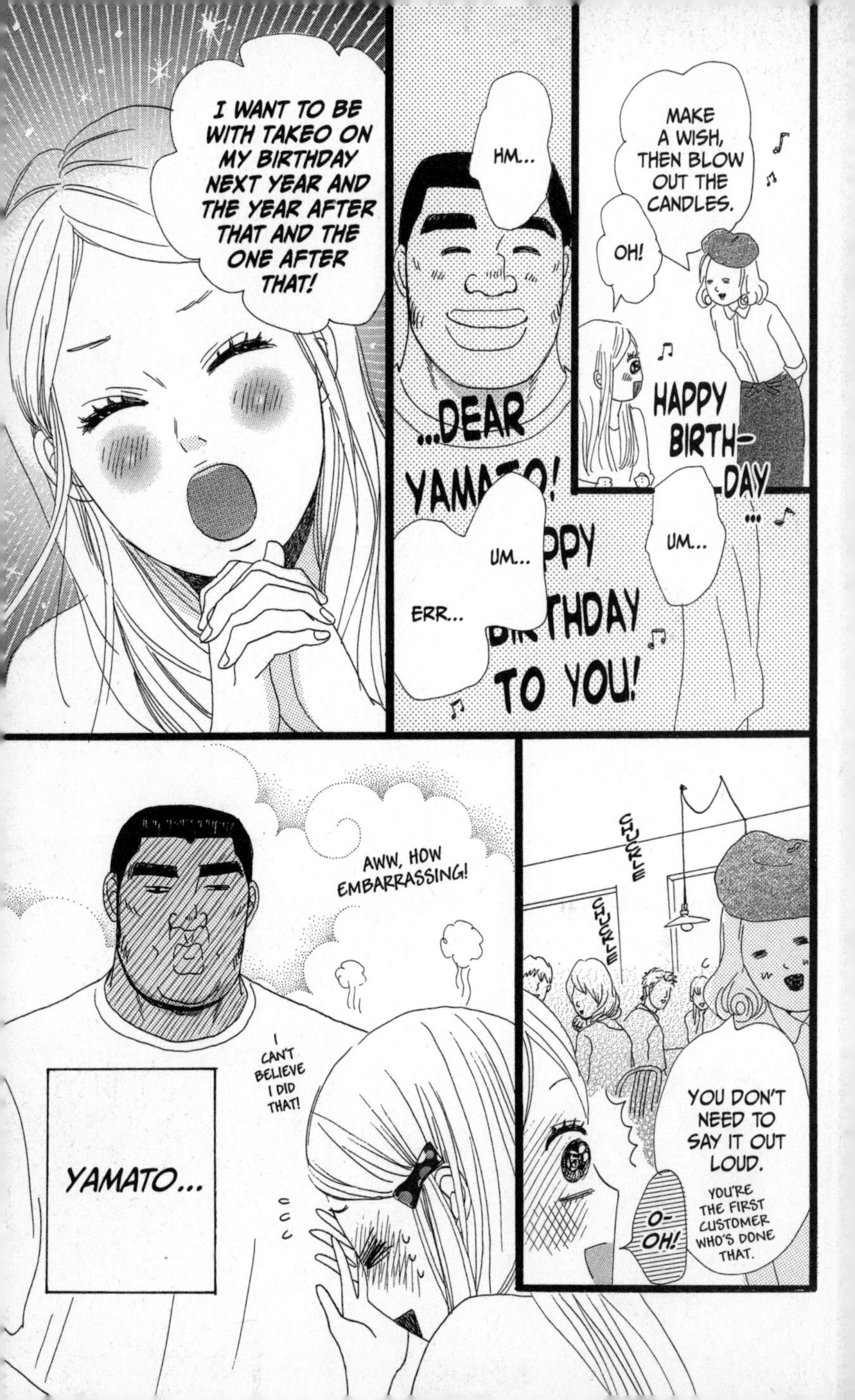

MAKE A WISH, THEN BLOW OUT THE CANDLES.
OH!
HAPPY BIRTH-DAY...
UM...
HM...
...DEAR YAMATO! HAPPY BIRTHDAY TO YOU!
UM...
ERR...
I WANT TO BE WITH TAKEO ON MY BIRTHDAY NEXT YEAR AND THE YEAR AFTER THAT AND THE ONE AFTER THAT!
CHUCKLE
CHUCKLE
YOU DON'T NEED TO SAY IT OUT LOUD.
YOU'RE THE FIRST CUSTOMER WHO'S DONE THAT.
O-OH!
AWW, HOW EMBARRASSING!
I CAN'T BELIEVE I DID THAT!
YAMATO...

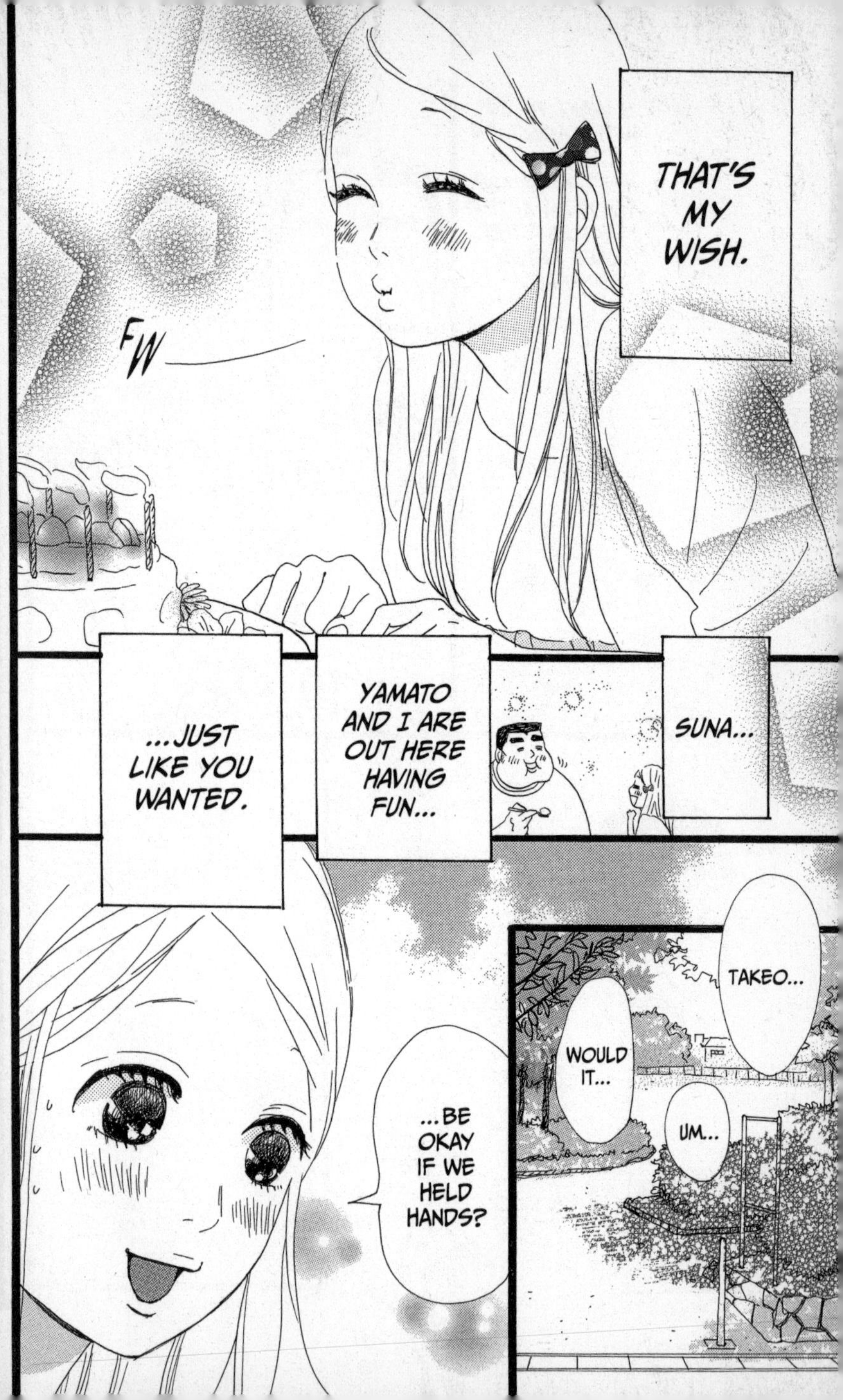
THAT'S MY WISH.
FW
SUNA...
YAMATO AND I ARE OUT HERE HAVING FUN...
...JUST LIKE YOU WANTED.
TAKEO...
UM...
WOULD IT...
...BE OKAY IF WE HELD HANDS?

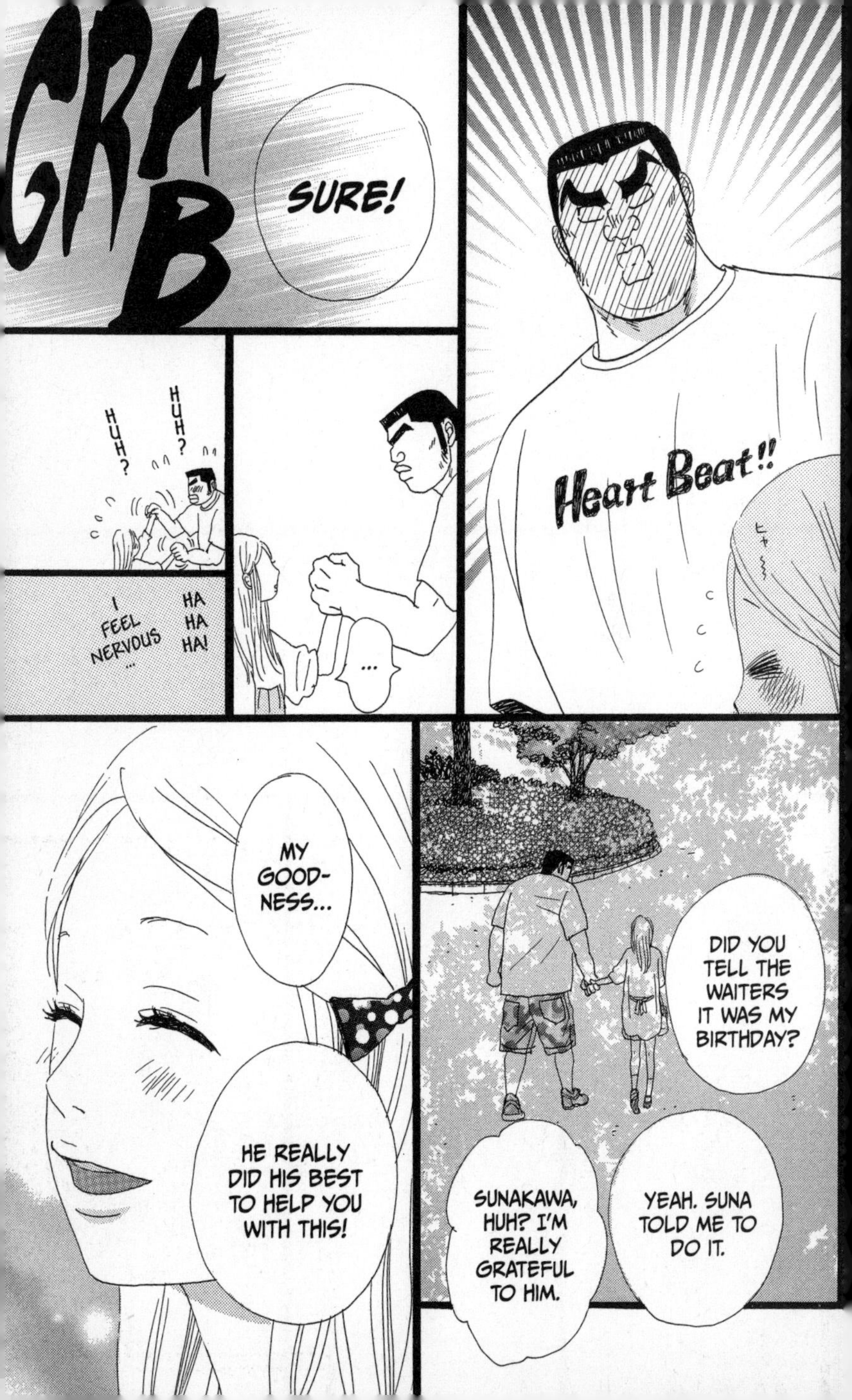
Heart Beat!!
GRAB
SURE!
...
HUH?
HUH?
I FEEL NERVOUS...
HA HA HA!
DID YOU TELL THE WAITERS IT WAS MY BIRTHDAY?
YEAH. SUNA TOLD ME TO DO IT.
SUNAKAWA, HUH? I'M REALLY GRATEFUL TO HIM.
MY GOOD-NESS...
HE REALLY DID HIS BEST TO HELP YOU WITH THIS!

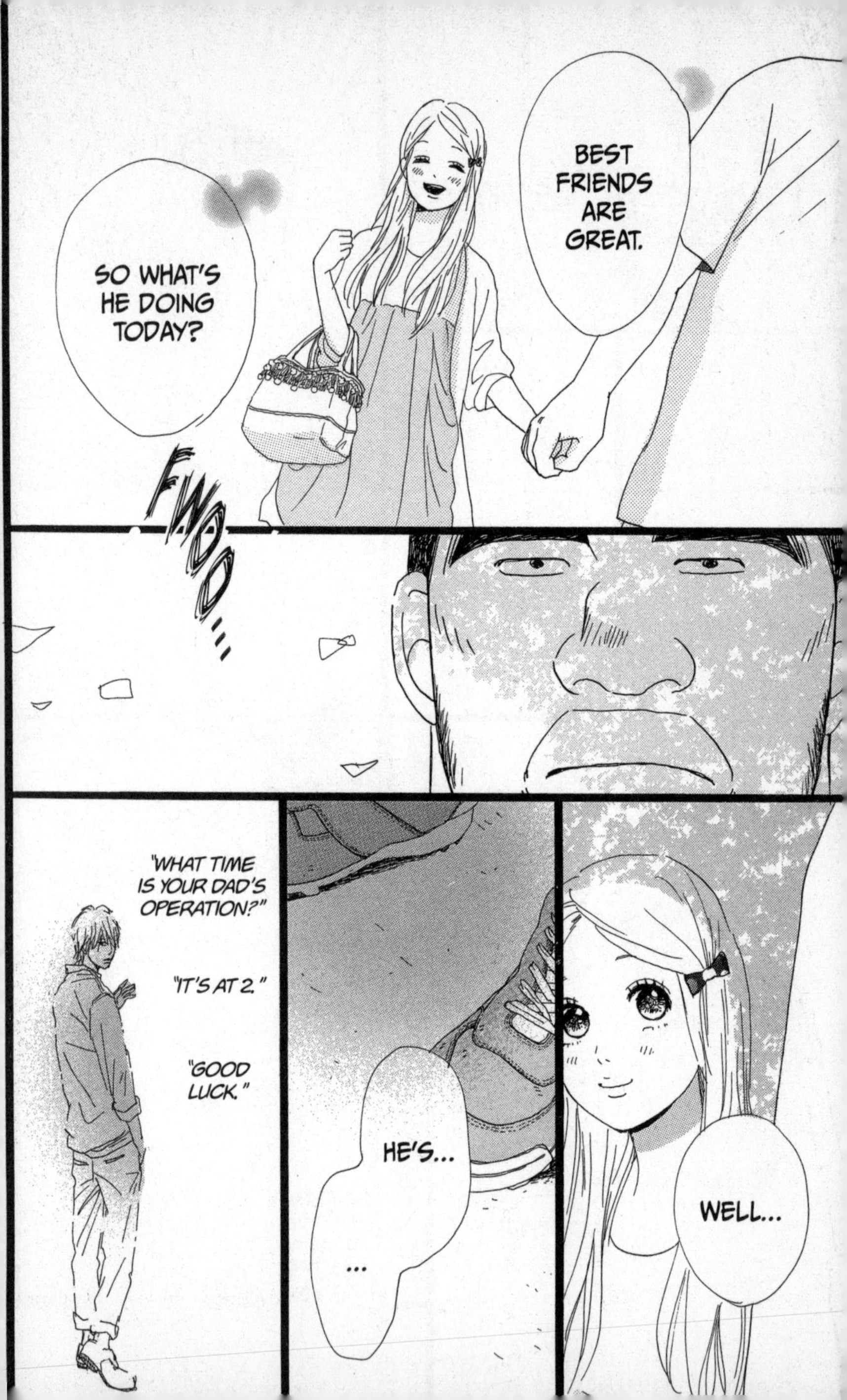
BEST FRIENDS ARE GREAT.
SO WHAT'S HE DOING TODAY?
FWOO...
WELL...
HE'S...
...
"WHAT TIME IS YOUR DAD'S OPERATION?"
"IT'S AT 2."
"GOOD LUCK."

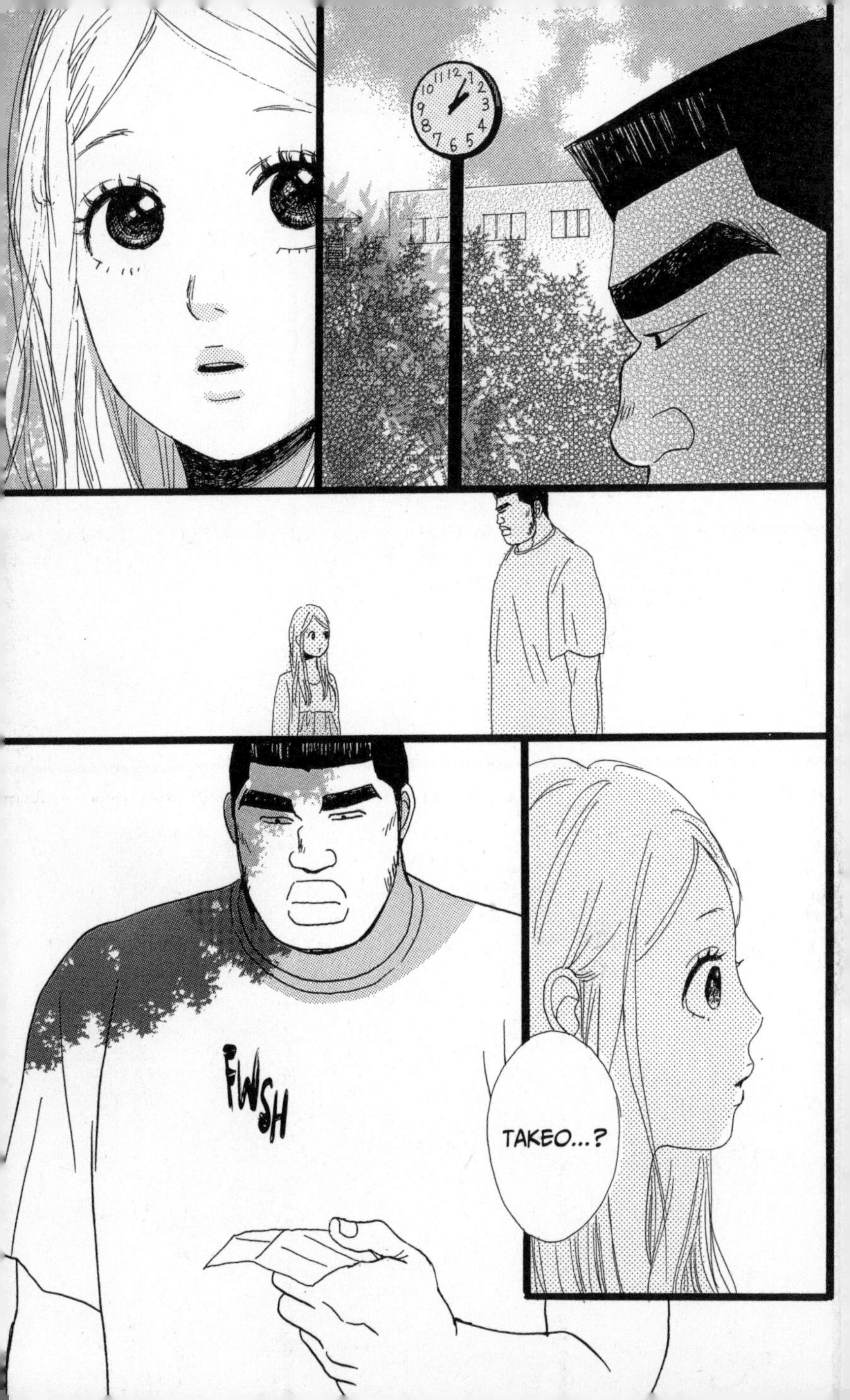
TAKEO...?
FWSH

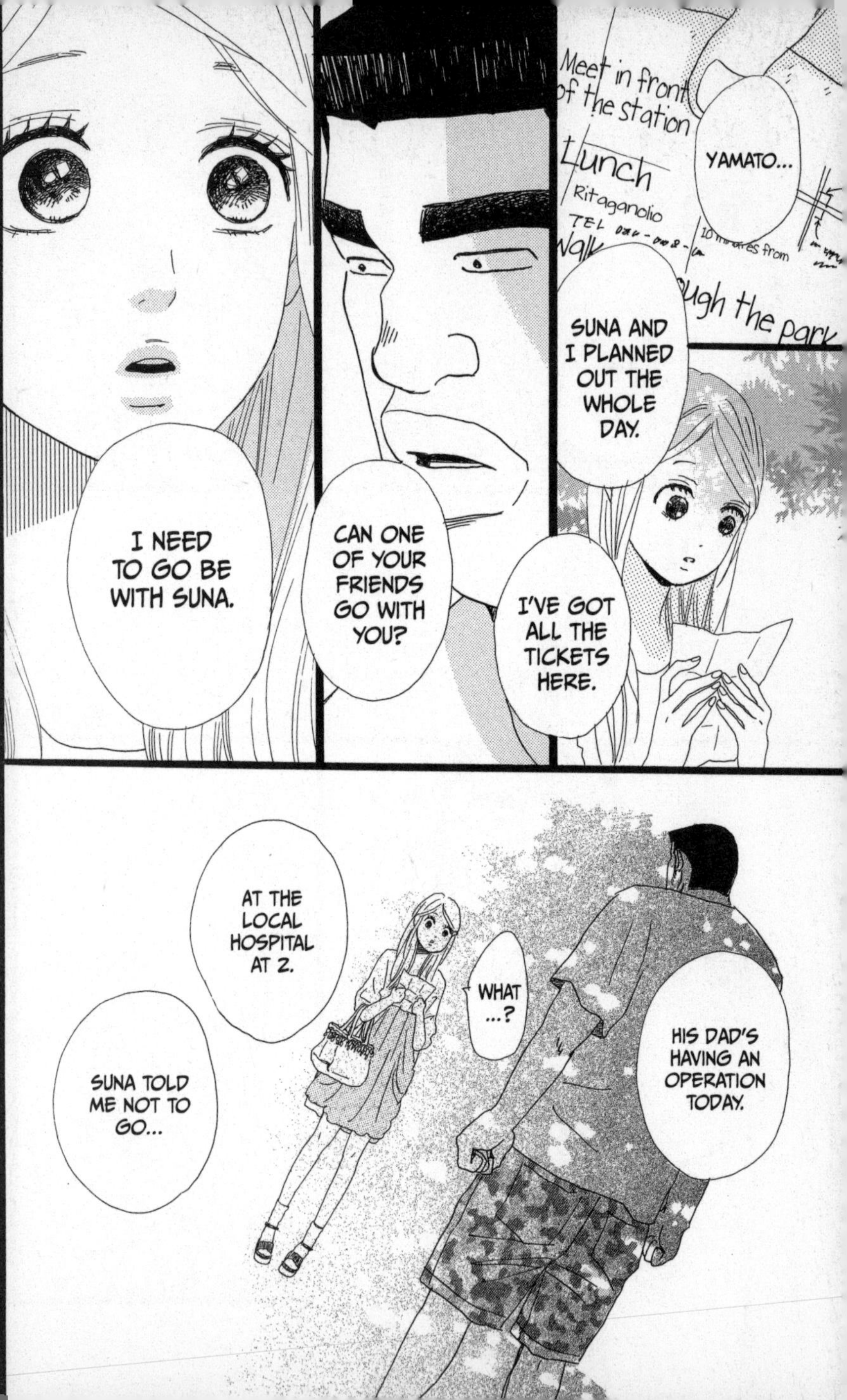
Meet in front of the station
Lunch
Ritaganolio
YAMATO...
SUNA AND I PLANNED OUT THE WHOLE DAY.
I'VE GOT ALL THE TICKETS HERE.
CAN ONE OF YOUR FRIENDS GO WITH YOU?
I NEED TO GO BE WITH SUNA.
HIS DAD'S HAVING AN OPERATION TODAY.
WHAT ...?
AT THE LOCAL HOSPITAL AT 2.
SUNA TOLD ME NOT TO GO...

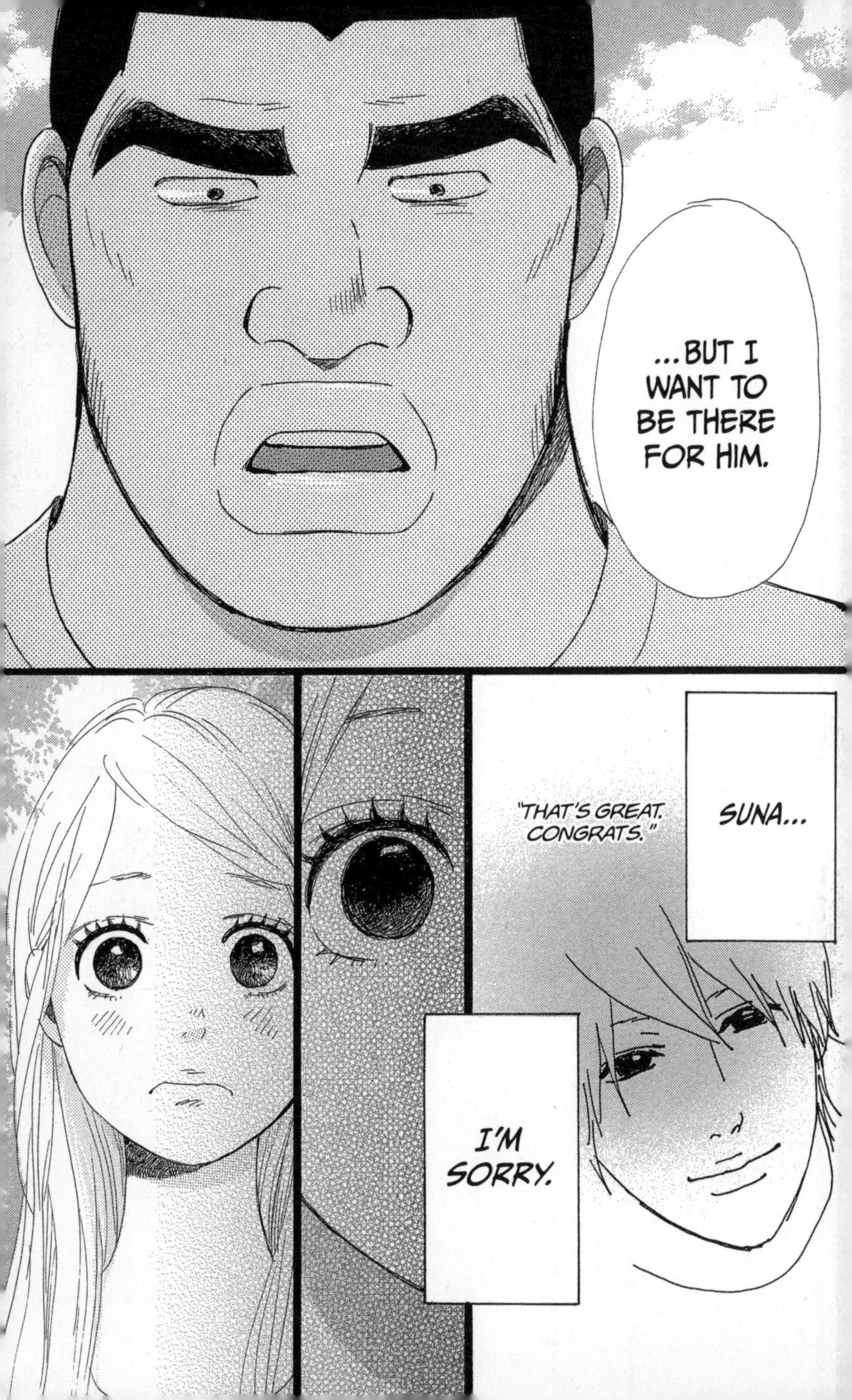
...BUT I WANT TO BE THERE FOR HIM.
SUNA...
"THAT'S GREAT. CONGRATS."
I'M SORRY.

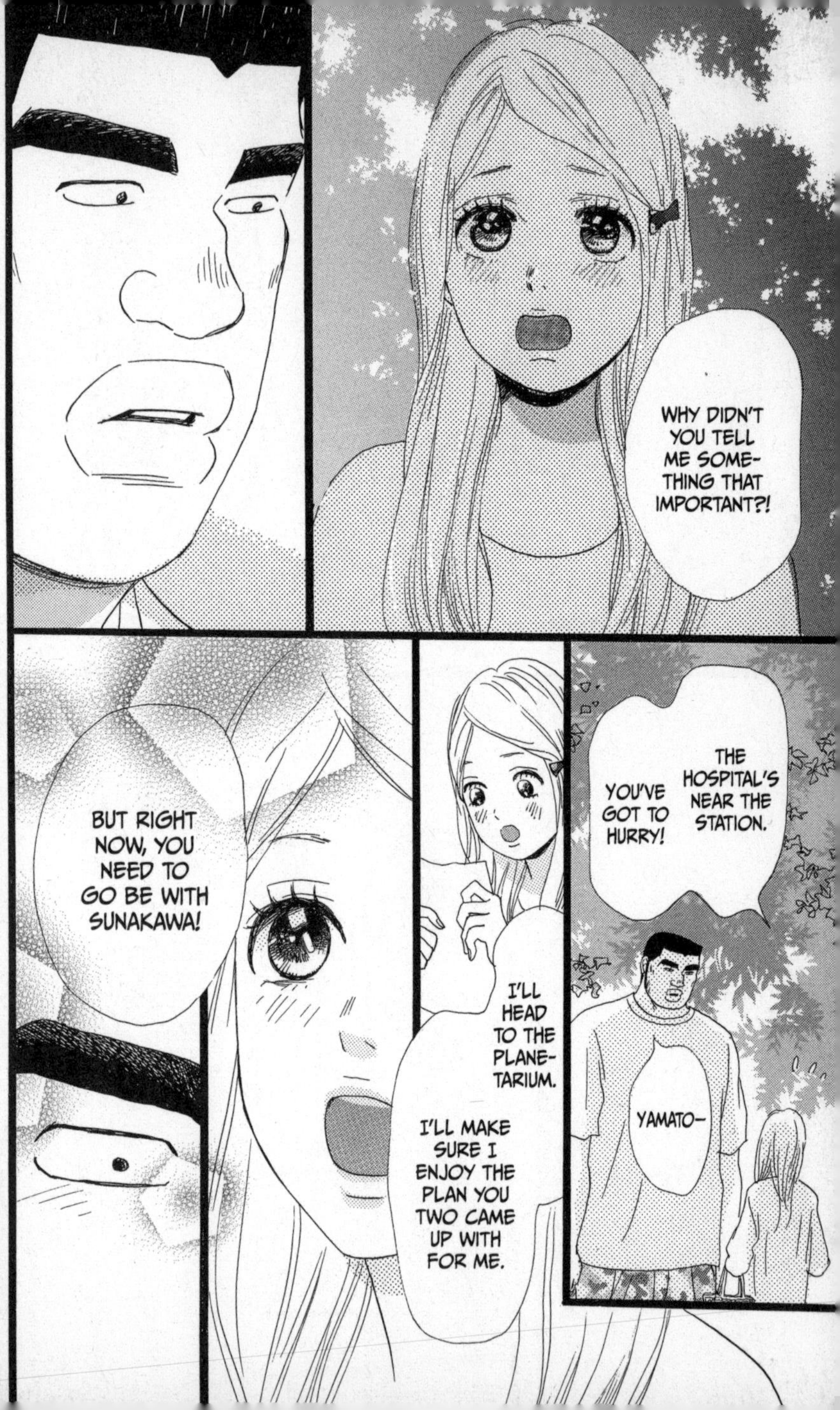
WHY DIDN'T YOU TELL ME SOME-THING THAT IMPORTANT?!
THE HOSPITAL'S NEAR THE STATION.
YOU'VE GOT TO HURRY!
YAMATO—
BUT RIGHT NOW, YOU NEED TO GO BE WITH SUNAKAWA!
I'LL HEAD TO THE PLANE-TARIUM.
I'LL MAKE SURE I ENJOY THE PLAN YOU TWO CAME UP WITH FOR ME.

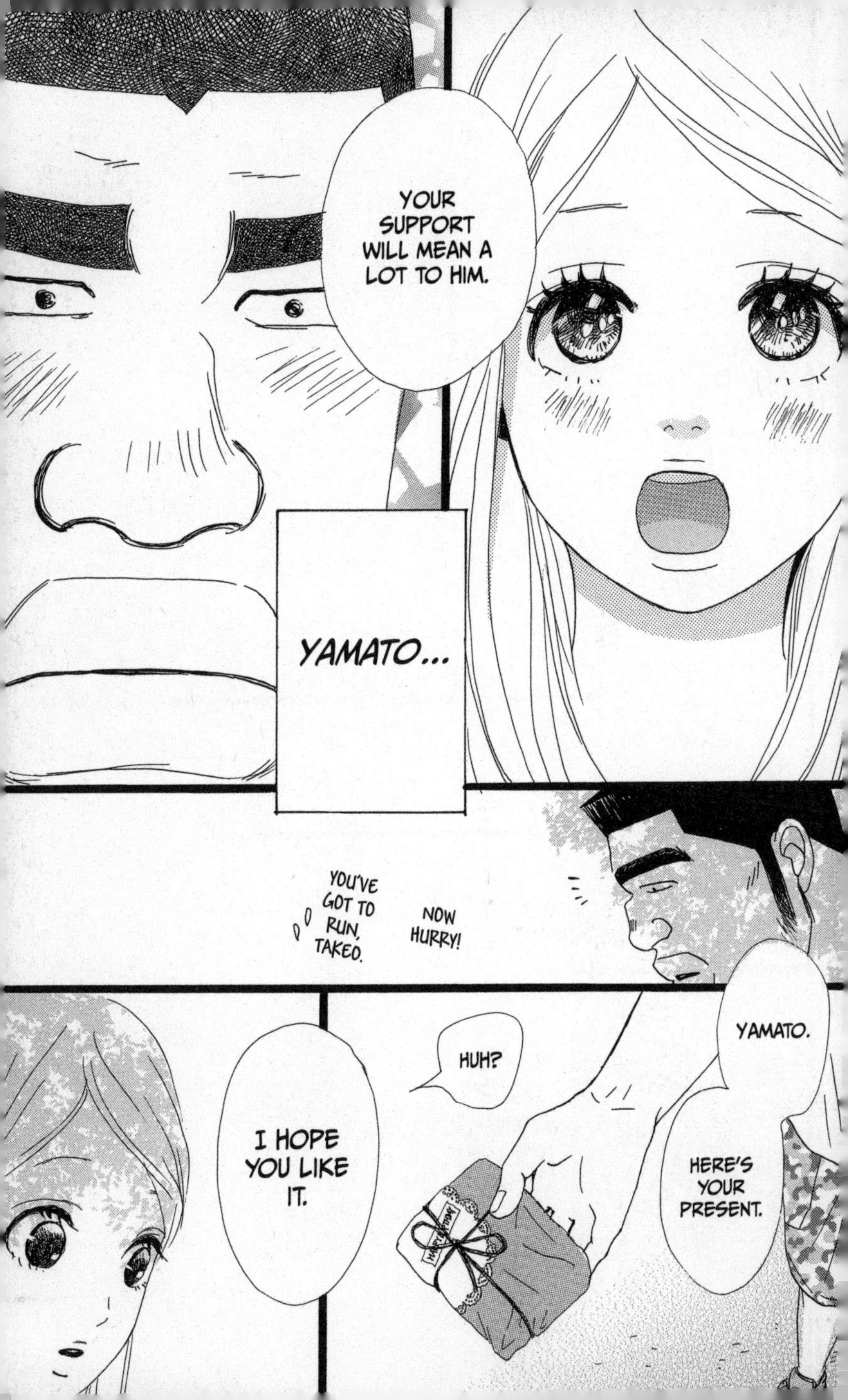
YOUR SUPPORT WILL MEAN A LOT TO HIM.
YAMATO...
NOW HURRY!
YOU'VE GOT TO RUN, TAKEO.
YAMATO.
HERE'S YOUR PRESENT.
HUH?
I HOPE YOU LIKE IT.

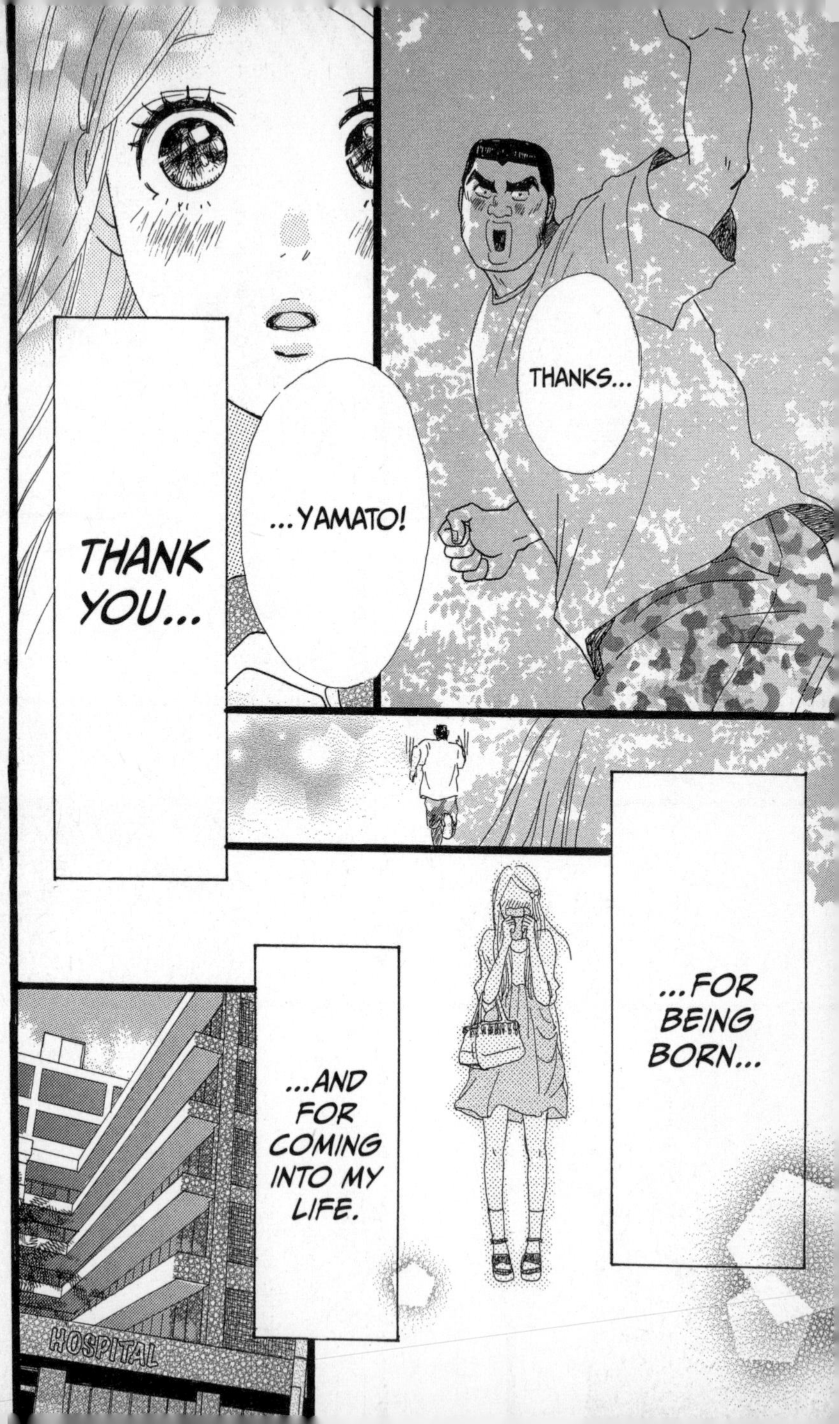
THANKS...
...YAMATO!
THANK YOU...
...FOR BEING BORN...
...AND FOR COMING INTO MY LIFE.
HOSPITAL

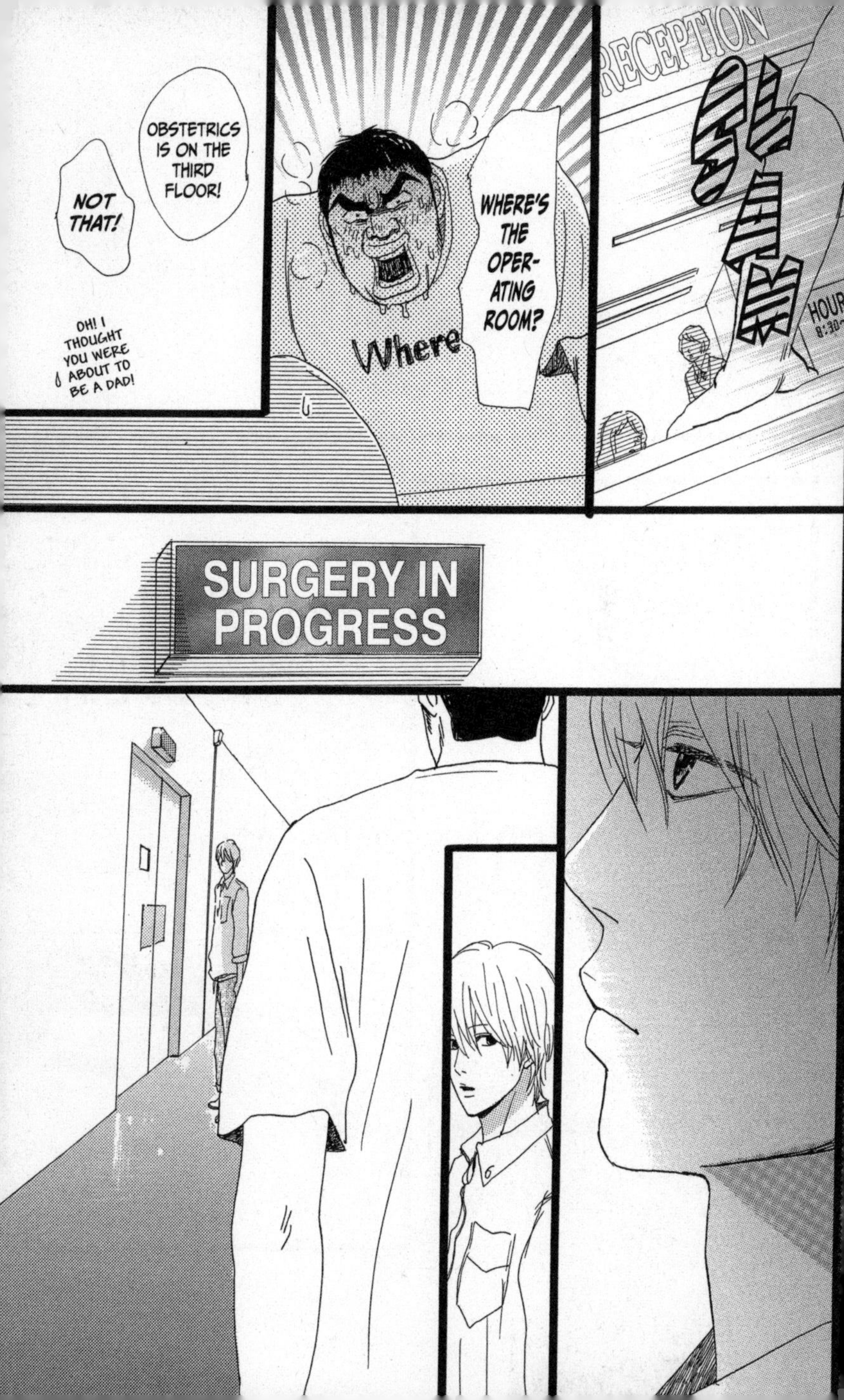
RECEPTION
WHERE'S THE OPERATING ROOM?
Where
OBSTETRICS IS ON THE THIRD FLOOR!
NOT THAT!
OH! I THOUGHT YOU WERE ABOUT TO BE A DAD!
SURGERY IN PROGRESS

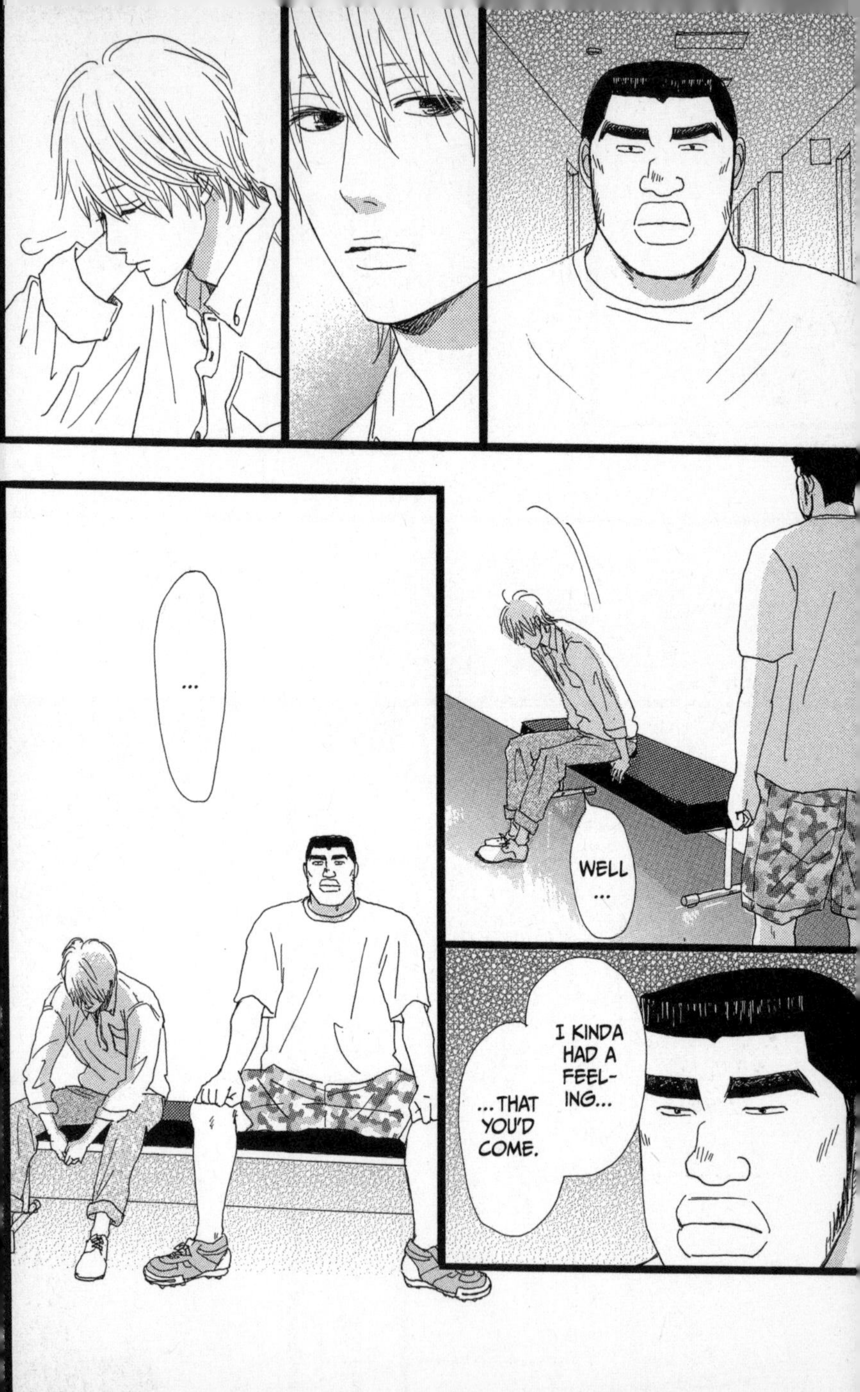
WELL ...
I KINDA HAD A FEEL-ING...
...THAT YOU'D COME.
...

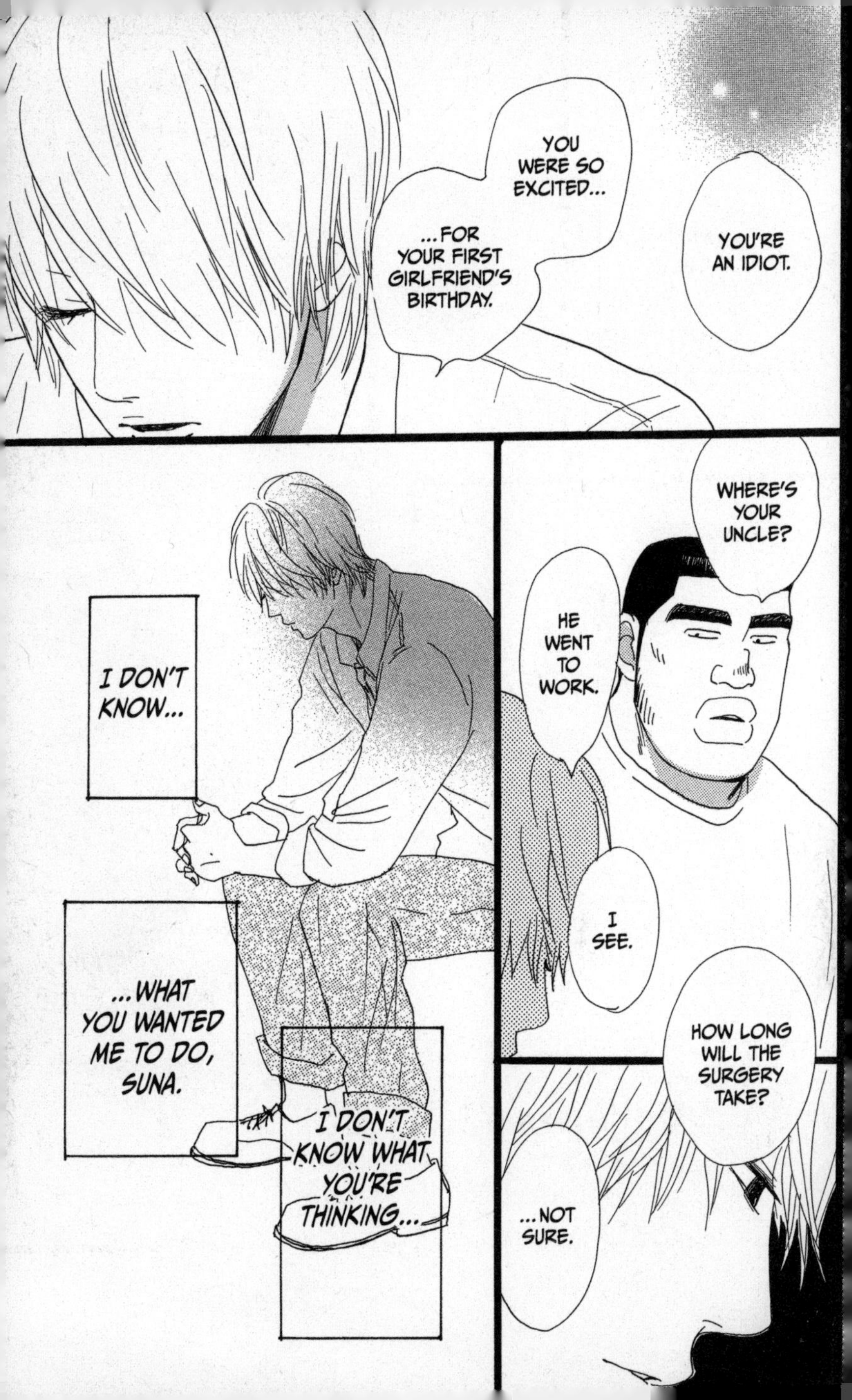
YOU'RE AN IDIOT.
YOU WERE SO EXCITED...
...FOR YOUR FIRST GIRLFRIEND'S BIRTHDAY.
WHERE'S YOUR UNCLE?
HE WENT TO WORK.
I SEE.
HOW LONG WILL THE SURGERY TAKE?
...NOT SURE.
I DON'T KNOW...
...WHAT YOU WANTED ME TO DO, SUNA.
I DON'T KNOW WHAT YOU'RE THINKING...

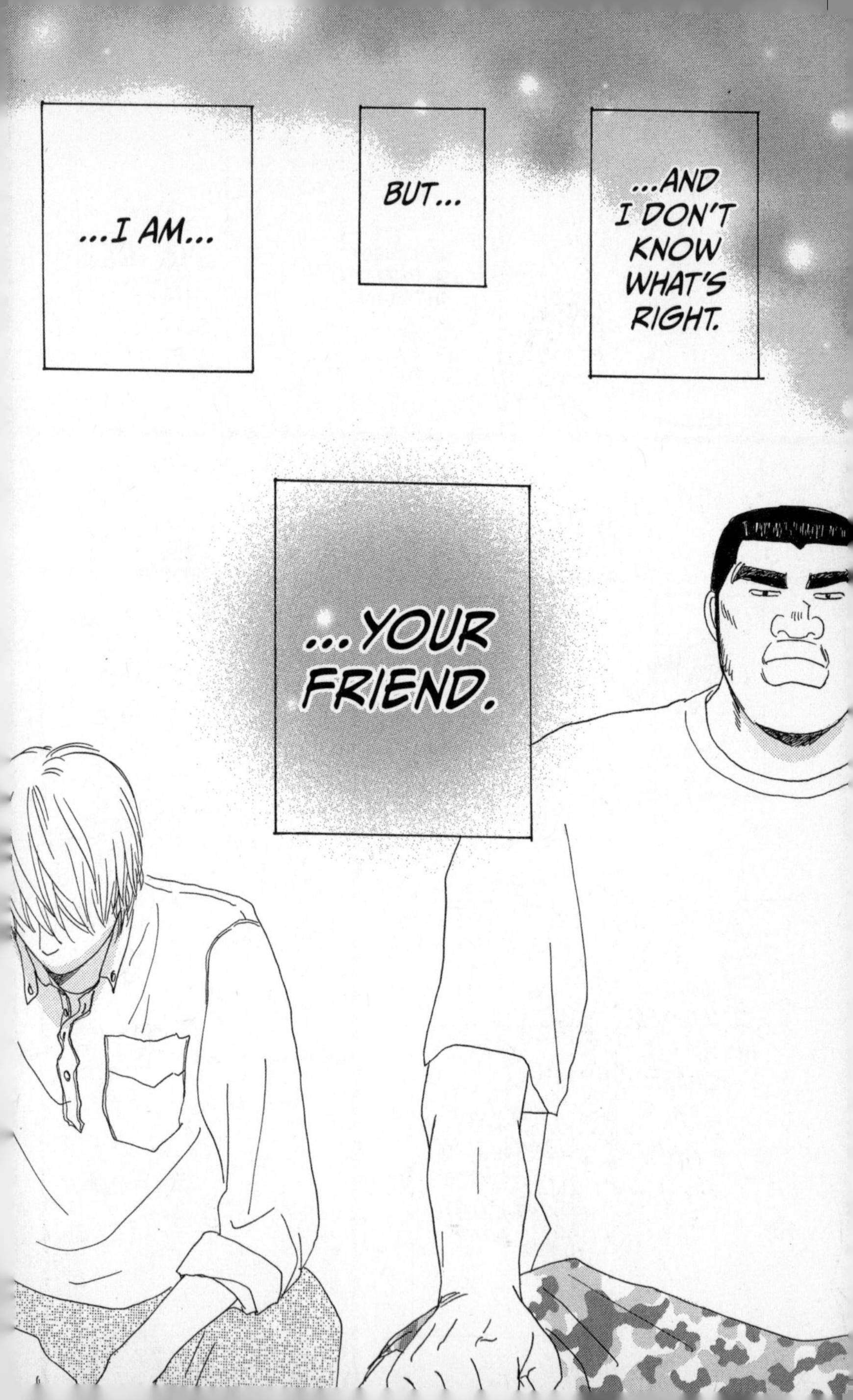
...AND I DON'T KNOW WHAT'S RIGHT.
BUT...
...I AM...
...YOUR FRIEND.

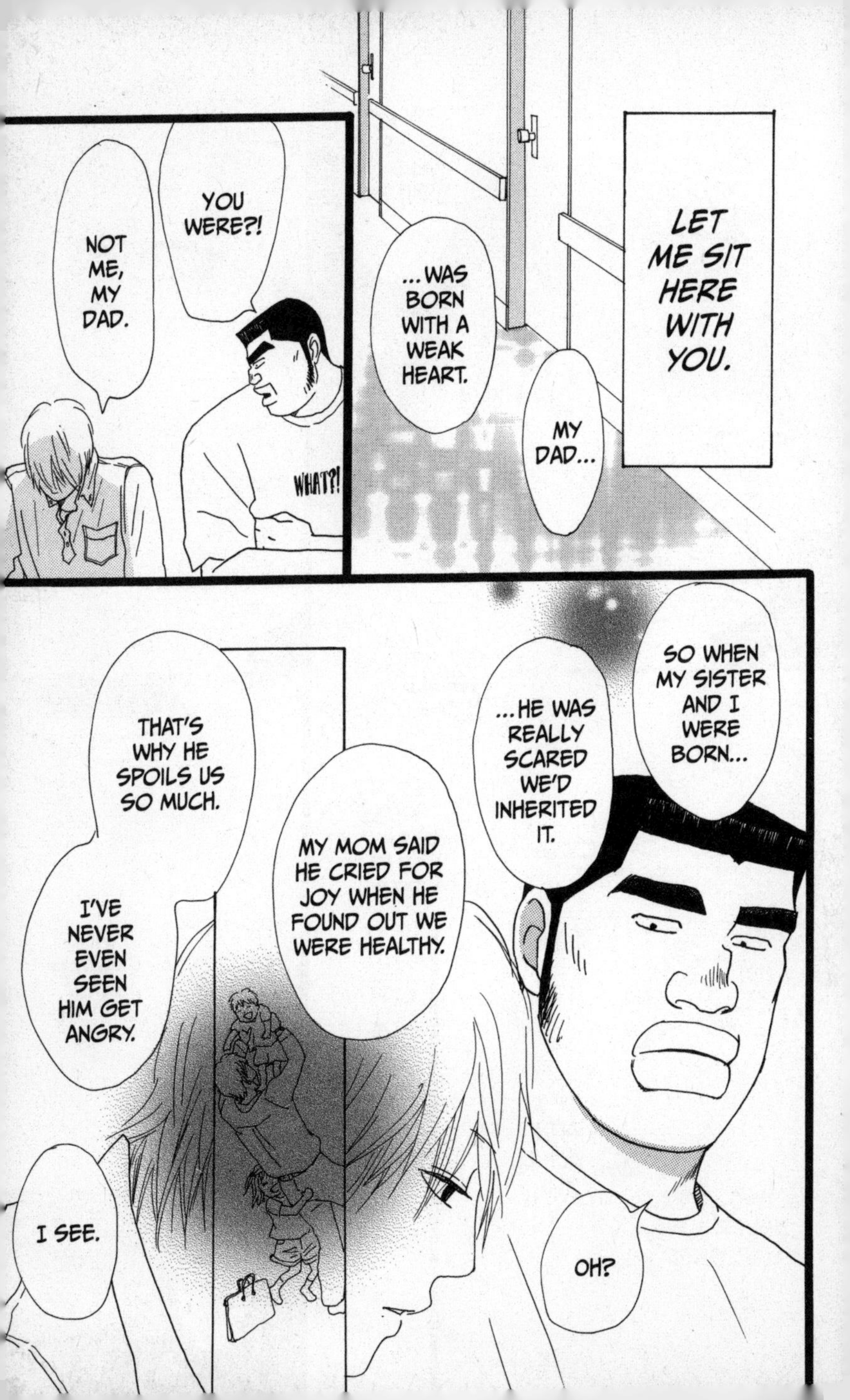
LET ME SIT HERE WITH YOU.
MY DAD...
...WAS BORN WITH A WEAK HEART.
YOU WERE?!
WHAT?!
NOT ME, MY DAD.
SO WHEN MY SISTER AND I WERE BORN...
...HE WAS REALLY SCARED WE'D INHERITED IT.
MY MOM SAID HE CRIED FOR JOY WHEN HE FOUND OUT WE WERE HEALTHY.
THAT'S WHY HE SPOILS US SO MUCH.
I'VE NEVER EVEN SEEN HIM GET ANGRY.
OH?
I SEE.

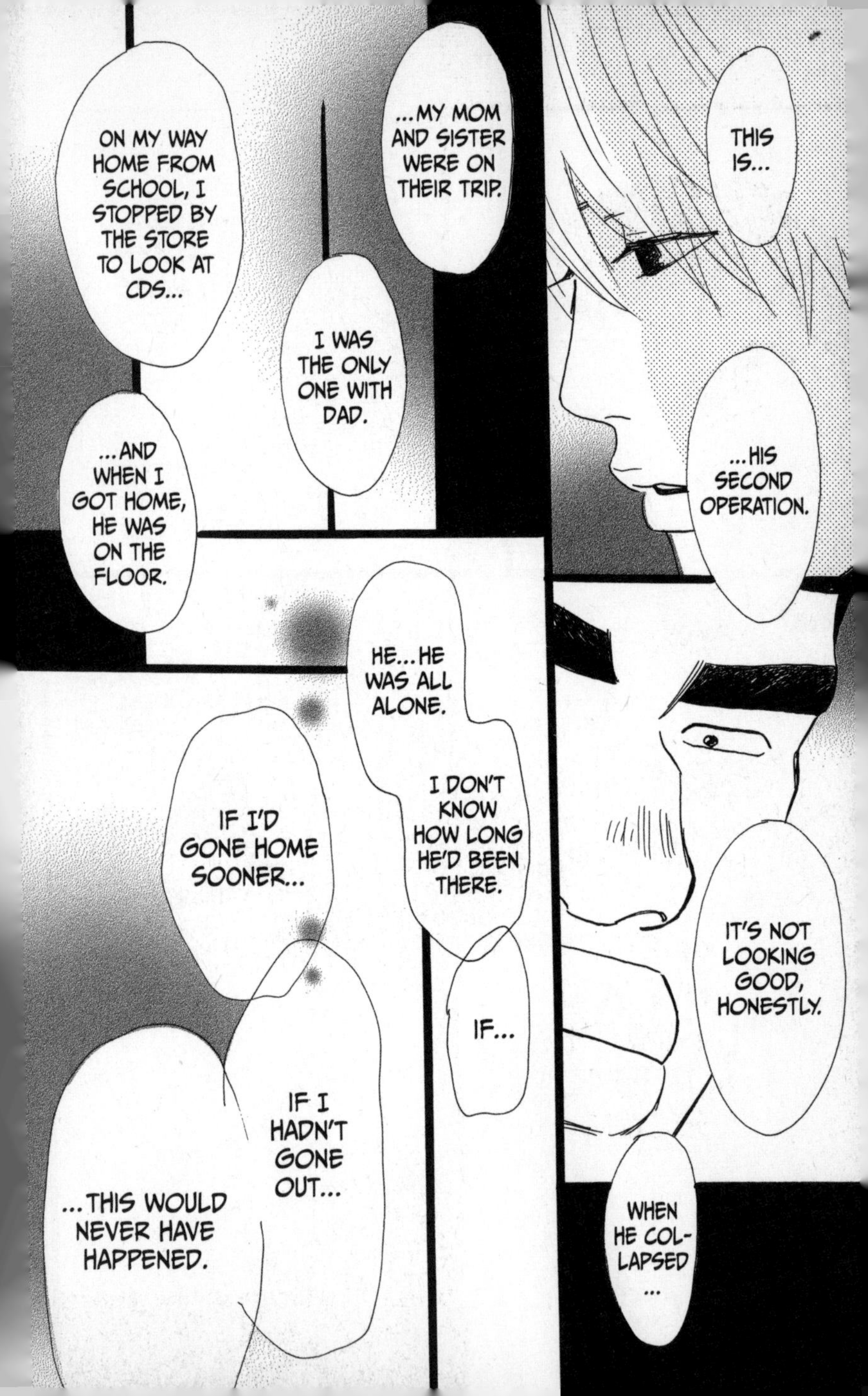
THIS IS...
...HIS SECOND OPERATION.
IT'S NOT LOOKING GOOD, HONESTLY.
WHEN HE COL-LAPSED...
...MY MOM AND SISTER WERE ON THEIR TRIP.
I WAS THE ONLY ONE WITH DAD.
ON MY WAY HOME FROM SCHOOL, I STOPPED BY THE STORE TO LOOK AT CDS...
...AND WHEN I GOT HOME, HE WAS ON THE FLOOR.
HE... HE WAS ALL ALONE.
I DON'T KNOW HOW LONG HE'D BEEN THERE.
IF...
IF I'D GONE HOME SOONER...
IF I HADN'T GONE OUT...
...THIS WOULD NEVER HAVE HAPPENED.

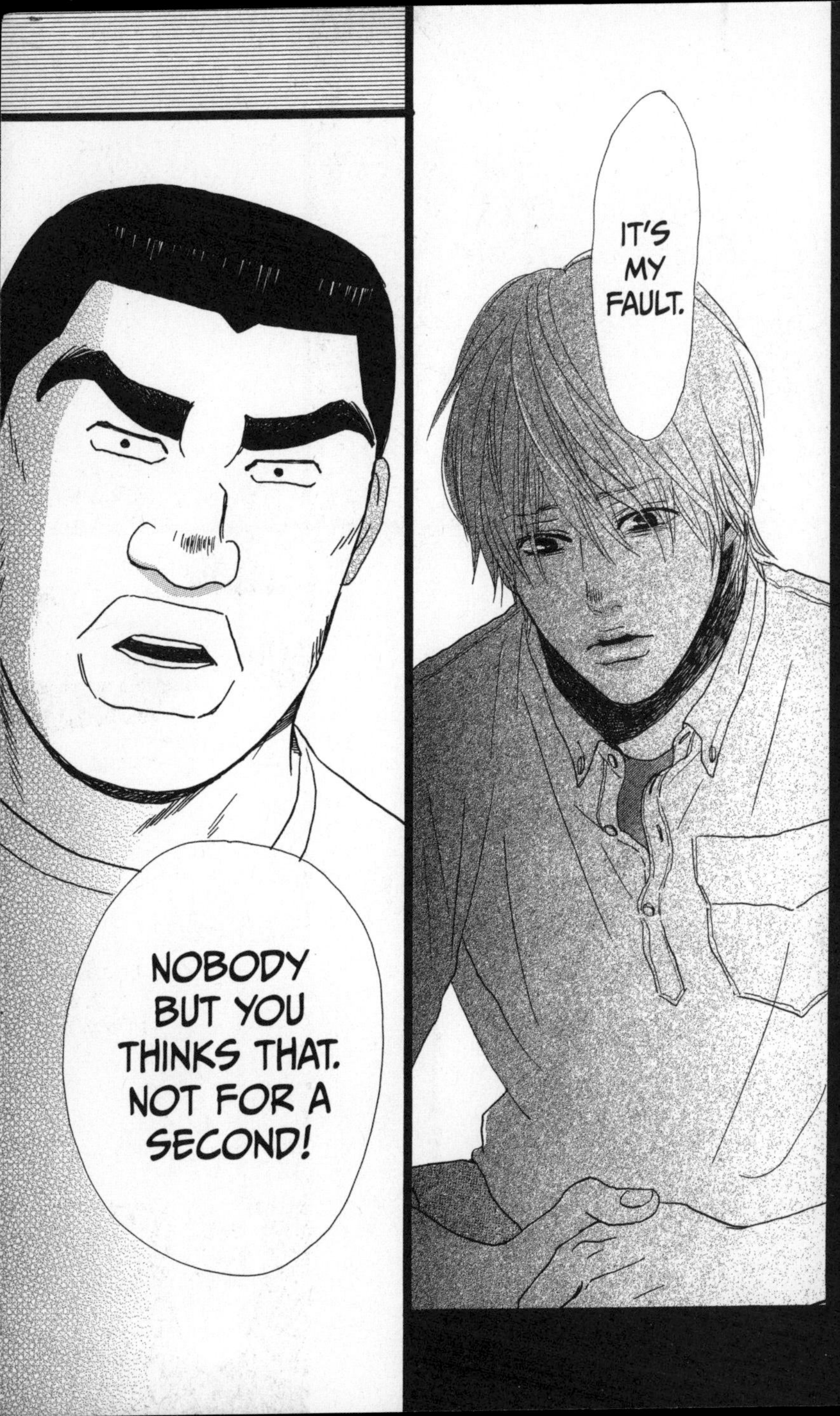
IT'S MY FAULT.
NOBODY BUT YOU THINKS THAT. NOT FOR A SECOND!

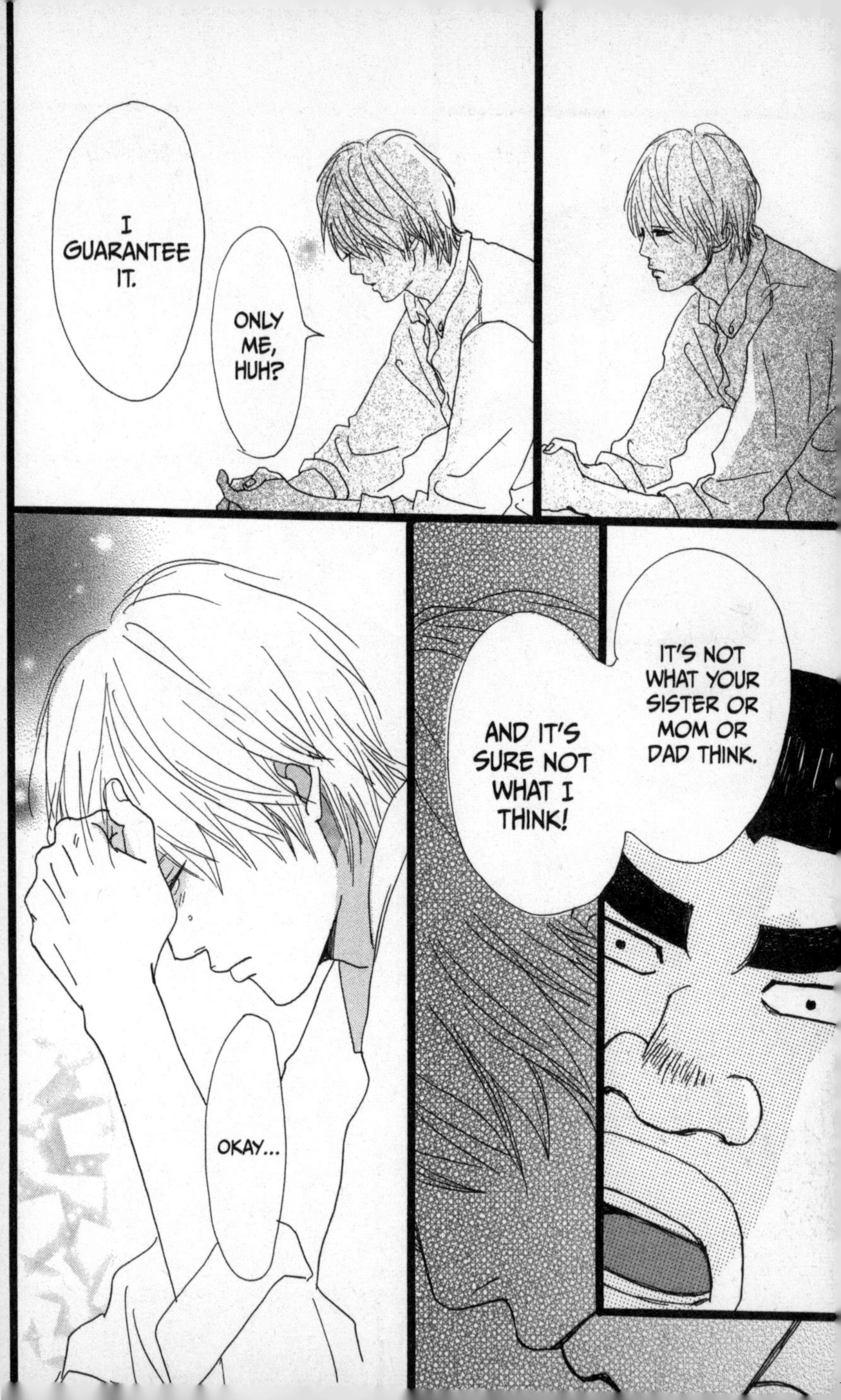
ONLY ME, HUH?
I GUARANTEE IT.
IT'S NOT WHAT YOUR SISTER OR MOM OR DAD THINK.
AND IT'S SURE NOT WHAT I THINK!
OKAY...

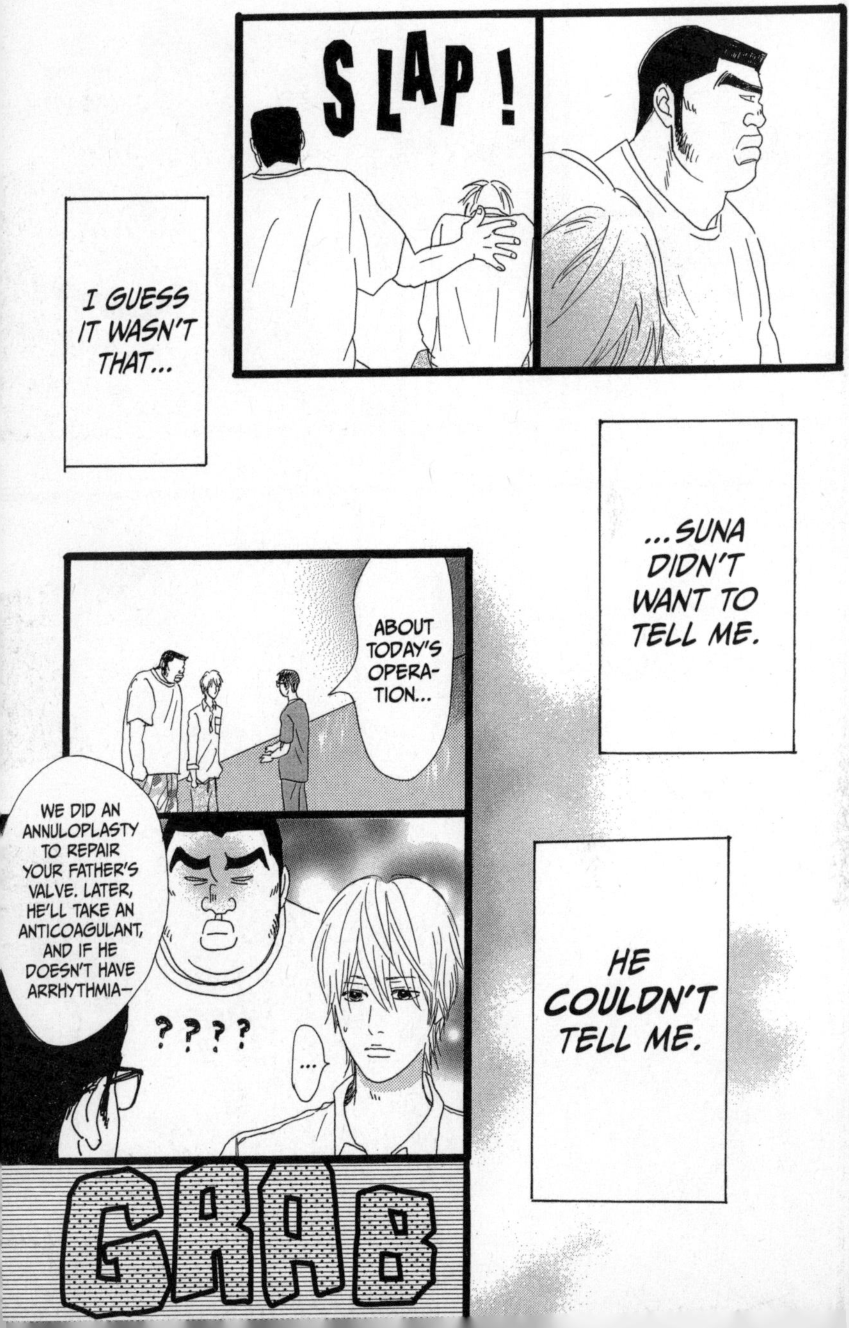
SLAP!
I GUESS IT WASN'T THAT...
...SUNA DIDN'T WANT TO TELL ME.
HE COULDN'T TELL ME.
ABOUT TODAY'S OPERATION...
WE DID AN ANNULOPLASTY TO REPAIR YOUR FATHER'S VALVE. LATER, HE'LL TAKE AN ANTICOAGULANT, AND IF HE DOESN'T HAVE ARRHYTHMIA—
????
...
GRAB

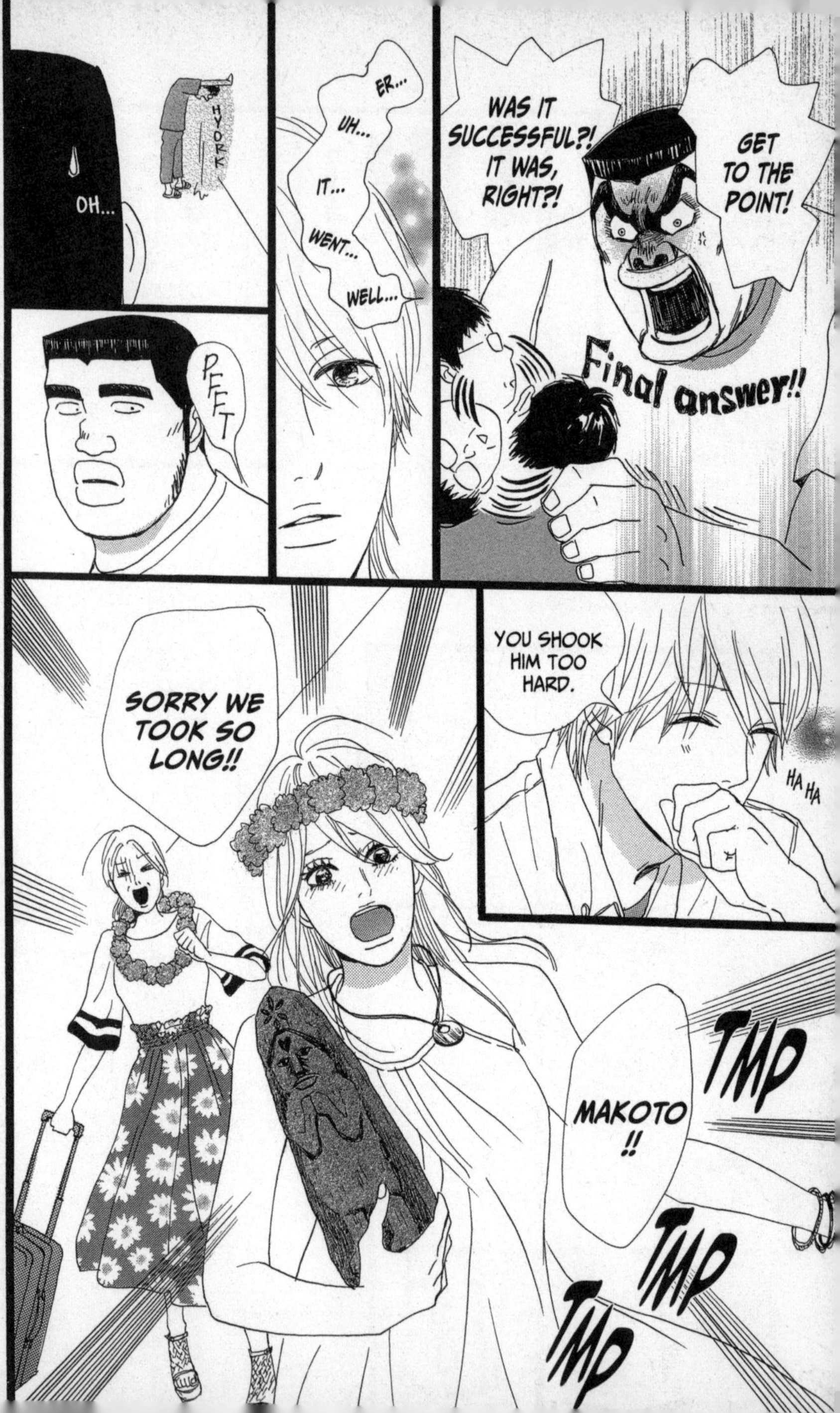
GET TO THE POINT!
WAS IT SUCCESSFUL?! IT WAS, RIGHT?!
Final answer!!
ER...
UH...
IT...
WENT...
WELL...
HYORK
OH...
PFFT
YOU SHOOK HIM TOO HARD.
HA HA
TMP
MAKOTO!!
SORRY WE TOOK SO LONG!!
TMP
TMP

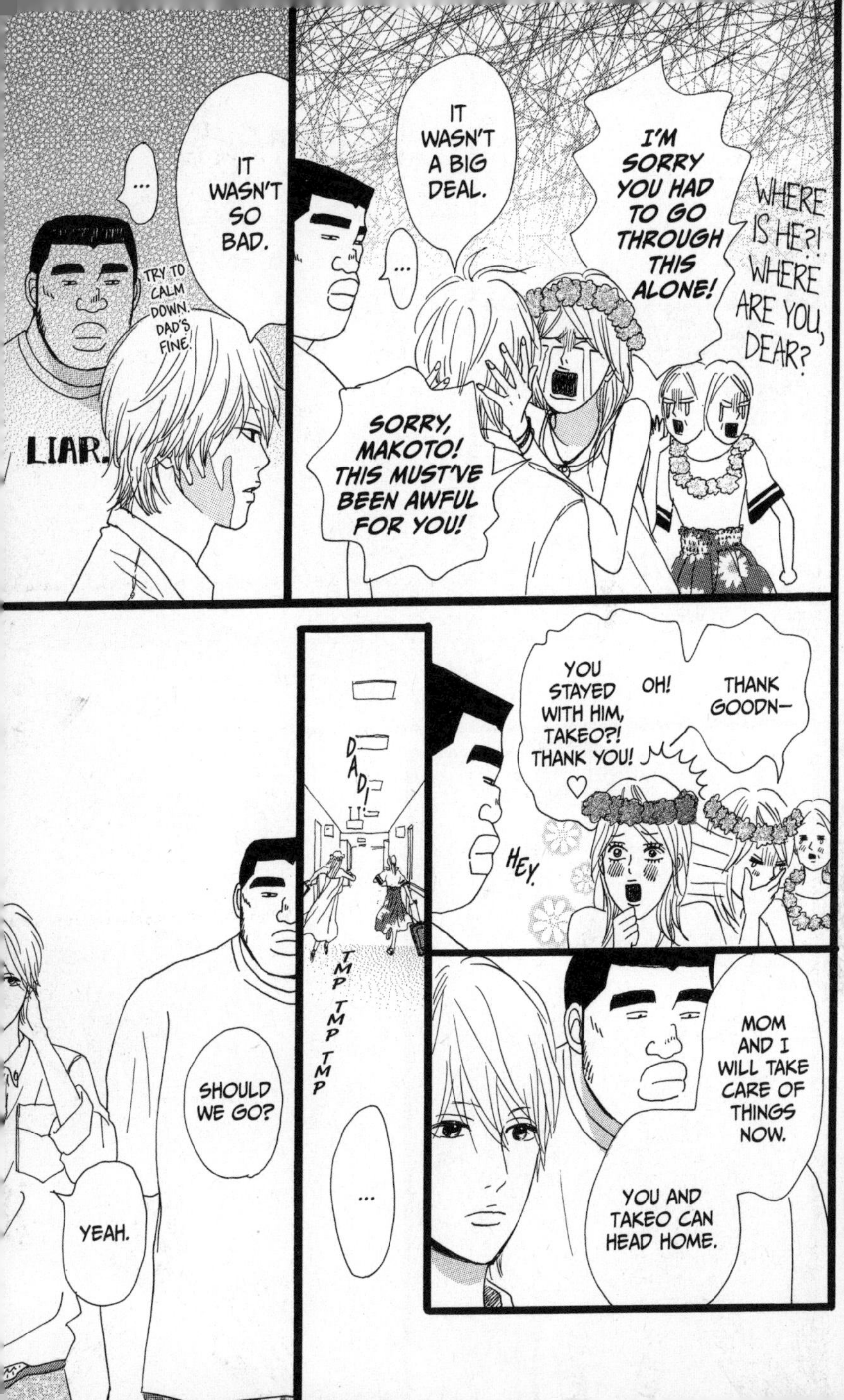
WHERE IS HE?! WHERE ARE YOU, DEAR?
I'M SORRY YOU HAD TO GO THROUGH THIS ALONE!
IT WASN'T A BIG DEAL.
...
SORRY, MAKOTO! THIS MUST'VE BEEN AWFUL FOR YOU!
IT WASN'T SO BAD.
...
TRY TO CALM DOWN. DAD'S FINE.
LIAR.
THANK GOODN—
OH!
YOU STAYED WITH HIM, TAKEO?! THANK YOU!
HEY.
MOM AND I WILL TAKE CARE OF THINGS NOW.
YOU AND TAKEO CAN HEAD HOME.
...
DAD!
TMP TMP TMP
SHOULD WE GO?
YEAH.

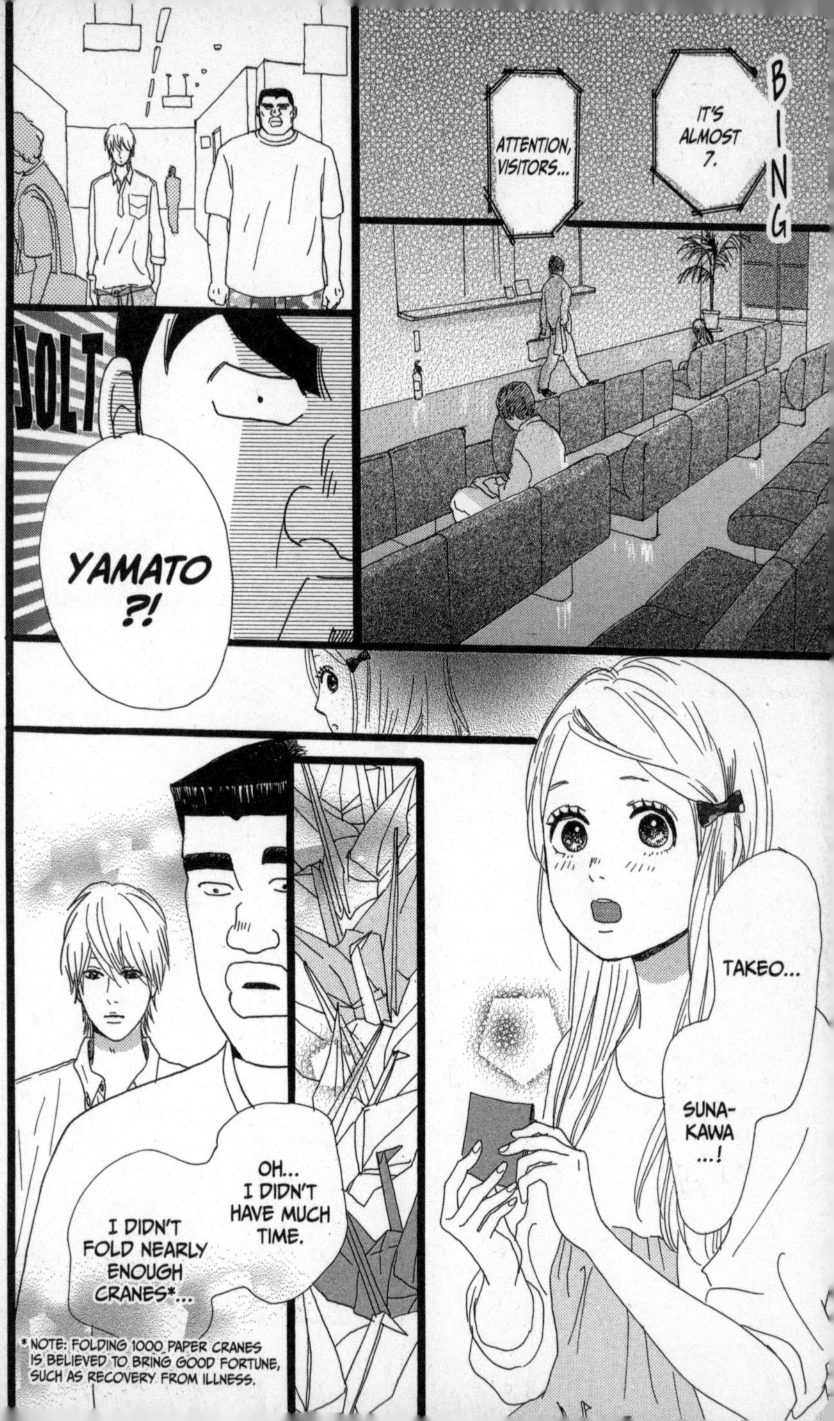
BING
IT'S ALMOST 7.
ATTENTION, VISITORS...
JOLT
YAMATO ?!
TAKEO...
SUNA-KAWA ...!
OH... I DIDN'T HAVE MUCH TIME.
I DIDN'T FOLD NEARLY ENOUGH CRANES*...
* NOTE: FOLDING 1000 PAPER CRANES IS BELIEVED TO BRING GOOD FORTUNE, SUCH AS RECOVERY FROM ILLNESS.

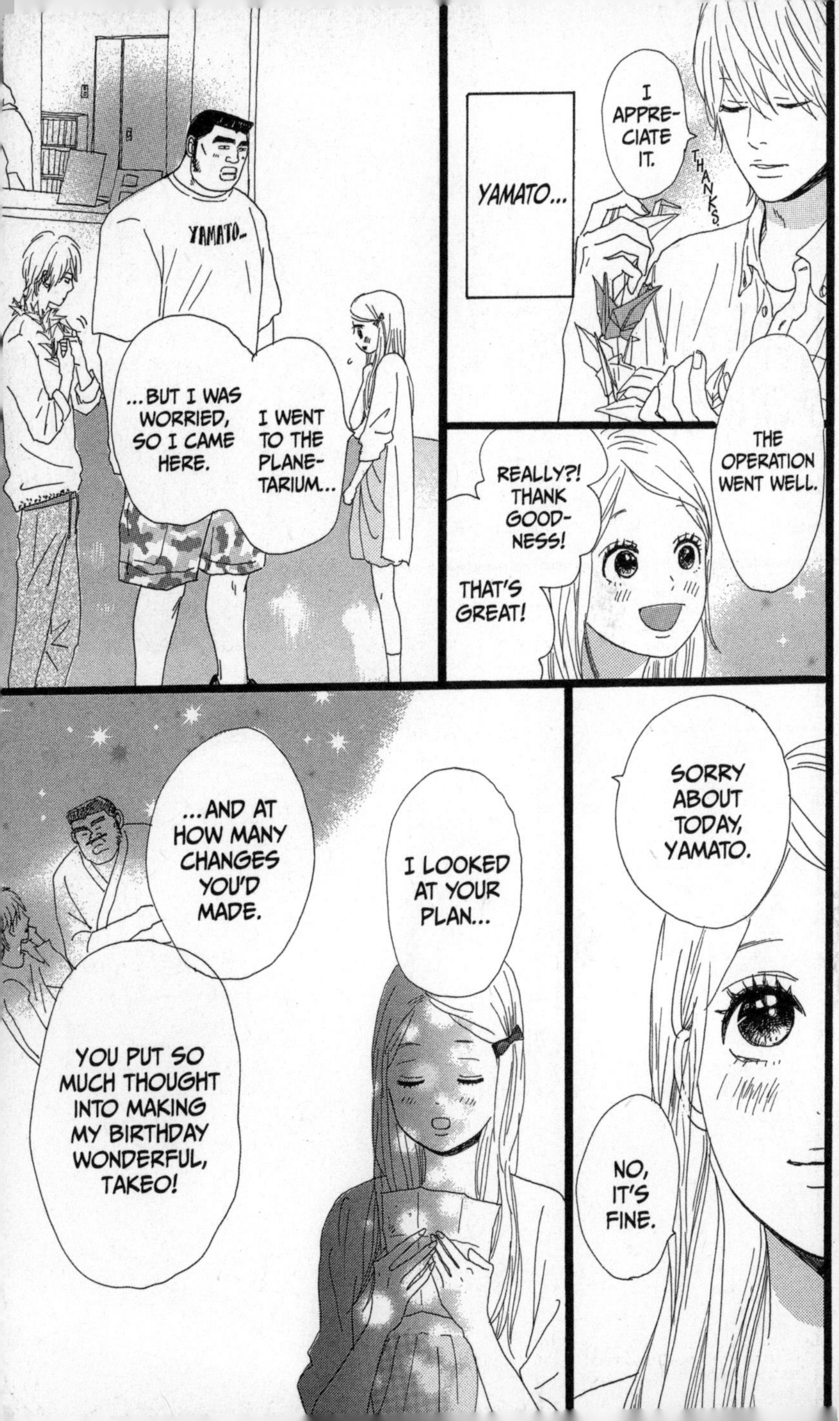
THANKS.
I APPRECIATE IT.
YAMATO...
THE OPERATION WENT WELL.
REALLY?! THANK GOODNESS!
THAT'S GREAT!
I WENT TO THE PLANETARIUM...
...BUT I WAS WORRIED, SO I CAME HERE.
YAMATO...
SORRY ABOUT TODAY, YAMATO.
NO, IT'S FINE.
I LOOKED AT YOUR PLAN...
...AND AT HOW MANY CHANGES YOU'D MADE.
YOU PUT SO MUCH THOUGHT INTO MAKING MY BIRTHDAY WONDERFUL, TAKEO!

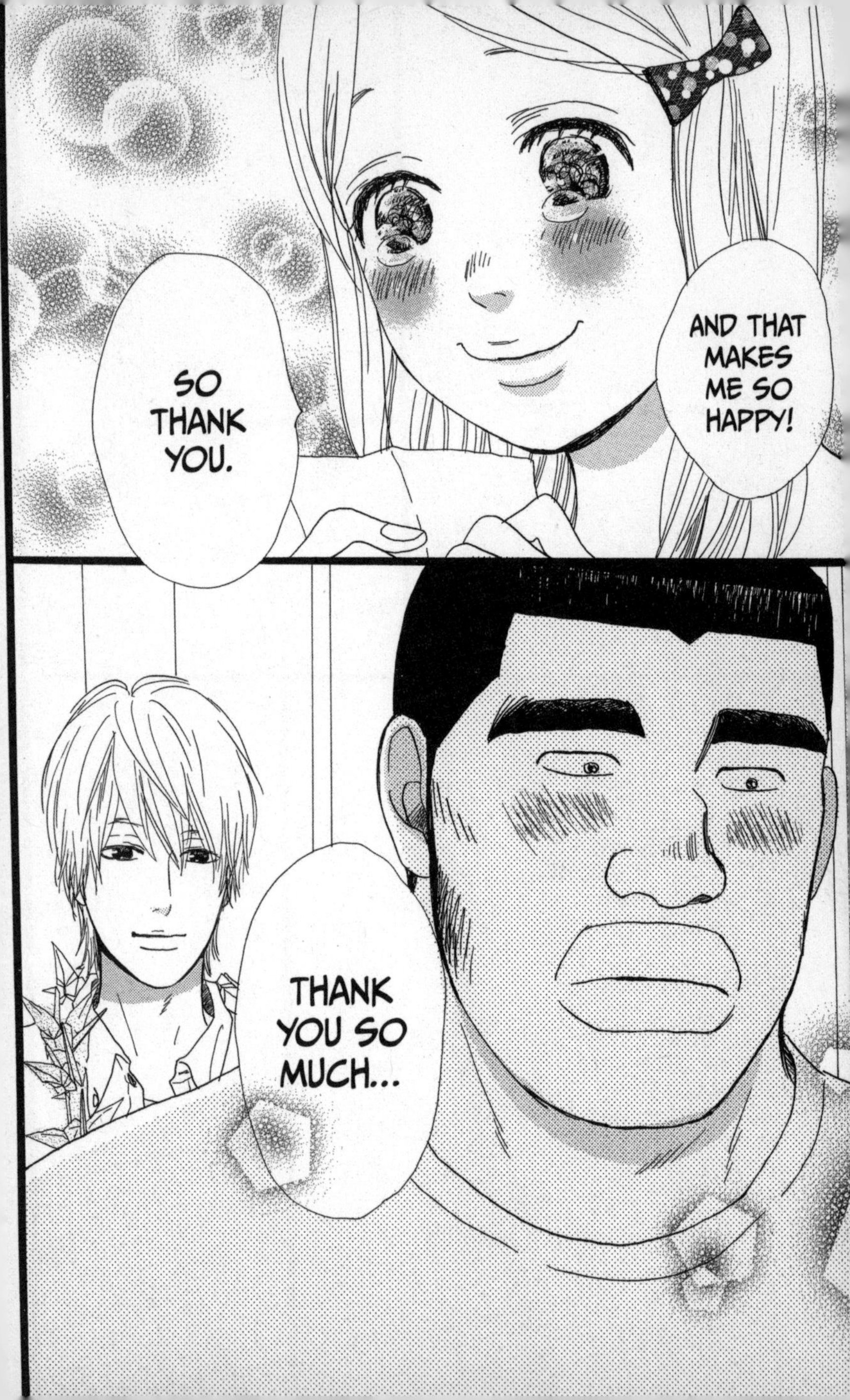
AND THAT MAKES ME SO HAPPY!
SO THANK YOU.
THANK YOU SO MUCH...

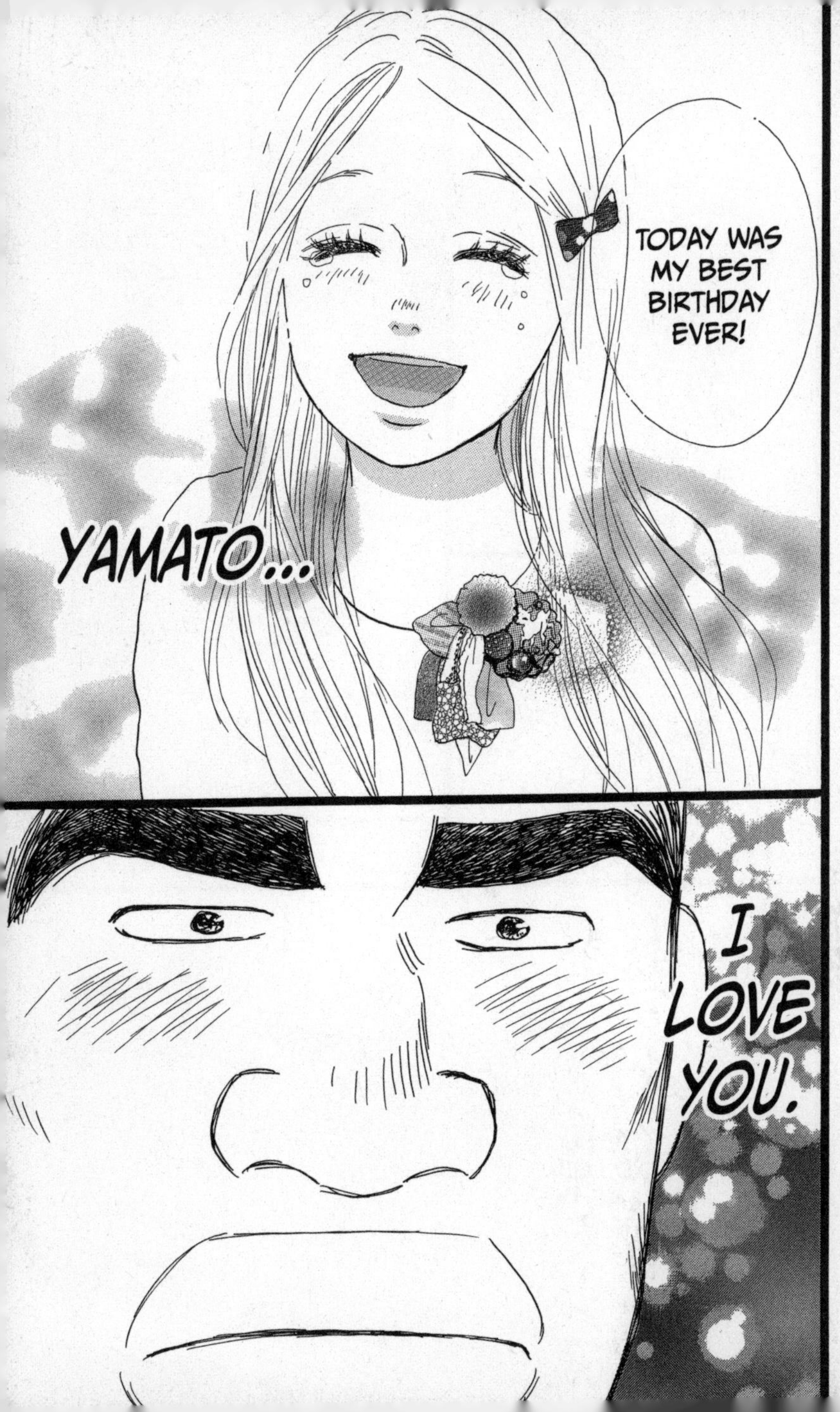
TODAY WAS MY BEST BIRTHDAY EVER!
YAMATO...
I LOVE YOU.

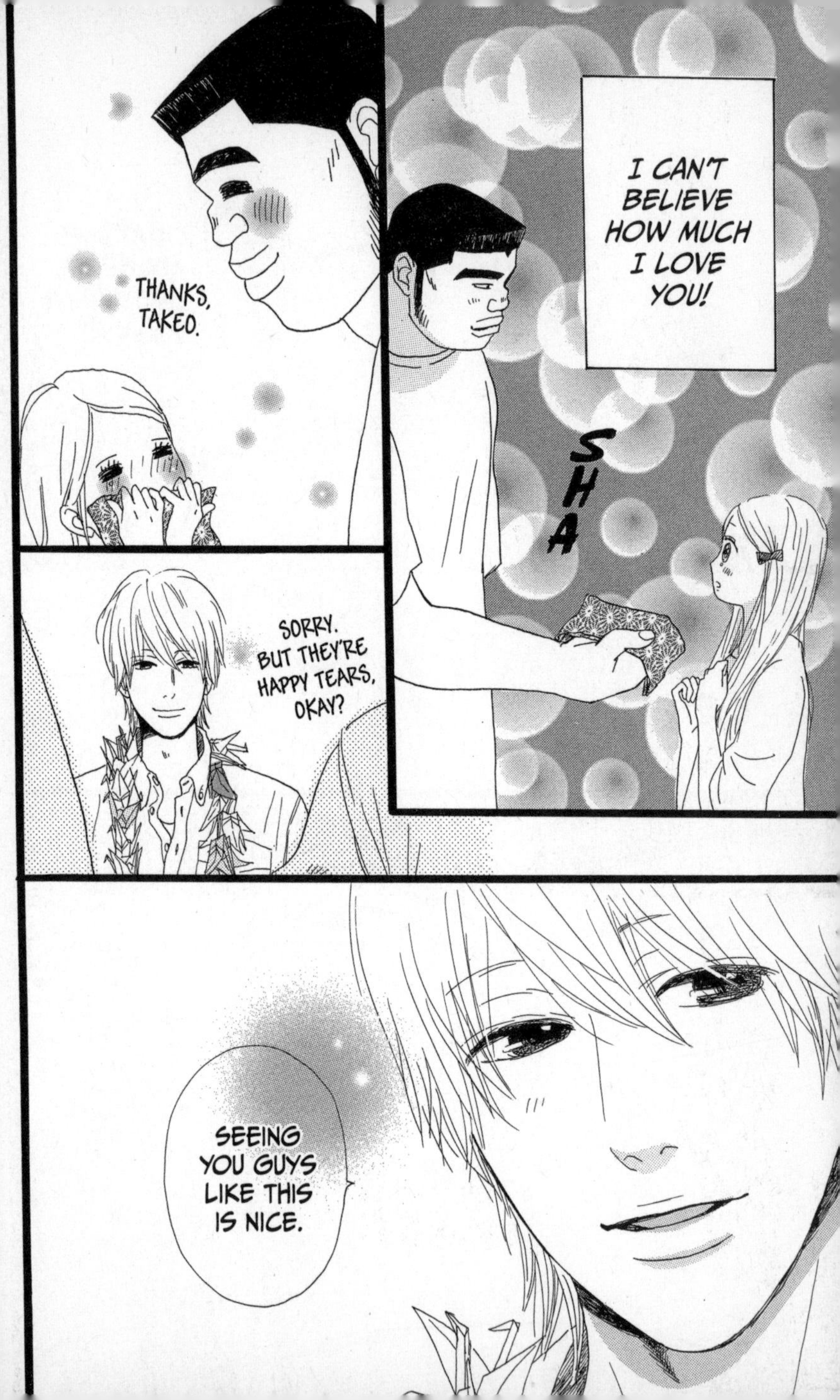
I CAN'T BELIEVE HOW MUCH I LOVE YOU!
SHA
THANKS, TAKEO.
SORRY. BUT THEY'RE HAPPY TEARS, OKAY?
SEEING YOU GUYS LIKE THIS IS NICE.

MY love STORY!!

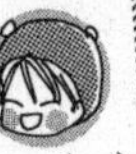

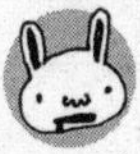

ARUKO & KAZUNE KAWAHARA

(Artist) (Author)

MY LOVE STORY!! SPECIAL CHAT ABOUT TAKEO!!

AN INSIGHTFUL INTERVIEW WITH ARUKO SENSEI AND KAWAHARA SENSEI, WHO ARE CAUSING A STIR IN THE WORLD OF SHOJO MANGA! THEY SAT DOWN WITH US TO DISCUSS THE APPEAL OF THE MAIN CHARACTER, TAKEO. THEY ALSO MENTIONED SOME THINGS TO LOOK FORWARD TO IN THE STORY! A MUST-READ FOR FANS!

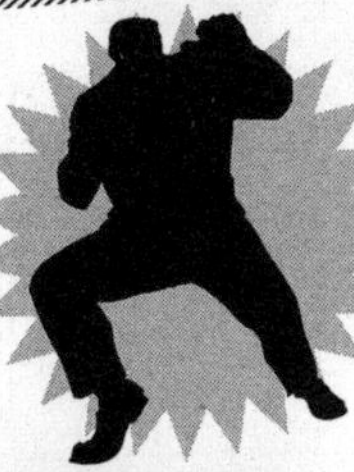

THE SECRET BEHIND THE CREATION OF *MY LOVE STORY!!* IT ALL STARTED WITH THE IDEA OF "MANLY MEN"!

-*My Love Story!!* is a shojo series that really stands out. Tell us how you began coming up with the story.

Kawahara Sensei ("K" from here on)**:** Well, I mentioned that I liked Aruko's work, and I was asked whether I'd be interested in collaborating on a story. That's what got things rolling.

Aruko Sensei ("A" from here on)**:** I was thrilled by the offer! I've liked Kawahara's work for a long time.

K: Thank you very much.

-How did you come up with the main character, Takeo?

K: Aruko has a book called *Shudensha*, and in the third story, there's a masculine girl who can do anything. I really liked her, so I wanted to create a boy who was similar to her.

A: Is that what happened?!

K: It is! *(Laughs)* But then I figured everyone would prefer a handsome guy, so when I wrote my first draft, Takeo was very trendy. But somewhere along the way, I realized I wanted him to be oozing with masculinity, and I rewrote his character. And I think Aruko brought that image of him to life.

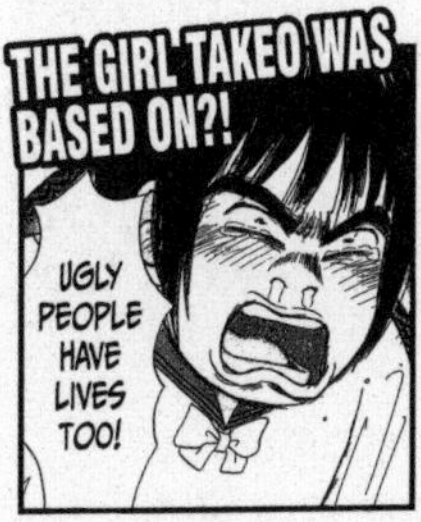
THE GIRL TAKEO WAS BASED ON?!
UGLY PEOPLE HAVE LIVES TOO!

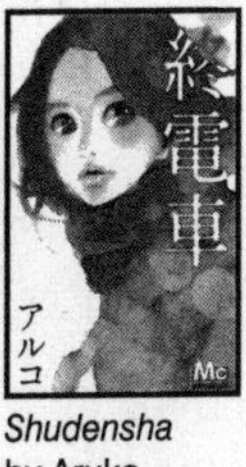
終電車
アルコ
Mc

Shudensha by Aruko

*Margaret Comics *Shudensha* (2010): A collection of short stories sharing the theme of "the last train." The girl who was the inspiration for Takeo is Yuria, the main character of the third story.

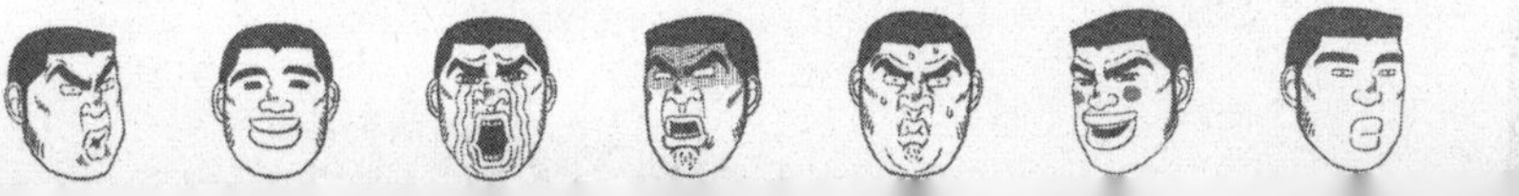

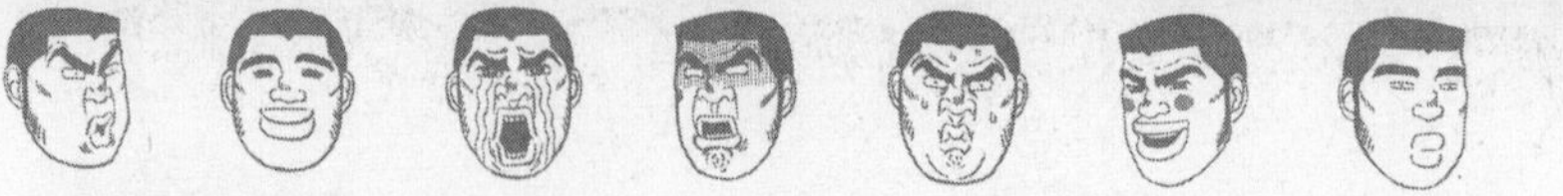

TAKEO'S WORLD KEEPS GETTING BIGGER!

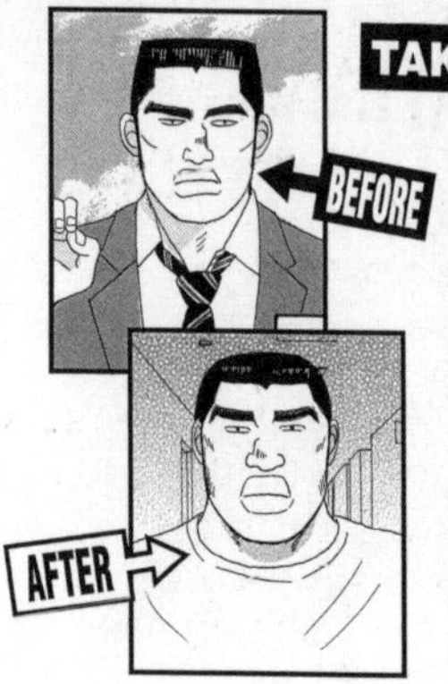
BEFORE
AFTER

-Who designed Takeo's looks?

K: That was Aruko Sensei! I only had a vague idea of what I wanted.
A: I thought it would be amusing to make him like a gorilla and someone who seems older than his actual age. In volume 1, his build is a bit square, but lately he's become rounder.
K: He's getting cuter. *(Laughs)* As I mentioned in the comments for volume 1, Takeo isn't ugly. He just doesn't have the kind of looks that girls go for—but it does make him popular with guys!
A: You really do see him as handsome, don't you?
K: I really do! Japan doesn't have many guys like him.
A: I visualized Takeo as a rather large guy, but when the editor mentioned in the summary of volume 1 that he was roughly 6' 6" tall and 265 lbs., I was shocked. As a result, Takeo is now even bigger than he was in volume 1.

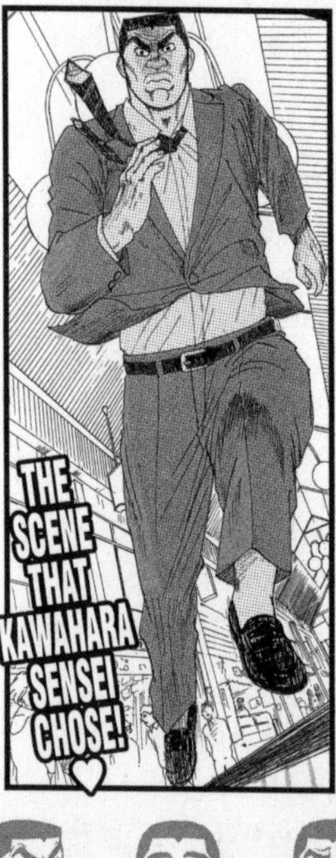
THE SCENE THAT KAWAHARA SENSEI CHOSE! ♡

K: I like that he stands out more when he's bigger.
His fashion sense is pretty unique, isn't it?
A: I get the feeling that he wears short sleeves all year round.
K: It seems natural for him to carry around a handkerchief too.

-Which of his scenes is your favorite?

K: I like every panel Takeo's in, but if I had to choose, it'd be the scene where he's running to Yamato. His pose is cool, but his face is even cooler!
A: This is how you run for short distances, and I thought it would be amusing to draw him doing that for a long-distance run. That's a bit off topic, but it really shows how single-minded Takeo is. I enjoyed drawing it.

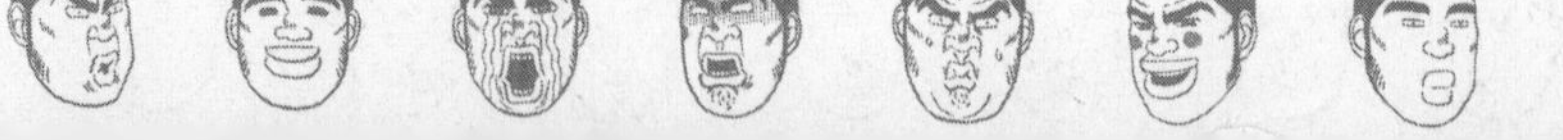

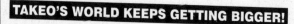

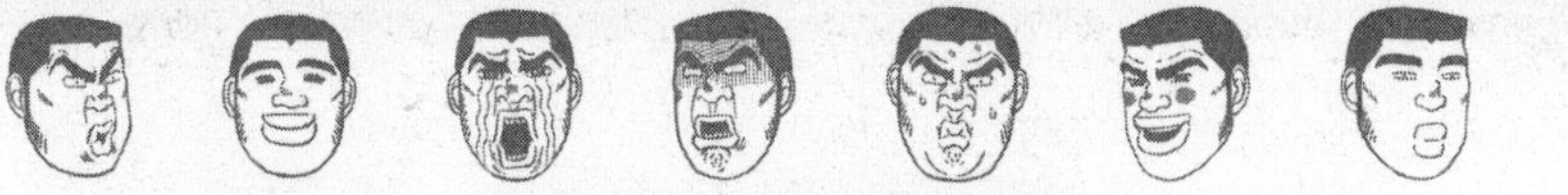

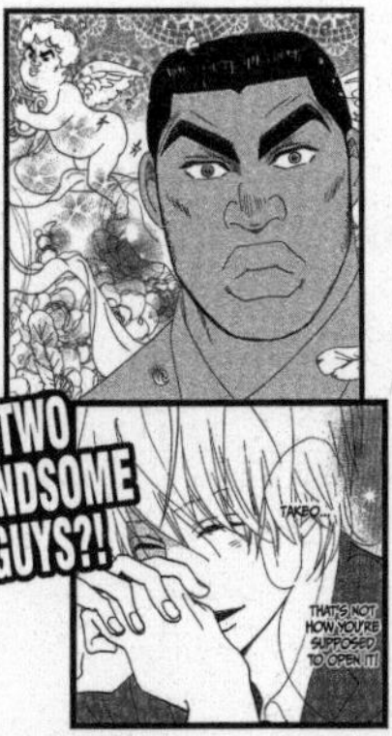
TWO HANDSOME GUYS?!
TAKEO...
THAT'S NOT HOW YOU'RE SUPPOSED TO OPEN IT!

TAKEO OR SUNAKAWA... WHICH IS YOUR TYPE?!

-By the way, would you rather go out with Takeo or Sunakawa?

A: Um... That's a tough one! *(Laughs)* Sunakawa, I guess? I don't think I could look after Takeo.
K: Sunakawa is a nice guy, isn't he?
A: He's a nice guy who always points out what Takeo's doing wrong. Which of them do you like, Kawahara-san?
K: Sunakawa can't be bothered with some things *(Laughs)*, so I'd prefer Takeo. But the downside to Takeo is that he's so big. I would prefer him to be a bit more compact.

I'M CURIOUS! WHAT KINDS OF THINGS CAN WE LOOK FORWARD TO?!

-Aruko Sensei, are there any stories that you'd like Kawahara Sensei to write for the series?

A: I want to know if Sunakawa gets a girlfriend or what kind of girl he'll fall in love with!
K: Well, now... I think he'd probably do well with someone like Takeo. But I still haven't decided on anything!
A: Are Takeo and Yamato ever going to kiss? Are they?!
K: Takeo practiced very hard (See volume 1, p. 174), but the right mood never seems to come along. And even if the mood was right, they probably wouldn't notice, and it would pass them by. I can't really imagine them kissing. *(Laughs)*

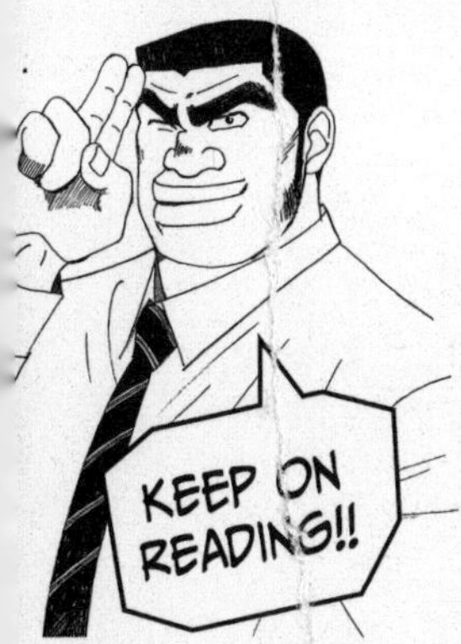
KEEP ON READING!!

A: I'm also very curious about what you're going to do when Takeo's mom gives birth!
K: You'd love to draw it all, wouldn't you? I'd like to see how you'd draw that!

-To wrap things up, is there anything you want to say to each other?

K: Thank you very much for always drawing with love! It makes me want to work hard too. I look forward to continuing to work with you!
A: I'm just glad I get to work with such a wonderful story. This really makes me remember how much fun it is to draw manga. And I'm looking forward to working more with you too!

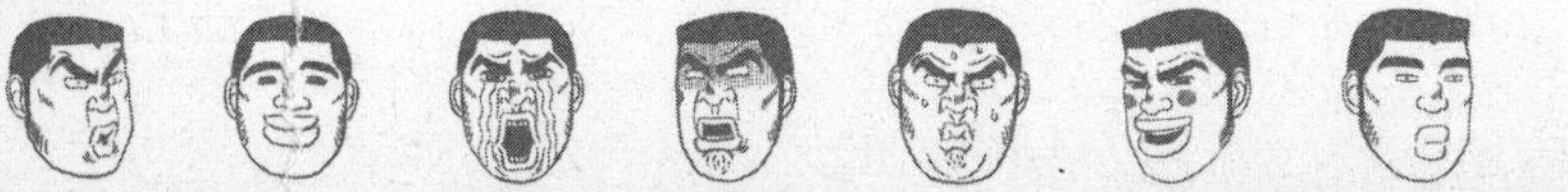

I'm glad we made it to volume 2! I love how cute Aruko draws Takeo, and I'd be thrilled if you like him too. I also think Sunakawa is really cool, so I hope you do too. Not to mention Yamato, Sunakawa's sister... Takeo's mom... I hope you love all of them!
– Kazune Kawahara

ARUKO is from Ishikawa Prefecture in Japan and was born on July 26 (a Leo!). She made her manga debut with *Ame Nochi Hare* (Clear After the Rain). Her other works include *Yasuko to Kenji*, and her hobbies include laughing and getting lost.

KAZUNE KAWAHARA is from Hokkaido Prefecture in Japan and was born on March 11 (a Pisces!). She made her manga debut at age 18 with *Kare no Ichiban Sukina Hito* (His Most Favorite Person). Her best-selling shojo manga series *High School Debut* is available in North America from VIZ Media. Her hobby is interior redecorating.

No problem! Don't worry! It'll be all right! Lately, I've been talking like Takeo. When I feel tired or down, I feel better just thinking about him. I'd be super happy if this manga has touched your heart.
– Aruko

MY LOVE STORY!!

Volume 2
Shojo Beat Edition

Story **KAZUNE KAWAHARA**
Art by **ARUKO**

English Adaptation ♡ **Ysabet Reinhardt MacFarlane**
Translation ♡ **JN Productions**
Touch-up Art & Lettering ♡ **Mark McMurray**
Design ♡ **Fawn Lau**
Editor ♡ **Amy Yu**

ORE MONOGATARI!!
© 2011 by Kazune Kawahara, Aruko
All rights reserved.
First published in Japan in 2011 by SHUEISHA Inc., Tokyo
English translation rights arranged by SHUEISHA Inc.

The stories, characters and incidents mentioned in
this publication are entirely fictional.

Printed in the U.S.A.

Published by VIZ Media, LLC
P.O. Box 77010
San Francisco, CA 94107

10 9 8 7 6 5 4 3 2 1
First printing, October 2014

www.viz.com

www.shojobeat.com

Is this girl a devil in disguise...
or a misunderstood angel?

A Devil and Her Love Song

Story and Art by Miyoshi Tomori

Meet Maria Kawai—she's gorgeous and whip-smart, a girl who seems to have it all. But when she unleashes her sharp tongue, it's no wonder some consider her to be the very devil! Maria's difficult ways even get her kicked out of an elite school, but this particular fall may actually turn out to be her saving grace...

Only $9.99 US / $12.99 CAN each!

Vol. 1 ISBN: 978-1-4215-4164-8
Vol. 2 ISBN: 978-1-4215-4165-5
Vol. 3 ISBN: 978-1-4215-4166-2
Vol. 4 ISBN: 978-1-4215-4167-9

Check your local manga retailer for availability!

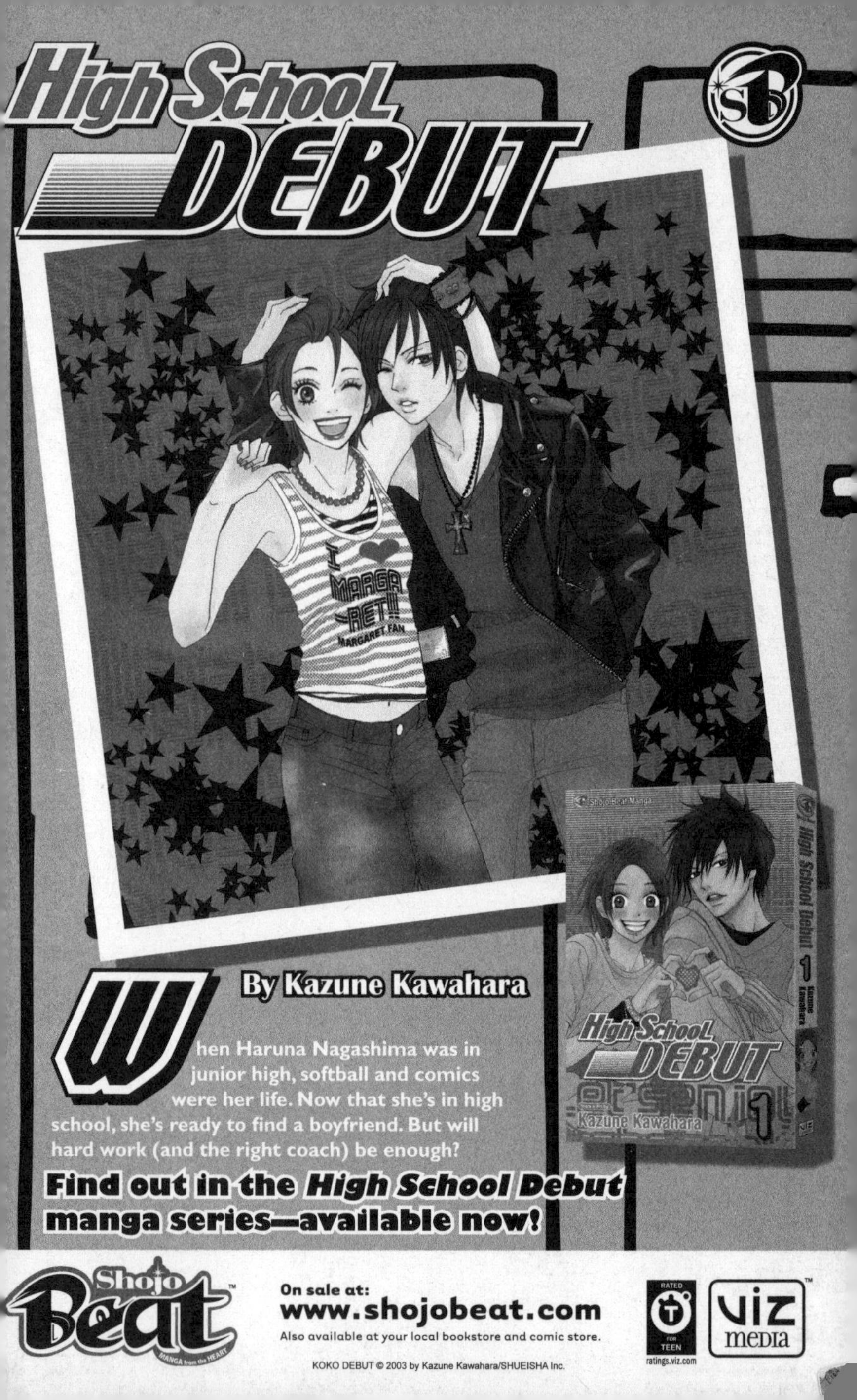

High School Debut
SB
I ♥ MARGARET!! MARGARET FAN
Shojo Beat Manga
High School Debut 1 Kazune Kawahara
By Kazune Kawahara
When Haruna Nagashima was in junior high, softball and comics were her life. Now that she's in high school, she's ready to find a boyfriend. But will hard work (and the right coach) be enough?
Find out in the High School Debut manga series—available now!
Shojo Beat™ MANGA from the HEART
On sale at:
www.shojobeat.com
Also available at your local bookstore and comic store.
RATED T FOR TEEN
ratings.viz.com
viz media™
KOKO DEBUT © 2003 by Kazune Kawahara/SHUEISHA Inc.

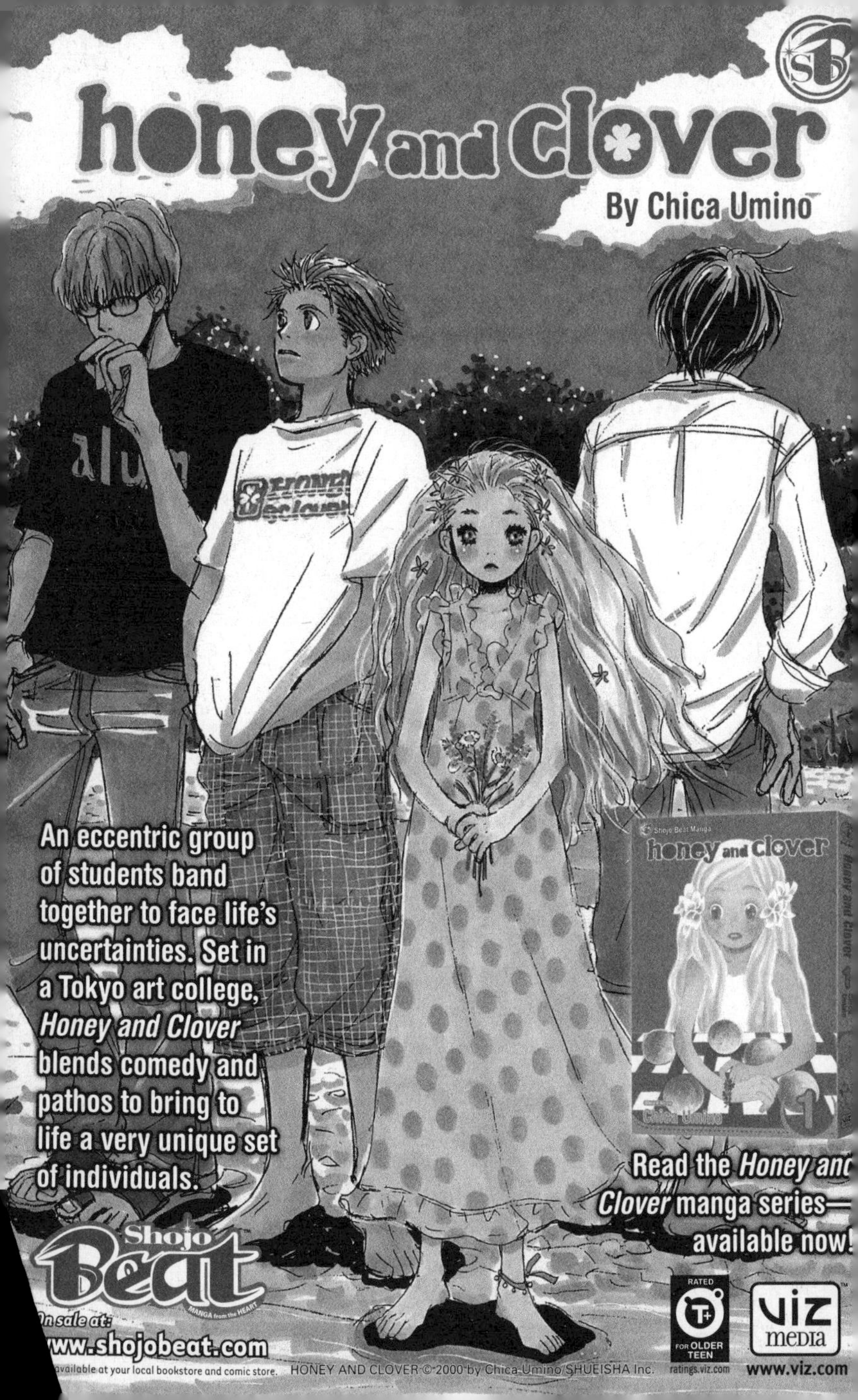
honey and clover
By Chica Umino
An eccentric group of students band together to face life's uncertainties. Set in a Tokyo art college, *Honey and Clover* blends comedy and pathos to bring to life a very unique set of individuals.
Shojo Beat Manga
honey and clover
Read the *Honey and Clover* manga series—available now!
Shojo Beat
MANGA from the HEART
On sale at:
www.shojobeat.com
available at your local bookstore and comic store.
HONEY AND CLOVER © 2000 by Chica Umino/SHUEISHA Inc.
RATED
T+
FOR OLDER TEEN
ratings.viz.com
VIZ media
www.viz.com

ᴠIZMANGA
Read manga anytime, anywhere!

From our newest hit series to the classics you know and love, the best manga in the world is now available digitally. Buy a volume* of digital manga for your:

- iOS device (**iPad®**, **iPhone®**, **iPod®** touch) through the **VIZ Manga** app

- Android-powered device (**phone or tablet**) with a browser by visiting VIZManga.com

- **Mac or PC computer** by visiting VIZManga.com

VIZ Digital has loads to offer:

- 500+ ready-to-read volumes
- New volumes each week
- FREE previews
- Access on multiple devices! Create a log-in through the app so you buy a book once, and read it on your device of choice!*

To learn more, visit www.viz.com/apps

* Some series may not be available for multiple devices.
Check the app on your device to find out what's available.

Aiwo Utauyori Oreni Oborero! Volume 1 © Mayu SHINJO 2010
DEATH NOTE © 2003 by Tsugumi Ohba, Takeshi Obata/SHUEISHA Inc.
NURARIHYON NO MAGO © 2008 by Hiroshi Shiibashi/SHUEISHA Inc.

You may be reading the **wrong way!!**

IT'S TRUE: In keeping with the original Japanese comic format, this book reads from right to left—so action, sound effects, and word balloons are completely reversed. This preserves the orientation of the original artwork—plus, it's fun! Check out the diagram shown here to get the hang of things, and then turn to the other side of the book to get started!

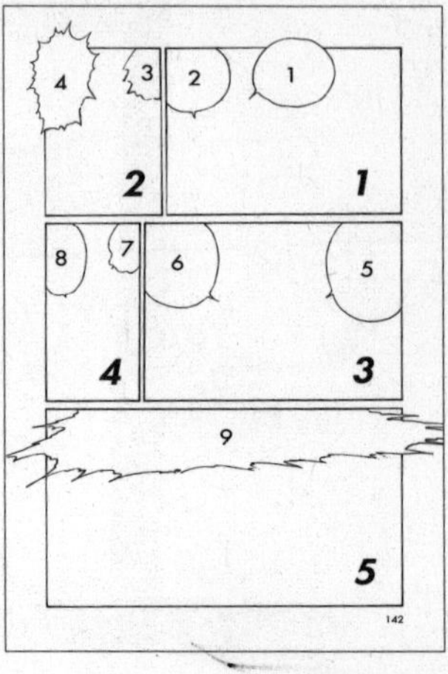

1
2
3
4
1
2
5
6
7
8
3
4
9
5
142

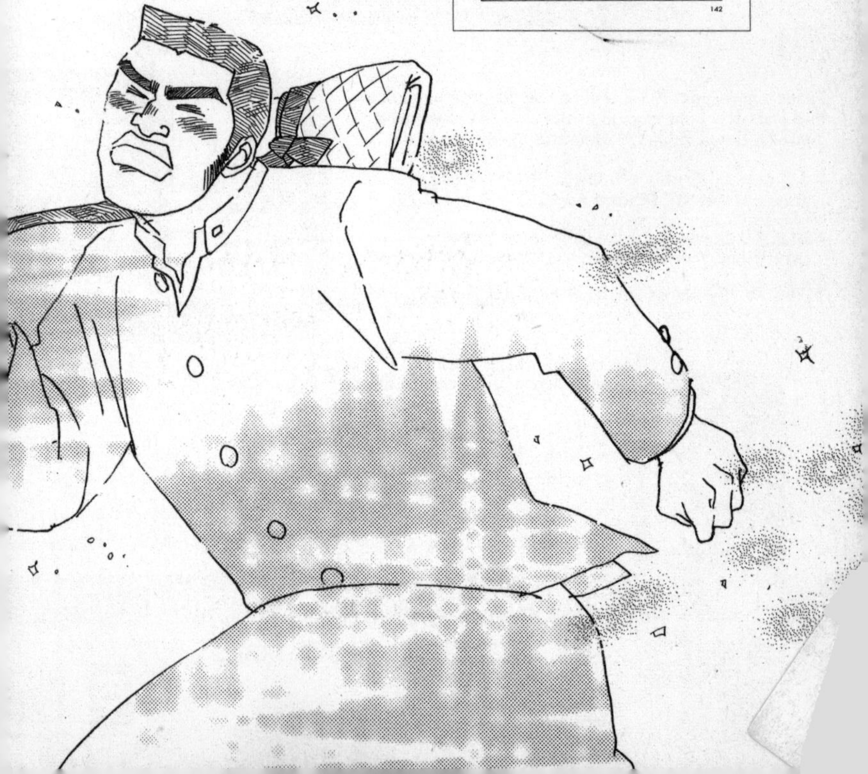